4818-8

THE FILMS OF
THE BOWERY BOYS

by David Hayes
and
Brent Walker

The Citadel Press   **Secaucus, N.J.**

ACKNOWLEDGMENTS

Edward Bernds
Gabriel Dell
Huntz Hall
Austen Jewell
Eddie LeRoy
Ernie "Sunshine Sammy" Morrison
Jane Nigh
Ben Schwalb
Gil Stratton Jr.
Elwood Ullman

Jeff Lenburg
Bruce Furman
Randy Skretvedt
Doris Walker
Greg Lenburg
Jordan Young
E.M. Nathanson
Charlie Christ
Vince Garofalo
Jeff Walton
Richard Roat
H. David Moss Agency
Academy of Motion Pictures Arts and Sciences
UCLA Film Archives

DESIGNED BY LESTER GLASSNER

First edition
Copyright © 1984, 1982 by David Hayes and Brent Walker

Published by Citadel Press
A division of Lyle Stuart Inc.
120 Enterprise Avenue
Secaucus, N.J. 07094
In Canada by Musson Book Company
A division of General Publishing Co. Limited
Don Mills, Ontario

Queries regarding rights and permissions should be
addressed to: Lyle Stuart Inc.
120 Enterprise Avenue, Secaucus, N.J. 07094

Manufactured in the United States of America

Library of Congress Cataloging in Publication Data

Hayes, David, 1962-
    The films of the Bowery Boys.

    1. Bowery Boys films.   2. Moving-pictures—Plots,
themes, etc.   I. Walker, Brent.   II. Title.
PN1995.9.B68H39   1984   791.43′09′09355   84-1700
ISBN 0-8065-0931-7

CONTENTS

Introduction	11
The Dead End Kids	19
Dead End (1937)	20
Crime School (1938)	24
Angels With Dirty Faces	26
They Made Me a Criminal (1939)	29
Hell's Kitchen	31
Angels Wash Their Faces	32
On Dress Parade	35
The Dead End Kids and Little Tough Guys	36
Little Tough Guy (1938)	38
Call a Messenger (1939)	40
You're Not So Tough (1940)	41
Junior G-Men	43
Give Us Wings	44
Hit the Road (1941)	45
Sea Raiders	46
Mob Town	47
Junior G-Men of the Air (1942)	48
Tough As They Come	49
Mug Town (1943)	50
Keep 'Em Slugging (1943)	51
Eastside Kids Primer	52
East Side Kids (1940)	56
Boys of the City	57
That Gang of Mine	58
Pride of the Bowery (1941)	59
Flying Wild	61
Bowery Blitzkrieg	62
Spooks Run Wild	63
Mr. Wise Guy (1942)	65
Let's Get Tough!	66
Smart Alecks	67
'Neath Brooklyn Bridge	68
Kid Dynamite (1943)	69
Clancy Street Boys	72
Ghosts On the Loose	73
Mr. Muggs Steps Out	74
Million Dollar Kid (1944)	76
Follow the Leader	77
Block Busters	78
Bowery Champs	79
Docks of New York (1945)	80
Mr. Muggs Rides Again	81
Come Out Fighting	82
The Bowery Boys Primer	85
Live Wires (1946)	87
In Fast Company	88
Bowery Bombshell	89
Spook Busters	91
Mr. Hex	92
Hard Boiled Mahoney (1947)	93
New Hounds	94
Bowery Buckaroos	95
Angels' Alley (1948)	96
Jinx Money	97

Smugglers' Cove	98	*Spy Chasers*	140
Trouble Makers	100	*Jail Busters*	142
Fighting Fools (1949)	101	*Dig That Uranium* (1956)	143
Hold That Baby!	103	*Crashing Las Vegas*	146
Angels in Disguise	104	**Primer For 1956-1958**	**147**
Master Minds	105	*Fighting Trouble*	150
Blonde Dynamite (1950)	107	*Hot Shots*	151
Lucky Losers	108	*Hold That Hypnotist* (1957)	152
Triple Trouble	109	*Spook Chasers*	155
Blues Busters	110	*Looking For Danger*	156
Bowery Battalion (1951)	112	*Up in Smoke*	158
Ghost Chasers	113	*In the Money* (1958)	159
Lets Go Navy!	115	**Biographies**	**161**
Crazy Over Horses	116	**Leo Gorcey**	**163**
Hold That Line (1952)	116	**Huntz Hall**	**169**
Here Come the Marines	119	**Gabriel Dell**	**175**
Feudin' Fools	120	**Billy Halop**	**179**
No Holds Barred	121	**Bobby Jordan**	**185**
Jalopy	123	**Bernard Punsly**	**187**
Loose in London	124	**David Gorcey**	**189**
Clipped Wings	126	**"Sunshine Sammy" Morrison**	**190**
Private Eyes	128	**Stanley Clements**	**195**
Paris Playboys (1954)	129	**Billy Benedict**	**201**
The Bowery Boys Meet the Monsters	131	**Bennie Bartlett**	**207**
Jungle Gents	134	**Bernard Gorcey**	**211**
Bowery to Bagdad (1955)	135	**The Others**	**214**
High Society	138	**Forerunners, Imitators and Offspring**	**221**

7

For Blair, Doris and Jack Walker

—Brent Walker

To the reader who is what I was at fourteen: an immense fan of the series with an intense desire to understand its characters' appeal. His questions were what I endeavored to answer.

—David Hayes

BLUES BUSTERS

INTRODUCTION

Slip yells at Sach.
Sach responds with a snappy comeback.
Slip hits Sach over the head with his hat.
The Bowery Boys have lived again.

Why have legions of fans and movie viewers been fascinated by the shenanigans of this group of teenagers? Answer: Because watching their activities is like visiting favorite friends.

Millions today don't mind that their films are in black-and-white, or that these pictures have never been appreciated by critics. Nowhere else is there a troupe who had their sense of honesty, their foibles and their virtues. No other films offer the wonderful personas of Slip Mahoney, Sach Jones or any of the characters in the sister series.

Slip tried to make the most of the world he lived in. Sach lived in his own world. Between these two we see layer upon layer of our selves.

Slip was always trying to realize himself, and thus tried to rearrange the elements of his world so that he could deal with it on his own terms. When he becomes an executive (as he does when he appoints himself one in *Live Wires, Smugglers' Cove* and other films), he does so on the condition that he will run things as he sees fit, subject only to his judgment.

In his efforts to achieve his ends, he fought battles while engaged in a continuous struggle with the English language. As anyone who has heard his efforts knows, his attempts to assimilate the locution of the elite resulted in some of the funniest malopropisms ever uttered on the screen.

This didn't reflect negatively on his character, however. Slip lived by a moral code, and went out of his way to help others.

Sach didn't. He would rather offend people than deny that he was anything other than what he was. He might make people shun him, but his consolation was that he knew better than they did; he maintained that every facet of his character contributed to his happiness, and that staying as he was offered intangible rewards which were worth risking the disapproval of the dour.

In *Crashing Las Vegas*, Sach is told, "The only thing that could improve your looks is plastic surgery." Sach's answer is "Thank you for the compliment." What he has done is interpret the remark to mean that his is such an exquisit appearance that only the most deliberate attempts to improve it could render a better image.

Such thinking has endeared Sach to many who rightly sense that adopting such egocentricity can lead to better mental attitudes. However, the exuberant Sach was not always like this, and during the early years of the Bowery Boys (1946-1951), his weak body housed a mind suppressed. Thus, in the earlier films, it is in detrimental circumstances that Sach executes his wonderful ideas.

Slip, Sach and the other boys always maintained that whatever they did was to be done to further their happiness. If they should open a business, their pleasure in operating it was the activity itself, not the profits. That was one of their principles whether they were the Dead End Kids, the Eastside Kids or the Bowery Boys.

As the Dead End Kids, they were unable to cope with society. Consequently they lashed out—at conscientious older sisters, authorities, supervisors, malcontents, and zealous character remolders—but they never had a genuine victory because they were always repressed.

Taught that they were low-life, they sought notoriety, took refuge in tough shells, and attacked the one thing each of them had: each other. The only way any of them could elevate themselves was by devaluing the others. In essence they told each other, "I can't do any better, so I'm staying around with you."

In much the manner that the Dead End Kids waited for circumstances to change their plight or for others to change their lives, the Butchs, Chucks and Whiteys of the Bowery Boys series had not yet taken charge of their lives. If there was one image of these "background" boys that could serve as the "master image," it would that of Butch, Chuck and Whitey waiting around at Louie's Sweet Shop for Slip and Sach to arrive. These three have sublimated themselves. Whatever opinions the others hold are the opinions they adopt for themselves.

For go-getters such as Slip and Sach, an unspeakable horror would be to find themselves entrapped in the world endorsed by Sidney Kingsley and Lillian Hellman, the authors of *Dead End,* whose society would stifle their goals as they expended pains for the common welfare. However, such efforts would benefit the type of person represented by the less integral Dead End Kids. And herein lies the key to the appeal each group has.

For those of us who can always be ourselves, Slip and Sach have found a permanent niche within us. For those of us who take to heart characters who might be intimidated by the Slips and Sachs of the world, the group of roughnecks would certainly be our favorites.

Most people agree on what the best films are. Few agree on what their favorites are. Favoritism is a personal matter, a reflection of what we hold to be true. Those of us who like the Bowery Boys hear in their voices the words we speak ourselves.

The Dead End Kids (from the left): Billy Halop, Bobby Jordan (seated,) Leo Gorcey, Huntz Hall, Gabriel Dell, Bernard Punsley.

HISTORY

In 1937, the juvenile cast members of a successful Broadway play, *Dead End*, were transported to Hollywood to make the movie version. Samuel Goldwyn had signed them to two-year contracts, and they seemed to be in Hollywood for good. Goldwyn chose not to keep them, however; they had started a rampage which destroyed studio property, culminating in the smashing of a truck into a sound stage. Goldwyn sold their contracts to Warner Brothers.

Warner Brothers starred them with such luminaries as Humphrey Bogart, Pat O'Brien, James Cagney, and John Garfield.

In 1938, Universal borrowed five of the six boys for the feature film *Little Tough Guy*. Meanwhile, back at Warner Brothers, the boys were launched as stars in their own right, albeit in low-budget pictures. Result: the strain of appearing in three pictures with no better support than Ronald Reagan led to their being dropped from the studio payroll.

From 1940 to 1943, Monogram Pictures used Bobby Jordan and Leo Gorcey as the leads in the Eastside Kids series. Universal resumed their "Little Tough Guy" series

That's a 20th Century-Fox poster on the wall. Was Samuel Goldwyn trying to degrade his competitors?

with Billy Halop, Bernard Punsly, and, for a short time, Bobby Jordan. Huntz Hall and Gabriel Dell appeared in both series.

In 1946, Leo and his agent, Jan Grippo, revamped the Eastside Kids, renamed them the Bowery Boys, and set out to make four entertaining pictures a year. Each had Huntz Hall as second banana. The chemistry of Slip (Leo) and Sach (Huntz) clicked, allowing for the imperceptible easing in of new cast members, glossing over departures by Bobby Jordan and Gabriel Dell.

In 1953, Ben Schwalb took over as producer from the retired Jan Grippo. Schwalb reshaped the series by bringing in comedy specialists from the short-subject field. But some things didn't change: Leo's brother David kept his Bowery Boy role, and Leo's father, Bernard, kept his role as the engaging sweetshop proprietor, Louie Dumbrowski.

In 1956, Stanley Clements was added to the cast, taking over the pinnacle position of Leo Gorcey. Gorcey had been saddened by the death of his father. Stanley Clements and the still active Huntz Hall continued to make pictures, with varying degrees of success, until 1958.

Warner Brothers teamed the kids with name stars such as James Cagney, here in Angels With Dirty Faces *(1938).*

The Little Tough Guys in Give Us Wings, *(1940). That's Shemp Howard on the right.*

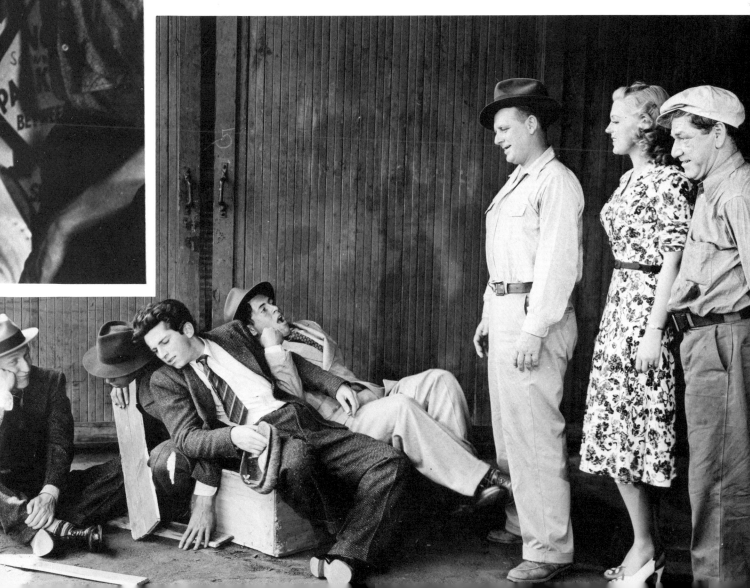

In 1946, the Eastside Kids became the Bowery Boys, with the emphasis on sheer entertainment. Leo Gorcey became top banana, with Huntz Hall second.

The comedy team of Leo Gorcey and Huntz Hall dominated the series during the early fifties.

Stanley Clements replaced Leo Gorcey in 1956, and he and the indefatigable Huntz Hall (left) went on to make seven more films until the series' demise in 1958.

Now Playing

The Dead End Kids

Bernard PUNSLY   Bobby JORDAN   Huntz HALL   Leo GORCEY   Gabriel DELL   Billy HALOP

Clockwise from upper left, Humphrey Bogart, Gabriel Dell, Huntz Hall, Billy Halop, Bernard Punsly, Bobby Jordan, Leo B. Gorcey. Gabriel Dell recalls, "Whenever you read about Bogart, he doesn't like anyone; but he liked us because we were kids and Bogie was basically a kid." The famous movie gangster and the kids played boxcar on the set between takes.

DEAD END

A Samuel Goldwyn Production, released August 27, 1937, by United Artists. Directed by William Wyler. Associate production by Merritt Hulburd. Screenplay by Lillian Hellman, based on the play by Sidney Kingsley. Photographed by Gregg Toland. Music by Alfred Newman. Art direction by Richard Day. Edited by Daniel Mandell. Set direction by Julie Heron. Costumes by Omar Kiam. Assistant direction by Eddie Bernoudy. Sound by Frank Maher. Dialogue direction by Frank P. Goodnow. Special effects by James Basevi. Also known as *Dead End; Cradle of Crime*. 8437 ft. 93 minutes.

Drina Gordon, Sylvia Sidney; *Dave Connell,* Joel McCrea; *Gil "Baby Face" Martin,* Humphrey Bogart; *Tommy Gordon,* Billy Halop; *Spit,* Leo B. Gorcey; *Angel,* Bobby Jordan; *T.B.,* Gabriel Dell; *Dippy,* Huntz Hall; *Milty,* Bernard Punsly; *Hunk,* Allen Jenkins; *Kay Burton,* Wendy Barrie; *Francie,* Claire Trevor; *Mrs. Martin,* Marjorie Main; *Philip Griswold,* Charles Peck; *Mr. Griswold,* Minor Watson; *Mulligan, cop,* James Burke; *Griswold doorman,* Ward Bond; *Mrs. Connell,* Elisabeth Risdon; *Mrs. Fenner, janitress,* Esther Dale; *Pascagli, diner owner,* George Humbert; *Governess,* Marcelle Corday; *Whitey,* Charles Halton; *Cop,* Robert E. Homans; *Drunk,* Bill Dagwell; *Milty's brother,* Jerry Cooper; *Milty's sister,* Kath Ann Lujan; *Old lady,* Gertrude Valerie; *Old man,* Tom Ricketts; *Women with poodle,* Charlotte Treadway, Maude Lambert; *Kay's chauffeur,* Bud Geary; *Well-dressed couple,* Frank Shields, Lucille Brown; *Tough boys,* Micky Martin, Wesley Girard; *Woman with coarse voice,* Esther Howard; *Man with weak voice,* Gilbert Clayton; *Griswold chauffeur,* Earl Askam; *Nurse,* Mona Monet; *Intern,* Donald M. Barry; *Little kids,* Sidney Kibrick, Larry Harris, Norman Salling.

In the slums near New York's East River, Drina Gordon is worried that her brother, Tommy, and his young gang of urchins will grow up to be like the mobsters they emulate, such as Baby Face Martin. Martin has returned to his old neighborhood to visit his mother and his old girlfriend after having achieved underworld notoriety. Dave Connell, a poor sign painter who is in love with Drina, is disturbed by Martin's presence. Dave spends most of his time with Kay Burton, the mistress of a playboy living in the luxurious apartments bordering the tenements. Tommy's gang roughs up a rich kid, and Tommy has to hide when he stabs the hand of the boy's father.

Martin is repudiated by his mother and shocked by the physical appearance of his former girlfriend. Depressed, he decides to kidnap the rich boy for ransom. His plans are thwarted by Dave, who survives a knife stabbing and guns the gangster down. In the ensuing riot, Spit, a member of Tommy's gang, is recognized as one of the boys who attacked the rich man. He clears himself by revealing that Tommy is the guilty delinquent. Tommy learns what Spit has done, and tries to brand him as a "squealer" with a tell-tale knife mark. Before he can slit Spit's cheek, he is restrained by Dave, who successfully convinces Tommy to give himself up. Dave promises Drin he will pay to have Tommy defended with reward money he received for Martin's slaying.

No film has done a better job than *Dead End* in depicting the squalor and treadmill cycle of Depression life in urban slums. Playwright Sidney Kingsley and screenwright Lillian Hellman—both liberals—advocated slum reform by presenting a world where despair breeds criminals, crowds of people share inadequate housing, and filth decorates the street and river. Seeing these elements made viewers sympathetic. Most reviewers failed to notice that the endless procession of emotionally-charged scenes obscured the intellectual issues involved. Thus, *Dead End* garnered prestige, which attracted independent film mogul Samuel Goldwyn.

A major part of the film's impact is due to the use of irony. Joel McCrea plays Dave (named Gimpty in the original play), an earnest young man who went to college with archectectual aspirations, but now barely makes a

living painting signs. Baby Face Martin (Humphrey Bogart) left school to pursue a career in crime, killing eight men in his rise to material success. The latter character is idolized by the kids, since he was "smart" instead of a "sucker." The plot denouement simply reverts the situation back to the beginning, with Baby Face gone, Dave no richer, the kids no better off, showing slum life as merely a vicious cycle in which all destinies lead to a "dead end."

The most disturbing effects of the movie come from seeing life regarded so cheaply. When Baby Face is asked whether he worries about getting shot, he answers, "You can't live forever." Drina considers bad shoes more dreadful than bad feet, and uses cardboard in the sole to preserve the leather. Drina's values have been corrupted by the slums. She looks upon marriage with Dave as financial security; she can't love him with the passion she accords her courteous dream man, and accepts Dave's excuses for not keeping their dates though she knows he's lying. She confides to Tommy that he, Tommy, is all she has.

Francie worships money, although she too was once uncorrupted and didn't always put money above everything else. As she recalls a moment when she and Baby Face were on a rooftop in their teens, she says, "The sky was full of stars and I was full of dreamy ideas." She is not like that when Martin sees her ten years later. As described in the film's script, "Martin draws back slightly, looks at her for a long time. Suddenly he sees her as she is. The nostalgic dream is finished. His face is full of disgust." Her eyes are on his money as he peels some bills from the roll. Everything about Francie suggests she has sold out to the almighty dollar. It is ominous of Martin's learning of Francie's prostitution that in the preceding scene he says, "I'm getting sick of what I can pay for."

Life looks terrible all around. In the opening shot, fog was added to a slum overview already on the camera negative. The original shooting script reveals that imagery such as this was intentional. The "shiny windows" and "beautifully arranged potted plants" of the rich Griswold's trellaced apartments (mentioned in descriptives for shots 5-6) are in contrast to the slum street below it. In shot 11, a light trick further suggests that the poor are slighted, as the sunlight emerges and "the contrast between rich and poor becomes sharper in the sharper light." The Griswold residence is impenetrable. It's as if an invisible wall begins at a crack in the sidewalk. In shot

24, "Spit . . . spits at the crack as if he knew that the doorman meant this crack to be a dividing line between the rich and poor." This division affects Dave and Kay, who inevitably break up because they belong to "different worlds."

The Dead End Kids are the axis of the film. Billy Halop is Tommy, the cynical leader, who, given the chance, could amount to something. He is a junior Baby Face, headed for reform school, ready to learn the same tricks Martin learned at the institution that launched his outlaw career. He is being sent to reform school by Mr. Griswold, the same judge who sentenced Martin to reform school.

Tommy's leadership is challenged by Spit (Leo Gorcey), who pictures himself as Führer. Bobby Jordan's Angel, the group runt, uses his wit to compensate for his lack of strength. Huntz Hall as Dippy is the comic stooge, and is so lacking in self-confidence that he slurs his

You'll notice that in none of these stills do the kids look in any way industrious. That was the point.

speech. Gabriel Dell plays T.B., who flaunts tuberculosis as though it makes him unique. Weaknesses fascinate him, as is evident when he is assisted by Spit and Dippy in imitating an old man's wayward walk. Member #6 is Milty (Bernard Punsly), who joins the gang in mid-film because joining seems worth the three cents he has in his pocket. The gang is first presented as a set of identifiable characters. It is only after we develop affection for them that they steal potatoes.

Parts of Sidney Kingsley's play were the target of the censors. One of the changes made for the movie surfaced in *Life* on July 18, 1938, in a piece titled, "Hays Office and U.S. Censors Cut These Things Out." Referring to the Hays Office production Code, the *Life* writer said, "Prostitutes may only be shown when essential to the plot and must be made unattractive. In *Dead End*, the prostitute's syphillis was changed to tuberculosis." This alteration leaves a conversation between Baby Face and Francie confusing.

It begins when Martin starts to reminisce and Francie says, "You're looking at me how I used to look." Martin notices her shocking appearance and asks her why she didn't get a job.

"They don't grow on trees."

"Why didn't you starve first?"

"Why didn't you?"

He hands her a roll of money and leaves. Coughs have been added to emphasise her "sickness." Her actual occupation is suggested elsewhere, when Monk, Baby Face's partner, refers to her as "That cheap little . . . ," and notes, "She's busy." Few facets of slum life escaped the playwright's eye.

Sidney Kingsley's original dialogue and stage directions paint a much grimmer portrait of slum life than the movie adaptation by Lillian Hellman. For instance, in his stage directions Kingsley directs attention to "the East River, covered by a swirling scum an inch thick . . . a hundred sewers vomit their guts into it." This water, the water the Bobby Jordan character dives into, is so pol-

luted that when Angel comes up with crud layered on his skin, he merely passes off that day's water as "dirtier than usual." After Spit dives in, swims and gets out, Dippy smells him and says, "Pee, ew."

The crudity of gutter speech (and thinking) was represented more acutely in the play than in the film. Tommy describes his reaction to the iciness of the water with the remark, "Gee, duh nuts." Dippy, after suffering from having Tommy pull out his chest hairs (an action seen in the film), is further chided when Tommy, noticing Dippy pick his nose, says, "Pick me a juicy one." When a taxi picks up the Griswolds, the French-speaking chauffeur answers *"Oui. Oui,"* Tommy repeats, *"Wee. Wee,* he's godda go wee wee." It is implied that reform school introduced T.B. and Angel to the illicit, notorious substance marijuana. "It gives yew dreams," says an alienated T.B.

Elements of Kingsley's play which gave physical, political and religious reasons for abolishing poverty were deleted in the adaptation. Physically, Gimpty (whose full name, Pete Gimpty, was changed to Dave Connell for the film) is a symbol. As a cripple (the result of an industrial accident), Gimpty represents the damage that such a wretched existence can do to both the physique and spirit. (By contrast, the film's Dave represents none of this, and in fact weakens the film's impact because he seems unlikely to have been bred in the slums.)

In the political sphere, a conversation betwen Baby Face and Gimpty advocating Socialism and Communism, stressing them as political alternatives, was deleted. Gimpty notes, 'Before you're an architect you've got to build a house, and before anyone'll let you build a house, you've got to be an architect."

On religious grounds, the play shows that slums must be cleared because God decreed (to Gimpty, who relates the story to Drina and the kids), "I gave you reason, I gave you a sense of beauty, I planted a God in your heart. Now let's see what you're going to do with them. And if you can't do anything with them, I'll take them away." (He took away "the head of the oyster," "the flight of the ostrich," and can make men "crawl on their bellies like snakes," according to Gimpty.) He suggests to the religious members of the audience that if man continues to muddle his existence, God will make man extinct like the dinosaur. Admittedly, it can be argued that these views were volatile, yet censorship should not have been regarded as the proper answer to them.

Lillian Hellman's screenplay *Dead End* works on an emotional level in ways that Sidney Kingsley's *Dead End* does not. Drina, who is very emotional in the film, was much less so (and less developed) in the play. Scenes of Drina and Tommy in their apartment were completely new or partially new, since the play never left the street. (Some conversations that take place in the apartment, notably those in which Drina explains why she is taking part in a strike, were in the play, but took place outdoors.)

The kids with Sylvia Sidney and Joel McCrea. As Dave, McCrea accepts the lawlessness of the street. He kills outlaw Bogart, but does so for personal reasons. He hates cops, as do all the street people.

Press copy made much out of the six youths' wild pranks and off-screen activities. Reports stated that on their westward journey, they disrupted fellow passengers by playing ball in the aisles. On the set, the kids disparagingly compared the film actors to the actors who had the roles on stage (they had been in the play since it opened at the Belasco Theater on October 28, 1935), and complained loudly about the expurgation of the lines they spoke in the play. They got out of attending the studio school by claiming imaginary rehearsals, and, while not filming, the boys were constantly causing problems in Los Angeles traffic. Gorcey got four traffic tickets in 18 days of shooting; Jordan, who was under the driving age, got one; Hall and Dell drove their Model T Ford into a telephone pole. Punsly spent most of his time reading, avoiding most of the trouble. William Wyler was a target; they added a fortune to his telephone bill by calling their mothers in New York from his office. ("Gabe gave a wonderful imitation of Mr. Wyler's voice," Gorcey recalled, explaining why the secretary accepted the calls.) Even Samuel Goldwyn didn't escape them. *Time* reported that the kids called him "Pop," and had a bone to pick with him because he wouldn't let them go swimming every day.

Publicity also made much of the purported $165,000 Goldwyn spent to buy the rights to the stage play. Director William Wyler wanted to shoot the film on location in New York, but Goldwyn, worried about having Wyler out of his reach, had a $50,000 set constructed in Hollywood. It was used for major shooting from May 3 to June 26, 1937, and for retakes shot July 6, 7, 8, 1937. About 175,000 feet of film were estimated to have been used.

Though it did not win an Oscar, *Dead End* received many Academy Award nominations: best picture, best director, best supporting actress (Claire Trevor), best art direction. Prestigious publications such as *Literary Digest* praised the film as the equal of the stage production.

Huntz Hall, Billy Halop and Gabriel Dell at the premier of Dead End.

Frankie (Billy), Spike (Leo) and Bugs (Gabe) make a deal with Junkie the Fence in the early scenes, before being sent to reform school, where . . .

CRIME SCHOOL

Released May 28, 1938, by Warner Brothers. Associate producer, Bryan Foy. Directed by Lewis Seiler. Screenplay by Crane Wilbur and Vincent Sherman. Story by Crane Wilbur. Music by Max Steiner. Photographed by Arthur Todd. Art direction by Charles Novi. Edited by Terry Morse. Gowns by N'Was McKenzie. Assistant direction by Fred Tyler. Dialogue direction by Vincent Sherman. Orchestrations by Hugo Friedhoffer and George Parish. Sound by Francis J. Scheid. *7793 ft. 86 minutes.*

Mark Braden, Humphrey Bogart; *Sue Warren,* Gale Page; *Frankie Warren,* Billy Halop; *Lester "Squirt" Smith,* Bobby Jordan; *Charles "Spike" Hawkins,* Leo Gorcey; *Richard "Goofy" Slade,* Huntz Hall; *George "Fats" Papadopolos,* Bernard Punsly; *Timothy "Bugs" Burke,* Gabriel Dell; *Cooper,* Weldon Heyburn; *Morgan,* Cy Kendall; *Red,* George Offerman, Jr.; *Judge Clinton,* Charles Trowbridge; *Old doctor,* Spencer Charters; *New doctor,* Donald Briggs; *Commissioner,* Frank Jacquet; *Mrs. Burke,* Hellen MacKellar; *Mr. Burke,* Al Bridge; *Mrs. Hawkins,* Sibyl Harris; *Nick Papadopolos,* Paul Porcasi; *Junkie the Junkman,* Frank Otto; *Officer Hogan,* Ed Gargan; *Schwartz,* James B. Carson; *Reporter,* John Ridgely; *Official,* Harry Cording; *Boy,* Hally Chester.

The Dead End Kids attack a junkman and the man suffers a concussion. The court wants to know which boy struck the fatal blow. When none confess, all are sent to reform school. Mark Braden, superintendant of the state reformatories, visits the boys' reformatory and finds that Morgan has been mismanaging it. He fires all of Morgan's ex-convict guards, save one with a good record.

Taking over as warden, Morgan atempts to parole the boys, combining his attempts with romancing Sue Warren, sister of Frankie, one of the boys. Office clerk Cooper, who had been the guard Braden spared, fears that Braden will discover Morgan's graft of the food budget, which would also implicate him. He discovers that Spike was the boy who delivered the fatal sledge-hammering to the junkman, and blackmails Spike into telling Frankie that Sue has been forced by Braden into paying for the preferential treatment the boys have received from Braden. This is untrue, but it induces the boys to break out.

The boys confront Braden on the outside and learn the truth. Morgan summons the police so that they will find the boys missing and decide that Braden is a lax warden. Braden and the boys reach the reform school before the police do. When the police arrive, Braden announces that he has evidence to convict Morgan.

Crime School is a film without pretensions, an unambitious sequence of scenes which offer nothing more than the pleasure of seeing the Dead End Kids in various situations. Setting up and building these scenes well is the main strength that the film shows during its 86 minutes.

The opening scenes are the funniest the Dead End Kids ever played in. They work for a fence, Junkie the Junkman, to whom they bring various pilfered items: Frankie (Billy) offers an orphaned tire, and Spike (Leo), a watch. Goofy (Huntz) invades the gathering with a second-hand bicycle, and Squirt (Bobby) trundles in the most personal loss, a bathtub. "There was a tootsie in it but she wouldn't go along." The episode is not only funny, but shows that the kids have advanced in social stature since *Dead End*; this time they are earning pay. Their mayhem (fighting) has direction, too; their assault on Junkie the Junkman is provoked by his refusing to pay them the money he owes them.

Humphrey Bogart, unconventionally cast on the right side of the law, is first seen 17 minutes into the film. As the film at this point is true to its purpose of maintaining attention on the kids, Bogart is not given much of anything to do. In typical scenes, he is seen sitting, or walking down the reformatory steps with Sue.

The other melodramatic roles are handled by Gale Page (playing a "typical sister" role) and Cy Kendall (one of the movies' most underrated meanies, a heavy-set gruff talker who brought the aura of a Nazi storm trooper to his roles).

The film maintains a gulf between the grim and the comic, but sometimes the two clash. In a coal-boilerroom scene the kids decide to sabotage the reform school operation, first by shoveling in so little coal that the temperature is sure to drop, and then by shoveling in too much. They cheerfully challenge each to make the Fahrenheit reading go up. Treating the task as an auction, one shouts, "80 [degrees]" and another shouts, "85." "Do I hear 90?" Frankie officiates. The scene quickly and abruptly changes from jovial to near-tragic when the boiler explodes, erupting into a fire that nearly claims Squirt.

Crime School parallels *Dead End* in some ways. Billy Halop once again has a hard-working sister, and Leo Gorcey again plays the wise guy who double-crosses Halop when circumstances force him to act against his will. Halop retaliates against Gorcey, in a scene that is virtually a carbon copy of the scene in *Dead End.* Apparently the Warner Brothers' writers felt that there was no better way for a young hoodlum to extract revenge than by pinning his adversary to the ground and inflicting scars on him. In both films Halop is restrained before he can inflict bodily harm.

The Warner Brothers executives had hoped that the public would now call the former Goldwyn players the "Crime School Kids." Although the name didn't catch on, trade paper advances for their next film, *Angels With Dirty Faces,* referred to them by that title.

Between *Crime School* and *Angels With Dirty Faces,* four of the Dead End Kids made a film at Universal titled *Little Tough Guy* (treated in the Dead End Kids and Little Tough Guys section of this book). Warner Brothers had dropped the contracts of Halop, Hall, Dell and Punsly, so they were free to work for the highest bidder. Jordan and Gorcey were retained by Warner Brothers for playing "boy" parts in their other stars' pictures. After the contracts of the other four were torn up, *Crime School* was released, and the excitement over it convinced Warners that more Dead End Kids pictures would be profitable. The four kids had been earning $275 a week when their contracts were cancelled, but they were able to renegotiate for $650 a week. The man who had let the four kids go, Mervyn LeRoy, was harshly dealt with by Warner Brothers, and he was soon to find employment with M.G.M.

Gabriel Dell, Bernard Punsly, Billy Halop.

Unbeknownst to them, their first warden has been substituting bad meat for good as part of a graft scheme.

25

Leo, Huntz, Billy, Bobby surround Pat O'Brien.

ANGELS WITH DIRTY FACES

Released November 24, 1938, by Warner Brothers. Produced by Samuel Bischoff. Directed by Michael Curtiz. Screenplay by John Wexley and Warren Duff. Story by Rowland Brown. Music by Max Steiner. Photographed by Sol Polito. Edited by Owen Marks. Song "Angels With Dirty Faces" by Fred Fisher and Maurice Spitalny. Art direction by Robert Haas. Assistant direction by Sherry Shounds. Dialogue direction by Jo Graham. Gowns by Orry-Kelly. Orchestrations by Hugo Friedhoffer. Technical advice by J. J. Devlin. Sound by Everett A. Brown. *8827 ft. 97 minutes.*

William "Rocky" Sullivan, James Cagney; *Jerry Connolly,* Pat O'Brien; *Laury Martin,* Ann Sheridan; *James Frazier,* Humphrey Bogart; *Mac Keefer,* George Bancroft; *Soapy,* Billy Halop; *Swing,* Bobby Jordan; *Bim,* Leo Gorcey; *Pasty,* Gabriel Dell; *Crabface,* Huntz Hall; *Hunky,* Bernard Punsly; *Steve,* Joe Downing; *Edwards, guard,* Edward Pawley; *Blackie,* Adrian Morris; *Rocky as a boy,* Frankie Burke; *Jerry as a boy,* William Tracy; *Laury as a girl,* Marilyn Knowlden; *Warden,* William Worthington; *Death row guard,* Jack Dwire; *Priest,* Earl Dwire; *Guard Kennedy,* Oscar O'Shea; *Bugs, gunman,* William Pawley; *Police captain,* John Hamilton; *Mrs. McGee,* Mary Gordon; *Soapy's mother,* Vera Lewis; *Railroad yard watchman,* James Farley; *Red,* Chuck Stubbs; *Johnny Maggione,* Eddie Syracuse; *Policeman,* Robert Homans; *Basketball captain,* Harris Berger; *Pharmacist,* Harry Hayden; *Gangsters,* Dick Rich, Stevan Darrell, Joe A. Devlin; *Italian,* William Edmunds; *Buckley,* Charles Wilson; *Poolroom boys,* Frank Coghlan, Jr., Dave Durand; *Norton J. White, editor,* Charles Trowbridge; *Prison guard,* Lane Chandler; *Death row guard,* Jack Perrin; *Girl at gaming table,* Poppy Wilde; *Newsboy,* Eddie Brian; *Themselves,* Robert B. Mitchell's St. Brendan Boy's Choir.

Warner Brothers advertised the kids as the "Crime School" Kids (so as not to publicize Dead End, *a Goldwin picture), but the public wouldn't accept the image.*

As boys, Rocky Sullivan and Jerry Connally had robbed a railroad car. Rocky was caught and sent to reform school, but Jerry escaped. Now a big time gangster, Rocky comes to New York to visit his old neighborhood, where Jerry is now a priest. Jerry runs a home intended to keep boys away from crime. Jerry's biggest project, a gang of six (Soapy, Swing, Bim, Pasty, Crabface and Hunky), discover Rocky and come to idolize him for his infamy.

Rocky elbows into a racket run by crooked lawyer Frazier and shady businessman Keefer. These two crooks try to bump Rocky off, but after trying unsuccessfully, are blocked when Rocky steals a record book Frazier has kept which would reveal that he bribes city officials. Jerry decides to expose the underhanded dealings, warning his childhood chum that if he's caught in the web, there will be no mercy shown by him. Rocky encourages Jerry to go ahead with his plan. Jerry rallies the public against the inside-government crime over radio, prompting Frazier and Keefer to plan to kill him. When Rocky overhears their plotting, he guns them both down.

Rocky is captured and convicted. Moments before his death sentence is to be carried out, he is visited by Jerry. Jerry asks Rocky, as a last favor, to die screaming, thus ending the kids' idolization of him. Rocky refuses, but at the last moment follows the request so thoroughly that he has to be dragged to the electric chair. The next day, the kids go with Jerry to mass.

Considered a classic of the gangster genre, *Angels With Dirty Faces* is centered around the characters played by James Cagney and Pat O'Brien, Rocky and Jerry. The talent in all departments is first rate, although the focus remains on the Cagney-O'Brien byplay.

Jerry and Rocky are compared and contrasted. Early in the film, Jerry wonders if they would have grown up the same way had both or neither been caught robbing the box car: "I've wondered, what if I was the boy caught that day." On this theme, at the end of the film, Jerry tells the kids, who he is leading to mass, "Let's give a prayer to a boy who couldn't run as fast as I."

By way of contrast, Jerry explains why he became an ordained priest with the unsure, "I was riding on the bus one day . . . the idea just came to me I guess." Rocky says he once got an idea on a bus: "That got me six years."

Jerry became an obscure priest while Rocky obtained the prominence accorded front-page lawbreakers. It is because of this that their close ties are broken. Rocky explains: "What was I going to say? Nothing happening on the inside. When I was on the outside, I figured you could always read the newspapers. I was always on the front page." At the plot twist, when Jerry breaks out of obscurity to become a powerful radio crusader, Rocky tells him that he has his permission to hurt him if he's in the way of Jerry's clean-up. Rocky regards Jerry's chance to succeed as nil.

The kids believe no deathhouse can hold Rocky. Rocky is the hero to them. More importantly, they live in Rocky's shadow; if it wasn't enough that Soapy, Bim, Crabface,

Dell, Punsly, Hall, Jordan, Gorcey, Halop.

Swing, Pasty and Hunky share what was once Rocky's hideout, the carved initials "R.S." are an ever-present reminder that they are growing up the same way as Rocky did.

When Rocky must explain why he is popular with the kids, he says, "I wear my collar frontwards." Rocky is not interested in helping the kids, however (except when he makes his final sacrifice). He merely has fun with them. He enjoys himself when he pulls a hold-up on them, using a fist-in-the-pocket to scare them. He later shows them that he carries no "rod."

The kids respect both Jerry and Rocky, but in different ways. The Dead Enders look up *to* Rocky, not up *at* him. With Jerry it's different. Although he sets up a basketball game for them, it's Rocky who steals their hearts, while Jerry slaps them for every cheatful move. The kids don't believe, as in the old cliché, that it's the way they play the game . . .

The ending weighs the two major characters' definitions of honesty. Rocky wants to sizzle in the electric chair unafraid, knowing that he can spit in a guard's eye and have the guard try to live it down for the rest of his life. He wants to view it as routine: "It'll be like sitting in a barber's chair." Jerry wants him to have another kind of courage: the courage to die cowardly, to forfeit his infamy, the only thing he has left. "Now you're going to be a hero in death," Jerry explains. As Sol Polito's silhouette shot shows, Rocky dies writhing, his voice high-pitched in cries for mercy. There is a special meaning for audiences—who know that only Jerry and a higher power are aware of Rocky's having faked dying "yellow "—when they hear Jerry say, "Goodbye: may God have mercy on you."

Critics have made much of this climactic scene. They have noted that Rocky is the honest one, because he wants to die as he feels, while Jerry comes across as unscrupu-

With James Cagney.

lous, using deception to forward his good intentions. It should be pointed out, however, that death seems to have played a part in shaping the characters' attitudes. Rocky was very dishonest through the picture up to the time of his death. He associated with company that crossed him when not threatened. In one scene Frazier tells his secretary that he doesn't want to see Rocky. When Rocky appears inside his door, he changes face and claims that he is pleased to see Rocky.

The kids' actions are small-scale versions of Rocky's. They are impressionable youths grasping for the easy route to money, and are on their way when Rocky pays each kid $50 for guarding an envelope. Soapy (Billy) exclaims, "Fifty dollars. It's burning a hole right through my hand!" With each kid toting this amount, the group goes to a bar, treats the neighborhood kids to beer, and "throw dollar bills around like it was confetti" (in the words of Laury, Rocky's girlfriend). Even Rocky is ashamed of these acts.

The kids are apprehensive of gangsters. When Rocky hands them the envelope they are to guard, and explains, "You know what happens to guys who talk," they swallow every word. They don't act kindly to the priest. Soapy explains for them all: "We don't fall for that pie-in-the-sky stuff anymore, Father." At the end of the film, when they learn that the character they emulated is gone, they are motionless. Huntz Hall explains:

"At the end of *Angels With Dirty Faces*, where the kids don't believe that Cagney went to the electric chair, and the priest comes in and tells us, we looked up and 'huh?' and we never answered. And the line starts up, 'These kids should be put out of pictures, they're bad, they don't even believe that the man finked out to go to the electric chair.' We got a lot of pressure. That was the time, the era. Every kid was growing up to be a gangster, and if they didn't have a war, there would have been machine guns in the street."

According to Bernard Punsly, there was a machine-gun atmosphere on the set. Whenever the Dead End Kids stalled production, Cagney would become the character he played on the screen and showed no leniency towards those who warranted his wrath. When Halop was (in Punsly's words) "acting up and wouldn't read his lines properly, Cagney 'taught him how.' He would put Halop's face to the script, apply his middle knuckle to his scalp and tell him to read his lines. It must have worked because word came down from Gorcey not to mess with Cagney." Gorcey too knew what it was to provoke the man who was enacting the role of Rocky Sullivan. During the scene in which Pat O'Brien "was trying to get us to come to church, Gorcey kept repeating his lines under his breath. Cagney stopped production, grabbed Gorcey by the hair and let him have it."

Bernard Punsly, Billy Halop, Huntz Hall, Gloria Dickson, Bobby Jordan, Leo Gorcey, John Garfield, and Gabriel Dell.

THEY MADE ME A CRIMINAL

Released January 28, 1939, by Warner Brothers. Produced by Hal B. Wallis. Directed by Busby Berkeley. Screenplay by Sig Herzig. Based on the story "They Made Me a Criminal," by Bertram Millhauser and Beulah Marie Dix, which had been filmed previously by Warner Brothers as *The Life of Jimmy Dolan* (1933). Music by Max Steiner. Photographed by James Wong Howe. Edited by Jack Killifer. Art direction by Anton Grot. Gowns by Milo Anderson. Musical direction by Leo S. Forbstein. Sound by Oliver S. Garretson. *8232 ft. 92 minutes.*

Johnny Bradfield, John Garfield; *Peggy,* Gloria Dickson; *Detective Monty Phalen,* Claude Rains; *Tommy,* Billy Halop; *Angel,* Bobby Jordan; *Spit,* Leo Gorcey; *Dippy,* Huntz Hall; *T.B.,* Gabriel Dell; *Milty,* Bernard Punsly; *Grandma Rafferty,* May Robson; *Goldie West,* Ann Sheridan; *Doc Ward,* Robert Glecker; *Charlie McGee,* John Ridgely; *Budgie,* Barbara Pepper; *Inspector Ennis,* William Davidson; *Lenihan, fight promoter,* Ward Bond; *Malvin, lawyer,* Robert Strange; *Smith,* Louis Jean Heydt; *Gaspar Rutchek,* Frank Riggi; *Rutchek's manager,* Cliff Clark; *Collucci,* Dick Wessel; *Sheriff,* Raymond Brown; *Fight announcer,* Sam Hayes; *Drunk,* Arthur Housman; *Ticket taker,* Clem Bevans; *Mrs. Williamson,* Doris Lloyd.

World champion fighter Johnnie Bradfield is thought to be dead and guilty of murder after his manager and girlfriend, the only people who could testify to his innocence, die in an auto crash. Police detective Phalen thinks Johnnie is still alive. Johnnie settles on Grandma Rafferty's date farm in Arizona. The farm is being used to rehabilitate juvenile delinquents who are under the guardianship of Peggy, the sister of one of the boys (Tommy).

Johnnie, remembering the advice of a lawyer who extorted his money, assumes the name "Jack Dorney." "Jack" encourages Tommy to get a gas pump as a sideline business for the farm. He plans to raise the money by staying in the boxing ring for three rounds at $500 per round against an up-and-coming challenger. Johnnie spots Phalen buying a ticket for the fight and, realizing that his trademark fight stance will give him away, he backs down. But his determination to help his ranch intimates is so strong that eventually he goes on with the match. "Jack" fights three rounds, but is defeated in the fourth. He surrenders himself to the detective. Phalen and Johnnie prepare to board a train for New York, but Phalen decides to let Johnnie stay where he is.

They Made Me a Criminal has a smattering of almost every staple used in the movies: romance, sports, detective yarn, urban setting, rural setting, cruel people, kind people, kids, philosophy. Certainly such an overload accounts for why there is not too much of any of these elements. For instance, there are no scenes letting us know what Johnnie, the champion prizefighter (who revels at being the champ in the opening scenes), feels about being Jack, the drifter. He may still be the same man, but he has a name he can never utter. Peggy never learns of his identity, although he could, by confessing his prowess, ease her fear that he will get hurt in the ring.

It's hard for us to believe what the screenwriter obviously believed: that Johnnie can be indifferent to his championship. The screenwriter tries to show that trophies can be meaningless, by creating a world champion who never learns that he has become world champion (the Arizona challenger, after defeating Johnnie/Jack in the fourth round, would, after all, be the new world champion). The audience is left with nagging doubts concerning the defeat and the victory (had Johnnie's training been better, would he have won?).

They Made Me a Criminal asserts that "everyone is a sucker." In the establishing scenes, Bradfield says he thinks that fight spectators are suckers for believing his spiel about "no booze or women." "It's a line, a line for suckers," he chortles as he drinks and fondles women. The same is true of his radio message to "Ma"—he has no mother. When he wants to pick up his prize money and learns from his lawyer that he must settle for only a fraction of the money due him, he asks, "Are you trying to make a sucker out of me?" When, in looking over the Rafferty Ranch, he learns that Peggy is reforming the boys without being paid to do so, he thinks she is a—you guessed it. The idea is carted out a last time at the end when Johnnie, watching Phalen return to New York without him, murmurs, "Goodbye, sucker."

Phalen (as played by Claude Rains) is the best element in this mixed bag. Phalen is bitter that he's on Morgue Detail, yet he is more analytical than the other detectives. When Phalen's captain and his fellow officers are celebrating the supposed death of Johnnie, Phalen lets the others know that he is not convinced that the body (or remains thereof) behind the wheel of the crashed car is Johnnie's. He recalls that Johnnie had his watch on his left wrist, while the accident victim had his on his right.

He maintains that no one would move his watch from wrist to wrist. "There are some things that a man always does the same, like the side he starts to shave on in the morning."

The Dead End Kids are clearly eclipsed by the other actors, for the second time in a row. Their plot function here is similar to that in *Angels With Dirty Faces*.

In one scene, "Jack" takes Tommy, Milty, Dippy and Angel swimming, without telling Peggy or Grandma. En route, Tommy says he is concerned that Mrs. Rafferty will lose her farm, and broaches to Jack the idea of installing a gas pump on the property, which would be an ideal location. The fivesome stop at an irrigation tank, which is gradually emptied as they swim. They must stand on one another's shoulders and help each other out. As Angel can't swim, the water level must be lowered, and Johnny and Tommy alternate between holding onto Angel and diving to the tank's bottom to open a release valve. The tank is drained only after Johnny and Tommy have traded off chores several times.

A moment isolated from the plot has the boys trying to raise enough money to buy Jack some boxing gloves. They get "J. Douglas Williamson, Jr.," a clean-cut rich kid whose manner is as eccentric as his name, into a game of strip poker to get his movie camera. The cards favor the rich kid, but Slip recommends disastrous plays. The boys trade the camera for a pair of "lucky leather."

They Made Me a Criminal was directed by Busby Berkeley. After making a name with musical spectaculars like *Footlight Parade* (1933), *Golddiggers of 1933*, and *Forty-Second Street* (1933), Berkeley persuaded Warner Brothers executives to let him do a dramatic picture. It was *They Made Me a Criminal*. He didn't shed his image entirely with it. The film contains an "in" joke: When Dippy operates the controls of a makeshift shower, he serenades the bathing Jack with "By a Waterfall," the hit number from *Footlight Parade*.

Warner Brothers cut their chances when they took on the director by assigning Berkeley a story that had already been shot. Berkeley could look at the 1933 *Life of Jimmy Dolan* for reference.

Punsly, Dell, Jordan, Hall (at top), Halop, John Garfield.

HELL'S KITCHEN

Stanley Fields, Ronald Reagan, Charley Foy, Frankie Burke, Huntz Hall. During the shooting of one of the two films the 40th president of the United States made with the Dead End Kids, the kids placed a burning hat on his head.

Released July 8, 1939, by Warner Brothers. Produced by Mark Hellinger and Bryan Foy. Directed by Lewis Seiler and E.A. Dupont. Screenplay by Crane Wilbur and Fred Niblo, Jr. Story by Crane Wilbur. Photographed by Charles Rosher. Edited by Clarence Kolster. Art direction by Hugo Reticker. Dialogue direction by Hugh Cummings. Gowns by Milo Anderson. Sound by Dolph Thomas. *7144 ft. 81 minutes.*

Tony Marco, Billy Halop; *Gyp Haller,* Leo Gorcey; *Joey Richards,* Bobby Jordan; *Bongo,* Huntz Hall; *Ace,* Gabriel Dell; *Patrick Henry "Ouch" Rosenbloom,* Benard Punsly; *Buck Caesar,* Stanley Fields; *Jim Donahue,* Ronald Reagan; *Beth Avery,* Margaret Lindsay; *Krispan,* Grant Mitchell; *Kid,* Frankie Burke; *Mike Garvey,* Fred Tozere; *Elmer Krispan,* Arthur Loft; *Sarah Krispan,* Vera Lewis; *Hardy,* Robert Homans; *Floogie,* Charley Foy; *Whitey,* Raymond Bailey; *Callahan,* Robert Strange; *Mr. Quill,* Clem Bevans; *Judge Chandler,* George Irving; *Bailiff,* Lee Phelps; *Mug,* Jimmy O'Gatty; *Maizie,* Ila Rhodes; *Chick,* Don Turner; *Nails,* Joe A. Devlin; *Roll Mop,* Jimmie Lucas; *Pants,* Jack Kenney; *Sweet Al,* Sol Gorss; *Guard,* Cliff Saum; *Henchmen,* Charles Sullivan, Jack Gardner; *Guards,* Max Hoffman, Jr., Dick Rich, Tom Wilson; *Announcer,* Reid Kilpatrick; *Usher,* George O'Hanlon; *Detective,* Jack Mower; *Mrs. Margaret Chandler,* Ruth Robinson; *Jury foreman,* George Offerman, Jr.

The Dead End Kids, in a crookedly operated reform school, see the chance of a better future in financial backer Buck Caesar. Buck, a paroled convict, contributes to the school at the suggestion of his nephew, lawyer Jim Donahue, who believes the boys need better guidance and thinks the contributions will create good will for his uncle. Superintendant Krispan doesn't want Caesar's contributions to lead to an audit. He arranges to have professional hockey players substitute for the boys' adversaries in an upcoming game so that Buck (a natural for placing a heavy bet) will get riled, become violent, and violate parole. Buck socks the opposing coach at the game, and goes on the lam to avoid arrest.

Krispan again takes his position as undisputed ruler of the reform school, which under Buck's influence had become a self-governing boys town. (Tony had been elected president, and Gyp chief of by police, by a majority of the 200 inmates.) Krispan locks Joey in a freezer as punishment and Joey dies. The kids start a revolt, and Buck hurries to the reform school when he learns of it. The boys find Krispan guilty of Joey's death and determine to make him "*join Joey,*" but Buck and the police he has brought with him stop them. Krispan is punished through legal channels; Buck is sent back to prison for violating parole.

Hell's Kitchen is intense melodrama. With a setting that is perfect for the Dead End Kids (they are optionless victims in the Hudson Shelter), it is an uprising tale told with vigor. Although "Hell's Kitchen" is the name of one of New York's districts, the force the two words carry make the combination a valid name for the Hudson Shelter. Tony (Billy Halop) explains. "We call it 'Hell's Kitchen' and sometimes we leave off kitchen."

Joey's death, the most powerful scene in the film, is the nadir of the boys' plight. Joey is a sick youth, sensitive to cold. When he badmouths Krispan for a fleeting moment, Krispan retaliates by placing him in an ice-house. He stays there for nine hours, until a concerned guard carries his stiff body to Tony and Gyp. Tony and Gyp each rubs his palms with Joey's to get

Joey's blood circulating, optimism blinding them to the truth visible in Joey's closed eyes. He is dead.

The first suggestion that anarchy could erupt occurs when Krispan decides to hold a private in-house funeral. He doesn't want the outside authorities to learn of Joey's death. Krispan delivers a nice eulogy, but can't resist making remarks designed to help him maintain his grip on the boys. As the boys draw away, Gyp and Tony realize that Krispan's sermon had layed responsibility for the tragedy on them. Gyp murmurs, "Krispan killed him. He killed Joey." "He killed Joey" is repeated in the same low tone by those around him. The chant "He killed Joey" spreads throughout the funeral procession. "HE KILLED JOEY" is repeatedly chanted in unison by the mob of 200 boys. Krispan tries to placate them but Gyp fires a gun at him. Krispan flees.

Ironically, *Hells's Kitchen* has comic moments, delivered by Stanley Fields. The opening moment sets the mood. The judge formally sentences Buck, but when he has finished his deliberated speech, Buck admits that he didn't understand the legalese His Honor spoke. The poorly educated Buck is then given a translation by a bailiff, who relates it in breakneck speed colored by mad gestures and Damon Runyon terms.

When Buck and Jim, accompanied by stooge aides, use hoses to squash a kids' riot at the shelter, the hydraulic gust blows all off their feet. Later, when Buck sits in a chair, it topples backward.

It may be said that Buck handles the comedy while the Dead End Kids perpetrate the melodrama.

Many Dead End Kids, Little Tough Guys, Eastside Kids and Bowery Boys films would receive the Adult ("A") rating from the British censorship board when they were reviewed prior to release in that country. (The "A" rating is equivalent to our modern-day "R." The British code must be used as reference for contemporary opinion, as the United States did not have a ratings code until 1968.) *Hell's Kitchen* is the only film in any of the four series to receive the "X" rating (which at the time was known as the "H" rating, for "Horrific"). Apparently the British censors were worried that children would get bad ideas from seeing the Dead End Kids try to seal the warden in a coffin.

ANGELS WASH THEIR FACES

Released August 26, 1939, by Warner Brothers. Produced by Hal B. Wallis. Directed by Ray Enright. Associate production by Max Siegel. Screenplay by Michael Fessier, Niven Busch and Robert Buckner. Story by Jonathan Finn. Photographed by Arthur L. Todd. Edited by James Gibson. Music by Adolph DeLitsch. Art direction by Ted Smith. Musical direction by Leo S. Forbstein. Sound by Dolph Thomas. Production title: *The Battle of City Hall. 8427 ft. 86 minutes.*

Huntz and Leo off-screen.

Billy Shafter, Billy Halop; *Gabe Ryan,* Frankie Thomas; *Leo Finnegan,* Leo Gorcey; *Bernie Smith,* Bobby Jordan; *Huntz Gartman,* Huntz Hall; *Luigi Batteran,* Gabriel Dell; *Luke "Sleepy" Arkelian,* Bernard Punsly; *Patrick Remson,* Ronald Reagan; *Joy Ryan,* Ann Sheridan; *Peggy Finnegan,* Bonita Granville; *A.H. Remson, Sr.,* Henry O'Neill; *William Kroner,* Bernard Nedell; *Alfred Martino,* Eduardo Ciannelli; *Mayor Dooley,* Berton Churchill; *H.J. Haines,* Cy Kendall; *Mrs. Hannaberry,* Margaret Hamilton; *Shuffle,* Dick Rich; *Gildersleeve,* Grady Sutton; *Mrs. Arkelian,* Margorie Main; *Maloney,* Minor Watson; *Alfred Goonplantz,* Jackie Searl; *Turnkey,* Aldrich Bowker; *Simpkins,* Robert Strange; *Joe Smith,* Egon Brecher; *Mrs. Smith,* Sibyl Harris; *Boy,* Junior Coghlan; *Reform school boy with knife,* Frankie Burke; *Merton,* John Hamilton; *Reporter,* John Ridgely; *Photographer,* William Hopper; *Prisoner,* Elliott Sullivan; *Man,* Charles Trowbridge; *Reporter,* John Harron; *Judge,* Howard Hickman; *Woman,* Sarah Padden; *Guards,* Lee Phelps, Jack Clifford, Tom Wilson; *Defense attorney,* Edward Keane; *Reporter,* Max Hoffman, Jr.; *Announcer,* Wendell Niles; *Assistant turnkey,* Harry Strange.

When Gabe Ryan gets out of reform school, his sister Joy takes him to a new neighborhood to start life anew. Immediately, Gabe joins the Beale Street Termites. A local mobster, William Kroner, allied with arsonist Martino, accuses Gabe of starting a fire on one of his properties. Martino, deciding that Gabe could be framed for any fire, sets one of his apartment buildings ablaze for insurance purposes. Invalid Sleepy dies in the flames.

Assistant District Attorney Patrick Remson is convinced that Gabe is innocent, and helps Gabe prepare his case, which also helps Remson get close to Joy. Joy also works hard preparing Gabe's defense, which consumes time that she would otherwise have spent rallying against corruption in city government; this pleases Martino very much. Gabe is convicted of arson and sentenced to prison.

In order to free Gabe, Billy competes for "boy mayor," and through hard study and the boys' tactics wins the top city position for a week. He has Kroner and a stooge arrested for a minor violation and places the two crooks in stocks. Billy, the kids and their neighborhood residents interrogate them to make them talk. They keep quiet, but when Remson shows them ship reservations which prove that Martino and the chief of the fire board (who is also involved) are about to skip the country, Kroner confesses. With Remson's help, Martino is later apprehended.

As the story shows, *Angels Wash Their Faces* follows the pattern of Warner Brothers crime drama, where the corruption is thick and victims are made of the innocent. (That had been the case with *Angels With Dirty Faces,* but, despite what the title implies, *Angels Wash Their Faces* is not a sequel.) But that's not the half of it.

With Ronald Reagan.

Gorcey, Jordan, Bonita Granville, Dell and Hall look at Billy Halop, who will get up again. This is the film in which the Dead End Kids lose their powerlessness.

33

At left, Bonita Granville and Frankie Thomas, both fixtures of Warner Brothers' "Nancy Drew" series. With Gabe, Huntz (seated), Billy, Bobby (seated), Leo.

Angels Wash Their Faces is a juvenile-aimed farce that shows that kids do everything right and the adults do everything wrong. Lines like a declaration made at the gallows by Mayor Billy—"We've got something here that might wake the grown-ups up and make them laugh out of the wrong side of their mouths"—undoubtedly endeared *Angels* to the adolescent audience. The film's value to adult cinema patrons was so negligible that no trade paper or major newspaper reviewed it. This is a shallow film for younger viewers who wouldn't guess that the film was calculated to capitalize on their sentiments.

The kids' first act as public officials is a jaunt to the jail to try unsuccessfully to free Gabe, an event made to seem "newsbreaking." Little has been spared to show the Dead End Kids as crusaders. With strengths like these, no wonder Remson (Ronald Reagan) remarks, "You've got to admit the grown-ups bawled things up. Give those kids a chance."

Perhaps if the situations weren't handled so ludicrously, it would be possible to empathize with these characters. The kids aren't the only ones who come off bad. The movie also makes monkeys out of its grown-up players.

Ronald Reagan fares worse than the kids do. To Gabe, he says, "I've come to the conclusion that all kids should be given a stretch in reform school—if they all come out as well as you did." A line saved for him to say to Miss Sheridan was: "You're the only person in the world who likes my dialogue." Miss Sheridan has some nifty lines

herself. When Ronnie makes advances to her, she says, "If you were to stop beating around the bush, and ask me if I have an evening free, I would . . . "

A dream sequence in which Billy has visions of the kids torturing his head while inundating him with tidbits of history and social science, some early moments showing the kids acting as kids, and a sequence in which various combinations of the boys rough up Billy's potential adversaries one after another are the only worthy scenes. Least worthy is a scene in which the Termites initiate Gabe into the club. They do this by dousing Gabe (who is blindfolded) with a liquid that he thinks is gasoline (it is water). They then give Gabe the impression that he's burning by using sound effects (match being lit, etc.). Apparently Gabe's senses couldn't tell him that there wasn't a flame touching him. Poor boy! The gang plays several such stunts on him, and each time he says, "You really had me fooled that time." The effects are obviously artificial, but then again, so is the film.

The kids smile at the wrong time and cheer at the wrong time. They stand up straight at a ceremony, and act as if they were being given orders under threat of pain. Which in fact they were. Warner Brothers, tired of the kids' pranks (they had painted obscene murals on the executives' office walls, thrown a lighted firecracker into Humphrey Bogart's dressing room, and set off the fire sprinklers in the wardrobe department), hired a guardian for them in the person of ex-football player Russ Saunders.

Leo Gorcey recalls in his autobiography: "While working on *The Battle of City Hall* [the production title for *Angels Wash Their Faces*] the kids really got out of line, Russ ordered a fire hose out, and let us have it full force.

"Anyone who has ever been hit point blank with the water from a full-size, high-pressure fire hose can understand that we were very nice kids while working on the rest of that picture." Maybe that's why they're not in character.

The notion that the Dead End Kids should have a chaperone was carried over into the script of the film. The chaperone is played by Grady Sutton. Sutton can be taken to be the same character on-screen that Saunders was off-screen. "I'm here to see that you don't get into any mischief," Sutton says. Yet Sutton, cast as the assistant to the genuine mayor, isn't equal to the task of controlling the kids. The kids jump him and lock him in a closet.

Just par for the course for the real Dead End Kids. One question does come up. Why did Warner Brothers approve a script calling for the kids to overpower and lock-up a guardian on film, while they didn't want the kids to do that to the real guardian? Was Warner Brothers saying that it was all right for the kids to attack a man on film, but not all right to do it in the studio?

Warner Brothers answered that when they dropped the kids after one more film.

ON DRESS PARADE

Released November 18, 1939, by Warner Brothers. Produced by Bryan Foy. Directed by William Clemens and Noel Smith (uncredited). Scenario by Tom Reed and Charles Belden. Photographed by Arthur L. Todd. Edited by Douglas Gould. Production title: *Dead End Kids at Valley Forge.* Also known as *Dead End Kids on Dress Parade* and *Dead End Kids at Military School. 5539 ft. 62 minutes.*

Cadet Major Rollins, Billy Halop; *Slip Duncan,* Leo Gorcey; *Cadet Ronny Morgan,* Bobby Jordan; *Cadet Johnny Cabot,* Huntz Hall; *Cadet Georgie Warren,* Gabriel Dell; *Dutch,* Bernard Punsly; *Colonel Mitchell Reiker,* John Litel; *Cadet Lieutenant Murphy,* Frankie Thomas; *Mrs. Neely,* Cecilia "Cissie" Loftus; *Captain Evans Dover,* Selmer Jackson; *Father Ryan,* Aldrich Bowker; *Hathaway,* Douglas Meins; *Dr. Lewis,* William Gould; *Colonel William Duncan,* Don Douglas.

Slip's father, a World War I hero on his deathbed, asks Colonel Reiker to take care of his boy after he's gone. Slip doesn't want to leave his poolhall existence, but is tricked into the Reiker-operated military school. Cadet Major Rollins tries to straighten out Slip's unruly ways, but is thrown out a window for his trouble. The other boys ostracize Slip, but his saving of Cadet Warren's life gains their respect.

The Dead End Kids have been cleaned up for *On Dress Parade,* an overly sentimental and mawkish picture, a quasi-precursor to the Monogram Eastside Kids stories that would follow it; even the running time is similar. Four of the kids are no longer from "the far side

of the tracks" (as *Variety* put it).

Slip (Leo) is the poolhall prodigy who succumbs to conformity before the final bell. At school, he is determined to upset things, and flaunts disrespect for all discipline. Collins (Halop), a cadet major, tries to stop Slip from abandoning his uniform, but in a fight that ensues, Slip pushes Billy through a second-floor window. Slip is remorseful, and works diligently in his classes and gets top grades. At the end of the picture, he is completely reformed. The silent treatment he received from the other boys has played a part in the transformation; he missed the companionship of Huntz, Gabe and Bobby (Bernard plays a street-wise kid), even though they are of different backgrounds, and wanted to re-instate himself with them.

The wrap-up of these 62 minutes rings false. Slip, the central character, rescues Gabe from a fire in a camp munitions storeroom, and is seriously burned in the process. He is thus made cadet major, and is given his father's distinguished service cross. To his comrades, Slip is a hero.

The Dead End Kids are not the ones we've come to know. Slip, had he been Spit or another former Gorcey characterization, would not be in tears after he pushes Halop out of the window. He would have scrammed. The business of Slip refusing to accept military discipline, and his isolation from the upper classmen, is not effectively handled. As for the Dead End Kids as a whole, they get along with the world and do not take sides against it. This is the only film in the Dead End Kids series in which that is the case. As *Variety* put it, "*On Dress Parade* looks like a partnership between Warner Brothers and the recruiting service."

Slip (Leo) observes wheelchaired Rollins (Billy), now his friend. Cissie Loftus looks on.

Now Playing

The Dead End Kids and Little Tough Guys

Billy BENEDICT   Hally CHESTER   David GORCEY   Harris BERGER   Norman ABBOTT

Huntz HALL   Billy HALOP   Bobby JORDAN   Gabriel DELL   Bernard PUNSLY

Ever see four kids aimlessly slap each other and jump on one another's back for sixty minutes?

That describes the typical film in the "Dead End Kids and Little Tough Guys" series. Those who've only heard of the nine hour-long features probably figure that these Universal films have the same substance as the concurrent Eastside Kids films released by Monogram. Anyone who assumes that the Universal films are equal to those of the Eastside Kids on a highlight-per-minute basis is going to be let down.

Another idea that those who have heard of this series might cling to is that the films are greyer and less attractively shaded than their counterparts. To these people it is hard to describe just how bad these films are. They are aimed at the four- to eight-year-old mentality. The Dead End Kids and Little Tough Guys films are meaningless, banal excursions into cinema's ghetto.

It is difficult to grasp the kids' roots here, as their background is seldom discussed. The Dead End Kids/ Little Tough Guys walk out of one film and into the next. Even when the Warner Brothers mob was in reform school, they had backgrounds. Universal did not develop such intricacies for the boys' characters. To be more exact, Universal did not develop characters.

Instead, Universal relied upon fast pacing to move the films. The effect is often like seeing a two-hour film whiz by at triple speed in forty minutes. The blurred figures leave the viewer baffled as to what was going on. Ideas (primitive ones) are thrown in and out but seldom elaborated.

To see how bad these films were, consider that film trade magazines—usually hesitant to debunk films that might lose money for the major studios, to which they were catering—issued warnings about the Little Tough Guys films. One 1941 trade review said: "Story pattern steers close to a formula previously used for the Little Tough Guys and Dead End Kids at Universal, and discarded because it proved *indigestible* as entertainment."

The Little Tough Guys do have one characteristic: they like to eat. Almost every film has at least one sequence at a dinner table, in a nightclub, or at a similar place of eating. The table usually appears during plot transitions, as the characters discuss possible forthcoming events while nibbling on chicken or box lunches. Dining sequences often gave rise to comic roughhousing, with the boys starting food fights (even fish fights) and practicing bad manners. This preoccupation with food shows that the writers were constantly thinking about what they wouldn't be able to enjoy had they been paid what their writing was worth.

So now with this warning, we go into our assessments of the adventures of Tom, Pig, Ape and String.

Clockwise (from top): Billy Halop, Gabriel Dell, Bernard Punsly, Huntz Hall, David Gorcey, Hally Chester.

David Gorcey, Huntz Hall, Robert Homans, Marjorie Main, Gabriel Dell, Helen Parrish, in the first film the boys made for Universal, which was produced between Crime School *and* Angels With Dirty Faces.

LITTLE TOUGH GUY

Released July 22, 1938, by Universal. Produced by Ken Goldsmith. Directed by Harold Young. Screenplay by Gilson Brown and Brenda Weisberg. Story by Brenda Weisberg. Additional dialogue by Lee Loeb. Photographed by Elwood Bredell. Edited by Philip Cahn. Musical direction by Charles Previn. Art direction by Jack Otterson. Assistant, N.V. Timchen. Assistant direction by Fred Frank. Sound by Bernard B. Brown. Sound engineered by Charles Carroll. *86 minutes.*

Johnny Boylan, Billy Halop; *Carl "Pig" Adams,* Huntz Hall; *String,* Gabriel Dell; *Ape,* Bernard Punsly; *Sniper,* David Gorcey; *Dopey,* Hally Chester; *Kay Bolan,* Helen Parrish; *Paul Wilson,* Robert Wilcox; *Cyril Gerrard,* Jackie Searl; *Mrs. Boylan,* Marjorie Main; *Rita Belle Warren,* Peggy Stewart; *Carl,* Edward Cehman; *Jim Boylan,* Edward Pawley; *Baxter,* Olin Howland; *Truant officer,* Robert Homans; *Cashier,* Eleanor Hanson; *Judges,* Charles Trowbridge, Selmer Jackson; *Kids,* Buster Phelps, George Billings; *Detectives,* Ben Taggart, William Ruhl; *Mr. Randall,* Hooper Atchley; *Mrs. Daniels,* Clara Macklin Blore; *Supervisor,* Jason Robards, Sr.; *Eddie,* John Fitzgerald; *Bud,* Richard Selzer; *Policeman,* Monte Montague; *Band leader,* Frank Bischell; *Usher,* Johnny Green; *Bertis,* James Zahner; *Clerk,* Stanley Hughes; *Secretary,* Raymond Parker; *Peddler,* Pat C. Flick; *Mrs. Wanamaker,* Helen MacKellar; *Mr. Gerrard,* Alan Edwards; *Domino, cop,* Jack Carr; *D.A.,* Edwin Stanley; *Superintendant,* Harry Hayden; *Dot LaFleur,* Janet McLeay; *Secretary,* Victor Adams; *Fat,* Edward Arnold, Jr.; *Chuck,* Paul Dubov; *Proprietor,* Paul Weigel; *Police sergeant,* J. Pat O'Malley; *Truck driver,* Bert Young; *Detective,* George Sherwood; *Woman,* Georgia O'Dell; *Office boy,* John Estes; *Salesgirl,* Gwen Seager; *Policemen,* Mike Pat Donovan, Jack Daley.

Jim Boylan is wounded in a strike protest riot and ordered to stand trial for incitement and a murder he didn't commit. He is found guilty and sentenced to die. His son, Johnny, tries to see the Attorney General, and, when he fails, vows to become a criminal. He and his gang of newsboy-cronies (Pig, String, Ape, Sniper and Dopey) start a local crime wave, abetted by Cyril Gerrard, the District Attorney's son, who the kids meet at a radio broadcast. His identity is unknown to them.

Johnny and Pig are surrounded in a shop by the police during a nighttime heist. Johnny, remembering the values taught to him by his mother, suggests to Pig that they give themselves up; adventurous Pig makes a break and is shot to death. Johnny, defended by family friends, is dismissed by the judge for charges of accessory in the death of Pig, but is sentenced for his crimes to a reform school stint equal to that of String, Ape, Sniper and Dopey. They meet Cyril at reform school.

Little Tough Guy routinely changes mood, and only becomes intelligent during its second half. It is disjointed, sometimes stupid, and treats its subject matter unevenly. It forces the characters in all of its independent plotlines (Johnny's sister in her plotline, the District Attorney and his people in theirs) to re-adapt each time it changes course.

The Dead End Kids are bland. They are established as inconsiderate urchins, and while their characters are developed more in the latter part of the film, the first impressions are maintained too long for the second impressions to stick.

The most unusual thing said by any of them during this early period is a response made by Pig (Huntz Hall) to a comment made by Ape (Bernard Punsly). Ape says, "You never gave me anything," to which Pig replies, "Except a punch on the nose."

The film often shifts its scenes away from the kids, but when they are returned to it's not to much purpose. Senseless fighting is for the kids a preoccupation. When they aren't fighting, their activities are equally senseless. When Cyril says, "I want to see what makes you tick," three of the boys (String, Ape and Sniper) go into an improvised dance, chanting "TIC-TOC-TIC-TOC" in unison.

The most defined character is that of Cyril, the rich kid. He describes himself to his urchin friends as the millionaire's son who is bored with life. As he tells this to the gang in his extensive playroom, the kids don't seem to understand him. He tells the gang that he envies them their being able to do what they want to when they want. When their same lackadaisical attitude results in the kids' cutting Cyril out of a job by throwing him out of the car, he stops admiring them and informs the police.

Johnny (Billy Halop) is not nearly so well defined. His character traits are often conflicting. (Perhaps the result of co-writers not working with the knowledge of the other? The film as a whole looks as if scenes which should have been discarded were included.) He and the other boys don't know each other at the beginning. When they meet, Pig tells him, "Mind your own business and you won't get hoit." When Pig challenges Johnny to a fight and is defeated by Johnny, what does Johnny do? Does he make demands on Pig? No. He offers friendship. (What kind of friendship will develop from this?) They then discover that they all sell newspapers, and being friends, they decide they won't intrude on each other's corners. Johnny says, "There are enough corners for us all to do business."

The film's lack of continuity is a burden the kids are forced to carry. In an out-of-place scene, the kids go to a "Youth of America" radio broadcast and are shunned by that sector of the audience not from the tenements.

The last half of the picture makes up for the slights in the first. It transcends the "B" movie with commentary, as when it presents a montage showing the six young hoodlums committing crimes, going over their booty, grinning. They act as if they considered the world their backyard, from which anything could be taken, from which goods could be lifted, as if the kids were in the wild and were taking deadfalls needed for firewood. Yet, the world closes in on them, and the world as they know it ends for Johnny and Pig in a cellar guaranteed to produce claustrophobia. They look at each other in glances. There isn't much light, shadows cover patches

Pig (Huntz) is pinned by Johnny (Billy). Making their first appearances: Hally Chester (above Billy's head) and David Gorcey (second from right).

Edward Pawley, Helen Parrish, Halop.

of their faces. We can see, though, what's going on inside them. Johnny is scared, but, as much as the circumstances permit, he is collected. Pig is death-defying, self-preserving. There are silent pauses, building intensity. Finally, Pig hot-heels it to the streets, and is shot full of holes. The differences in their outlooks has brought about this.

The skill of this scene makes it possible to forgive Universal. The company chose the idea for this film and made it the same way it did all of its films at the time. By committee. And you know what they say about committees. Universal wasn't then the big studio that it is today, or that it would be a few years later. Financially, the studio remained solvent due to annual revivals of *Dracula* and *Frankenstein*, both made under the care of Carl Laemmle (Universal's founder) in 1931. (No other studio at that time allowed the public to see its "lost treasures," so people couldn't expect to see many old films after initial release.) In 1941 Universal would be saved when it hired a pair of burlesque comics who performed "Who's on First?" It then became a studio that turned its attention to comedy and attracted the top writers in the field. Sadly, they weren't used for the kids.

Billy Benedict (second from right) makes his first appearance with the kids. Billy Halop is fourth from left. To the right from him: Huntz, Hally Chester, Billy B., Harris Berger.

CALL A MESSENGER

Released November 3, 1939, by Universal. Produced by Ken Goldsmith. Directed by Arthur Lubin. Screenplay by Arthur T. Horman. Story by Sally Sandlin and Michael Kraike. Photographed by Elwood Bredell. Edited by Charles Maynard. Musical direction by Hans J. Salter. Art direction by Jack Otterson. Assistant direction by Henry Spitz. Sound by Bernard B. Brown. *65 minutes.*

Jimmy Hogan, Billy Halop; *Pig,* Huntz Hall; *Yap,* David Gorcey; *Trouble,* William Benedict; *Kirk Graham,* Robert Armstrong; *Marge Hogan,* Mary Carlisle; *Frances O'Neill,* Anne Nagel; *Ed Hogan,* Victor Jory; *Chuck Walsh,* Larry "Buster" Crabbe; *Baldy,* El Brendel; *Bob Pritchard,* Jimmy Butler; *Big Lip,* George Offerman Jr.; *Al,* Jimmy O'Gatty; *Nail,* Joe Gray; *Sgt. Harrison,* Cliff Clark; *Lt. Nelson,* John Hamilton; *Gardner,* Anthony Hughes; *Virginia,* Kay Sutton; *Cop,* James C. Morton; *Sweeney,* Sherwood Bailey; *Clerk,* Joey Ray; *Miss Clarington,* Ruth Rickaby; *Barber,* Frank Mitchell; *Desk sergeant,* James Farley; *Cop,* Frank O'Connor; *Clerk,* Lyle Moraine; *Kid,* Payne Johnson; *Paymaster,* Jack Gardner; *Police officer,* Kernan Cripps; *Watchman,* Russ Powell; *Butler,* Wilson Benge; *Black maid,* Louise Franklin; *Messengers,* Harris Berger, Hally Chester.

Jimmy takes the rap for the other boys when he is caught robbing a branch of the Postal Union. To avoid reform school, he accepts a job as a messenger boy. The other kids razz him about his uniform, but he coerces them to join the company as well. Jimmy tries to steer his sister Marge away from gangster Chuck Walsh. When their brother Ed returns from a stretch in the pen, Jimmy and Marge try to keep him straight. Ed gets involved with Walsh, and the duo start robbing branches of the Postal Union. When Walsh decides to hold up Jimmy's branch, Ed goes straight and attempts to warn Jimmy, but is shot by Walsh. Jimmy and the boys nevertheless rout the crime ring.

Call a Messenger is an unpretentious follow-up to *Little Tough Guy,* although not as somber as that previous film. Director Arthur Lubin keeps the plot and action moving, with a ration of humor on the side. But the film is mainly a rehash of formulas from the gangster film cycles, with the boys playing it honest through much of the picture.

Halop and Hall are the only original Dead End Kids here, and are the focus of the film's action. The plot has the Little Tough Guys (after three vehicles of their own) shoved to the background. (The Little Tough Guys had appeared in *Little Tough Guys in Society, Newsboys' Home* and *Code of the Streets* between this and the previous Dead End Kids films. These solo films are covered in the chapter "Forerunners, Imitators and Offspring.") Halop's part in the plot is integral, while Hall is given responsibility for the humor. Contemporary trade reviewers recognized that Huntz had developed into a decent comedian, and he shows it here within the boundaries of a lighthearted portrayal. Pig had been a tough guy in the first Universal picture, but he is mellow here and would remain so for the rest of the series. Halop was not a comic actor, so he was held to playing the tough, fed-up kid (a part he played well). His character and Hall's were therefore to clash in the films to come. His interaction with Pig often was nothing more than slaps and pokes. In this film and in the others, these slaps and pokes are not funny and do not fit well into the film. (Slaps and pokes would have been fine if they had been delivered in the Gorcey manner—somehow combining hitting with humor and warmth—but this was not the case.)

The gang gets some laughs when they fight over the attentions of bank manager Frances O'Neill, but on the whole the gang has little funny business to perform, and pale in comparison to El Brendel, king of the Scandanvian comics, who, although well along in years, was cast as a messenger boy.

The *Motion Picture Herald* best summed up *Call a Messenger*: "The film is neither tremendous or trivial, mighty nor meager, but a sanely, sensibly constructed item of product."

Pig, Tommy and Mama Posita (Rosina Galli) confront the representatives of the packing company (Harry Hayden, Joe King).

YOU'RE NOT SO TOUGH

Released July 26, 1940, by Universal. Associate producer, Ken goldsmith. Directed by Joe May. Screenplay by Arthur T. Horman. Based on story "Son of Mama Posita," by Maxwell Aley. Contribution by Brenda Weisberg. Photographed by Elwood Bredell. Musical direction by Hans J. Salter. Art direction by Jack Otterson. Sound by Bernard B. Brown and Frank Gross. Assistant direction by Phil Karlstein (Karlson). 65 *minutes.*

Tommy Abraham Lincoln, Billy Halop; *Pig (Albert),* Huntz Hall; *Rap,* Bobby Jordan; *String,* Gabriel Dell; *Ape,* Bernard Punsly; *Millie,* Nan Grey; *Salvatore,* Henry Armetta; *Mama (Lisa) Posita,* Rosina Galli; *Griswold,* Cliff Clark; *Collins,* Joe King; *Marshall,* Arthur Loft; *Lacey,* Harry Hayden; *Les,* Eddy Waller; *Bianca,* Evelyn Selbie; *Brakeman,* Joe Whitehead; *First picker,* Harry Humphrey; *Conley,* Don Rowan; *Second newsboy,* Hally Chester; *Jake,* Harris Berger; *First worker,* David Gorcey; *Valley truck driver,* Ralph Dunn; *Guard,* Kernan Cripps; *Jorgenson,* Eddie Phillips; *Third picker,* Ralph LaPere; *Second picker,* Marty Faust; *Third worker,* Frank Bischell; *Store proprietor,* Heinie Conklin; *Truck driver,* Harry Strang, *Carstens,* Ed Peil Sr.

The boys are hoboes who travel from ranch to ranch to grab meals and win money at dice games. They are locked up after a fight induced by their cheating at craps, and are put to work sawing wood. A local girl, Millie, teases Tommy Lincoln, the boys' leader, and in his fury he saws the wood in record time. Thus having "proved" himself as a good worker, he (along with Pig) is taken to Mama Posita's Ranch to work for pay.

Tommy learns that Mama Posita hasn't seen her only son since he was an infant, so he lets it be known that he is an orphan (which he is) and leads Mama Posita to believe that he is her son. He is given the easy job of foreman. He also is given a share of Mama Posita's wealth. This was his initial aim in starting the ruse, but he grows fond of the woman who becomes the mother he never had, so much so that when she offers him money to buy a used car, he finds that he can't accept.

A packing company boycotts Mama's crops and a growers' association refuses to let her use its trucks because she refuses to cut her wages, so Mama resigns herself to not having her crops make it to market. But Tommy devises an idea. With the help of the boys and the ranch workers, he breaks through a barricade of growers' association trucks by using tractors and sprays, and races to market with the produce.

This third entry may be the best film of the series. It makes good use of its Salinas Valley location by placing the boys in an environment in which laziness isn't as accepted as it is in New York. Tommy develops considerably during the story, and because the story develops as he does, the film is quite satisfying.

As the film opens, it appears that the kids are driving a car. When the camera pulls back, we find that the car is perched on a moving train. Moments later they are chased away, but we have learned from their conversation that they refuse to work. "What? Break our back for a dollar a day?"

They are shrewd. They deliberately avoid mooching from the rich because the rich couldn't empathize with

Tommy, Millie (Nan Grey), Ape, String (seated), Rap, Pig, at an auto court. Millie is reacting as she customarily does to beggars.

them. "When you mooch," Tommy says, "you mooch from someone who knows what it's like to be hungry."

What's more, they feel entitled to food. "We want what's coming to us," Tommy tells the sheriff who arrests them. "Three squares a day and a place to sleep. We have that coming to us. We're Americans."

No wonder they're arrested. They hasten their own downfall when they claim that they have been working. The sheriff asks to see their hands. No calluses. They're sentenced.

Of course this doesn't change them. When Tommy gets himself and Pig paroled into paying work, Pig says to him, "Now look what you've got us into! Jobs!"

Tom begins to change when he learns that his employer is the best one a worker could have. A co-worker tells him: "You haven't cropped much. Most places treat a worker like a hog, except they take a whole lot better care of their hogs. Mama Posita figures workers are people."

Mama Posita feels so intensely that her workers are people that she takes their side against the growers' association. The growers' association's position is that other workers will demand higher wages if her wages stand as an example of what an employer can pay. She insists that her pay rates are warranted, as her workers are wonderful workers.

It is because Mama Posita is so kind to her workers that Tommy first becomes fond of her. He is impressed by word that she plants a variety of crops instead of one so that her workers (who elsewhere would be dismissed

without a moment's notice) can continue working all year round. Naturally this is a woman he cannot bilk. He rationalizes about his scheme: He is an orphan, so he may be Mama Posita's son after all, regardless of the scheme he used to make her think so.

The faults that Tommy has when he comes to the ranch are overlooked by Mama Posita. She is happy to accept him as he came to her if it means she has a son. She showers him with gifts and a generous allowance.

Of course, the other boys horn in on Tommy when he has the allowance. They have always been looters, and will loot from Tommy now that he has money. The boys' behavior now embarrasses Tommy. He is no longer one of them. He maintains himself with what is given to him gladly.

Tommy makes up for his earlier behavior towards Mama Posita when he saves the crops at the end of the film. He had taken freely, but now he gives. His unruliness turns out to be what saves the crops, his tough nature being a match for the unscrupulous instigators of the truck barricade. He complements Mama Posita where it counts; he is an appropriate business partner for her.

"That's a nice boy you got here," the sheriff tells Mama. Yes, she agrees, "but he's not my son." Here the film takes care of the one hitch that has not been cleared up: Mama Posita reveals that she has known all along that the boy she had taken in was not her son. But Tommy had enjoyed being her son, so she played along.

It's a tender moment that wraps up an attractively wrapped film package.

Notice that the "super-thrills" are all depicted by sketches!

JUNIOR G-MEN

First chapter released in August, 1940, by Universal. Associate producer, Henry McRae. Directed by Ford Beebe and John Rawlins. Scenario by George H. Plympton, Basil Dickey and Rex Taylor. Photographed by Jerome Ash. Edited by Alvin Todd, Louie Sackin and Joseph Glick. Editing supervised by Saul A. Goodkind. Art direction by Ralph DeLacy. Dialogue direction by Jacques Jaccard. *12 chapters (approximately 20 minutes each).*

Billy Barton, Billy Halop; *Gyp,* Huntz Hall; *Terry,* Gabriel Dell; *Lug,* Bernard Punsly; *Buck,* Kenneth Lundy; *Sailor,* Harris Berger; *Murph,* Hally Chester; *Harry Trent,* Kenneth Howell; *Jim Bradford,* Phillip Terry; *Colonel Barton,* Russell Hicks; *Brand,* Cy Kendall; *Severn,* Ben Taggart; *Midge,* Roger Daniels; *Corey,* Victor Zimmerman; *Evans,* Edgar Edwards; *Foster,* Gene Rizzi; *Mary,* Florence Halop; *Flaming Torch member,* Ralph Peters.

1. "Enemies Within"
2. "The Blast of Doom"
3. "Human Dynamite"
4. "Blazing Danger"
5. "Trapped by Traitors"
6. "Traitor's Treachery"
7. "Flaming Death"
8. "Hurled Through Space"
9. "The Plunge of Peril"
10. "The Toll of Treason"
11. "Descending Doom"
12. "The Power of Patriotism"

The Dead End Kids join forces with the FBI and its sub-group, the Junior G-Men, to track down the Order of the Flaming Torch, a group of would-be dictators who have kidnapped the scientist-father of Billy, the kids' leader.

Were there no "thrills" here, there would be almost nothing. *Junior G-Men* is a 12-chapter, 240-minute fist-throwing and gas-exploding spectacle that will leave any sensible viewer aghast. Seeing Billy Halop's seemingly futile efforts to find his father through 23 reels is enough to make anyone declare that he will never watch a serial again.

Essentially, the serial progresses from potential death in a chemical explosion to a fisticuffs-encounter with the villains.

Considering that Billy and Gyp are in the same house as Billy's father in the second installment, it is rather far-fetched that Billy and his father don't meet until Chapter 11. During the time in-between, the serial—like most serials—goes from one certain-death situation to another. *Junior G-Men* uses the common serial trick of ending one chapter with a given ending, only to open the next chapter showing some detail conveniently left out of the previous one's ending.

This cheats the audience. But there is another way this particular serial does this: The "evolution" of the kids from street kids to law enforcement agents is chronicled without any answer as to how these trouble-makers feel in shedding their brass knuckles and under-handed fighting techniques for the devices of law and order.

Inasmuch as the Dead End Kids and Little Tough Guys were hardly hero-types, it's strange that they were cast in it at all. The scene most deserving of them occurs at the beginning, when in a comic moment they unleash a poultry truck's load of chickens into a black man's cab. The most exciting scene is the plane ride that occurs in the ninth chapter.

GIVE US WINGS

Released December 20, 1940, by Universal. Directed by Charles Lamont. Associate producer, Ken Goldsmith. Screenplay by Arthur T. Horman and Robert Lee Johnson. Based on the story "Crop Dusters," by Eliott Gibbons. Photographed by John Doyle. Edited by Frank Gross. Music conducted by Hans J. Salter. Art direction by Jack Otterson. Assistant direction by Charles S. Gould. Costumes by Vera West. General music direction by Charles Previn. Sound by Bernard B. Brown. *62 minutes.*

Tom, Billy Halop; *Pig,* Huntz Hall; *Ape,* Bernard Punsly; *String,* Gabriel Dell; *Rap,* Bobby Jordan; *Arnold Carter,* Victor Jory; *York,* Wallace Ford; *Julie Mason,* Anne Gwynne; *Buzz,* Shemp Howard; *Tex Austin,* Milburn Stone; *Link,* William Benedict; *Bud,* Harris Berger; *White,* James Flavin; *Captain Stern,* Addison Richards; *Mammy,* Etta McDaniel; *Servant,* Paul White; *Gas station attendant,* Milton Kibbee; *Foreman,* Ben Lewis.

The kids build airplane engines, but they long to fly planes. Carter, a crooked crop-dusting agent who uses dilapidated planes and illegal pilots to cut costs, hires the boys to fly for him. York, Carter's foreman, implores Carter to buy new planes, and tells the kids that they would be foolish to continue to work for Carter. Tom, Pig, Ape and String become crop dusters, but Rap is kept on the ground at less pay because he is younger than the others.

When a dangerous job is turned down by the other boys, Rap is secretly enticed to do it when Carter offers him a pay raise and the opportunity to fly regularly. Rap is killed while doing the job. Vowing revenge, Tommy tracks down Carter to even the score. Carter flees by car and Tommy chases him by airplane. Carter switches to a plane and takes to the air, where Tommy engages him in a dogfight. After the fight, Carter is captured.

This meager entry in a meager series offers little and often takes away what it has offered. It may show some nice attributes in the kids or in one kid, but it will take away those attributes before the film has advanced much further.

The only solid element this film has is the quality of its aerial photography and aerial stunt work. The dogfight scene, despite its clichés, is decently done. The rest of the film isn't.

At the beginning, we know the kids want to fly. Fine, why shouldn't these kids, who seem like conscientious workers, be given air jobs? After the next scene, though, no one could care less. Suddenly these conscientious workers are rash and unstable. They become hostile to each other, and remain so throughout the film.

During a series of test flights, each kid is taken up into the air. When Tom is told by foreman York that he must continue to practice flying before he may do any serious flying, he becomes indignant.

"He thinks I gotta practice practice," Tom says. "It comes natural to me. I've got bird blood in me."

"You said it," Pig fires back. "You just laid an egg."

Rap is the only one not affected. He has the intelligence to question the integrity of the pilots who fly the "museum piece" planes and calls their group a "suicide club." He is full of sorrow when he sees a pilot burn to death while trapped in his cockpit. Why Rap should be vulnerable to accepting the dangerous job is not explained. His last words are those of a man who has given up his life for nothing: 'Mr Carter [sob] said if I did the Andrews job [sob] I would be a pilot like the rest of you guys.'

There's something to be said about Pig here: He develops his first elaborate weapon in this film. (It was the first developed by any Huntz Hall character.) The weapon is a fish that conceals a heavy knife. It is used to clobber nemeses during the fish fry fight.

The fish fry fight? This is the longest unnecessary scene in the entire canon of Dead End Kids–Little Tough Guys–Eastside Kids–Bowery Boys films. The fish fry is a rural social. Music is provided by a band whose smiles are pasted on their faces. A fight erupts and a lot of seafood is thrown about, but it is for naught. Not a laugh in a netload; it's just a scaly mess.

Smaller fights break out throughout the film. They start with little provocation:

York [to a girl]: Let's let these monkeys climb
    back into the trees.
Pig: Do I look like a monkey?
String: Not to me you don't. You ain't got a
    tin cup. [Sock!]

The funniest person in the film is Shemp Howard, who plays Buzz, a mechanic. He is involved in some wild gags: in one, his hat flies off when the boys shout at him in unison; in another, he clings to a ceiling fan as it spins.

Huntz Hall's progress as a comedian in this film was a direct consequence of Shemp's being in it. "He was like my father. He taught me comedy," Huntz says about Shemp.

Shemp rightfully gets the fade-out joke. Pig (Huntz) sits on a two-by-four. When he gets up he sees that there was a nail protruding from it. Shemp cracks, "Lucky it wasn't a finishing nail."

Unfortunately, this scene didn't put the "finishing" nail in the boys careers at Universal. What was to come was worse.

String, Ape, Rag, Pig (hidden) and Tom cross the Mason-Dixon line.

HIT THE ROAD

Released June 27, 1941, by Universal. Associate producer, Ken Goldsmith. Directed by Joe May. Screenplay by Robert Lee Johnson and Brenda Weisberg. Story by Robert Lee Johnson. Photographed by Jerome Ash. Edited by Bernard Burton. Musical direction by Hans J. Salter. Art direction by Jack Otterson. Assistant, Harold H. MacArthur. Costumes by Vera West. Set decorations by R.A. Gausman. Sound by Bernard B. Brown. Sound engineered by William Heddcock. *61 minutes.*

Tom, Billy Halop; *Pig Grogan,* Huntz Hall; *Ape,* Bernard Punsly; *String,* Gabriel Dell; *Molly Ryan,* Gladys George; *James J. Ryan (alias Valentine),* Barton MacLane; *Patience Ryan,* Evelyn Ankers; *Paul Revere Smith,* Charles Lang; *Pesky,* Bobs Watson; *Spike the Butcher,* Edward Pawley; *Dingbat,* Shemp Howard; *Creeper,* John Harmon; *Colonel Smith,* Walter Kingsford; *Cathy Crookshank,* Eily Malyon; *Rufus,* Jess Lee Brooks; *Martin,* Charles Moore; *Sullivan, chauffeur,* Charles Sullivan; *Trusty,* Hally Chester; *O'Brien, first guard,* Ernie Stanton; *Second guard,* Lee Moore; *Guard,* Kernan Cripps; *Mrs. Hickridge (part cut from film),* Grace Hayle.

Tom, Pig, Ape, String and Pesky, four of whom are parentless after their fathers are killed in a mob massacre, are paroled into the custody of the father of the fifth. They go to live on a ranch owned by an ex-con pal of the boys' fathers. When a rival mob threatens the lives of the ex-con's family, the kids save the man, his wife and his daughter.

If one ignores what *Hit the Road* doesn't have—a credible plot-line—one can look at what it does have: a string of scenes for the Dead End Kids to play in, and an unwanted screen presence in the person of child-actor Bobs Watson.

Bobs Watson could be taken to be the star of the film, if the number of close-ups is taken into account. A close-up of him ends every scene he's in, whether he has something to react to or not. He gets two early minutes in which to prepare to join the other boys at the car that will take them from Hillsdale, where the law has relinquished custody of them, to their guardian's ranch. In another scene, he puts on a badge (we're talking about a little kid here!), stops a car, and "plays sheriff."

The kids' scenes are of the following type: One kid slaps another, who in retaliating slaps a third. The third pokes the one who hit him and the one he had intended to hit. And so on. (For the record, Tommy starts it, he hits Pig, and String is brought into it next, he being the one who starts the warfare going on a mass scale.)

It may be said that the *Hit the Road* crew didn't know what to do with any of their materials. Just as they used

Huntz Hall, Bernard Punsly and Gabriel Dell don't look very enthusiastic in this scene in which they confront Barton MacLane. And why should they, considering the script.

Bobs Watson too extensively, and the Dead End Kids inappropriately, they wasted the considerable talents of Shemp Howard. Howard here plays a deadpan (called Dingbat) who is a member of the rival mob. He is seen only in passing, never moves a muscle, and is never alone. He has only one line.

Pig does what he can for comic relief when he mistakes a twig (which he has backed into) for a gun. He goes through a multitude of facial expressions. Every time he moves, the twig, which is tied to a rope that is stuck to Pig, moves with him. Thinking that he is being led by gunpoint, Pig climbs a tree and is at the end of a branch overhanging a ravine when he realizes his mistake.

Ape gets a laugh when the kids are swabbing a floor. He sprinkles soap flakes into the air, creating the effect of snowflakes falling.

As usual, the Billy Halop character (Tommy) participates in both the kids' scenes and the adults' scenes. (For the viewer, "adults' scenes" can be taken to mean "desperation time.") He hears all of the clichés these movies say about underpriviledged youngsters. When the ex-con's daughter (Evelyn Ankers) paints rosy-pink images with her words, Tommy says, "I've heard so much of that baloney I could eat it with mustard."

So have we.

SEA RAIDERS

First chapter released in August, 1941, by Universal. Associate producer, Henry McRae. Directed by Ford Beebe and John Rawlins. Scenario by Clarence Upson Young and Paul Huston. Art direction by Ralph DeLacy. Editing supervised by Saul A. Goodkind. Photographed by William Sickner. *12 chapters (approximately 20 minutes each).*

Billy Adams, Billy Halop; *Toby Nelson,* Huntz Hall; *Bilge,* Gabriel Dell; *Butch,* Bernard Punsly; *Swab,* Hally Chester; *Brack Warren,* William Hall; *Tom Adams,* John McGuire; *Aggie Nelson,* Mary Field; *Elliott Carlton,* Edward Keane; *Leah Carlton,* Marcia Ralston; *Carl Tonjes,* Reed Hadley; *Captain Olaf Nelson,* Stanley Blystone; *Jenkins,* Richard Alexander; *Zeke,* Ernie Adams; *Anderson,* Jack Clifford; *Krans,* Richard Bone; *Captain Lester,* Morgan Wallace; *Captain Meredith,* Eddie Dunn; *Lug,* Joe Recht.

1. "The Raider Strikes"
2. "Flaming Torture"
3. "The Tragic Crash"
4. "The Raider Strikes Again"
5. "Flames of Fury"
6. "Blasted from the Air"
7. "Victims of the Storm"
8. "Dragged to Their Doom"
9. "Battling the Beast"
10. "Periled by a Panther"
11. "Entombed in a Tunnel"
12. "Paying the Penalty"

The kids, working to learn the identity of the dreaded "Sea Raider" who has been sinking Allied ships, are aided by Billy's scientifically minded brother Tom. Tom works for Captain Carlton, who unbeknownst to all is the infamous traitor.

Sea Raiders cast the Dead End Kids as more than stick figures—they have humor-tinged talks, amusing infighting, a rational patriotic zeal, and are wiser than the cops who chase them for no reason—but after a few chapters they have little to do which develops these characterizations. Although the first few chapters offer solid plot development and first-rate thrills (directors Ford Beebe and Jack Rawlins knew how to stage action sequences that left out just enough details to make them exciting), the last chapters are so lacking in these elements that they undermine the buildup. During these chunks of time, the story develops little (and in two chapters, not at all) as it plods from one animal attack to another.

MOB TOWN

String tells Tommy to scram after Tommy has been ousted in the "kangaroo court." Darryl Hickman is the "Shrimp."

Released October 3, 1941, by Universal. Associate producer, Ken Goldsmith. Directed by William Nigh. Scenario by Brenda Weisberg and Walter Doniger. Photographed by Elwood Bredell. Edited by Arthur Hilton. Musical direction by Hans J. Salter. Art direction by Jack Otterson. Associate, Ralph M. DeLacy. Assistant direction by Howard Christie. Set decorations by R.A. Gausman. Costumes by Vera West. Sound supervised by Bernard B. Brown. Sound engineered by Robert Pritchard. *60 minutes.*

Tom Barker, Billy Halop; *Pig,* Huntz Hall; *Ape,* Bernard Punsly; *String,* Gabriel Dell; *Sgt. Frank Conroy,* Dick Foran; *Marion Barker,* Anne Gwynne; *Butch ("Shrimp"),* Darryl Hickman; *Judge Luther Bryson,* Samuel S. Hinds; *Uncle Lon Barker,* Victor Kilian; *Cutler, cop,* Truman Bradley; *Rummel, auto junker,* John Butler; *Mr. Loomis,* John Sheehan; *Boys,* Roy Harris, Peter Sullivan; *Girls,* Dorothy Darrell, Elaine Morley, Beverly Roberts; *Police chief,* Cliff Clark; *Monk Bangor,* Paul Fix; *Pawnbroker,* Will Wright; *Mrs. Minch,* Eva Puig; *Mrs. Flynn,* Dorothy Vaughan; *Nutsy,* Edward Emerson; *Women,* Rosina Galli, Mary Kelly; *Manager,* Dick Rich; *Police officer,* Bob Gregory; *Mrs. Simpson,* Claire Whitney; *Henderson,* Terry Frost; *Brick,* John Kellogg; *Woman,* Clara Blore; *Charlie, paper boy,* Harris Berger; *Burly man,* Duke York; *Boys,* Hally Chester, Joe Recht; *Court clerk,* Ed Dew; *Man,* Pat Costello.

Tom Barker idolizes the memory of his brother, Eddie, who was sent to the death house. He and his gang also look up to gangster Monk Bangor, who was Eddie's partner in crime. Policeman Frank Conroy tries to keep the boys from turning to the streets by setting up a recreational project. He gains the confidence of Pig, Ape and String, but fails to motivate Tom.

Conroy gets the foursome jobs in an auto wrecking yard, where they prove themselves. He gets them out of a scrap when two of Monk's henchmen use them as pigeons in a jewelry robbery. However, Tom learns that it was Frank who had arrested Eddie. Though the other boys remain with Frank's youth group, Tom sides with Monk and is used in a jewel robbery. Monk hires Tom to drive him out west, but on the way, the gangster pulls a hold-up in a drug store. Angered, Tom deliberately crashes the car and returns to Frank with a promise to go straight.

Mob Town looks as though it had been written by a committee whose members weren't speaking to each other. The film merely presents exposition scenes (the type usually seen only at the beginning of a picture) for fifty minutes. Only in its last ten minutes does it develop anything resembling a plot. (Elsewhere in the movie there are other suggestions that *Mob Town* deliberately went against traditional moviemaking wisdom. It's possible that the movie was made the way that it was as an experiment, to see the effect of breaking the rules—not telling a story in recognizable terms, etc.)

The outlandish opening scene.

Mob Town spends sixty minutes getting started, then the "end" title flashes on.

The first scene is at a dance. The Dead End Kids and some other people are fighting. Whose side should we be on? We aren't told. Why are they fighting? No explanation is given. This "introduction" to the movie is not an introduction at all. It makes the film seem already in progress. It sets the tone for what is to follow.

The next scene takes place on a staircase. Tom and grade-school-aged Butch meet on it. Butch says, "Don't call me 'Shrimp.' " They go up to the Barkers' (Tom's family's) apartment, where we find Tom's sister and their uncle (they have no parents), about whom we learn little or nothing. (We have to listen carefully just to find out that the uncle is an uncle.) Officer Conroy (the villain!) bursts in and arrests Tom for his part in the fight.

In the next scene Marion Barker, the sister Tom is saddled with, takes over the screen. She tries to arrange a job for Tom, and then visits the police station—where she is joined by Butch—to see Tom. Officer Conroy (the hero!) steps in and suggests that the police start a program to reform young hoodlums. Butch says, "Don't call me 'Shrimp.' "

The movie is as bad at comedy as it is at drama. Pig, Ape and String are set up to be laughted *at*, not laughed *with*. The humor is at the kids' expense. There are two scenes that are more prominent than the rest. One has the four boys being taught judo, the other has the boys working in an auto wrecking yard. Both scenes rely on roughhousing and face-slapping.

The way that this film destroys the boys' characters is evident at the obligatory dinner table sequence. The boys try some "play-acting," with String assuming the role of a radio quiz announcer, spewing off such bits of comic dialogue as:

String: Can you tell us what year the War of 1812 was fought?

Pig: 1776

Next film please.

JUNIOR G-MEN OF THE AIR

First chapter released in June, 1942, by Universal. Associate producer, Henry McRae. Directed by Ray Taylor and Lewis D. Collins. Scenario by Paul Huston, George H. Plympton and Griffin Jay. Photographed by William Sickner. *12 chapters (approximately 20 minutes each).*

Billy "Ace" Holden, Billy Halop; *Bolts Larson,* Huntz Hall; *Stick Munsey,* Gabriel Dell; *Greaseball Plunkett,* Bernard Punsly; *Eddie Holden,* Gene Reynolds; *The Baron,* Lionel Atwill; *Jerry Markham,* Frank Albertson; *Don Ames,* Richard Lane; *Jack,* Frankie Darro; *Araka,* Turhan Bey; *Beal,* John Bleifer; *Monk,* Noel Cravat; *Comora,* Edward Foster; *Augar,* John Bagni; *Dick Parson,* Paul Phillips; *Double-Face Barker,* David Gorcey; *Jed,* Eddy Waller; *Oriental chemist,* Paul Bryar; *Colonel,* Fred Burton; *Flyer,* Jack Arnold; *Official,* Mel Ruick; *Dogaro,* Jay Novello; *Ito,* Angelo Cruz; *Sergeant,* Lynton Brent; *Conductor,* J. Pat O'Malley; *Whitey, newsboy,* Billy Benedict; *Newsboy,* Ken Lundy; *Soldiers,* Guy Kingsford, Win Wright; *Alien Japanese-American,* Jimmy O'Gatty; *Man,* Joey Ray; *Policemen,* Bill Moss, Bill Hunter, Charles McAvoy; *Patrolman,* Dick Thomas; *Japanese clerk,* Rico de Montez; *Uamalka,* Edward Colebrook; *Customers,* Rolland Morris, William Desmond; *Senator,* Guy Usher; *Scientist,* Bert Freeman; *Lieutenant, State Guard,* Hugh Presser; *Watchman,* Heenan Elliott; *Corporal,* Ben Wright; *Instructor,* George Sherwood.

1. "Wings Aflame"
2. "The Plunge of Peril"
3. "Hidden Danger"
4. "The Tunnel of Terror"
5. "The Black Dragon Strikes"
6. "Flaming Havoc"
7. "The Death Mist"
8. "Satan Fires the Fuse"
9. "Satanic Sabotage"
10. "Traped in a Blazing 'Chute"
11. "Undeclared War"
12. "Civilian Courage Conquers"

When the kids chase gangsters—who disappear on the desert, leaving behind their truck—they have their first clue to the identity of Black Dragon saboteurs who use airplanes to kidnap Billy's inventor-brother Eddie. The saboteurs' efforts to cripple American defense are thwarted by the kids.

After warring with spies on land and sea, the boys predictably took to the air in their next serial, a sequel to

Junior G-Men. The character names of the kids are different, and Harry Trent of the Junior G-Men has become Jerry Markham of the same organization, but the two serials have a great deal in common. To begin with, both spend about the same amount of time on land. Despite its title, *Junior G-Men of the Air* doesn't have much to do with the air.

In both serials a member of Billy Halop's family is an inventor; in both that member is kidnapped. In both serials Billy and the gang at first will have nothing to do with law enforcement, but in both cases he and they change their minds when Billy is treated fairly by the Junior G-Men. In both Billy has an important trinket on his person in the first chapter (in the first serial, it was a medal belonging to Billy's father; in the latter, it was a Black Dragon charm left in the gangsters' crashed car). In both serials there is a warehouse explosion in Chapter 6. In both there is a hideout that's like a farm, and which is in a rural area. In both that hideout is located by air. In both serials, Billy's family member (be it his father or his brother) tells off his kidnapper in Chapter 7. In both serials, the kids gain access to the hideout by hiding in the back of a truck.

And both serials have a chapter entitled "The Plunge of Peril."

The most interesting aspects of *Junior G-Men of the Air* are those created for the serial—and not just because they were new. The notion that a formula could be added to gasoline that would ruin the engines of the machines using it is a scary one, so the material comes off well. Also, the business of the explosion of the dam crippling the war effort is a fear-provoking one. Both play on the understandable fear that not everyone in our society will take precautions against nefarious infiltrators (to use the language of the serial's characters).

Showmen's Trade Review took note of an imaginary Tough Guy Code which forbade trust in helpful officers of the law. Of course, it is difficult to trust authoritative figures as cardboard as those in *Junior G-Men of the Air.*

The three seemingly minor-league Dead End Kids in one of their thirty-second alleged comedy bits. Pig is wearing his plumber's jacket, the uniform for the job we never see him performing.

TOUGH AS THEY COME

Released June 5, 1942, by Universal. Associate producer, Ken Goldsmith. Directed by William Nigh. Screenplay by Lewis Amster and Albert Bein. Photographed by Elwood Bredell. Edited by Bernard W. Burton. Musical direction by Hans J. Salter. Art direction by Jack Otterson. Assistant art direction by Martin Obzina. Assistant direction by Howard Christie. Costumes by Vera West. Sound supervised by Bernard B. Brown. Sound engineered by Charles Carroll. *61 minutes.*

Tommy Clark, Billy Halop; *Pig (Albert),* Huntz Hall; *Ape,* Bernard Punsly; *String,* Gabriel Dell; *Ann Wilson,* Helen Parrish; *Ben Stevens,* Paul Kelly; *Frankie Taylor,* Ann Gillis; *Mrs. Clark,* Virginia Brissac; *Mike Taylor,* John Gallaudet; *Gene Bennett,* Jimmy Butler; *Esther,* Mala Powers; *Ma,* Giselle Werbiseck; *Eddie,* Clarence Muse; *Eddie's wife,* Theresa Harris; *Rogers,* John Eldredge; *Process server,* James Flavin; *Dave,* George Offerman, Jr.; *Fruit vendor,* Antonio Filauri; *Jim Bond,* Dick Hogan; *Collector,* Frank Faylen.

Law school student Tommy Clark gets a job with the crooked Apex Financing Company instead of a $3-a-week job as a legal-aid attorney. Although Tommy is in love with sophisticated Ann, he is loved by a local girl, Frankie. Frankie's father, Mike Taylor, is a cabdriver in debt to the Apex Company. Tommy is dispatched to repossess the cab, and does so despite the efforts of his

Frank Albertson, as the leader of the Junior G-Men (at left), and the Dead End Kids regulars confront a Black Dragon chemist (Charlie Lund).

former friends, Pig, Ape and Sting. Distraught, Mike attempts to jump off a building, but he is deterred by Tommy and Pig.

The neighborhood folk want to lynch Tommy, but local philosopher Ben Stevens points out that what should be eliminated is dishonest work, not the person who accepts it. Tommy decides to get the goods on the finance company, and enlists Pig, Ape and String to help. They ransack the office for incriminating evidence. After a fight, they get the evidence and take it to the D.A.'s office. Tommy helps Frankie to understand that each of them should love someone else. He wins Ann when he vows to form a people's credit union.

Tough as They Come is an action drama without much action. Once again, Halop is separated from the rest of the boys. It is he alone who faces the challenges. It is he who is despised by the entire district of the city.

The other boys squeeze as much out of their half-minute sequences as possible. In this film, Pig, Ape and String are purported to have careers. Ape is a would-be fighter, with String as his manager. Pig, according to dialogue and an insignia on his jacket, is a plumber's assistant, although he is never seen on the job.

There is a bit more humor and slightly fewer clichés than in *Mob Town,* but the humor often turns to rough-house antics. Minor low-jinx occur in Ape's mock fight scenes and in String's pretending to a be a carnival barker promoting Pig in a mock high-wire act.

During the usual dinner table scene, Tommy attempts to appear older for Ann (the effect is as if he had put on a mardi-gras mask). Before this develops very far, food gags take over (String hits Pig with a grapefruit, etc.). Ape becomes the center of attention. It is to him that Ann says one of the poorest lines of the movie: "What are you training for, *Mr. Ape?"* Ape's appetite becomes a topic (Ape: "I eat like a bird." Pig: "Yeah, a vulture.").

These squabbles among the kids leaves a question: Which is harder to accept? The scenes, or the kids?

MUG TOWN

Released January 22, 1943, by Universal. Associate producer, Ken Goldsmith. Directed by Ray Taylor. Screenplay by Brenda Weisberg, Lewis Amster, Harold Tarshis and Harry Sucher. Story by Charles Grayson. Photographed by Jack McKenzie. Edited by Ed Curtis. Musical direction by Hans J. Salter. Art direction by Jack Otterson. Assistant, E.R. Robinson. Assistant direction by Charles S. Gould. Costumes by Vera West. Sound by Bernard B. Brown. Sound engineered by Paul Neal. *60 minutes.*

Tommy Davis, Billy Halop; *Pig,* Huntz Hall; *String,*

The Dead End Kids have picked up Tommy Kelly (between Halop and Punsly) as a travelling companion.

Gabriel Dell; *Ape,* Bernard Punsly; *Norene Seward,* Grace McDonald; *Clinker,* Edward Norris; *Alice Bell,* Virginia Brissac; *Mack Seward,* Jed Prouty; *Don Bell,* Dick Hogan; *Shorty,* Murray Alper; *Marco,* Paul Fix; *Mr. Perkle,* Lee "Lasses" White; *Steve Bell,* Tommy Kelly; *Drunk,* Syd Saylor; *Waiter,* Sidney Melton; *Matilda, fat girl,* June Bryde (Gittleson); *Cop,* Ralph Dunn; *Singer,* Napoleon Simpson; *Bouncers,* William Hall, Matt Willis; *Thief,* Ernie Adams; *Waiter,* Paul Dubov; *D.A.,* William Forrest; *Man in flophouse,* Danny Beck; *Detective #1,* William Gould; *Manager,* John Sheehan; *Chef,* Danny Seymour; *Detective #2,* John Bagni; *Detective,* Jack Marvin; *Girls,* Joline Westbrook, Evelyn Cooke, Dorothy Cordray; *Hatchet-faced woman,* Clara Blore; *Motorcycle cop,* Eddie Parker; *Crap shooter,* Johnny Walsh.

Our four vagrants check into a rural flophouse and meet a sick boy. They invite him to roam with them and he accepts, but he is unable to climb in and out of boxcars as they do without help and is killed while escaping from a railroad official. The boys locate his mother and try to break the news, but her kindness overcomes them. The boys stay on at her house thanks to a fabricated story of Tommy's, but Tommy earns his keep working at a gas station. Trucking racketeers blame stock shortages on Tommy, but he catches on to them and pursues them in an auto chase. When he drives a wounded adversary to a private doctor, as requested by the crook, instead of to a hospital, Tommy is indicted, but the mother clears him by telling the judge that he's honest.

Mug Town has the look of a lowlife scene on a soiled canvas, and it is pleasing. None of the films in the kids' previous three years of output succeed as well as this one does. The opening ten minutes—which includes a bunkhouse fight, with pillow feathers flying about once the fight is started after the kids prevent a napsack-snatching hobo from pilfering the sick kid's belongings—are ingeniously photographed to fill the screen with action; they have the flavor of fisticuffs, a proper feel for a film tailored to the rural double-bill or the city Saturday-afternoon kid-pleaser program.

Pig, String and Ape are given space to grow. They have a career sideline in this one: selling magazine subscriptions. This occupation spawns a worthy sequence. In it, String and Ape practice their sales pitch on Pig, who pretends to be a housewife. Or at least that's what they agree to do. String and Ape start out by saying "knock-knock," but Madam Pig doesn't receive her callers (which she must do in pantomime, as all three parties are outdoors). When asked why by the others, he says that "she" didn't hear the knock the first time. The trio agrees to try again. This time Madam Pig doesn't answer because she wants to tidy up the house before accepting visitors. String and Ape make continued efforts to get Pig to answer, but they are for naught. Pig suggests through pantomime that the lady is taking a shower.

At a restaurant, Pig, Ape and String make fun of its poshness. When their waiter removes a goblet from Pig's coat, Pig praises the waiter for having a magician's talents. When String learns that Coca-Cola costs twenty-five cents, he asks, "Anything off for good behavior?"

Tommy doesn't come off as well. He has many tear-jerking scenes, but his inability to command the frame is noticeable. By contrast, Pig has complete command of the frame. He is hilarious in a nightclub scene in which he dances with a portly girl. The girl's stomach repeatedly bounces Pig flat onto his back.

Patriotism abounds. Although we don't know it at first, the picture takes place in 1941, a fact revealed when Pig turns on a radio to listen to a "Flash Gordon" imitator and a bulletin comes on announcing the bombing of Pearl Harbor! The fade-out line is an unabashed appeal to patriotism. All four boys strut about in military garb. After they have stomped around some, Tommy speaks to the audience. It is Billy Halop's last line in a Dead End Kids film. He says, apparently in regard to enlisting, "AND *we're* not *kidding*!"

KEEP 'EM SLUGGING

Released August 2, 1943, by Universal. Associate producer, Ben Pivar. Directed by Christy Cabanne. Screenplay by Brenda Weisberg. Story by Edward Handler and

Tommy (Bobby Jordan) and his department store clerk girlfriend (Elyse Knox) meet Pig, String and Ape (Norman Abbott).

Robert Gordon. Photographed by William Sickner. Edited by Ray Snyder. Musical direction by Hans J. Salter. Art direction by John B. Goodman. Associate, Ralph M. DeLacy. Assistant direction by Gilbert Valle. Costumes by Vera West. Sound by Bernard B. Brown. *60 minutes.*

Tommy, Bobby Jordan; *Pig,* Huntz Hall; *String,* Gabriel Dell; *Ape,* Norman Abbott; *Sheila,* Evelyn Ankers; *Suzanne,* Elyse Knox; *Frank,* Frank Albertson; *Jerry,* Don Porter; *Binky,* Shemp Howard; *Mr. Carruthers,* Samuel S. Hinds; *Lola,* Joan Marsh; *Duke Rodman,* Milburn Stone; *Detective sergeant,* Joseph Crehan; *Police sergeant,* Wade Boteler; *Mr. Meecham,* Paul McVey; *Scott,* Joe King; *Miss Billings,* Minerva Urecal; *Mr. Quink,* Arthur Hoyt; *Macklin,* Cliff Clark; *Matron,* Alice Fleming; *Mrs. Meegan,* Dorothy Vaughan; *Mrs. Banning,* Mary Gordon; *First detective,* William Gould; *Customer,* Mira McKinney; *Young girl,* Janet Shaw; *Bingo,* Dave Durand; *Shorty,* Jimmy Dodd; *Sammy,* Dick Chandlee; *Dugan,* Ernie Adams; *McGann,* Milton Kibbee; *Lady in "poiple,"* Fern Emmett; *Fat Man,* Harry Holman; *First student,* Johnny Walsh; *Second student,* Budge Patty; *Jailer,* Lew Kelly; *Sharkey,* Ben Erway; *Thug #1,* Anthony Warde; *Thug #2,* Joey Ray; *Young lovers,* Peter Michael, Harryette Vine; *Second detective,* Frank O'Connor; *Languid customer,* Caroline Cooke; *Personnel managers,* Rex Lease, Bob Hill, Howard Mitchell; *Mike,* Bob Spencer; *Policeman,* Jack C. Smith; *Waiter,* Roy Brent; *Stars in moviehouse film,* Jane Frazee, Robert Paige.

Having spent plenty of time in and out of reformatories, the kids decide that they'll go straight and get legitimate jobs during school vacation in order to free draft-age men for fighting duty. However, their past records cause all prospective employers to discard their applications. Finally, Tommy is able to land a job in the shipping department of a department store where his sister Sheila is employed as a clerk. Frank, the shipping superintendent, has been giving nightclub owner and hijacker Duke Rodman tips on valuable shipments. When Tommy refuses to help the hijackers, Frank frames him for jewel theft to get him out of the way. With the aid of the boys and a firehose, Tommy rounds up the ring. The store hires the other boys.

The final film of the Universal congregation, *Keep 'Em Slugging* ironically may be the most enjoyable. Bobby Jordan is the lead, playing the role of Tommy, Billy Halop's former role. The use of Jordan, as noted by *Motion Picture Daily,* resulted in "somewhat less of the slapping and cuffing which is their specialty."

The comedy is more abundant here than in any previous entry. Hall gets to display his comic skills in a number of scenes, including one in which he masquerades as a female dress mannequin. His disguise is exposed when unsuspecting Evelyn Ankers pricks him with a pin, and he runs screaming through the store. There are also laughs when Shemp Howard, playing a soda jerk, has to contend with the boys' orders.

For the fan, *Keep 'Em Slugging* offers the spectacle of Bobby Jordan playing full-fledged leader for the only time in his combined Dead End Kids–East Side Kids– Little Tough Guys–Bowery Boys career. He is marvelous.

Tommy's character is intricate and likable. He is assertive when he should be, as when he exhorts the boys: "We're not old enough to fly a bomber, drive a tank or man a machine gun. We all know there's a war going on. Get legitimate jobs! Keep things moving over here." He has an adult approach to the extent to which his family is responsible for him, and is aware of needs other than tangible ones. When his mother and sister offer to help him prepare a defense for his trial on charges of jewel robbery, and hire a lawyer, he cries out to them, "I don't want your help. I don't want your lawyer either. A guy's gotta have someone believe in him." That someone is pretty clerk Suzanne, his girl, who inspires him to act in his own behalf.

Director Christy Cabanne can be commended for a good job in combining the melodrama with the comedy, something previous directors of this series proved unable to do. *Keep 'Em Slugging* shows that the makers of the Universal output were finally paying attention to what was going on at Monogram. But why now?

EASTSIDE KIDS PRIMER

MUGGS (Leo Gorcey) was honest, lived by a code of ethics. However, he could be deceptive when he had a goal to achieve. In *Follow the Leader,* he is with a gangster who introduces him to his boss. To impress the hood when the latter has ordered a double shot of bourbon, Muggs orders a triple. The gangster leaves, and the drinks arrive. Muggs takes one sip of his and reacts as if were going to die. He orders a ginger ale chaser (which has the same color), and sips at it until it is at the boubon's level. The 80-proof stuff is hidden. When the underworld man returns, Muggs gulps the "alcohol" and exclaims, "that's good bourbon."

GLIMPY (Huntz Hall) is what Shakespeare referred to as "a fantastic." This "mouse-man," whose headgear is always the upturned-baseball-cap, and who seems to be suffering from early muscular dystrophy, has weird thinking. In *Mr. Muggs Steps Out,* Muggs has delegated a car polishing task to him. Glimpy tells Muggs that he will get *the gang* to do it. "Here, Skinny," Glimpy says as he hands Skinny a sponge, "you'll get fat." He's not dumb. He simply believes that if hard work can reduce the waistline of a fat person, the same chore will also create desirable results for a thin person.

GINSBERG: The name Ginsberg pops up on at least six occasions in Eastside Kids films: as a turkish bath owner and lemonade vendor (not shown) in *Mr. Muggs Steps Out,* as a trombone retailer mentioned in *Clancy Street Boys,* as a soda store proprietor in *Million Dollar Kid,* and as a delicatessen owner in *Follow the Leader.* This last role was played by Bernard Gorcey, Leo Gorcey's father. Ginsberg was a name out of Leo's past. One day, when he was 15, some of his friends living in his New York City neighborhood asked him to participate in robbing a neighborhood store. Leo resisted, but they told him that all he had to do was signal them with a knock if the cops should come. Leo kept his bargain, but neglected to rap on the wall when the cops did arrive. The other boys were sent to reform school. Two weeks later they were released and laid for Gorcey, and they threw him from one end of his apartment building hall to the other. The name of the delicatessen owner was Ginsberg.

NOAH BEERY'S COURT: When Leo came to Hollywood, he garnered 25 traffic tickets in two years. Taking a tip from other Hollywood residents, he used his clout to avoid a court appearance. One time when the judge insisted on seeing him, he paid an official 50 dollars to square matters. The official ran off with the fifty dollars and $200,000 of the city's funds, so Gorcey was forced to appear on the stand. According to Gorcey, it took the judge a full *eight minutes* to read the entire record of Gorcey's 25 offenses. When the judge was finished, he looked down, smilingly, and said, "Well, sonny, what

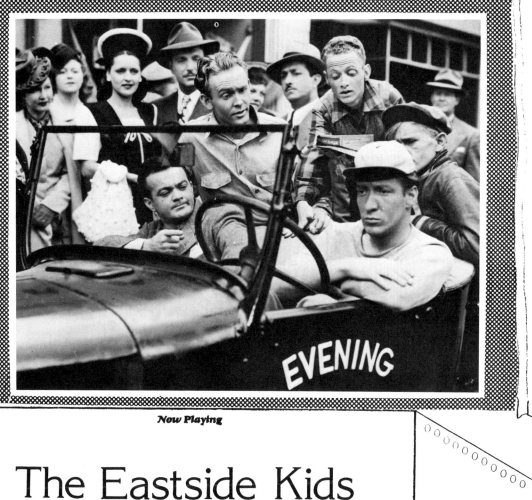

EVENING

Now Playing

The Eastside Kids

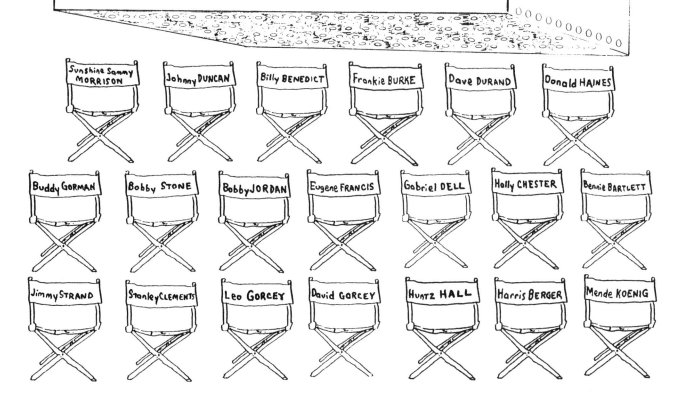

Sunshine Sammy MORRISON

Johnny DUNCAN

Billy BENEDICT

Frankie BURKE

Dave DURAND

Donald HAINES

Buddy GORMAN

Bobby STONE

Bobby JORDAN

Eugene FRANCIS

Gabriel DELL

Holly CHESTER

Bennie BARTLETT

Jimmy STRAND

Stanley CLEMENTS

Leo GORCEY

David GORCEY

Huntz HALL

Harris BERGER

Mende KOENIG

have you got to say for yourself?" Gorcey put on a smile bigger than the judge's, and answered, "Judge, that report is a little longer than most novels I've read." The judge said, "Son, you have a wonderful sense of humor, and upstairs we have a mess of prisoners that really love to be entertained. I'm going to give you the priviledge of spending five days telling them jokes." For the next five days he was a guest of the county.

This incident was adapted into several Eastside Kids films. The definitive judge was Noah Beery, Sr., who assayed the role in *Mr. Muggs Steps Out* and *Block Busters*. In both, Gorcey (Muggs) is charged with a multitude of infractions. In the former, the case ahead of him is that of Joan Marsh, who is charged with a multitude of driving violations.

FEDORA BRIMS: If you were to start a gang of outlaws, you would not want your comrades or yourself to be flagrantly obvious. You would not want anyone to suspect you engaged in illegal activities. This kind of logic did not occur to the gangsters who popped up with regularity in Eastside Kids films. Always wearing Fedora hats, these guys showed up everywhere! It could be said that the theme the Eastside Kids writers tried to convey was, "There's a gangster on every corner."

UP-TO-DATE SCRIPTING: The Eastside Kids films were current on developments in World War II, as they were shot close to release. In *Docks of New York*, a character says it's obvious the Allies are going to win the war, and two months after release, Germany surrendered. By contrast, the Bowery Boys films had a wide gap between production and distribution. *Dig That Uranium* was released early in 1956, although one of the lead characters was incapacitated in late August 1955.

FIGHT SCENES: Leo Gorcey said:

"The fight scenes are probably the most dangerous, especially when there are about thirty guys in a hotel room all swinging at once. I have never gotten through one of those scenes unscathed.

"I averaged a broken bone about every four pictures."

Edward Bernds (Bowery Boys director):

"Leo knew from long experience how to throw those fake punches and make them look real. Hall was the one who hid under the table."

Sunshine Sammy Morrison:

"When the fighting started, I got out of there."

. The fight scenes were enhanced by Edward J. Kay's "fight music" composition. When the fights were resumed in the Bowery Boys pictures, the loss of Kay's tune was sorely missed. In the Bowery Boys' later years, music editor Marlin Skiles brought in a theme that was a match for it. Used to score some of the fights, but not all

(the sword fight in *Paris Playboys* was one that did), it was the introduction to Lully's opera *Armide* (1686).

THE GORCEY-HALL RELATIONSHIP. Scenes here from *Mr. Muggs Steps Out* (upper) and *Docks of New York* (below) show the Leo Gorcey-Huntz Hall relationship as seen on the screen. Their off-screen relationship helped to shape their working association.

Huntz Hall: "We (all of us) got along fabulously, or else we couldn't have lasted twenty-two years. We went our own ways when we were not working together. Like I used to go on the road for personal appearances, do theater. We'd see each other a couple of times a year socially. What we tried to do was avoid the problems of other comedy teams, like Abbott & Costello and Martin & Lewis. If we worked together all the time, and were always together, it could have caused problems. I did a lot of work with Gabe on the road. We did a nightclub act and theaters in Mississippi, Alabama, Texas, all over. We did one-nighters, which today they call concerts."

In reference to Leo, he says, "We dug one another."

STUDIOS: The exterior in Eastside Kids films were shot at Republic, Warner Brothers and Hal Roach Studios. (The photo here from *Kid Dynamite* was shot at Roach.) Monogram Pictures, which produced the series, didn't have many sets of their own. They employed short production schedules. The schedules were for seven days, with some films shot in five or six. Gabriel Dell recalls, "People don't know it, but those films were shot in six to seven days, seven for the good ones."

THE KIDS' HONESTY: The Eastside Kids pictures brought a new dimension to the former Dead End Kids' characters. They were respectable. This dialogue from *Block Busters,* between kind-hearted grandmother-figure Amelia Norton (Minerva Urecal) and an indignant woman visiting her shows the high regard in which the kids were held by those who came to know them.

Madam: Amelia! How can you tolerate these creatures. I never thought a woman of your breeding would lower herself to associate with such riffraff.

Amelia: Aren't you being a trifle snobbish?

Madam: Have you forgot your position, your background, your debt to society?

Amelia: My backgr— Have you forgot that I was born in this neighborhood, and if Charlie hadn't made a lucky investment, I woul have never left it.

Madam: Do you mean you consider these creatures—your equal?

Amelia: My equal? Why they make me feel ashamed of myself. There's no sham attached to them. They're real and honest, and if I were you I'd move here too before my arteries become too hardened and my mind warped.

Muggs faces Noah Beery, Sr.'s court. The actor Leo Gorcey was not too conscientious about the reform aspects of this scene: barely visible is a cigarette between his finger! Also pictured are Fred Pressel (on stand) and Minerva Urecal.

Two of many encounters the kids had with fruit vendors. The idea of the kids fighting an Italian pitchman would be carried on into the second Bowery Boys film.

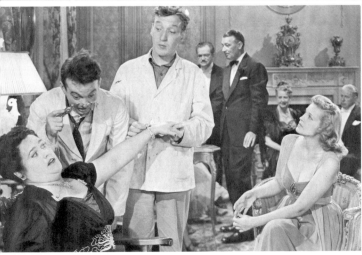

EAST SIDE KIDS

A Four-Bell Production, released February 10, 1940, by Monogram. Produced by Sam Katzman. Directed by Robert F. Hill. Associate producer, Glenn Cook. Scenario by William Lively. Photographed by Art Reed. Edited by Earl Turner. Production managed by Ed W. Rote. Music by Johnny Lange and Lew Porter. Sound by Glen Glenn. *5600 ft. 62 minutes.*

Danny Dolan, Harris Berger; *Fred "Dutch" Kuhn*, Hally Chester; *Skinny*, Frankie Burke; *Peewee*, Donald Haines; *Mike*, Eddie Brian; *Pete*, Sam Edwards; *Officer Pat O'Day*, Leon Ames; *Milton Mileaway*, Dennis Moore; *Molly*, Joyce Bryant; *Algernon "Mouse" Wilkes*, Jack Edwards; *Knuckles Dolan*, David O'Brien; *Whisper*, Vince Barnett; *Schmidt*, Richard Adams; *May*, Maxine Lewis; *Captain Moran*, James Farley; *Cornwall*, Robert Fiske; *Joe, detective*, Alden "Stephen" Chase; *Mr. Wilkes*, Fred Hoose; *Eric*, Eric Burtis; *Tony*, Frank Yaconelli; *Boy*, Dave Durand.

Knuckles Dolan is in jail. His friend, Pat O'Day, who became a policeman when he realized that crime wasn't right for an ex-Eastside Kid, tries to uncover evidence to vindicate him. Dolan's gang has pierced New York, and is attempting to distribute counterfeit money by using a neighborhood gang of kids. One of the boys is Dolan's brother, Danny, who is chased by the police as a counterfeiting suspect and eventually joins the counterfeiters. He changes his mind when he learns that his brother had taken the rap for a murder their leader (Mileaway) had committed. He leads the crooks into a police trap, where O'Day captures them, exonerating Knuckles.

East Side Kids is an ordinary low-budget crime melodrama with no more pretentions than the product of any studio trying to ape Warner Brothers. The film is an action showcase with police situations leading to a tense climax.

Violence is prevalent. There is little regard for human life; six persons die in the course of the narrative. When Dutch (who is the co-leader in this initial entry) is claimed in the climax, during which he and gangster Mileaway fall to their deaths while in a stranglehold with each other, he is gone for good. A wall-plaque

Leon Ames, Joyce Bryant, Harris Berger, Frankie Burke, Alden Chase, Richard Adams, James Farley (seated), unidentified, Dennis Moore, Hally Chester.

perpetuates his memory in the boys' gym.

The kids themselves are common urchins who are introduced on the street playing dice. They don't have much to do that is original. One scene has them recite the Pledge of Allegiance virtually in toto. Like many other elements in the film, the kids' characters were lifted from *Dead End.* The two lead gangsters, Mileaway and Whisper, are fuzzy reflections of Baby Face and Hunk. Likewise, Pat and Molly (Danny's sister) draw their inspiration from Dave and Drina.

Monogram was known for fast-paced, quickly produced action films. It was formed in 1924 as Rayart to produce films for the bottom half of double-feature bills. (Such movies are called "B" movies.) They changed their name to Monogram in 1931, which is the name under which they merged with Mascot to form Republic in 1935. Two of their board members were unsatisfied with the way things were going at Republic, so they re-formed Monogram in 1936. The Monogram we know today is the corporation re-formed by W. Ray Johnson (the man who formed the studio originally). They made such films as *I Am a Criminal, Mutiny in the Big House* and *Gang Bullets*, as well as release-charts full of Frankie Darro and Jackie Cooper films. The lines in this 1940 film, "Whatsamatter kid, ya yellow?" and "I ain't no stoolie," are typical of the dialogue in these pictures. Finding out just what Monogram produced can require detective work. Once known as Continental Talking Pictures, Syndicate Film Exchange and Lone Star (all before the Mascot merger), it was also known as Interstate Television Corporation and—its final identity—Allied Artists.

Sam Katzman had had his own studio, Victory, when he came to Monogram and set up his own unit, Four-Bell Productions, later called Banner, in 1940. *East Side Kids* was the first project. Katzman, a former theatrical producer, had an eye for public tastes. On his four-decade resumé were nine Bela Lugosi vehicles, the *Jungle Jim* series with Johnny Weissmuller, *It Came From Beneath the Sea* (an early work by special effects genius Ray Harryhausen) and a gaggle of exploitation pictures (*Rock Around the Clock, Riot On Sunset Strip*, etc.). *East Side Kids* was his first attempt at cashing in. He soon acquired the services of Leo Gorcey and Bobby Jordan, a deal which was to launch his most endurable motion picture series.

BOYS OF THE CITY

A Four-Bell Production, released July 15, 1940, by Monogram. Produced by Sam Katzman. Directed by Joseph H. Lewis. Scenario by William Lively. Photographed by Robert Cline and Harvey Gould. Edited by Carl Pierson. Production managed by Ed W. Rote. Assistant direction by Robert Ray and Arthur Hammond. Music by Johnny Lange and Lew Porter. Settings by Fred Preble. Sound by Glen Glenn. Concurrently released as *The Ghost Creeps* in the Northeast. *5649 ft. 63 minutes.*

Mugs, Leo Gorcey; *Danny Dolan*, Bobby Jordan; *Scruno*, "Sunshine Sammy" Morrison; *Peewee*, David Gorcey; *Skinny*, Donald Haines; *Johnny*, Hally Chester; *Peter*, Frankie Burke; *Knuckles Dolan*, David O'Brien; *Louise Mason*, Inna Gest; *Giles*, Dennis Moore; *Simp*, Vince Barnett; *Algernon "Algy" Wilkes*, Eugene Francis; *Judge Malcolm Parker*, Forest Taylor; *Agnes*, Minerva Urecal; *Jim Harrison*, Alden "Stephen" Chase; *Tony*, George Humbert; *Cook*, Jerry Mandy.

Constantly in trouble, the gang (led by Mugs and Danny) is sent to camp in the Andirondacks by Algy's rich father. Also heading for the mountains is Judge Malcolm Parker, who is being threatened by a mob. Accompanied by his attorney (Giles), his bodyguard (Simp) and his niece Louise, the judge crosses paths with the kids' entourage (which includes Danny's brother, Knuckles, and Algy) and invites them to spend the night at his mansion. During the eerie night, the judge is murdered; Louise (a possible witness) has been kidnapped. Knuckles is accused by Giles due to Knuckles' having been incorrectly sentenced by the judge a year earlier. Knuckles and the gang tie up Giles and Simp while they investigate. Mugs and Danny discover a passageway hidden behind the organ, and find evidence that the housekeeper deliberately tried to scare them out of the place. Knuckles captures a stranger cloaked in black, who turns out to be not the murderer but a special investigator. Giles and Simp are released, but Simp is soon caught transporting Louise. The investigator recognizes him as a member of the mob which threatened Parker; Giles is arrested too on complicity.

This second Monogram entry can be considered the first true Eastside Kids film. This is the first film to have the standard characters, and the first to have any Dead End Kids in the cast (Leo Gorcey and Bobby Jordan, but two others were to join the series later). This also has the leisurely pace that the series would adopt (although this particular film is a bit too leisurely). *Boys of the City* is a neat little murder mystery containing situations for the juvenile delinquent kids.

The film gives the kids the lion's share of the action,

Inna Gest and Dave O'Brien ("Mish-Mash the Mutton-Head" in the Pete Smith shorts, and the reefer-smoking menace in Tell Your Children *[a.k.a.* Reefer Madness, *1936] are at left.*

and their characters are fully explored. They release the nozzle of a fire hydrant in their first scene, which not only shows that they are willing to be a public nuisance just for the sake of getting wet, but forwards the plot by giving the police and wealthy Mr. Wilkes an impetus for sending them to the mountains.

Mr. Wilkes's character was one that would be a convenience for setting up plots in the films to come. It was he in *East Side Kids* who gave the kids a clubroom. It is he in *Boys of the City* who still believes he can help the kids rehabilitate themselves, and it is he who has the mountain camp. His son Algy is also one who defies convention.

Algy was the member of the gang who could be both part of it and a spectator to it. He was the only member who could have chosen his companions from higher social circles had he so pleased. He had become part of the gang in *East Side Kids* (although the role had been played by blasé Jack Edwards, not by the cheerfully debonair Eugene Francis).

Peewee is one of five kids whose characters weren't spotlighted. It was to be a trait of this series that several boys would do no more than follow the two leaders.

Mugs (Leo Gorcey) and Danny (Bobby Jordan) develop a wonderful rapport. They create an atmosphere for each other that is relaxed, easygoing, carefree. They are given to banter, and are not supportive. While they search near the organ, Muggs remarks that the mansion's decor is just the type to have a secret passage. Danny tells Mugs that he's suffering the after-effects of too many movies. "Movies!," Mugs exclaims as he realizes that he can be a detective patterned after those he's seen on the screen. "Hey, what's the 'Thin Man' got that I haven't got?" "Myrna Loy," answers Danny.

"Give me a little time, bub, give me a little time," Mugs cautions him.

Mugs and Danny's foray into the secret passage takes them past paneling and weapons. They're timorous about going further. Shots of their candle show a

Frankie Burke, David Gorcey, Donald Haines, Hally Chester, "Sunshine Sammy" Morrison (as Scruno) and Eugene Francis (as Algy).

nervous hand shaking beneath it. In a frightening moment their candle is snuffed out and is re-lit by an unknown source. The film builds up the situation so that the cloaked man's first appearance later on has been anticipated.

The cloaked man is a red herring. For all the shots of him hiding behind bushes, peeking behind corners, he turns out to be an agent of the District Attorney. Suspicion had been thrown too on the housekeeper, and her guilt is more palpable by the fact that she had played the ghost to scare the boys.

The first malaprop delivered in an Eastside Kids film is in *Boys of the City.* But while Leo Gorcey was to deliver most of the malaprops in years ahead, Bobby Jordan delivers this historic one. His line is: "Don't jump to confusions."

"Sunshine Sammy" Morrison was to play a comic character who, though not on the level of Bobby Jordan and Leo Gorcey, was not relegated to the sidelines like the other boys. He plays that character here, where he shines in isolated cases, and is spotlighted in a scene in which he is forced into racial stereotypes. For instance, he is given a black man's supposed favorite dessert by the housekeeper. "Now I don't like that woman, and I don't like that graveyard," he explains, "but watermelon is, uh, watermelon anytime."

As Scruno and Mugs did not appear in *East Side Kids,* and Bobby Jordan didn't play Danny in that film, you would not think that the filmmakers would put any obvious tie-ins to the previous film in this one, but such was not the case. *Boys of the City* takes up where *East Side Kids* left off, and no two films in any of the series have such strong ties to each other as these two. Dave O'Brien carries over his character of the incarcerated Knuckles Dolan to the exonerated brother-guardian he plays here. The judge who is murdered is the same judge who sentenced him for the crime he didn't commit. There's no question that he's innocent of the judge's murder. He is rehabilitated. He is unlike the hard character he had been in *East Side Kids.*

And what's more, early in the film we see Giles plant a bomb meant to kill Parker. However, *it's possible* to miss the implications of this, as these scenes move fast while the rest of the film moves slowly. The same is true of the insert shots of the man from the D.A.'s office. The audience can miss him completely.

THAT GANG OF MINE

A Four-Bell Production, released September 23, 1940, by Monogram. Produced by Sam Katzman. Directed by Joseph H. Lewis. Associate producer, Pete Mayer. Screenplay by William Lively. Story by Alan Whitman. Photographed by Robert Cline and Harvey Gould. Edited by Carl Pierson. Production managed by Ed W. Rote. Assistant direction by Arthur Hammond and Herman Pett. Musical direction by Lew Porter. Settings by Fred Preble. Sound by Glen Glenn. *5567 ft. 62 minutes.*

Mugs Maloney, Leo Gorcey; *Danny Dolan,* Bobby Jordan; *Scruno,* "Sunshine Sammy" Morrison; *Peewee,* David Gorcey; *Skinny,* Donald Haines; *Ben,* Clarence Muse; *Knuckles Dolan,* David O'Brien; *Louise,* Joyce Bryant; *Algernon "Algy" Wilkes,* Eugene Francis; *Conrad Wilkes,* Milton Kibbee; *Blackie Towne,* Richard R. Terry; *Nick Buffalo,* Wilbur Mack; *Mrs. Wilkes,* Hazel Keener.

Though scoffed at by the gang, Mugs wants to be a jockey. His hopes are realized when a poor black man, Ben, and his thoroughbred racehorse are discovered in a barn. Ben puts up his horse on condition that the boys raise money for entry fees. Algy's father is persuaded to put up the money. Mugs trains to be a jockey, but he fails miserably in his first race. Mr. Wilkes's friend tells him that the horse is an excellent one, but needs a better jockey. Jimmy Sullivan, whom Mugs dislikes for his arrogance, is a natural choice. Mugs assaults him to keep him from riding, but relents before the big race in order to help Ben and Mr. Wilkes. He even fights Sullivan to get him to ride. The horse crosses the finish line first.

That Gang of Mine improved on *Boys of the City* by being more sophisticated and by having a solider story line, but it was less interesting. On the positive side, each scene builds on the one before. Also, the camera technique has improved.

When Mugs approaches Jimmy Sullivan to persuade him to ride Ben's horse, Jimmy is just as stubborn as Mugs. Mugs tests his knuckles, then saunters over to Jimmy, his figure filling the picture's frame. When the camera has been completely blocked by Mugs, the scene cuts. The film doesn't show what happens next; it doesn't have to. The film has made it very clear what will occur.

Mugs is thus shown to be full of determination but lacking in talent. To be more accurate, he is full of determination to seem to have determination. If he had true determination, he could develop talent.

Mugs desires to have the admiration of the gang, but he shuns practice. He submits to a training program, but doesn't push himself at any of the exercises. To the gang, he is living out a dream.

The gang sets up a special racetrack for Mugs after he announces his plans. Mugs sits on a sawhorse on which he imagines a forthcoming victory; Dany uses a beer can to simulate a microphone on which he gives a radio commentator's version of the events; Skinny uses a box to simulate a Newsreel camera with which the victory is recorded. After the mock race, Danny assumes the part of a Southern horse magnate praising Mugs's victory.

There are some character changes resulting from the kids' association with horses and Ben. They become easygoing. When Danny ribs Mugs about the kids' betting money on him ("Do you know an easier way to lose money?"), you know he does so because he cares about his friend.

Ben's character suffers from stereotyping. The film is condescending to him not just in making note of the color difference (with dialect), or in placing him in the series' always uneasy atmosphere (anti-black lines showed up throughout the series: In this film Scruno says, "If I's yellow, you'se colorblind"), but in creating for him a character that runs the gamut of racial clichés. He is superstitious; he thinks the difference between a horse winning or losing a race can be made by his singing "All God's Chil'run Got Shoes." He and his fellow black attach themselves to each other for no reason other than color. And then he says, "Why I just came from Kentucky, and—" at which point Scruno exclaims, "Why my pappy came from Kentucky." They exchange facts from their family trees, and it is suggested that they have a common ancestry. What's made of this? If you answered "nothing," you're correct.

William Lively (the screenwriter) created some of the most helpless females ever written for the movies when he wrote the script. One of them is Louise, Knuckle's girlfriend. (Whether or not she is supposed to be the same Louise kidnapped in *Boys of the City* is not explained, although the Louise in each film is just as helpless.) She can't sit still while Knuckles learns from brother Danny that the gang has part-interest in a horse. She nudges Knuckles when opportunity permits and reminds him, "We were going to a movie." This fact is unmistakable. She says it enough times. The second helpless woman is Mrs. Wilkes, whose husband lives in fear that she'll discover that he bets money on horses. (Why he should fear such a mindless nonentity is unknown.) When Algy's friends become involved with the horse, she has a suitable reason to see her first race, and she discovers that she likes them! She also seems not to understand them: When the horses leave the starting gate, she exclaims, "They're moving."

PRIDE OF THE BOWERY

A Banner Production, released January 31, 1941, by Monogram. Produced by Sam Katzman. Directed by Joseph H. Lewis. Associate producer, Pete Mayer. Screenplay by George Plympton. Story by Steven Clensos. Adapted by William Lively. Photographed by Robert Cline. Edited by Robert Golden. Production managed by Robert Tansey. Assistant direction by Arthur Hammond and Herman Pett. Musical direction by Johnny Lange and Lew Porter. Sound by Glen Glenn. British title: *Here We Go Again. 61 minutes.*

Leo and Mary Ainslee.

Mugs Maloney, Leo Gorcey; *Danny,* Bobby Jordan; *Scruno,* "Sunshine Sammy" Morrison; *Peewee,* David Gorcey; *Skinny,* Donald Haines; *Willie,* Bobby Stone; *Alan,* Kenneth Howell; *Norton,* Carlton Young; *Elaine,* Mary Ainslee; *Captain Jim White,* Kenneth Harlan; *Algy,* Eugene Francis; *Ranger,* Nick Stuart; *Doctor,* Lloyd Ingraham; *Man,* Steve Clensos.

Danny, managing boxer Mugs, books him into a Civilian Conservation Corps (CCC) camp for training. Mugs's arrogant manner soon alienates him from the other boys. When one boy, Willie, announces that he needs money for his ill mother, Mugs enters a boxing tournament in town. When Mugs loses, the boy resorts to robbing the camp safe. Mugs is accused, but Danny (who learns that Willie's mother is not sick) exonerates him by capturing Willie.

Pride of the Bowery is possibly the worst entry of the Eastside Kids series due to its simplistic plot development and lack of set diversity. What there is of plot is hard to follow, and there is little of the gang's shenanigans to lift the film.

Like its predecessor, this is a "Mugs" picture, but one is left wondering whether to be for or against him. Like *On Dress Parade*, this film shows Gorcey at odds with a regimental system. This time Kenneth Howell replaces Billy Halop as the boy sergeant who tries to straighten Gorcey out. He ends up fighting Mugs in a boxing match. The fight is a draw, but Mugs refuses to admit it, so he gets the silent treatment from the other boys. As in the previous film, Gorcey redeems himself by rescuing a boy (Howell) from certain death (a falling tree).

Danny gets a little spot which turns out to be the funniest scene in the picture. He finds out that if he feigns illness he will not have to dig ditches like the other boys. But, after initiating the ruse, he learns he will have to stay in the camp and saw firewood. The other boys, boarding the truck-bus for transport to their ditch-digging site, break out in laughter as they see Danny's seeming good fortune turn sour.

The most notable quality of *Pride of the Bowery* is the lack of sets. It was shot mostly outdoors (a great deal of this takes place around a tree-shaded lake), with the indoor sets consisting of the captain's office, the boys' barracks, their mess hall, and the downtown boxing arena.

The film apears to have been made for the sake of doing a film about the CCC camps. The Civilian Conservation Corps was a part of President Franklin Roosevelt's New Deal, initiated in 1933. It provided a chance for underpriviledged boys to earn money by digging irrigation ditches, building dams and making fire breaks. Monogram made a similar film in 1937 called *Blazing Barriers*, where the idea should have remained. A year later, the CCC was discontinued by the government due to the war.

FLYING WILD

A Banner Production, released March 10, 1941, by Monogram. Produced by Sam Katzman. Directed by William West. Associate producer, Pete Mayer. Scenario by Al Martin. Photographed by Fred Jackman. Edited by Robert Golden. Production managed by Ed W. Rote. Assistant direction by Arthur Hammond and Herman Pett. Music by Johnny Lange and Lew Porter. (Fight music: excerpts from the ballet "Don Juan," by Gluck.) Set direction by Fred Preble. Sound by Glen Glenn. Production title: *Air Devils. 5693 ft. 64 minutes.*

Mugs, Leo Gorcey; *Danny Dolan,* Bobby Jordan; *Scruno,* "Sunshine Sammy" Morrison; *Peewee,* David Gorcey; *Skinny,* Donald Haines; *Louie,* Bobby Stone; *Helen Munson,* Joan Barclay; *Tom Larson,* David O'Brien; *Dr. Richard Nagel,* George Pembroke; *Algernon "Algy" Reynolds,* Eugene Francis; *Mr. Reynolds,* Herbert Rawlinson; *George,* Dennis Moore; *Forbes,* Forrest Taylor; *Woodward,* Bob Hill; *Jack,* Alden "Stephen" Chase; *Maisie,* Mary Bovard.

Dr. Nagel owns a flying ambulance which he uses to transport secret information from an aviation factory to airports near an international border. Mugs, who watches the gang work at the airplane plant, suspects Nagel, but when he presents his suspicion to the airfield owner he is dismissed as having too much imagination. Danny becomes convinced of Mugs's theory when the two boys find part of a blueprint on board the plane during an unscheduled flight. Mugs substitutes Danny as the doctor's fake patient and accompanies him to the border. The gang, having been flown there by their friend Tom Larsen, meet them to rout the spies.

A melodrama told with tongue firmly in cheek, *Flying Wild* is an unusual entry because it goes through so many cliffhangers. In leading up to them though, it has many comic moments and many savory moments of drama.

The boys get in and out of trouble. When Mugs and Danny burst in to Dr. Nagel's office to ask him to lend them his plane to fly wounded Peewee to a hospital, they do so not trusting the doctor. They make a convincing case, however, Mugs telling the doc, "That's the reason you built that plane, to fly people back and forth." The hesitant doctor relinquishes. As the boys go out, Mugs mutters that the doctor is a real prince of a guy. "Just to think," he says. "I thought he was a spy." A Nagel henchman overhears, and the message is relayed to Dr. Nagel, who tries to have the boys killed.

Mugs is an intelligent youngster who is getting an idea of what he wants. He knows he doesn't want a job, but he will diligently do something if it appeals to him; he will conduct an investigation of Nagel because that's important. He will also claim triumphs for himself that he doesn't deserve. He can't rightfully claim to have a flying ambulance, but he does.

"I'm going into the humatarian business," he tells Danny, trying to elicit the same amazed reaction from Danny as he had when he was told what a humanitarian did.

"Humatarian," muses Danny. "I've heard of vegetarians, they only eat vegetables. But a humatarian!!"

Mugs makes a remark about Danny's mentality being that of the working class, then haughtily says, "I have to do something to help these poor, gullible invalids."

He takes Danny and the boys on a tour of Dr. Nagel's airplane, passing it off as his. The gang is impressed. After they have fiddled with various medical devices, the doctor arrives and hustles them out. Since Scruno has inhaled ether, he skips out in a deluded state. Afterward he does a dance in slow-motion on the airfield.

(This last scene is one of the cleverest in the series in terms of execution. The slow-motion perfectly captures Scruno's state. The writer, Al Martin, had been a top comedy creator in the Twenties, so he knew how to apply the advanced techniques of silents to this film.)

Director William West keeps not only a balance between comedy and tension, but a balance between human touches and thrills throughout the film.

As Mugs and Danny fly back from Peewee's hospital, they have a warm conversation about girlfriends. Mugs and Danny recall the ones each has had. "She was a waitress," Danny recalls. "Boy, how she could flip hotcakes." Mugs adds to the topic by reminiscing about the girl he knew best. "I went with a girl there once, she was a little manicurist. We used to hang out at . . ." Their conversation holds the ear.

Moments later there is the sequence in which the plane is forced down, an action sequence which holds the eye.

This is the first film in which Leo Gorcey's character says openly that he despises work. In both Eastside Kids and Bowery Boys films he would say that he was allergic to work. The topper to this running gag came in the 1955 Bowery Boys film *Jail Busters*: When he hears the word "job," he says, "Job? What's that?"

This was also the first film in which Gorcey used malaprops. He confuses "humility" for "humidity" ("The humility is getting a little warm") and says "hallucinations" with a hard "c."

A film in which the action never lets up, *Flying Wild* is one of the best films in the Eastside Kids series.

BOWERY BLITZKRIEG

A Banner Production, released September 8, 1941, by Monogram. Produced by Sam Katzman. Directed by Wallace Fox. Associate producer, Peter Mayer. Screenplay by Sam Robins. Story by Brendan Wood and Don Mullahy. Photographed by Marcel Le Picard. Edited by Robert Golden. Production managed by Ed W. Rote. Assistant direction by Harry Slott and Arthur Hammond. Musical direction by Johnny Lange and Lew Porter. Set direction by Fred Preble. Sound by Glen Glenn. Released in Britain as *Stand and Deliver*. 62 minutes.

Muggs McGinnis*, Leo Gorcey; *Danny Breslin,* Bobby Jordan; *Limpy,* Huntz Hall**; *Scruno,* "Sunshine Sammy" Morrison; *Skinny,* Donald Haines; *Peewee,*

David Gorcey; *Tom Brady,* Warren Hull; *Mary Breslin,* Charlotte Henry; *Monk Martin,* Bobby Stone; *Clancy,* Keye Luke; *Mrs. Brady,* Martha Wentworth; *Slats Morrison,* Eddie Foster; *Dorgan,* Dennis Moore; *Dutch,* Tony Carson; *Lieutenant,* Dick Ryan; *Boxing trainer,* Pat Costello; *Reform school officer,* Minerva Urecal; *Officer Sherrill,* Jack Mulhall.

Danny, a good kid who plans to go to college, is training for an amateur boxing tournament sponsored by the police, but he gets involved with cheap crook Monk Martin. Muggs, Danny's sister Mary, and her beau, cop-on-the-beat Tom, are all sure that Danny can still study to be a lawyer and at the same time be a contender in the boxing tournament. Under Monk's influence, Danny becomes hostile towards his sister and Tom, and participates in Monk's robberies. Muggs takes over Danny's position as the local police department's entry in the boxing tournament. Fight fixers approach Muggs, but he refuses to sell out. Nevertheless, public opinion has it that he will throw the fight. Danny and Monk are chased by Officer Tom after a holdup. Monk is shot to death and Danny is shot and wounded, but is saved by a blood transfusion from Muggs. Muggs goes ahead with the fight although he is advised not to exert himself. He takes a licking, but stays on his feet and wins. The fight fixers are apprehended in the audience.

Bowery Blitzkrieg is a cheap imitation of *Dead End*. It

Leo and Eddie Foster.

emphasizes the tenement surroundings, the boys' rough background, the boy-girl relationship between another Dave and Drina. It has a gangster who meets his death at the hands of a "Dave" midway through the film. It

---

*The spelling of Muggs's name (with one g or two) seems to have been strictly up to whoever wrote or designed the credits for Monogram. With *Mr. Muggs Steps Out* and *Mr. Muggs Rides Again*, however, the two g's became the accepted version, although occasionally the credit writer reverted to the single g.
**Appearing in his first of 65 consecutive Monogram/Allied Artists series entries.

differs from *Dead End* in its use of a Muggs vs. Danny plot. It might just as well have borrowed more from *Dead End*, considering the results of the Muggs vs. Danny business. The problem with the plot is that it pigeonholed one of the two (in this case Danny) into the role of a bad guy. No sale. It's hard to accept either one of them as bad. (Two later Eastside Kids films would use this plot, and both would elect Muggs as baddie.)

Bowery Blitzkrieg never leaves the Bowery, but it depicts a Bowery that is strange. It is one that is peopled. It is one where the Irish poolhall proprietor is played by Keye Luke, who played number one son in the Charlie Chan films.

Director Wallace Fox gets interesting drama from these streets. Fox, who was a veteran of Westerns, directed action that seems to be a hybrid of what took place in *Dead End* and what took place on the frontier. The most peculiar sequence is the one in which Tom shoots the two robbers. It is midday, but for once the streets aren't peopled. There isn't a pedestrian within blocks. Tom yells "Hey" when he sees Monk and Danny, and then pursues them on foot. Monk and Danny run huffing and puffing for several blocks. (Again, not a pedestrian in sight.) Tom follows, his feet hitting the pavement with thunderous sounds. The drama is intense. But it comes at a cost. How can one accept the triumph of good over evil as real when the scene that presents it is so obviously distorted?

The lesser Eastside Kids don't fare too well. Muggs and Danny do everything there is to be done. Perhaps the status of the lesser Eastside Kids can be summarized best by citing that Scruno is confined to mimicking Danny's reciting his lessons. "Economics," Scruno quotes Danny as saying, "is the science of man's activities devoted to obtaining the material means to the satisfaction of his wants."

Huntz Hall makes his first appearance as an Eastside Kid in this film. He comes off little better than Scruno. Director Wallace Fox's entries never gave Huntz a chance to show his comic gifts. In *Bowery Blitzkrieg*, Huntz plays a character who speaks in a tough voice, says stupid things (not funny-stupid, but things that are incoherent) and appears deadpan most of the time. His name is Limpy (the G was added onto the beginning of the first name in the next film).

Mary is played by Charlotte Henry, who played Alice in *Alice in Wonderland* (1933) and Bo Peep in *Babes in Toyland* (1934) with Laurel and Hardy. Roles dried up after her fairy-tale films, but she launched a comeback campaign in 1941. This was her only film after her return to the screen.

Tom, the cop on the beat, understands things. When he tells Mary that he is committed to changing the tenements (he's "Dave," remember?), he says, "It's like a leaky faucet. If you don't fix it it gets worse. Then the whole building is affected, then it's too late to do

anything about it."

The same could be said for the script of *Bowery Blitzkrieg*. No one caught on in time that it couldn't be another *Dead End*.

SPOOKS RUN WILD

A Banner Production, released October 24, 1941, by Monogram. Produced by Sam Katzman. Directed by Phil Rosen. Associate producer, Pete Mayer. Scenario by Carl Foreman and Charles R. Marion. Additional dialogue by Jack Henley. Photographed by Marcel Le Picard. Edited by Robert Golden. Production managed by Ed W. Rote. Assistant direction by Arthur Hammond. Musical direction by Johnny Lange and Lew Porter. Sound by Glen Glenn. Production title: *Ghosts In the Night*, which later became the British release title for *Ghosts on the Loose. 5821 ft. 69 minutes.*

Mugs, Leo Gorcey; *Glimpy,* Huntz Hall; *Danny,* Bobby Jordan; *Scruno,* "Sunshine Sammy" Morrison; *Skinny,* Donald Haines; *Peewee,* David Gorcey; *Nardo,* Bela Lugosi; *Jeff Dixon,* David O'Brien; *Linda Mason,* Dorothy Short; *"Von Grosch",* Dennis Moore; *Luigi, the dwarf,* Angelo Rossitto; *Lem Harvey,* P. J. Kelley; *Constable,* Guy Wilkerson; *Margie,* Rosemary Portia.

The boys are sent to a mountain camp. Stranded in a small rural town, they hear about a "Monster Killer" roaming the New England countryside. At night, they sneak away from camp. Peewee is shot by a gravedigger, and they are forced to seek aid at an old mansion. The

Dracula himself, Bela Lugosi, is at left. In the ten years since playing the Transylvanian count on film, Lugosi had dwarfed his stature by accepting most roles offered to him (partly to buy medicine to recuperate from previous drug abuse), leading to a nine-picture contract with Sam Katzman and Banner Productions. Spooks Run Wild *was the third, which inspired a reunion with the kids,* Ghosts on the Loose, *his sixth.*

strange inhabitant gives Peewee a sedative, and insists that the boys spend the night. After seeing Peewee walk through the house in a trance, the boys decide that the man turned Peewee into a zombie. The boys gang up on their host and tie him up. Th nurse at the boys' camp, Linda, sets out to find the missing boys, and enters the mansion with a certain Dr. Von Grosch, who has come to town to rid it of the Monster Killer. The boys find Peewee cured. They hear a scream from elsewhere in the house. They run there in time to save Linda from Dr. Von Grosch, who turns out to be the Monster Killer. The mansion's resident turns out to be Nardo, a well-known magician.

Spooks Run Wild is comedy, pure comedy, a banquet of slapstick and farce. It has sight gags, and it lampoons the horror genre that is its format.

Horror film giant Bela Lugosi is cast as Nardo. The man who created *Dracula* on film (1931), he adds greatly to the film. He turns out to be a red herring, but he helps to rib the form that gave him his fame.

Glimpy is very prominent in the film. His gift for comedy is central to many of the episodes. In camp, Glimpy reads in the darkened camp bunkhouse. "How can you read in the dark?" Danny asks. "I went to night school," Glimpy replies. He has become a full-fledged comedian and principal member in this film. The script by Carl Foreman and Charles R. Marion emphasized him. Foreman, who was to co-write the prestigious *High Noon* (1952) and the Academy Award-winning *Bridge on the River Kwai* (1957), was under personal contract to Huntz Hall at the time this picture was made. Marion was to write many of the Bowery Boys most comedy-oriented pictures.

Lugosi obviously relished his part in *Spooks Run Wild*,

and seems to enjoy himself. He was in the midst of a nine-picture deal with Sam Katzman. Most of the films were below par for the man who had played the definitive Count in *Dracula*. He had few chances to put on his cape again, but he enjoyed doing so.

The highlight of the film occurs when the tables are turned on Lugosi. He backs away in fright when he encounters a horrifying figure played by the kids. The kids have assembled pyramid-style behind a sheet, and are totally masked behind a skull image. Glimpy is at the top, and petrifies Lugosi with a ghastly story: "Twenty years ago in this very house, I was a living being. I used to have flesh on my bones, blood ran through my veins, but you . . . you," Glimpy says, "scared the *health* out of me."

Spooks Run Wild has only modest production values (when a match is lit, the lights that simulate it come on a moment too late and actually capture the shadow of the match itself!). Nonetheless, the sets are most adequate. *Spooks Run Wild* would not be the last film to offer Eastside Kids fans a chance to see these backgrounds. Some of these sets were to be used in Eastside and Bowery stories shot into the fifties.

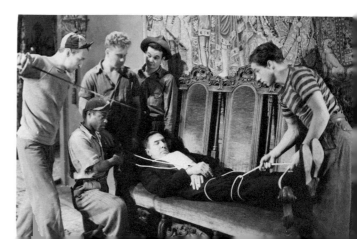

"Mr. Horror Man," as Muggs calls Bela Lugosi's character, has been subdued.

MR. WISE GUY

A Banner Production, released February 20, 1942, by Monogram. Produced by Sam Katzman and Jack Dietz. Directed by William Nigh. Associate producer, Barney A. Sarecky. Screenplay by Sam Robins, Harvey Gates and Jack Henley. Story by Martin Mooney. Photographed by Art Reed. Edited by Carl Pierson. Production managed by Ed W. Rote. Assistant direction by Arthur Hammond and Gerald Schnitzer. Musical direction by Johnny Lange and Lew Porter. Art direction by G.C. Van Marter. Sound by Glen Glenn. Sound engineered by Buddy Meyers. *6303 ft. 70 minutes.*

Ethelbert "Muggs" McGinnis, Leo Gorcey; *Danny Collins,* Bobby Jordan; *Glimpy Stone,* Huntz Hall; *Peewee,* David Gorcey; *Scruno,* "Sunshine Sammy" Morrison; *Skinny,* Bill Lawrence; *Bill Collins,* Douglas Fowley; *Ann Mitchell,* Joan Barclay; *Rice Pudding Charlie,* Gabriel Dell; *Chalky Jones,* Bobby Stone; *Knobby,* Billy Gilbert; *Dorothy Melton,* Ann Doran; *Luke Manning,* Guinn "Big Boy" Williams; *Jim Barnes,* Jack Mulhall; *Jed Miller,* Dick Ryan; *Dratler,* Warren Hymer; *Waiter,* Benny Rubin; *"Charlie Horse,"* Sidney Miller; *Bit,* Joe Kirk.

The gang helps a truckdriver load a barrel onto a truck. Minutes later they are charged with stealing the truck. They are sent to reform school. Danny's brother Bill, ready for the army, is arrested for a robbery-killing, of which he is innocent, and is sentenced to death. The killing was actually committed by Luke Manning, a prominent mobster recently escaped from Blackwell's Island and presumed dead. At reform school, the gang is mistreated by guard Jed Miller, who gives favorable treatment to inmate Rice Pudding Charlie, who is a nephew of Manning's. Manning wins $5000 in a lottery and sends out his moll Dorothy and dumb henchman Knobby to pick up the loot. The kids see a newsreel of Knobby collecting the cash and recognize him as the truckdriver they had helped. Deducing that Luke Manning had been in the barrel they handled, they break out of reform school and go to Dorothy's apartment, following information furnished by Charlie. They find Knobby with Dorothy, get Knobby to confess, and save Bill from the electric chair with only minutes to spare.

Mr. Wise Guy has a lot of gaps. Example:

The gang is sentenced to reform school even though nobody testifies that they stole the truck? Neither Knobby nor Luke appears at the trial. (And there is no trial!) Also, they are charged with stealing the truck when they never actually drive it.

And, between Knobby's collecting the sweepstakes money and his spending of it that very night, a newsreel (of Knobby) is assembled. Did they have Polaroid back then, or video editing, or . . . ?

Leo, Huntz, Ann Doran, Billy Gilbert, David Gorcey, Jordan, Lawrence.

Blame for these oversights must be placed on director William Nigh. He had committed these same artistic transgressions at Universal, where he directed the equally confusing *Mob Town.* (Fortunately this was his only Eastside Kids film.) Under his hands, *Mr. Wise Guy* has holes ten and fifteen minutes long during which no plot or characterization occurs.

Billy Gilbert is wasted in his role as blustery mobster Knobby. The role does not show off his considerable comedic skills well, and his being a gangster makes it hard to accept his humor. For anyone who has seen Gilbert in full comic action (as in *His Girl Friday* [1940] with Cary Grant, or in several Laurel and Hardy comedies), it is sad to see Gilbert treated as he is, especially when Manning continually tells him, "Lay off that bourbon!"

Mr. Wise Guy introduced a running gag to the Eastside Kids series. In juvenile prison, each member of the gang is called up to the desk by sour guard Jed Miller. The last name called is that of an "Ethelbert McGinnis." No response. Glimpy observes, "We have a McGinnis, but no Ethelbert." McGinnis, Muggs, wakes from a nap, and, hearing the name, sheepishly answers, "I'm Ethelbert." The gang is stunned. Glimpy says, "Now I'm completely disillusioned." Muggs's shame over his given name of Ethelbert was to be a subject frequently recalled in the series.

Gabriel Dell makes his first appearance in the series that his old Dead End Gang had started without him. He is cast here as an adversary. Observing his and Leo's fight are Bobby Stone (far left), Bobby Jordan (center), "Sunshine Sammy" Morrison (beneath Leo's chin)

Glimpy is grabbed by Danny, while Danny's brother (Tom Brown) is about to be klunked by Mugs.

LET'S GET TOUGH

A Banner Production, released May 22, 1942, by Monogram. Produced by Sam Katzman and Jack Dietz. Directed by Wallace Fox. Associate producer, Barney A. Sarecky. Screenplay by Harvey Gates, based upon his story "I Am an American." Photographed by Art Reed. Edited by Robert Golden. Production managed by Ed W. Rote. Assistant direction by Arthur Hammond and Gerald Schnitzer. Art direction by David Milton. Musical direction by Johnny Lange and Lew Porter. Sound by Glen Glenn. Production title: *Little MacArthurs. 5599 ft. 62 minutes.*

Ethelbert "Muggs" McGinnis, Leo Gorcey; *Glimpy,* Huntz Hall; *Danny Collins,* Bobby Jordan; *Scruno,* "Sunshine Sammy" Morrison; *Skinny,* Bobby Stone; *Peewee,* David Gorcey; *Phil Connors,* Tom Brown; *Nora Stevens,* Florence Rice; *Officer "Pops" Stevens,* Robert Armstrong; *Fritz Hienbach,* Gabriel Dell; *Joe Matsui,* Philip Ahn; *Hienbach Sr.,* Sam Bernard; *Music teacher,* Jerry Bergen; *Navy recruiter,* Pat Costello.

The kids want to do something to help their country, so they break into a Mr. Keno's antique shop to break it up. (Keno is believed to be a Jap.) They find the owner stabbed. They pay their condolences to the widow, and see a Japanese man snatch a pen from a locker the widow had opened for him. Glimpy lifts the pen from him and the boys find an oriental message inside. To have it translated, they take it to Mr. Matsui, a Japanese tea

shop proprietor, who tries to steal it, and, when he fails, stabs himself in front of their eyes. The boys report this to the police, but when they return to the shop, Matsui's son is standing in for his late father. On this trip, Glimpy notices a violin case the boys had already sold to another party. He takes from it a packet that turns out to be an explosive. The boys break into Matsui's shop at night and expose a Black Dragon Society that is about to launch a plot to overthrow the United States.

Let's Get Tough! is a superb entry. Its plot logically draws from itself, with each event leading to the next, and it is pleasing, innocuous entertainment.

Let's Get Tough! has a strong dose of Americanism. The kids want to do everything they can for Uncle Sam. After seven reels, we think they have, but in the end we learn that Danny's brother Bill is leading an F.B.I. investigation which would have netted the Axis plotters anyway.

Let's Get Tough! sometimes caters to the tastes of children. In the Black Dragons' house the kids sneak into, they encounter a set of window bars that lock them in only moments after they have entered, a swinging panel that hides the way to the rest of the house, a trapdoor that opens over a deep body of water (when Scruno drops an object into it, moments elapse before the splash is heard, prompting him to say, "That bathtub must be in China"), and a seemingless endless supply of staircases and passageways. Costumes are worn by the kids as they listen to the leader of the Black Dragons lecture against America.

This is one of the few Eastside Kids films that

children in Britain were permitted to see. The British Board of Film Censors, which normally gave the films in the series the "A" (adult) rating, approved this film for all audiences. Today, however, Japanese communities, sensitive about the way their race is depicted, have requested that this film be withdrawn. Television stations in Los Angeles, San Francisco and Las Vegas won't run it.

Oddly enough, *Let's Get Tough!* is not objectionable. It is an *anti*-racist film. In one of the film's "censorable" scenes, the kids learn that the man that they had attacked was not Japanese, as they had thought, but Chinese. This teaches that one should not direct hostility towards an ethnic group (in this case Orientals) because the violence would be or might be misdirected. End of lecture. Nonetheless, the film continues to be objected to.

"Sunshine Sammy" Morrison gives some insight into the atmosphere in which this series was shot in recalling how an adlibbed bit made it to the final negative:

"The scene where nobody had any money, and we wanted to get some flowers—the scene ended with everybody's leaving, going to get some money, and I stayed, and they kept the camera rolling. I reach into my pocket and pull out a big wad. Then they pick up with me counting all the money [same shot], and when I look up the other guys see me with all this money; 'goddamn,' I take off. They used it. I just happened to stay there.

"Cameramen will keep going. They found out that a lot of things they [editors] can use will happen after the 'cut.' "

Huntz Hall, Robert Armstrong, David Gorcey, Leo Gorcey, Bobby Jordan, Bobby Stone, "Sunshine Sammy" Morrison.

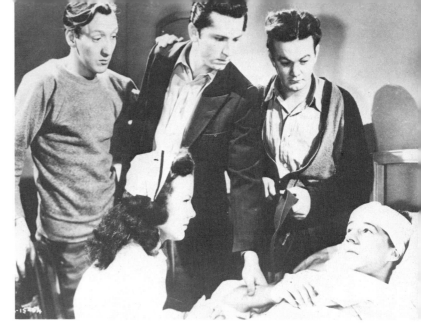

TV's "My Little Margie"—Gale Storm—was ingénue in this picture, but fame didn't come until long after this 1942 Monogram release.

SMART ALECKS

A Banner Production, released August 7, 1941, by Monogram. Produced by Sam Katzman and Jack Dietz. Directed by Wallace Fox. Associate producer, Barney A. Sarecky. Scenario by Harvey H. Gates and Jack Dietz. Photographed by Mack Stengler. Edited by Robert Golden. Assistant direction by Arthur Hammond and Gerald Schnitzer. Art direction by David Milton. Musical direction by Edward Kay. Sound by Glen Glenn. *5940 ft. 63 minutes.*

Ethelbert "Muggs" McGinnis, Leo Gorcey; *Danny Stevens,* Bobby Jordan; *Glimpy,* Huntz Hall; *Henry "Hank" Salko,* Gabriel Dell; *Stash,* Stanley Clements; *Scruno,* "Sunshine Sammy" Morrison; *Peewee,* David Gorcey; *Skinny,* Bobby Stone; *Butch Brocalli,* Maxie Rosenbloom; *Ruth Stevens,* Gale Storm; *Officer Joe Reagan,* Roger Pryor; *Dr. Ornsby,* Walter Woolf King; *Captain Bronson,* Herbert Rawlinson; *Mike,* Joe Kirk; *Dr. Thomas,* Sam Bernard; *Prison warden,* Dick Ryan; *Nurse,* Marie Windsor; *Receptionist,* Betty Sinclair.

The gang wants to buy baseball uniforms, but the only way they can get enough money is by accepting dishonest work from ex-member Hank, who is sent to jail for aiding a notorious criminal. The criminal, Butch Brocalli, remains at large, but when he steals the boys' baseball, Danny creates a scene with him, and cop-on-the-beat Reagan arrests him. Danny gets a reward, with which he intends to buy baseball uniforms, but Muggs thinks that Danny wants to keep the money for himself. Muggs leads the gang to Danny's apartment, where they

The gang offers the doctor $90 derived from the sale of their car. Not coincidentally, the Dead End Kids paid that very amount for a Model A when they arrived in Hollywood. Walter Woolf King (whose career had petered out) is at left.

break in and take the money. Danny refuses to press charges, so the kids keep the money and buy a dilapidated car.

Hank and Brocalli escape jail, and Hank warns the gang to hide Danny so that Brocalli can't find him. The advice comes too late; when the gang finds Danny he has been critically injured. To help Danny, the kids obtain expert brain surgeon Dr. Ornsby, who refuses the money they raised by selling the car. He asks them to buy uniforms. After Danny recovers, Brocalli locates him again, but he is subdued by the gang, Hank and Officer Reagan. Hank is paroled for participating in the capture.

The screenplay of *Smart Alecks* was as inappropriate for the kids as the film's title. A throwback to *Bowery Blitzkrieg*, this also has Muggs and Danny hating each other for no plausible reason. There is an older sister for Danny, a boyfriend who is a cop, a gangster who comes close to infiltrating the kids' lives, a hospital where Danny is admitted, and a tenement setting that is never left.

What makes this film especially disturbing is seeing Muggs lead the others to steal. The scenes before they commit the robbery suggest that they are of good character. The Muggs in the early scenes won't accept crooked jobs. When the kids hide Hank from Officer Reagan, and are then offered a present for doing so, Muggs tells Hank that they won't touch his tarnished money. So what comes over them? They utter something about each being entitled to one-seventh of the money, and then climb up a fire escape, squeeze through a window and enter an apartment unwelcomed. What kind of kids are these?

Also damaging the film is the casting of former-heavyweight-Boxer-turned-pug-comedian Maxie "Slapsie" Rosenbloom as the main villain. What does he do while his henchman beats Danny? He puts cotton in his ears!

Walter Woolf King wins the schmaltz award. A respected stage actor and superb singer, he had been sensational in the Marx Brothers' *A Night at the Opera* (1935). Here he appears in the role of the open-hearted surgeon Dr. Ornsby. When he hears semi-conscious Danny mutter something about unfinished business with Muggs, and is told by the patient's sister that Danny was talking about a misunderstanding he had with his friends, Ornsby delivers the line: "I think your brother is suffering from more than one kind of wound."

Gabriel Dell (as Hank) played his first gangster role in *Smart Alecks*. He would play the part often.

The kids can't do much with the script, but there are a couple of cases where they overcome their material. Gorcey does this in a scene where he prays for Danny and has trouble finding the words.

Case of the Missing Kid: In *Smart Alecks*, the size of the gang after Danny leaves varies from five to six members—not because one of the members left in support of Danny, but because one of the kids mysteriously appears and disappears. The kid is Peewee, who is, or had been, played by David Gorcey. The most likely reason for his disappearances is that he walked out on the film, but whether or not he did, and if so his reason for doing so, is unknown. The other actors playing the kids actually make cracks (ad-libs on the part of Huntz Hall and "Sunshine Sammy" Morrison) about this shortcoming: when the (five) boys are riding in their Model T, Huntz says, "Good thing there's only five of us because the limousine only holds five." While the (six) boys rob Danny, Scruno explains it's because "we's entitled to six-sevenths."

It may be said that the missing member of the gang is symbolic of the film. However, *Smart Alecks* is missing something much more integral.

'NEATH BROOKLYN BRIDGE

A Banner Production, released November 20, 1942, by Monogram. Produced by Sam Katzman and Jack Dietz. Directed by Wallace Fox. Associate producer, Barney A. Sarecky. Scenario by Harvey H. Gates. Photographed by Mack Stengler. Edited by Carl Pierson. Art direction by David Milton. Musical direction by Edward Kay. Assistant direction by Arthur Hammond. Sound by Glen Glenn. *5529 ft. 61 minutes.*

Muggs McGinnis, Leo Gorcey; *Glimpy,* Huntz Hall; *Danny Lyons,* Bobby Jordan; *Scruno,* "Sunshine Sammy" Morrison; *Stash,* Stanley Clements; *Skinny,* Bobby Stone;

How to pad a film: The voiceless sole witness to a murder (J. Arthur Young) blinks out Morse Code for 'M-C-G-A-F-F-E-Y K-I-L-L-E-D M-O-R-L-E-Y," taking two minutes of screen time to do so.

Sylvia, Ann Gillis; *Butch,* Noah Beery, Jr.; *McGaffey,* Marc Lawrence; *Skid,* Gabriel Dell; *Sergeant Phil Lyons,* David O'Brien; *Sniffy,* Jack Raymond; *Morley,* Bud Osborn; *Glimpy's mother,* Patsy Moran; *Bunny,* Betty Wells; *Police captain,* Dewey Robinson; *Sergeant Clancy,* Jack Mulhall; *Skipper,* J. Arthur Young; *Saleswoman,* Betty Sinclair; *Soup customer,* Snub Pollard; *Babies: Slaine, Chowderhead,* Leo Gorcey, Huntz Hall.

Danny, Muggs and the kids hear a scream come from an apartment. They enter and find a girl, Sylvia, and the corpse of her guardian, a man named Morley, who had mistreated her. Saloon-keeper McGaffey had killed him after the two crossed each other in a deal. The kids hide stray Sylvia in their club. Circumstantial evidence points to the kids, and Danny is locked up as a murder suspect. McGaffey has the stick he used to club Morley with, which has Muggs's fingerprints on it. He uses this to blackmail Muggs into helping him rob a warehouse a few nights later. The boys' sailor pal Butch returns to New York on leave and finds Sylvia in the boys' clubroom. He agrees to help her and the boys find out who her guardian's murderer was. She introduces Butch to her paralyzed grandfather, Skipper, who saw the murder but is unable to speak. Butch observes that Skipper communicates by blinking his eyes to form messages in Morse code. He translates Skipper's blinks into "McGaffey killed Morley." Muggs goes to the warehouse to keep his bargain with McGaffey, but at Muggs's instruction the kids rout McGaffey and his gang.

'Neath Brooklyn Bridge is amusing, consistently brisk entertainment, though its plot is hard to accept. It's hard to picture Danny *seriously* accused of murder, so the film falls apart there. The film doesn't make too much of many of its plot elements: The gangsters, for instance, proceed with their plans without much interference.

Some idea of the film's haphazard nature can be gained from the opening scene. In it, Glimpy and his mother are moving to a new apartment in order to beat the rent. The kids help. Glimpy's mother says she and

Glimpy may be moving again next month. Are we supposed to think that these people are wonderful?

The police certainly don't. Not only do they lock up Danny, although he didn't do anything (and even though Danny's brother, an officer on the force, admits that the police don't think Danny is guilty), but they try to eavesdrop on the boys' conversation when they visit Danny in the visiting room, which is wired with a hidden microphone. Fortunately Muggs finds the microphone and stuffs it with a handkerchief before the police captain decides to listen in on them.

Seeing Muggs triumph over sneaky people like the police captain is one of the factors making 'Neath Brooklyn Bridge enjoyable. Also enjoyable is the repartee between Muggs and Glimpy. Glimpy is given a solo comedy scene in this one (he gets a meal of pilfered soup and swiped vegetables for Sylvia); his stature was growing.

KID DYNAMITE

A Banner Production, released February 12, 1943, by Monogram. Produced by Sam Katzman and Jack Dietz. Directed by Wallace Fox. Asociate producer, Barney A. Sarecky. Screenplay by Gerald J. Schnitzer. Based on the *Saturday Evening Post* story "The Old Gang," by Paul Ernst. Additional dialogue by Morey Amsterdam. Photographed by Mack Stengler. Edited by Carl Pierson. Art direction by David Milton. Musical direction by Edward Kay. Assistant direction by Arthur Hammond. Sound by Glen Glenn. Production title: *Little Mobsters. 5969 ft. 67 minutes.*

Ethelbert "Muggs" McGinnis, Leo Gorcey; *Danny Lyons,* Bobby Jordan; *Glimpy McGleavey,* Huntz Hall; *Scruno,* "Sunshine Sammy" Morrison; *Harry "Stony" Stone,* Bobby Stone; *Beanie Miller,* Bennie Bartlett; *Joe "Skinny" Collins,* Dave Durand; *Ivy McGinnis,* Pamela Blake; *Harry Wyckoff,* Gabriel Dell; *Louis Gendick,* Henry Hall; *Nick,* Charles Judels; *Klinkhammer,* Vince Barnett; *Tony,* Wheeler Oakman; *Mrs. McGinnis,* Daphne Pollard; *Mrs. Lyons,* Margaret Padula; *Scruno's dad,* Dudley Dickerson; *Kay, Mugs's dancing partner,* Kay Marvis [Mrs. Leo] Gorcey; *Judge,* Minerva Urecal; *Themselves,* Mike Riley's Orchestra; *Band singer,* Marion Miller; *Dance official,* Snub Pollard; *Thug,* Ray Miller; *Man,* Jack Mulhall.

When Muggs is kidnapped by gamblers to keep him out of a boxing match, Danny is substituted. Muggs thereafter accuses Danny of collaborating with the gamblers. Danny protests his innocence, but when Danny is hired

as the gas station attendant that Muggs wanted to be, an all-out war begins between Muggs and Danny. Muggs attempts to show up Danny in a dance contest, but is disqualified on a technicality. Danny is decreed the winner, a bitter defeat for Muggs, since Danny's partner was Muggs's sister, Ivy. Danny joins the Army, and returns on furlough a month later. Muggs attempts to disgrace the boy in uniform by coercing Danny into taking part in a robbery (of the gas station) in which Danny is sure to be caught. Danny foils Muggs's plans, tells him off, then fights Muggs. Danny, motivated by the desire to marry Ivy, wins. Muggs concedes that he always said the guy who married his sister had to beat him first.

The Muggs in this picture is one who was recreated for this episode. He is self-assuming. He is cruel. He is also someone the outside world knows it has to reckon with. (When the bookmakers first hear the proposal that Muggs be kidnapped, they mention that they were going to bet on him.)

Muggs does his utmost to humiliate Danny. He puts up a sign reading, "Muggs dares Danny to fight him," and parades through the street in a caravan displaying the banner.

Glimpy (playing a tough character) makes a speech about Muggs to a crowd that gathers to see the challenger. Glimpy says, "He's so tough, he told Joe Louis [the reigning boxing champion] where to get off."

Mr. and Mrs. Leo Gorcey are about to hit the dance floor. Snub Pollard, Bobby Jordan, Vince Barnett and Pamela Blake are to the right of them.

Wheeler Oakman is socked by Dave Durand. Gabe Dell is on the phone, Bobby Stone beneath him. Leo Gorcey and Bennie Bartlett attack bookies as Huntz Hall watches.

"He told Joe Louis where to get off?" queries an astonished Scruno.

"Well, they were riding on the same streetcar together." Glimpy believes in Muggs, as do most people in this film.

Two people who don't are Gendick, the garage owner, and Mugg's skeptical mother, mature characters who are prominent only in the last half-hour; the gangsters appear only in the first.

Just as characters are shuttled in and out, situations are brought in and out of play. The boxing match at the beginning of the film leads to no further bouts; the gangsters' bookmaking stops after the villains are sentenced. The dance contest is another area in which the film develops a situation and then leaves it behind.

The dance contest may be the most aesthetically enjoyable scene in the film. The kids perform crazy variations with their jitterbug partners. Marion Miller sings "Coming Through the Rye;" the band plays a toe-tapping melody perfectly five times. And why shouldn't they be perfect five times. They're performing to sound coming from a recording!

The characters of Ivy, Gendick and Mrs. Lyons (Danny's mother) were created by Paul Ernst in his story "The Old Gang." The plot of *Kid Dynamite* was also carried over from that story, which had been published in the *Saturday Evening Post* in its July 11, 1942 issue. Muggs, Danny and Glimpy also appear in the story, though they are called Ozzie, Stevie and Crab.

Kid Dynamite has an in-joke tying it to "The Old Gang." Muggs says in trying to con Danny, "I hate to see *the old gang* break up."

The man in the cowboy hat is Noah Beery, Sr. To the right, surrounding Amelita Ward, are the supposed "McGinnis clan": Benny (Bennie Bartlett), Muggs, Dave (Eddie Mills, hidden), Glimpy—dressed as "Annabelle"—Stash (Dick Chandlee), "re-adopted" Scruno, Danny.

CLANCY STREET BOYS

A Banner Production, released April 23, 1943, by Monogram. Produced by Sam Katzman and Jack Dietz. Directed by William Beaudine. Associate producer, Barney A. Sarecky. Scenario by Harvey H. Gates. Photographed by Mack Stengler. Edited by Carl Pierson. Art direction by David Milton. Musical direction by Edward Kay. Assistant direction by Arthur Hammond. Sound by Glen Glenn. *5930 ft. 66 minutes.*

Ethelbert "Muggs" McGinnis, Leo Gorcey; *Glimpy,* Huntz Hall; *Danny,* Bobby Jordan; *Scruno,* "Sunshine Sammy" Morrison; *Benny,* Bennie Bartlett; *Stash,* Dick Chandlee; *Dave,* Eddie Mills; *Pete Monahan,* Noah Beery Sr.; *Judy Monahan,* Amelita Ward; *Molly McGinnis,* Martha Wentworth; *George Mooney,* Rick Valin; *Butch,* Billy Benedict; *Cherry Streeters,* Jimmy Strand, Johnny Duncan; *Flanagan,* J. Farrell MacDonald; *Violinist,* Jan Rubini; *Williams,* George DeNormand; *Bar owner,* Bernard Gorcey; *Henchman,* Jack Normand; *Head waiter,* Gino Corrado.

Muggs's "Uncle" Pete is coming to visit. Since Muggs's late father had bragged that he and Muggs's mother had seven kids, Muggs recruits the other six boys to pose as his brethren. One was a girl named "Annabelle," and Glimpy plays this role. Pete treats the family well, taking them to a nightclub. All goes fine with Pete and his daughter Judy until gangster George Mooney exposes the scheme. Pete tells Muggs that he can forget he ever had an Uncle Pete, and Mooney kidnaps Pete. Muggs and the kids investigate into Pete's whereabouts and rescue him. Pete treats the kids to a stay on his ranch in Texas.

Clancy Street Boys is a pure comedy, a bright, brisk film that moves from one amusing situation to another at a good steady pace.

The pace was so well set that it was duplicated by several subsequent Eastside Kids films over the next three years. It roughly allows for a new situation to develop each ten minutes.

In *Clancy Street Boys,* the first ten minutes are devoted to mischief. It is Muggs's birthday. The other kids are looking for him. Muggs hides behind a corner, behind posts, and behind a fat man walking on the sidewalk. When the man he is walking behind changes direction, his cover is blown without his knowing it. The other kids spot him, but don't let on. Silently, they walk up behind Muggs and tip-toe as Muggs tip-toes. At the right time they jump him.

Thus the film has developed a comic situation without entangling it in a story. This was the technique of silent comedy and short-subject comedy. *Clancy Street Boys'* director William Beaudine had thirty years' experience directing this kind of comedy. It works well for the Eastside Kids.

The second ten minutes develops a more serious

situation, although like the previous scene, it doesn't crack open the story. Muggs's mother is worried because Mr. McGinnis's false story about having seven kids will finally have to be exposed, since his friend Pete is coming from Texas and will discover the truth. Muggs has other ideas.

The third ten minutes introduce more characters: George, Pete, Judy. Nonetheless, there are plenty of opportunities for the kids to do funny things. Glimpy (now dressed as Annabelle) and Muggs have a recurring problem keeping Glimpy's pants from unrolling below his dress. They go into a telephone booth to remove the pants for good. Some indignant women watch them struggle behind the glass doors. They conclude that something entirely different is going on inside!

The fourth ten minutes of the film take place in a nightclub. This sequence is isolated from the scenes occurring before and after, and makes a nice break from the action.

The fifth ten minutes sets up the story for the kidnapping. George gets Pete's confidence by letting him know that Muggs was making a fool of him. He thus has an easy time kidnapping Pete. (The part of George was created along the lines of those Gabe Dell had been playing. It's possible that the role was written for him. Dell was in the service during the making of this film and the next one.)

The sixth (and last) segment has the boys saving Pete. A brawl takes place. The kids bring plenty of reinforcements in the form of a rival gang (Glimpy has them chase him to the fight location) and the police.

In several coming Eastside Kids films, the plots were to develop in the same manner, by creating ten-minute segments that were ordered as follows:

    1st) unrelated scenes
    2nd) plot development
    3rd) introduction of new aspect
    4th) isolated sequence
    5th) transitory scenes
    6th) bam! pow! sock!

Clancy Street Boys moves from funny situation to situation. Muggs often completely drops his tough shell when he can make a joke. When Uncle Pete, who is a cattleman, tells Muggs that he just sold a thousand head of cattle to the Army, Muggs asks him, "What do you do with the rest of the cow after you've sold the head?"

Humor pops up throughout the film. When the gang gives Muggs a birthday cake, it is inscribed "Happy Boithday."

Clancy Street Boys is a treat for the Eastside Kids fan.

GHOSTS ON THE LOOSE

A Banner Production, released July 30, 1943, by Monogram. Produced by Sam Katzman and Jack Dietz.

Directed by William Beaudine. Associate producer, Barney A. Sarecky. Scenario by Kenneth Higgins. Photographed by Mack Stengler. Edited by Carl Pierson. Art direction by David Milton. Musical direction by Edward Kay. Assistant direction by Arthur Hammond. Sound by Glen Glenn. Released in Britain as *Ghosts in the Night. 5893 ft. 70 minutes.*

Muggs McGinnis, Leo Gorcey; *Glimpy Williams,* Huntz Hall; *Danny,* Bobby Jordan; *Scruno,* "Sunshine Sammy" Morrison; *Skinny (a.k.a. Benny),* Billy Benedict; *Stash,* Stanley Clements; *Rocky (a.k.a. Dave),* Bobby Stone; *"Sleepy" Dave,* Bill Bates; *Emil,* Bela Lugosi; *John "Jack" Gibson,* Rick Vallin; *Betty Williams Gibson,* Ava Gardner; *Hilda,* Minerva Urecal; *Tony,* Wheeler Oakman; *Monk,* Frank Moran; *Bruno,* Peter Seal; *Lieutenant Brady,* Jack Mulhall; *Bridesmaid,* Kay Marvis Gorcey; *Minister,* Robert F. Hill.

The kids try to make life more tranquil for Glimpy's sister Betty and Jack Gibson, who have just married. Mistaking an address on a card that fell out of Jack's pocket, they go to what they believe is Jack's new house to decorate. The house is actually owned by Nazi spies, who are trying to buy Jack's house (next door) so that their espionage activities can go on unnoticed. In their search of the Nazi house, the kids come across a printing press and Nazi propaganda. Believing the house to be Jack's, they move the press and pamphlets to the house next door, then learn from Jack that the house is his. They move the press back and Jack summons the police, but when the police arrive the Nazis have moved the press. Jack and the kids find the press and call the police back. All participate in routing the agents.

Where are the ghosts? There are no ghosts in *Ghosts on the Loose.* There are only Nazis.

Ava Gardner appears here. Rick Vallin, her movie hubby, was heading for obscurity, here in the second of his two Eastside Kid roles. In Clancy *he played a Gabriel Dell part. Here he has a role obviously written for Dave O'Brien.*

Only a writer of musicals (Kenneth Higgins) would write in a singing scene for the Eastside Kids. They sing "To Celia" by Ben Jonson (1613). With Hall, Gorcey, Jordan and Stone are Stanley Clements, Billy Benedict and Bill Bates (at organ).

Some of the writing in *Ghosts on the Loose* is laughable. Late in the film, the cops' patrol car is radioed to "Return to 322 Elm Street." One cop looks at the other and says, "That's where we just came from." When they do arrive, one notices an open hall door. "Was that door there when we first came here?" he inquires of his companion. "No, it just this minute grew!" When Muggs and Glimpy are held captive by the Nazis in a room accessible only by an underground hall, Jack, hearing the boys' screams through a door, deduces, "There must be somebody in there!"

Writer Kenneth Higgins makes everybody look bad, even the producer, who the dialogue takes a potshot at. When Muggs and Glimpy visit police headquarrters to ask for a police escort for the wedding, Glimpy expresses fear that the ceremony will be invaded by a notorious and infamous mob, the "Katzman mob." (Higgins had never before worked for Monogram and never would again.)

Ghosts on the Loose has earned some notoriety itself as the film in which Bela Lugosi sneezes out a four-letter word. Director William 'One-Take" Beaudine didn't re-shoot the scene.

The biggest problem with *Ghosts on the Loose* is that the Eastside Kids don't play Eastside Kids. They play middle-class kids. There are no references to the slums. They drive a fairly respectable car.

The lack of a slum setting was not so much by design as by circumstance. The series had been using Hal Roach Studios for backgrounds. In 1943 the Army moved in and turned the studio into a center for making training films. Commercial filmmakers were turned away. Katzman needed to find a new studio backlot before he could use exteriors again.

The film has a few neat touches: the beginning of the wedding dissolves to the minister anouncing, "Is there anyone here who has just reason why this couple should not be wed?" Muggs, acting as if he had been officially appointed, stands up and scans the assembly to make sure no one objects. Dissolve again to the two lovebirds being pronounced man and wife.

However, most of the gags don't come off. For example, Glimpy contracts a case of German measles, and the pox marks take the shape of swastikas.

MR. MUGGS STEPS OUT

A Banner Production, released October 29, 1943, by Monogram. Produced by Sam Katzman and Jack Dietz. Directed by William Beaudine. Associate producer, Barney A. Sarecky. Scenario by William X. Crowley and Beryl Sachs. Photographed by Marcel Le Picard. Edited by Carl Pierson. Set design by Ernest Hickerson. Musical direction by Edward Kay. Assistant direction by Arthur Hammond. Sound by Gilbert E. Meloy. *5893 ft. 63 minutes.*

Elthelbert "Muggs" McGinnis, Leo Gorcey; *Glimpy,* Huntz Hal; *Pinky (a.k.a. Skinny),* Billy Benedict; *Speed,* Bobby Stone; *Skinny,* Bud Gorman; *Danny,* Dave Durand; *Rocky,* Jimmy Strand; *Brenda Murray,* Joan Marsh; *Maisie O'Donnell,* Patsy Moran; *Dips Nolan,* Gabriel Dell; *Butch Grogan,* Eddie Gribbon; *Charney,* Halliwell Hobbes*; *Virgil Wellington Brooks III,* Stanley Brown; *Margaret Murray,* Betty Blythe; *John Aldredge Murray,* Emmett Vogan; *Diamonds Hamilton,* Nick Stuart; *Judge,* Noah Beery, Sr.; *Elizabeth, dowager,* Lottie Harrison; *Dancer,* Kay Marvis Gorcey.

*Name misspelled "Holliwell Hobbs" in credits

Muggs works as a chauffeur for the Murray women (Joan Marsh, Betty Blyth).

Muggs is ordered by a judge to get work. While he is still in the courtroom, Mrs. Murray, a woman in the habit of hiring servants in court, hires Muggs as her chauffeur. Her husband is furious, but resigned. The Murray house is already a mad one with two unruly servants, and the couple's daughter, Brenda, has a penchant for getting into trouble. An engagement party is thrown for the daughter, and Muggs's gang is hired to be the extra servants. During the festivities, a valuable necklace is stolen. Mr. Murray wants to hold Muggs, the gang, and the two court-hired servants for a police inquiry, but the maid, Maisie, remembers seeing a man at the party who didn't belong. The kids and she go to a nightclub where they pick up the trail of the thief. They follow him to his West Side apartment, where they recover the necklace after a fight.

"Should a dish of coffee be held with the right or left hand? Do gentlemen take off their hats before hitting a lady? Get the hilarious lowdown on high society from your favorite rascals, the Eastside Kids in *Mr. Muggs Steps Out* opening Thursday."

—ad copy for the original release
of *Mr. Muggs Steps Out*

Mr. Muggs Steps Out puts the Eastside Kids into their first domestic comedy, an above-average film that is as entertaining as a "B" feature ever was.

Its comedy comes at a furious pace. At the party, the boys take their instructions about handing out snacks a little too seriously. Glimpy becomes a salesman, refuses to let people miss their opportunities at his treats. Muggs follows him around to see that he does his job. When one guest thanks Skinny for one of his hors d'oeuvres, Skinny answers, "I didn't pay for them, I just hand them out."

The Murray household is a crazy one. One servant (Butch) eats the boss's leftovers while clearing the table. Mrs. Murray suggests to her husband that they have a duty to assist the underpriviledged: "We must give these poor unfortunates a chance to express themselves." "I'd like to express them," he tells her, "—to Africa."

Only one adept servant exists in the household, Charney, who speaks in snooty Bostonian tones. Naturally Muggs deflates this overbred Custodian-of-the-Tray. He argues that Charney doesn't use the words "who" and "whom" correctly. He says of Charney to the other servants, "Ignorant, never loined no gramma'."

Mr. Muggs Steps Out, the title of which spoofs Grand National's *Mr. Boggs Steps Out* (1937), is one of the kids' best films.

MILLION DOLLAR KID

A Banner Production, released February 28, 1944, by Monogram. Produced by Sam Katzman and Jack Dietz. Directed by Wallace Fox. Associate producer, Barney A. Sarecky. Scenario by Frank Young. Photographed by Marcel Le Picard. Edited by Carl Pierson. Settings by Ernest Hickerson. Musical direction by Edward Kay. Assistant direction by Arthur Hammond. Sound by Gilbert E. Meloy. *65 minutes.*

Muggs McGinnis, Leo Gorcey; *Glimpy McClosky,* Huntz Hall; *Skinny,* Billy Benedict; *Herbie,* Al Stone; *Rocky,* Bobby Stone; *Danny (a.k.a. Dave),* Dave Durand; *Slug (a.k.a. Pinky),* Jimmy Strand; *Lou (a.k.a. Stinkie),* Bud Gorman; *John Cortland,* Herbert Heyes*; *Roy Cortland,* Johnny Duncan; *Louise Cortland,* Louise Currie; *Lefty,* Gabriel Dell; *Lt. Andre Duprée,* Stanley Brown; *Captain Matthews,* Noah Beery, Sr.; *Maizie Dunbar,* Iris Adrian; *Spike,* Pat Costello; *Spevin,* Robert Greig; *Mrs. McGinnis,* Mary Gordon; *Mrs. McClosky,* Patsy Moran; *Messenger,* Bernard Gorcey.

*Misspelled "Hayes" in credits

The gang befriends millionaire John Courtland after they save him from a mugging. They suspect that his son Roy is one of the three who committed the misdeed. The kids investigate and find evidence that Roy is a mugger. Knowing that the father, distressed that one son was lost to WWII, will be heartbroken if he learns that his remaining son is a crook, the gang set out to reform Roy. Roy's mugging partners kidnap Skinny to prevent Roy's confession, but the boys fight and defeat the muggers. Roy turns himself in to the police commissioner, who, after hearing Muggs's plea in Roy's behalf, tells Roy that he can expect a suspended sentence if the boys do as well before the jury.

When the kids learn that Roy is the person they tangled with in that dark alley, Muggs exibits compassion for Roy, whom he then fights for Roy's own good. Afterwards, Muggs tells him, "You took a beating there, but I didn't have to beat you, because all the time you're beating yourself." Muggs has matured.

Million Dollar Kid presents the interesting notion that a rich kid can become so bored with life that he'll turn to the same life of crime that poverty-area kids are believed to lead.

Muggs and Glimpy are at their comic best when only the two of them are together. Their funniest exchange occurs when they are following the scoundrel out to bilk Mr. Courtland's daughter, "Loutenant" Andre Duprée. As they see him meet his burlesque-entertainer girl-friend (Iris Adrian, who is pictured in the film-reference book *Who Is That?* as the archetypical "cheap blonde"), Glimpy notices a billboard of the girl. On it is the slogan "Fantastic." Muggs deduces that this means that she does a fan dance.

"With no clothes on?" asks Glimpy. Glimpy points to a line reading "No Cover." Muggs takes Glimpy's arm from the billboard to reveal that "No Cover" was actually "No Cover Charge," the last line having been hidden by Glimpy's arm.

Muggs explains the slogan, "That means you don't pay nothing for the table cloth."

The comedy in the film was taken from other sources. The theater-sign bit had its roots in Fatty Arbuckle's *Back Stage* (1918). An amusing dialogue between Leo Gorcey (Muggs) and Leo's father, Bernard (cast as the messenger who delivers the telegram that tells of the older Courtland boy's having been killed), goes like this:

Muggs: There's no smoking
Messenger: I'm not smoking
Muggs: You've got a cigar in your mouth
Messenger: I have shoes on my feet but I ain't walking.

It had been used before, by Abbott and Costello.

One joke had roots in the boys' past. In the police station where Courtland has convinced the police captain to release the boys, Muggs lets the police captain know that there are no hard feelings by saying, "Everyone makes mistakes; that's why they put erasers on lead pencils." The line was used in the play *Dead End*. (It had been deleted from the film.)

Another two jokes weren't stolen, but had roots in the boys' *present*. Glimpy says (discreetly) in two scenes that he has a bad eye. Huntz Hall did, and for this reason he was excused from duty in the Army. (Gorcey too avoided Army duty. One wouldn't know it, but for a year during the war, he was in a body cast. He had been severely hurt in a motorcycle accident, after which his heart was laterally displaced. Bobby Jordan didn't have such luck. He was in the Army while this film was made. His part was taken by Dave Durand.)

FOLLOW THE LEADER

A Banner Production, released June 3, 1944, by Monogram. Produced by Sam Katzman and Jack Dietz. Directed by William Beaudine. Associate producer, Barney A. Sarecky. Scenario by William X. Crowley and Beryl Sachs. Story by Ande Lamb. Photographed by Marcel Le Picard. Edited by Carl Pierson. Set design by Ernest Hickerson. Musical direction by Edward Kay. Assistant direction by Arthur Hammond. Sound by Glen Glenn. Production title: *East of the Bowery*. 65 *minutes*.

Muggs McGinnis, Leo Gorcey; *Glimpy Freedhoff,* Huntz Hall; *Danny,* Dave Durand; *James Aloysius "Skinny" Bogerty,* Bud Gorman; *Speed,* Bobby Stone; *Dave,* Jimmy Strand; *W.W. "Fingers" Belmont,* Gabriel Dell; *Larry,* Jack LaRue; *Millie McGinnis,* Joan Marsh; *Spider O'Brien,* Billy Benedict; *Mrs. McGinnis,* Mary Gordon; *Ginsberg,* Bernard Gorcey; *Clancy,* J. Farrell MacDonald;

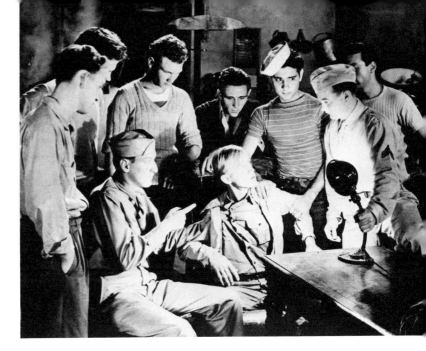

Billy Benedict gets a third degree in Follow the Leader.

Colonel, Bryant Washburn; *Entertainers,* Gene Austin, Sherrill Sisters; *Scruno in dream,* "Sunshine Sammy" Morrison.

Back home from the Army, Muggs and Glimpy learn that Danny was sent to jail in connection with a warehouse robbery. The one who really opened the trap door to let the thieves in was Spider, a new member whom Muggs dislikes. Muggs pretends to like Spider, and learns from him the set-up, after which Spider is killed by Fingers and Slug. Muggs obtains Spider's old job, conspiring to capture the crooks by working for them. Muggs is found out, and is scheduled to be shot. Muggs's sister Millie detains boss Larry by exposing a leg. The boss tells her she "ain't seen nothing yet . . ." and he's right, as Glimpy leads the gang and Army authorities into the crooks' nest.

Follow the Leader has an excellent assortment of comedy, and a good characterization of Muggs.

It opens with an outlandish comedy scene, satirizing jungle movies. Glimpy walks through a jungle island clad in his tenement clothes. A girl approaches him. "Will you follow me, no?" "I'll follow you, yes." He is terrorized by native Muggs and the gang, who throw him into a kettle. A dissolve reveals that it was a dream. Muggs attempts to wake him by shouting, but when this doesn't work, Muggs whispers, and Glimpy is aroused in a second.

Glimpy asks him about the guys who were chasing him. "You were dreaming," Muggs says. Glimpy responds, "I know I was, but you were there, don't you remember?"

Good jokes, bad jokes, they're all included, and the film seems funnier for having both. When Muggs and Glimpy leave after having a visitors' session with the incarcerated Danny, Muggs tells him that he'll get on the case. "Sit tight, don't move," Muggs instructs. Danny,

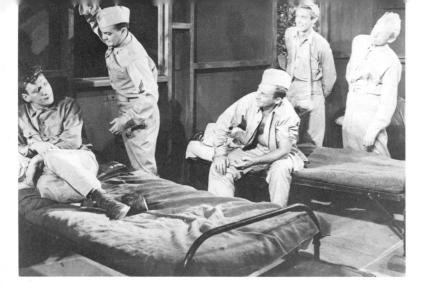

realizing where he is, asks, *"Are you kidding?"* Muggs, studying the situation, answers, "I guess I was a little superfluous."

Huntz Hall was added to the list of comedians who ribbed Brooklyn for declaring itself independent of New York:

Muggs: Where are you from?
Spider: Brooklyn.
Glimpy: Brooklyn. That's one of our allies.

Billy Benedict was given another irregular role. In the previous film he was kidnapped. In this film he is murdered. At this time he was alternating between playing one of the gang's members and being one of their antagonists. In the credit titles and one sheet posters the four actors who received billing under the name "East-side Kids" were Gorcey, Hall, Dell and Benedict. Of these, only Gorcey and Hall were consistently cast as Eastside Kids.

Follow the Leader has topform "B" entertainment values. There are two songs catering to wartime tastes. One is the moody "Now and Then" (performed by Gene Austin), the other is the jazzy "All I Want to Do is Play the Drums" (The Sherrill Sisters).

Follow the Leader shows some signs that the series was wearing thin. Ideas from *Let's Get Tough* and *'Neath Brooklyn Bridge* form most of the plot. A scene in which Gabriel Dell's character is sheltered by the boys was lifted from *Smart Alecks*, which, like the other two, dated from 1942.

BLOCK BUSTERS

A Banner Production, released July 22, 1944, by Monogram. Produced by Sam Katzman and Jack Dietz. Associate producer, Barney A. Sarecky. Directed by Wallace Fox. Scenario by Houston Branch. Photographed by Marcel Le Picard. Edited by Carl Pierson. Art direction by David Milton. Musical direction by Edward Kay. Assistant direction by Arthur Hammond. Sound by Harold McNiff. *5445 ft. 60 minutes.*

Ethelbert "Muggs" McGinnis, Leo Gorcey; *Glimpy,* Huntz Hall; *Pinky, group member,* Gabriel Dell; *Danny,* Jimmy Strand; *Jean Rogers,* Frederick Pressel; *Amelia Norton,* Minerva Urecal; *Irma Treadwell,* Kay Marvis; *Jinx,* Roberta Smith; *Tobby Dunn,* Bill Chaney; *Lippman,* Bernard Gorcey; *Higgins,* Harry Langdon; *Butch,* Billy Benedict; *Judge,* Noah Beery, Sr.; *Meyer,* Tom Herbert, *Doctor,* Robert F. Hill; *Umpire,* Charlie Murray, Jr.; *Five Pointers' batter,* Jack Gilman; *Themselves,* Jimmy Noone and His Orchestra; *Dancers,* The Ashburns.

When Muggs has a fight with French-bred Jean, both are hauled to court. The Judge makes each boy responsible for the conduct of the other. Muggs decides to try being friendly, and Jean accepts his efforts, especially when Muggs teaches him American games, which his grandmother had hoped he would learn. Jean is put onto

The ad says of Kay Marvis, "She's a killer." And she was—in a divorce court. See biography section.

the boys' baseball team, but is thrown off after his enthusiastic plays are taken as showing-off. At the big game, the boys play poorly without Jean. Their sponsor offers to send a sick friend of theirs to the mountains if they win. They re-instate Jean, with whom they go on to win the game.

Block Busters has the shape and feel of a classic comedy short subject. It delicately adapts the short-subject formula to the one-hour format. It has comedy situations galore, and develops each for as long as necessary, letting it breathe without the intrusions of a plot.

The kids are unlike they were in their other films. They are earnest; they listen. When Jean comes to them during the big game and tells them that he didn't want to be a show-off, Muggs thinks about what he has to say. Muggs then thinks something that he hadn't thought before, that showing off was an integral part of Jean, something he could grow out of.

The baseball diamond is the scene of much of the short-subject-style comedy. Glimpy takes the bat, promises "I'll hit the ball so far it'll take Hitler to get it." He doesn't notice three balls fly by while he takes what he thinks are practice swings. He's declared out. He explains to team sponsor Lippman that he didn't feel well. "Didn't feel well?," Lippman asks. "What did you have for breakfast?" Upon hearing that Glimpy had forty of Lippman's pretzels and a cup of coffee, Lippman deduces that the coffee did it, and gives Glimpy a pretzel to counteract the effects of the coffee.

Lippman is played by Bernard Gorcey, later to play Louie Dumbrowski in the Bowery Boys. Louie was vulnerable, whereas Lippman is not. Bernard is more sharp-minded here than he is in his more familiar characterization.

Muggs and Glimpy have only one scene alone, but it is a funny one. It is the one in which they crash a party which Jean is attending. (It is the film's "isolated sequence.") They enter the party by crawling under a curtain, and discover that they have crashed a masquerade party. Glimpy boasts to Muggs that he can scare a girl. Wearing a mask, he walks up to a young woman, growls at her, but she is not bemused. He then takes *off* the mask. She screams in fright.

Two piquant moments occur in the next few minutes. The party's costume judge announces that the prize for the best gentleman's costume goes to "the young man dressed as a Bowery toughie." Muggs and Glimpy don't know to which of them he refers. They decide that they will "choose" to determine who will go up.

They shake their fists and put out a number of fingers. Glimpy wins the first round. "That's one for me."

> They go again. "That's twice for me."
> Again. "That's three for me."
> Muggs has lost.

This dialogue sequence was one that Spit and Dippy had in the stage version of *Dead End.* (It is not in the movie.) Muggs and Glimpy's enactment of it was about the four-hundredth time it was performed by Gorcey and Hall.

As *Block Busters* continues, Muggs goes up to collect his prize. It is a kiss from the prize-winner for best ladies' costume. He is ecstatic after the kiss. "Oh Mother! I'll vote for masquerade every day and twice on Sunday." He is reacting to the kiss of a character played by his wife, Kay Marvis (Gorcey).

The person who expects a typical Eastside Kids outing gets something other than what he bargained for. *Block Busters* has no gangsters. It is unique among Eastside Kids film in this regard. It is also unique in placing its emphasis on comedy.

BOWERY CHAMPS

A Banner Production, released November 25, 1944, by Monogram. Produced by Sam Katzman and Jack Dietz. Directed by William Beaudine. Associate producer, Barney A. Sarecky. Scenario by Earl Snell. Additional dialogue by Morey Amsterdam. Photographed by Ira Morgan. Edited by John Link. Art direction by David Milton. Musical direction by Edward Kay. Production manager, Ed W. Rote. Assistant direction by Arthur Hammond and Clark Paylow. Sound by Tom Lambert. Special effects by Ray Mercer. Production title: *Mr. Muggs Meets a Deadline.* 5573 ft. 62 minutes.

Ethelbert "Muggs" McGinnis, Leo Gorcey; *Glimpy,* Huntz Hall; *Skinny,* Billy Benedict; *Danny,* Jimmy Strand; *Shorty,* Bud Gorman; *Jim Linzy,* Gabriel Dell; *Gypsy Carmen,* Evelyn Brent; *Jane,* Ann Sterling; *Lester Cartwright,* Frank Jacquet; *Ken Duncan,* Ian Keith; *Diane Gibson,* Thelma White; *Himself,* Bobby Jordan; *Mr. Johnson,* Bernard Gorcey; *McGuire,* Fred Kelsey; *Lieutenant,* William Ruhl; *Tom Wilson,* Wheeler Oakman; *Henchman,* Kenneth MacDonald; *Sports writer,* Francis Ford; *Brother,* Eddie Cherkose; *Apartment manager,* Betty Sinclair.

Strand, Gorman, Evelyn Brent, Gorcey, Hall.

Muggs works as an *Evening Express* copy boy with aspirations of being a top reporter, like his pal Jim Linzy. He gets his chance when Linzy isn't on the job when a big murder story breaks. Muggs and Glimpy visit the home of the deceased Thomas Wilson, and learn that the man's ex-wife had been seen running from the house after the murder was committed. By asking cabdrivers, the boys locate the ex-wife, Gypsy Carmen. They become convinced that she didn't commit the crime, so they hide her from the police in their clubroom while they investigate. Skinny overhears a conversation between Wilson's lawyer (Ken Duncan) and girlfriend (singer Diane Gibson). He tracks them to Duncan's nightclub, then calls the boys. They visit the nightclub, find incriminating evidence in Duncan's desk, and rout him.

Newspaper work is wonderful for Muggs, who takes it seriously and thus has less bite than ever before. This is shown in the opening scene. He is a copy boy (a well-dressed one, attired in a suit), but the blood of a potential reporter is in his veins. He tears apart a sports columnist's copy, assessing that the column has "no feeling." He shows the veteran newspaperman how he can enliven the column. "You make it sound like he's asking for a second helping of applesauce," Muggs confidently tells him. Muggs prepares his own version of the columnist's baseball game story. He writes until he wants to use the word "catastrophe."

"How do you spell 'cat-astrofey?' " he asks a literate reporter.

"If you're referring to the word 'catastrophe,' " the reporter says, "from the Latin and Greek origins . . . "

"I'm not talking about the Latins and the Greeks. I'm talking about a baseball game!"

In this manner, Muggs and the other kids conduct a matchless investigation which is operated at full-throttle up to the end.

The fight scene (the kids rallying the crooks) has a special treat. Muggs is fighting one of Duncan's nightclub employees, having trouble doing it. Up comes a stranger who knocks Duncan's henchman off the balcony on which Muggs and he were fighting. Muggs looks up at his benefactor. It is Bobby Jordan! They shake hands, and Muggs says that he will take him to see the other kids. Bobby tells him that he hasn't the time. "I only have a twelve-hour pass and I've been chasing you guys all over town."

Indeed he has. He has seen everyone the kids saw that day (the newspaper office people, the friendly policeman at Wilson's, a cabdriver they questioned, the manager of Gypsy's apartment building), and has always missed the kids by minutes. Bobby makes us see how fast the kids have moved—how much like a chase the film has been.

An Eastside Kids film that whizzes by, *Bowery Champs* is one of the best of the series.

Does Muggs have lock jaw? He would like the police to think so. In his mouth is a diamond. Pierre Watkin probes.

DOCKS OF NEW YORK

A Banner Production, released February 24, 1945, by Monogram. Produced by Sam Katzman and Jack Dietz. Directed by Wallace Fox. Scenario by Harvey Gates. Photographed by Ira Morgan. Edited by William Austin. Art direction by David Milton. Musical direction by Edward Kay. Assistant direction by Mel DeLay. Sound by Tom Lambert. Special effects by Ray Mercer. *5543 ft. 62 minutes.*

Ethelbert "Muggs" McGinnis, Leo Gorcey; *Glimpy,* Huntz Hall; *Skinny,* Billy Benedict; *Sam,* Mende Koenig; *Danny,* Bud Gorman; *Saundra,* Gloria Pope; *Marty,* Carlyle Blackwell, Jr.; *Mrs. Darcy,* Betty Blythe; *Compeau,* Cyrus Kendall; *Prince Egor Mallet,* George Meeker; *Millie,* Joy Reese; *Captain Jacobs,* Pierre Watkin; *Mrs. McGinnis,* Patsy Moran; *Kessel,* Bernard Gorcey; *Peter,* Leo Borden; *Patriot,* Maurice St. Clair; *Woman at pawnshop,* Betty Sinclair.

Glimpy finds a necklace alongside a dead body in an alley and takes it to Muggs. They go to the spot where Glimpy found it, but retreat when they are pursued by a man carrying a cane-sheathed knife. They visit Muggs's neighbors, Mrs. Darcy and Saundra, learn that the necklace belongs to them, and agree to keep it for them. Delegates of Tuscania are looking for the two women; Saundra is to be made ruler of that duchy. Compeau has been conducting the delegates' search, but hasn't told them that he has found them. He wants to get their necklace first. He kills a pawnbroker whom he believes to have the necklace, but what the pawnbroker had was an imitation. When the boys are held by the police for carrying a stone from the original article, Compeau claims ownership, and, later, comes to them for the whole necklace. He takes it at gunpoint. His cohort, Mallet, traces Mrs. Darcy and Saundra and attempts to strangle Saundra so that he can claim the throne of Tuscania. He is thwarted by the boys. The police lead Mrs. Darcy and Saundra to their country's delegates. The boys see them entering the delegates' headquarters and think that they are being forced in. The kids break in, find and subdue Compeau and Mallet, and summon the police.

Docks of New York breaks all of the standing rules about how the plot of an Eastside Kids film can be constructed. It comes off as a flavorful unconventional "B" intrigue film.

The repartee between Muggs and Glimpy is wonderful. They could be the Eastside Kids all by themselves; for the first twenty minutes of the film they are. There are no other Eastside Kids during these minutes.

After Glimpy breaks in on Muggs during the black hours, Muggs tells Glimpy of the dream he had.

"Was I in it?," Glimpy asks.

"I said a dream, not a nightmare."

Muggs gets to the dream. "I was dreamin' I was a bookmaker, and all the horses people were betting on were breaking their legs, and I was making money. I had limousines and yachts, then you had to come around and spoil it."

This is off-character for Muggs. But this is also the Muggs who, after Mrs. Darcy tells him that she is afraid of the police (she knew the wrath of the Gestapo), tells her, "Glimpy and I aren't exactly on interregular terms with the police, but they're right guys, and I think they can help."

(Compare this to the Mugs in *Boys of the City.* When he learned that his car-party will be giving a lift to a judge, he says, "Five-million guys thumbing their way along the road, and we've got to pick up a judge. That's fate.")

Docks of New York was something different for the series; it was a mystery story treated with intrigue-film technique, and it took the series closer than ever to a Muggs-Glimpy mold.

John H. Allen, Bud Gorman, Mende Koenig, Huntz, Milton Kibbee, Leo, Minerva Urecal, Johnny Duncan.

MR. MUGGS RIDES AGAIN

A Banner Production, released July 15, 1945, by Monogram. Produced by Sam Katzman and Jack Dietz. Directed by Wallace Fox. Scenario by Harvey H. Gates. Photographed by Ira Morgan. Edited by William Austin. Art direction by David Milton. Musical direction by Edward Kay. Assistant direction by Mel Delay. Sound by Glen Glenn. Special effects by Ray Mercer. *63 minutes.*

Ethelbert Aloysius "Muggs" McGinnis, Leo Gorcey; *Glimpy,* Huntz Hall; *Skinny,* Billy Benedict; *Squeegie Robinson,* Johnny Duncan; *Danny,* Bud Gorman; *Sam,* Mende Koenig; *Nora "Ma" Brown,* Minerva Urecal; *Elsie,* Nancy Brinkman; *Gaby O'Neill,* Bernard B. Brown; *Dollar Davis,* George Meeker; *Scruno,* John H. Allen; *Dr. Fletcher,* Pierre Watkin; *Veterinarian,* Milton Kibbee; *Steward Farnsworth,* Frank Jacquet; *Meyer,* Bernard Gorcey; *Mike Hanlin,* I. Stanford Jolley; *Joe English,* Michael Owen; *Nurse,* Betty Sinclair.

Muggs is barred from horseracing. His suspension is based on false evidence submitted by gamblers. Grateful to Ma Brown for letting him jockey her horses, he takes up a collection from the gang so that she won't lose

Cy Kendall looks for the boys who absconded with his booty.

her stable to debt. Ma's niece (Elsie) attracts one of the gamblers, Gaby, who goes straight, befriends Muggs, and agrees to confess that the gamblers lied about Muggs. The gangsters shoot Gaby, dope Ma's horses, and bet heavily on their favorite, confident that they will win the big race. They are upset when Gaby recuperates and confesses, one horse recovers, and Muggs wins. The gangsters are arrested at the track.

Mr. Muggs Rides Again, which adheres to the six-segment story format (which is not a bad thing in itself), is a mawkish, sometimes bland entry, composed of clichés, although it has some interesting individual scenes.

The racetrack scenes have no action other than that of the horses running (film taken from a stock-shot library), interspersed with shots of Muggs on horseback and of the boys cheering him from the grandstand.

The gangsters don't have any special traits either. The hardened ones (all but Gaby) wear obligatory pencil mustaches and fedora hats, as if there were a dress code.

The best scene is a carnival scene. (It is the fourth segment, the "isolated sequence.") Muggs, Glimpy and Squeegie find the fortune-teller passed out, bottle at side. "He's been consulting the spirits," Glimpy notes. Glimpy supplants the real swami, and Elsie and Gaby come in to the fortune-telling parlor to have Elsie's fortune told. Wearing the swami's clothes and mask, Glimpy tells Elsie that in her life is a woman who loves her like a mother, and a group of young men. Elsie is amazed that the "stranger" could know this. The crystal-ball gazer continues by telling her that the group is "trying to protect her from a very ugly young man, a floorflusher [Gaby]. He crossed them." She storms out. Says Muggs to Glimpy afterwards (about Gaby), "You not only fixed him with Elsie, but you made him pay for it."

Mr. Muggs Rides Again is an average entry in the series which does not borrow from the other horse-racing film, *That Gang of Mine.*

COME OUT FIGHTING

A Banner Production, released September 29, 1945, by Monogram. Produced by Sam Katzman and Jack Dietz. Directed by William Beaudine. Scenario by Earl Snell. Photographed by Ira Morgan. Edited by William Austin. Art direction by David Milton. Musical direction by Edward Kay. Production managed by Mel Delay. Sound by Tom Lambert. Special effects. *5582 ft. 62 minutes.*

Muggs McGinnis, Leo Gorcey; *Glimpy,* Huntz Hall; *Talman, group member,* Gabriel Dell; *Skinny,* Billy Benedict; *Danny Moore,* Mende Koenig; *Sammy,* Bud Gor-

man; *Gilbert Mitchell,* Johnny Duncan; *Rita Joyce,* Amelita Ward; *Jane Riley,* June Carlson; *Commissioner James Mitchell,* Addison Richards; *Silk Henley,* George Meeker; *Pete Vargas,* Pat Gleason; *Chief Tom Riley,* Robert Homans; *Mr. McGinnis,* Fred Kelsey; *Mrs. McGinnis,* Patsy Moran; *Mayor,* Douglas Wood; *Whitey,* Alan Foster; *Officer McGowan,* Davidson Clark; *Jake,* Meyer Grace; *Commissioner's stenographer,* Betty Sinclair.

The gang appeals to the police commissioner to return their clubroom rights after a policeman padlocks the door. The commissioner consents, and later, as a return favor, asks that his son be made a member of the gang so that he will lose his sissiness. The boy, Gilbert, gets led on by a gambler's (Silk Henley's) girlfriend, Rita Joyce. She arranges that Gilbert be caught gambling when Silk's operation is raided. The kids break into the gambling room to save him, and they do, but Muggs is caught. Since Muggs may not box in a tournament because of his alleged gambling ties, and since Danny busted his hand during the raid, Gilbert takes Muggs's place. Gilbert wins, impresses his father, and confesses that it was because he was in Henley's place that Muggs went there, thus vindicating Mugs.

An idea of what *Come Out Fighting* is like can be gathered from the opening scene. The boys' basement clubhouse is noisy. They are training a member for the upcoming boxing bouts. A neighbor complains to a cop, "Those kids and their club have been bad enough all along, but lately nobody had been able to hear himself think." The cop agrees. The kids, who we've thought to be good kids, are inconsiderate rowdies trampling upon others' rights.

The next scene is just as bad. The kids go to visit the police commissioner at his headquarters. Muggs becomes unjustifiably angered when another motorist takes the parking place he had picked out for himself. He prepares to fight the "intruder," but is talked out of it by Glimpy. "How do you expect to make a hit with the police commissioner when you start a fight right in front of his building?" Glimpy's words are all that keep Muggs from starting a fight.

These scenes set the tone for the mixed-up picture that follows.

Some special notes:

Muggs has permitted a girl to join the club. This is a bold step, although he had a girlfriend in *Docks of New York.* The idea of Gorcey's character having a girlfriend was carried through 1946 (in the Bowery Boys series), then dropped after the sixth entry.

A plumbing scene returns Gorcey back to an employment he had in his youth. In this scene, Muggs (whose father is a plumber) and Glimpy install fixtures for a gangster. When one of his henchmen gets antagonistic, Muggs punches him out.

The commissioner (Addison Richards) pays a visit to the gang's clubroom. The gang consists of Dell, Hall, Gorman, Gorcey, June Carlson and Mende Koenig. They give the commissioner such a welcome that their shouts summon a cautioning officer.

Come Out Fighting doubles as a crusade against alcohol. Gilbert has a brown tongue and is sick after a night of drinking the new-type "Orange-aide" fed to him by Joyce. The symptoms of his hangover (his stomach does "flip-flops") are new to his nutty mother, who calls Gilbert's father to find out what ails him.

The idea behind *Come Out Fighting* was not bad, but it was not for the Eastside Kids. Fans might have appreciated the idea more had it been saved for the Beach Party gang.

Huntz, Leo, Pat Gleason, Amelita Ward, George Meeker.

Now Playing

The Bowery Boys

Eddie LeROY | Gil STRATTON Jr. | Bennie BARTLETT | Gabriel DELL | Jimmy MURPHY | Buddy GORMAN

David GORCEY | Stanley CLEMENTS | Bobby JORDAN | Leo GORCEY | Huntz HALL | Billy BENEDICT | Bernard GORCEY

THE BOWERY BOYS PRIMER

"THEIR WORLD"

The Bowery Boys were . . . Leo Gorcey hitting Huntz Hall over the head with his hat . . . Four to six boys in a dilapidated 1910 car going to a rendezvous with underworld figures . . . A union of non-workers who sit all day at Louie's Sweetshop sipping on sodas they can't pay for . . .

The Bowery Boys had their own "world." Girls were creatures who might be trusted or distrusted, but always turned out to be worthy of suspicion. Lawyers and salesmen had a habit of walking into Louie's to whisk the boys off to all corners of the world, and, in fact, the list of places the boys visited is quite impressive: London (twice, each time a different adventure), Africa, Baghdad, the West, the Nevada plains and Las Vegas, prison, the South Seas, the Deep South, haunted houses, and, in one off-beat entry, the past! The Bowery Boys comedies were a series in which people could do the impossible and have the impossible happen to them four times a year for twelve years.

Whereas the early Bowery Boys films (1946-50), the gangster melodrama ones, show the boys meeting the challenges posed by living among gangsters, the latter ones, the pure comedies, adhere to an old rule of comedy: "Make the audience feel superior to you." For instance, when Whitey (Billy Benedict) turns off a radio, as requested by Slip (Leo Gorcey), in *Blues Busters*, he's horrified when the sound of singing continues (he doesn't know that Sach [Huntz Hall] is singing), and says that the radio must be broken. The audience knows that if the radio knob doesn't deactivate it, disconnecting its power source will. Slip pauses for a moment before lecturing Whitey, "In an emergency like this, all you gotta do is pull out the plug."

MALAPROPS: Webster's might say: "The contortion of influential sounding words, often used for comic effect." Slip Mahoney was characterized by a vocabulary that was rarely correct. Watches were "sympathized," not "synchronized;" a counteracting remedy was an "anecdote;" deep mental thoughts required "concecration." Perhaps no one summed it up better than Slip in *Hold That Baby!*: "Sometimes I doubt my own verbosity [veracity]—whatever that means."

MOTORLIPS: Every comedian has his trademark piece of funny business. With Huntz Hall, it was the way he gyrated his lips whenever he pleased.

ROUTINE —: The Bowery Boys had their own fight signals. One would call out "routine" and a number which corresponded to a specific fight plan. This gave them an edge in their fight, as the boys' plans were intricately worked out, with patterns that appeared disorderly but were contingent upon the wholehearted fighting spirit of all the boys.

IOUs: The boys' inability to pay for their sodas didn't faze them: they simply handed Louie a piece of paper promising a future payment of the debt. As the series progressed, the bill increased. In the earliest mention, the amount owed was $3.80. In 1952, Slip said they owed Louie for 136 banana splits. In 1953, the bill was $21.15. And in one of the last films, they owed the Bowery Café (now owned by Mike) $66.

LOUIE'S SWEET SHOP: The "home base" of the boys. They could never wander too far away from it. Whenever an episode absented itself from Louie Dumbrowski's establishment for too long—as in *Clipped Wings* and *Here Come the Marines*—Louie would pop up wherever the boys were. In the cases of both *Clipped Wings* and *Here Come the Marines,* there is a substitute ice cream parlor where Slip, Sach, the boys and Louie congregate. Louie's was located at 3rd and Canal.

THE BOYS' NAMES: The developers of the Bowery Boys series dipped into history for the names of three of the characters. The two main Bowery Boys were named after Ancient Roman poets: Terence (Gorcey) and Horace (Hall). The third name was Homer, after the Greek bard.

(Curiously, the name of Horace was not given as Sach's first name until the seventh film of the series. It is first spoken when a bailiff calls it out. Sach at first doesn't recognize the name as his. This parallels a situation in the Eastside Kids series. Muggs's first name was not given as Ethelbert until the seventh film in that series. And he too didn't instantly respond to it. And he also was in a courtroom when the name was first spoken!)

THEIR STUDIO'S STATURE: A survey in 1946 revealed how many movie-goers recognized studio trademarks. With the studio names blocked off, patrons were asked to name the studio. Here are the results:

Columbia	MGM	Monogram	Paramount	RKO	Universal	Warner Brothers	
24%	76%	32%	61	28%	23%	7%	Men
15	72	17	51	14	14	5	Women
19	74	25	56	21	19	6	Total

(Note: Twentieth Century-Fox was excluded from the survey because its logo was inextricable from its name.)

(Figures from *Hollywood Looks at its Audience,* University of Illinois Press, 1950.)

As this shows, Monogram was a studio to be reckoned with in 1946, the year the Bowery Boys came into being. Monogram's was the third most-recognized logo.

Monogram, it should be noted, now found the kids more worthwhile. They allowed production schedules on the first two years' releases to go as long as two weeks.

MONOGRAM PICTURES CORPORATION

Presents

LEO GORCEY

AND

The Bowery Boys

LIVE WIRES

Released January 12, 1946, by Monogram. Produced by Lindsley Parsons and Jan Grippo. Directed by Phil Karlson. Scenario by Tim Ryan and Joseph Mischel. Based on an original story by Jeb (Dore) Schary. Photographed by William Sickner. Edited by Fred Maguire. Art direction by David Milton. Musical direction by Edward Kay. Production managed by Glenn Cook. Assistant direction by Theodore "Doc" Joos. Set decorations by Charles Thompson. Sound by Tom Lambert. *64 minutes.*

Terrence "Slip" Mahoney, Leo Gorcey; *Sach,* Huntz Hall; *Bobby,* Bobby Jordan; *Whitey,* Billy Benedict; *Homer,* William Frambes; *Mary Mahoney,* Pamela Blake; *Jeannette,* Claudia Drake; *Patsy Clark,* Mike Mazurki; *Mabel,* Patti Brill; *Herbert L. Sayers,* John Eldredge; *John Stevens,* Pat Gleason; *Jack Kane,* Bernard Gorcey; *Red,* Frank Marlowe; *Ann Clark,* Gladys Blake; *Construction foreman,* William Ruhl; *George,* Rodney Bell; *Boyfriend,* Bill Christy; *Girlfriend,* Nancy Brinkman; *Barton,* Robert Emmett Keane; *Barker,* Earle Hodgins; *Cop,* George Eldredge; *Shill,* Eddie Borden; *Ditch diggers,* Charlie Sullivan, Henry Russell; *Bouncers,* John Indrisano, Steve Taylor; *First pretty girl,* Beverly Hawthorne; *Head waiter,* Jack Chefe; *M.C. and announcer,* Malcolm McClean.

With an already poor employment record, Slip loses his job with Herbert L. Sayers' construction company by socking his foreman. Since his sister is secretary to Sayers, Slip finds it necessary to make amends to him. Slip gets a new job working for the District Attorney, who also employs Sach. His first task is to reposses a car from a singer who hasn't met her payments. Having succeeded, Slip is entrusted to find "Patsy Clark"; Sach has to serve a warrant to "the Pigeon." Clark turns out to be a mammoth gangster who uses Slip and Sach as playmates for "airplane." They find out from him that the Pigeon is Slip's old boss Mr. Sayers, and that he is about to skip off to Mexico. Slip leads Sach and the boys to a rendezvous at the airport, reaching it just before the Pigeon is about to take off with Slip's sister.

Live Wires is a "nightclub film." The first entry of the Bowery Boys series, it established the tone for the films to be released for the rest of the year. Monogram, anxious to establish their top drawing cards in popular post-war entertainment, embellished *Live Wires* and two subsequent films, *Bowery Bombshell* and *Mr. Hex* (from the same year), with pretty chorines and nightclub songs. *In Fast Company* (also 1946) also fit into the group, by complying with the there-must-be-Fedora-hatted-gangsters code. *Live Wires* set the standard.

The gangsters are not played for their hissing value. The leads, Mike Mazurki (as Patsy) and John Eldredge (as

Whitey (Billy Benedict), Bobby (Bobby Jordan), Slip (Leo Gorcey), Sach (Huntz Hall), Slip's sister Mary (Pamela Blake) and Homer (William Frambes).

Sayers), are made to complement the tone rather than the plot. (Hence, they seem at home in the film, although they are caught in the end.) Mazurki (the hulking giant in *Murder My Sweet* [1944]), whose character enjoys playing "airplane" (wherein he throws everyone else around), and who dominates the lasts ten minutes by throwing the comparatively puny Slip around his penthouse, gets laughs also. Eldredge is the guy you'd never expect to be a crook, but who turns out to be one in the end. The impression left by this is one that the series often left: that those who are higher bred don't necessarily enrich the social fabric, while the boys are honorable.

The script pages detailing the chorine numbers were prepared from new notes, whereas the pages containing the dialogue were yellowed with age. Dore Schary (later to become president of MGM) wrote the first version of the story in 1933 for a Monogram production, *He Couldn't Take It.* It was used again for an Eddie Qualen vehicle, *Here Comes Kelly,* an episode of Monogram's *Kelly* series, in 1943. Phil Karlson's direction keeps the film moving smoothly, he being a master who would tackle the very successful "B" sleeper *Black Gold* (1947) and the popular naturalistic *Phenix City Story* (1955).

However, neither the re-writers nor the director refashioned the story in such a way that it would be a true Bowery boys film. Schary's story remains one with only one major role, which goes to Gorcey; Hall has little to do.

Leo virtually has a solo film. The gangsters are seen more often than the secondary Bowery Boys. Slip Mahoney, Leo's character, is established early: he hates work, uses malaprops, is mothered by his sister, and starts fighting with little provocation. It is this pugnaciousness that causes him to lose jobs.

Bowery Boys fans who are accustomed to the later films are often amused to see Bernard ("Louie") Gorcey appear briefly in two scenes as a small-time bookmaker. He started playing Louie in the next film.

Live Wires is a sprightly introduction to Slip Mahoney and the gangster world he would delve into.

IN FAST COMPANY

Released June 22, 1946, by Monogram. Produced by Lindsley Parsons and Jan Grippo. Directed by Del Lord. Scenario by Edmond Seward, Tim Ryan, Victor Hammond and Ray Schrock. Story by Martin Mooney. Photographed by William Sickner. Edited by William Austin. Editing supervised by Richard Currier. Technical advice by David Milton. Musical direction by Edward Kay. Assistant direction by Theodore "Doc" Joos. Sound by Tom Lambert. Production title: *In High Gear. 61 Minutes.*

Terrence "Slip" Mahoney, Leo Gorcey; *Sach,* Huntz Hall; *Bobby,* Bobby Jordan; *Whitey,* Billy Benedict; *Chuck,* David Gorcey; *Mabel Dumbrowski,* Judy Clark; *Marian McCormick,* Jane Randolph; *Steve Trent,* Douglas Fowley; *Father Donovan,* Charles D. Brown; *Patrick McCormick,* Paul Harvey; *Sally Turner,* Marjorie Woodworth; *Mr. Cassidy,* Frank Marlowe; *Mrs. Cassidy,* Mary Gordon; *Nora Cassidy,* Judy Schenz; *Pete,* Dick Wessel; *Gus,* William Ruhl; *Tony,* Luis Alberni; *Meredith,* Charles Coleman; *Louie,* Bernard Gorcey; *"Blind" man,* Stanley Price; *Officer,* George Eldredge; *Chauffeur,* Marcel de la Brosse; *Old gentleman,* Walter Soderling; *O'Hara,* Lee Phelps; *Cop,* Jack Cheatham; *Customer,* Fred Aldrich; *Cop,* Mike Pat Donovan; *Bit,* John Indrisano.

Tragedy strikes: John Cassidy's cab is overturned in a collision with another cab. Father Donovan knows that this will bring hardship to Cassidy, but he figures that Cassidy will be able to support his family if his cab is driven by someone with free time: Slip. Slip refuses, but after the Father gets him out of a scrape with the law, he relents. Slip is unhappy that his driving forces him to cancel dates with his girl friend, and he tries to profit from the arrangement by withholding money, but as he learns that Trent has been ordering his Red Circle Cabs to wreck the cabs of competing firms, he decides to fight the offending firm. He enlists the other boys. Slip and the boys go to McCormick, president of Red Circle Cab, to talk to him about manager Trent, but he won't listen to them. The boys persist, and are able to get through to McCormick's daughter. She arranges for her father to be in a cab driven by Slip, and as he tells McCormick about Trent, a Red Circle Cab attempts to force Slip's cab off the road. McCormick fires Trent and replaces him with Cassidy, who is given a higher salary than he earned on his own.

In Fast Company is a third-rate entry in the Bowery Boys series which substitutes differing forms of drama for genuine Bowery Boys entertainment. The film's only appeal is to Bowery Boys fans, as the film has a passable number of amusing situations.

It is because the boys give varying impressions that this film can't be recommended to non-fans. In the boys' first scene, they are parasitic creatures. They munch on bananas for which they aren't going to pay. Slip is the worst offender: He argues with the fruit salesman that there is no reason for him to pay, since the vendor wouldn't have any profit after paying taxes and the wholesale costs of the fruit. It's hard to sympathize with the boys.

Director Del Lord seemed an odd choice to handle a film that was short on action and long on melodramatics. He was a veteran of Mack Sennett slapstick comedies, and was fondly remembered by Sennett for his aptitude with automobiles.

Lord's major contribution to the film turned out to be

Judy Clark hugs Slip as Sach looks on from cab.

its climax: the duel between the two cabs, during which wheels collide, hubcaps rub.

In Fast Company was a remake. The Martin Mooney story had been shot by Monogram eight years earlier.

For the Bowery Boys fan, one of the most exciting scenes is the one that introduces Louie. This genial Jew isn't too prominent, and his last name isn't yet given as Dumbrowski, but he would become more prominent as the series progressed.

BOWERY BOMBSHELL

Released July 20, 1946, by Monogram. Produced by Jan Grippo. Directed by Phil Karlson. Screenplay by Edmond Seward. Story by Edmond Seward and Victor Hammond. Additional dialogue by Tim Ryan. Photo-

Leo with Dawn Kennedy

Teala Loring and Leo try to convince investigating James Burke that the concealed Huntz is Teala's grandmother. Although Burke is suspicious, he doesn't catch on to this "Whistler's Mother" imposter.

Sheldon Leonard plays deadpan to Leo. Wee Willie Davis looks on. At this time, Sheldon was doing radio (Jack Benny Show," "Maisie," "Parkyakarkus"), as was Leo, who lent his voice to "The Bob Burns Show."

graphed by William Sickner. Edited by William Austin. Editing supervised by Richard Currier. Musical direction by Edward J. Kay. Assistant direction by Theodore "Doc" Joos. Makeup by Harry Ross. Sound by Tom Lambert. 65 *minutes.*

Terrence "Slip" Mahoney, Leo Gorcey; *Sach,* Huntz Hall; *Bobby,* Bobby Jordan; *Whitey,* Billy Benedict; *Chuck,* David Gorcey; *Cathy Smith,* Teala Loring; *Ace Deuce*

Baker, Sheldon Leonard; *Moose,* William "Wee Willie" Davis; *Louie Dumbrowski,* Bernard Gorcey; *Officer O'Malley,* James Burke; *Street cleaner,* Vince Barnett; *Dugan,* William Newell; *Professor Schnackenberger,* Milton Parsons; *Featherfingers,* Lester Dorr; *Mug number 1,* William Ruhl; *Officer O'Hara,* Eddie Dunn; *Johnson,* Emmett Vogan; *Maisie,* Dawn Kennedy; *Newsboy,* Bud Gorman.

While Sach is having his picture taken (by street photographer Cathy) near a bank, a robbery is committed and Sach becomes the prime suspect. The boys learn that Ace Deuce is the actual culprit, but since he is a sly one, implicating him and vindicating Sach will be troublesome. A gangster whom Ace Deuce fears is Midge Casalotti, and since no one has actually seen Casalotti, Slip and the boys pose as Casalotti and his mob. They visit Ace's nightclub and secretly shoot incriminating pictures. One of the mobsters catches on and leads some of his comrades to them, but the boys' professor friend gives the hoodlum a serum which makes him a human bomb, so he is forced to turn his mob away. The boys extract a confession from him in return for their help in saving his life.

Bowery Bombshell is a crazy comedy whose plot throws a curve to that segment of the Bowery Boys fanship which expects the stories to be simple. The *Bowery Bombshell* plot gives no hint as to where it's going next. The continuity—showing Sach hiding from the police, the boys' attempts to trap the culprits by imitating their rivals, their encountering the crooks in a science lab— feeds off of its most inconspicuous elements. It allows for some riotous situations: Slip and Cathy trying to hide Sach from a police gumshoe, and finally succeeding by disguising Sach as Cathy's grandmother, for one.

Where *Bowery Bombshell* fails is in its credibility. For most of the picture, the characters get in and out of situations through possible methods. But during the last ten minutes plausibility is buried as the focus turns to the "human bomb" gangster. The gangster knows that he has drunk an explosive because everytime he spits, an explosion occurs where his saliva lands. The logic, that once he drank the serum he was a dead duck, is bypassed. What's more, in the end, it turns out that the serum he drank was "perfectly harmless," leaving us to wonder how his spit could have caused explosions.

Interesting anecdote: In the last shot, Slip and Sach have their heads in an inner tube reading "Dead End," the name of the play and movie that launched their careers.

Also, James Burke, who played a cop in *Dead End,* appears as a cop here.

These are interesting observations considering that this film was released on the threshold of the boys' tenth year in pictures.

SPOOK BUSTERS

Released August 24, 1946, by Monogram. Produced by Jan Grippo. Directed by William Beaudine. Scenario by Edmond Seward and Tim Ryan. Photographed by Harry Neumann. Edited by William Austin. Editing supervised by Richard Currier. Musical direction by Edward J. Kay. Production managed by Glenn Cook. Makeup by Harry Ross. Sound by Tom Lambert. Alleged production title: *Ghost Busters*. 6143 ft. 68 minutes.

Terrence "Slip" Mahoney, Leo Gorcey; *Sach*, Huntz Hall; *Bobby*, Bobby Jordan; *Whitey*, Billy Benedict; *Chuck*, David Gorcey; *Gabe, mature friend*, Gabriel Dell; *Dr. Coslow*, Douglass Dumbrille; *Mignon*, Tanis Chandler; *Louis Xavier Dumbrowski*, Bernard Gorcey; *Dr. Bender*, Maurice Cass; *Mrs. Grimm*, Vera Lewis; *Stiles*, Charles Middleton; *Brown*, Chester Clute; *Ivan*, Richard Alexander; *Dean Pettyboff*, Charles Millfield; *Herman*, Arthur Miles; *Police Captain Ryan*, Tom Coleman.

The boys went to school to learn exterminating and have opened shop. Their first assignment is to exterminate ghosts in a spooky mansion. There, Sach encounters a mad scientist who wants him for an experiment. The boys find Sach, free him from the operating table, and unleash an anaesthetic that knocks out the doctor and his cronies . . . at least that's the story Slip tells the police chief when asked what the boys were doing in the house.

After three relatively mature and complex films, *Spook Busters* is unprecedented. It is a pure comedy. It is a film of situations that are funny in themselves, and are made funnier by the jokes and incidences contained within them. Naturally, this makes the film easy to understand for youngsters. There is no complex plot to follow, nor are the characters' motivations above anyone's comprehension.

The fight scene in *Spook Busters* is one of the funniest the Bowery Boys ever participated in. It is done in slow motion, since the combatants have inhaled ether. The fist-and-knuckles confrontations take seconds instead of frames, magnifying the impact of every slug.

Spook Busters obviously doesn't resemble its three predecessors, but it doesn't resemble its three "spook film" counterparts in the Eastside Kids series either. Although there is a superficial resemblance to *Spooks Run Wild* and *Ghosts on the Loose*, the similarity is limited to the design of the studio sets.

Spook Busters revives an element from the Eastside Kids. Gabriel Dell is back. He plays a mature friend of the boys, the type of role he would play in most of the episodes after this one. In *Spook Busters*, Gabe plays

Sach confronts the gorilla whose heads and body he will receive. He tells the mad scientist that he would like to postpone the operation to Wednesday—"Wednesday 1982!"

Huntz Hall, Billy Benedict, Leo Gorcey, David Gorcey, Bobby Jordan.

Gabe, who has just returned from service in the Navy. He goes to Louie's, finds out that the boys are at the house, then goes to see the boys. He has a French wife.

William Beaudine directed. A veteran of six Eastside Kids films (including several of the best), he applies to *Spook Busters* the know-how that earned him the admiration of the "B" movie community. This film was his first with the Bowery Boys. He was to direct 25 of the 48 episodes.

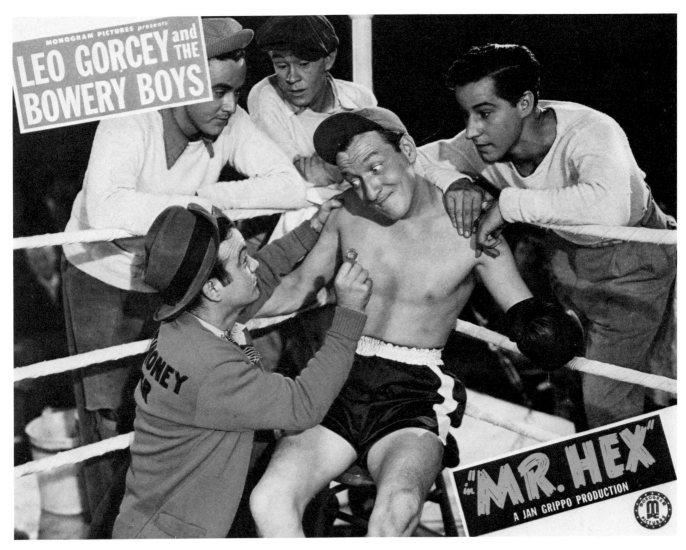

Chuck, Whitey and Bobby surround Slip and Sach.

MR. HEX

Released November 9, 1946, by Monogram. Produced by Jan Grippo. Directed by William Beaudine. Associate producer, Cyril Endfield. Screenplay by Cyril Endfield. Story by Jan Grippo. Photographed by James Brown. Edited by Seth Larson. Editing supervised by Richard Currier. Art direction by David Milton. Musical direction by Edward J. Kay. Set decorations by Raymond Boltz, Jr. Assistant direction by Wesley Barry. Songs "A Love Song to Remember" and "One Star-Kissed Night" by Louis Herscher. Technical advice by John Indrisano. Makeup by Milburn Morante. Sound by Tom Lambert. *63 minutes.*

Terrence "Slip" Mahoney, Leo Gorcey; *Sach Sullivan,* Huntz Hall; *Bobby,* Bobby Jordan; *Whitey,* Billy Benedict; *Chuck,* David Gorcey; *Gabe,* Gabriel Dell; *Louie Dumbrowski,* Bernard Gorcey; *Gloria Williams,* Gale Robbins; *Bull Laguna,* Ben Welden; *Raymond the Hyp-* *notist,* Ian Keith; *"Evil Eyes" Fagin,* Sammy Cohen; *Ray Teasdale (alias Billy Butterworth),* Joe Gray; *Mob leader,* William Ruhl; *Danny the Dip,* Danny Beck; *Margie,* Rita Lynn; *Blackie,* Eddie Gribbon; *Referee Joe McGowan,* John Indrisano; *Henchman,* Gene Stutenroth; *Waiter,* Jimmy Aubrey; *Truck driver,* Dewey Robinson; *Henchman,* Meyer Grace.

Sach takes on superhuman strength when put into a trance by a magician. Slip learns the technique and uses it to get Sach into prize-fights. Sach wins against all opponents. It becomes known that the boys use a hex on Sach to make him win. Bull Laguna decides to promote his own boxer and use a hex on him. He hires Ray Teasdale, a champion who has had a face lift that makes him unrecognizable as his old self; he's re-named Billy Butterworth. Laguna hires "Evil Eyes" Fagin to use his hypnotic eyes to hex Butterworth. Gabe is hired to accept bets on Sach, who Laguna thinks is sure to lose against Butterworth in an upcoming match. Gabe tells Laguna that Slip can't hex Sach without a special coin, and Laguna has that coin snatched. Nonetheless, when the time of the fight comes, Slip finds a coin that Sach accepts as the special one, and Bobby and Whitey fix Fagin so that he can't hex Teasdale/Butterworth. Sach wins. Gabe decides to tell the judges that Butterworth is Teasdale and is unqualified. He is shot, but makes it to the authorities. Gabe survives, the gamblers are arrested.

Mr. Hex was the fourth "nightclub/gangsters" film, but the established formula is twisted so that it downplays the serio-comic melodrama in favor of purer comedy.

The melodrama is concentrated in the early scenes, in which a key character is Gloria, whose plights will lead the boys to seek the prize money.

In the last half of the film, when the hex becomes the main focus, the comedy takes on a juvenile air. Not that the idea of two boxers, both of whose consciousnesses are controlled, coming head-on is bad, but the film doesn't present many variations on the derived hypnosis. The freshest bit has Whitey exploding a flashbulb in the eyes of the hexer of Sach's opponent. As Whitey predicted, "Evil Eyes" Fagin is incapacitated. For the most part, the fight is kid stuff, and sluggish due to unnecessary length.

The story writer was Jan Grippo, a professional magician who knew the subject of magic. He also produced the film.

Production values are good. The song "One Star-Kissed Night" is nicely handled. The photography by James Brown is also good. The scene in which the boys talk about helping Gloria demonstrates this. It opens with a view of Slip, the first to speak, and the camera pulls back as the others speak. *Mr. Hex* was bigger on talent than script.

Sherlock Slip confronts his Doctor Watson, Sach, as Betty Compson tries to find them a safe escape route.

HARD BOILED MAHONEY

Released April 26, 1947, by Monogram. Produced by Jan Grippo. Directed by William Beaudine. Scenario by Cyril Endfield. Additional dialogue by Edmond Seward and Tim Ryan. Photographed by James Brown. Edited by William Austin. Editing supervised by Otho Lovering. Art direction by David Milton. Musical direction by Edward J. Kay. Set decorations by George Milo. Assistant direction by Frank Fox. Production managed by William Calihan. Production supervised by Glenn Cook. Sound by Eldon Ruberg. Special effects by Augie Lohman. *5689 ft. 63 minutes.*

Terrence "Slip" Mahoney (alias Robert Westerfield), Leo Gorcey; *Sach (AK 9),* Huntz Hall; *Bobby,* Bobby Jordan; *Whitey (AK 7),* Billy Benedict; *Gabe, club member,* Gabriel Dell; *Chuck,* David Gorcey; *Eleanor Williams,* Teala Loring; *Dr. Armand,* Dan Seymour; *Louie Dumbrowski,* Bernard Gorcey; *Alice (AK 13),* Patti Brill; *Selena Webster,* Betty Compson; *Lennie the Meatball,* Danny Beck; *Dr. Rolfe Carter,* Pierre Watkin; *Hasson,* Noble Johnson; *Dr. Armand's secretary,* Carmen D'Antonio; *Professor Quizard,* Byron Foulger; *Thug,* Teddy Pavelec; *Police lieutenant,* Pat O'Malley; *Police sergeant,* Jack Cheatham; *Bits,* William Ruhl, Tom Faust.

Slip and Sach go to a detective's office to collect salary earned there by Sach. A woman, Selena Webster, mistakes them for sleuths and hires them to find a missing woman. Slip learns that his client hasn't been on the level with him when he locates the woman she hired him to find and learns that she has no connection with Selena.

Raymond the Hypnotist (Ian Keith) places Sach in a state of hypnosis.

Betty Compson, Leo Gorcey, Noble Johnson, Dan Seymour.

The second woman, Eleanor Williams, mentions a man named Armand, but she won't tell him any more. Slip visits fortune-teller racketeer Armand. Armand knows that Slip is investigating him, so he has him knocked out. Selena, who works for Armand, revives Slip and tells him that Armand's fortune-telling is a ruse for getting information which he can use for blackmail. Armand arrives the next night at Louie's to see Eleanor, but the boys round him up with "routine nine."

Hard Boiled Mahoney is a special episode: it is a dark movie, incorporating elements of multi-layered crime more associated with *Maltese Falcon, Murder My Sweet* and *Lady in the Lake.* (It isn't until late that we learn why Selena wanted Slip to find Eleanor: Eleanor had come into possession of letters Selena needs to become free of Armand.)

Although the *film noir* ("dark film") genre had been popular since the middle of World War II, the Bowery Boys had never been in a film containing its elements: desperation, psychology, confusion. (Monogram made a specialty of making this type of film, though.) What we see here is the Bowery Boys facing uncertainty and danger. Slip becomes the target of killers. He is in Eleanor's apartment when he is knocked unconscious. When he awakes, he is disoriented, in a room he doesn't remember, surrounded by people he has never seen before. One has a gun.

In the true spirit of *film noir,* we share Slip's harrowing process of making sense of what he sees while recovering. The screen (which had gone black when Slip was blackjacked) fades-in as Slip awakens. Out-of-focus objects circle about. We see what Slip sees.

Abrupt action such as that in *Hard Boiled Mahoney* has fascinated French cinema figures since film was young. The French consider action that starts abruptly to be "true to life," an honest depiction of the way things are. As Monogram films usually had much abrupt action, the studio was (and is) revered in France. Famous French director Francois Truffaut is one of the French figures who have written in praise of Monogram. He admits that he is not blind to the structural flaws of many of their films, but he has an answer, an answer that he says Monogram resident Charlie Chan would have given: "Folly is the Sister of Genius."

NEWS HOUNDS

Released August 13, 1947, by Monogram. Produced by Jan Grippo. Directed by William Beaudine. Screenplay by Edmond Seward and Tim Ryan. Story by Tim Ryan, Edmond Seward and George Cappy. Photographed by Marcel Le Picard. Edited by William Austin. Editing supervised by Otho Lovering. Art direction by David Milton. Musical direction by Edward J. Kay. Set decorations by Raymond Boltz, Jr. Production supervised by Glenn Cook. Assistant direction by William Calihan, Jr. Sound by Tom Lambert. *6111 ft. 68 minutes.*

Terrence J. Montgomery "Slip" Mahoney, Leo Gorcey; *Horace Debussy "Sach" Jones,* Huntz Hall; *Bobby,* Bobby Jordan; *Whitey,* Billy Benedict; *Chuck,* David Gorcey; *Gabe, hoodlum,* Gabriel Dell; *Louie Dumbrowski,* Bernard Gorcey; *John Burke,* Tim Ryan; *"Dapper Dan" Greco,* Anthony Caruso; *Jane Ann Connelly,* Christine McIntyre; *Mark Morgan,* Bill Kennedy; *Mack Snide, lawyer,* Robert Emmett Keane; *Dutch Miller,* Ralph Dunn; *Judge,* John H. Elliott; *Timothy X. Donlin,* John Hamilton; *Red Kane,* Leo Kaye; *Defense attorney,* Emmett Vogan; *Mame,* Nita Bieber; *Copy boy,* Bud Gorman; *Johnny Gale,* Emmett Vogan, Jr.; *Sparring partner,* Meyer Grace; *Dutch's henchman,* Gene Stutenroth; *Bits,* Terry Goodman, Russ Whiteman.

Slip and Sach work for the *Daily Chronicle,* Slip as a copy boy who wants to become a reporter, Sach as a photographer. Slip is told by mob-member Gabe that his boss, Dapper Dan Greco, is a sly one who can't be caught. Slip ignores Gabe's advice and goes with Sach to see Greco. Slip and Sach pretend to be agents of Greco's old friend, Dutch Miller, and use this ploy to learn about the underworld's fixing of sports events. They return to Greco's at an appointed time, but this time Dutch Miller is in Greco's office and he denies knowing them. The boys escape the gangsters, and Sach takes a picture of them. However, the camera is lost as they make their getaway. Slip types a story linking philanthropist Timothy X. Donlin to organized crime, which is accidentally published after Gabe types a sports columnist's name onto it. Donlin, Greco and Miller file a libel suit against the *Chronicle.* In court, they contend that they've never met, but the boys find Sach's pictures, which prove that they're lying.

News Hounds borrows from *Bowery Champs,* but it isn't as good. While most Bowery Boys films that treat the same subject as an Eastside Kids film are better than their predecessors, *News Hounds* is an exception. Its best scenes (Slip hammering out a sports column, Slip planning investigation strategy) are taken from the previous film.

News Hounds suffers from having too much plot. More occurs in just the first half of the film than normally occurs in a whole Bowery Boys episode. In fact, the film has a mini-climax at the half-way point, at

Mame (Nita Bieber) says that she has to watch her figure. Gabe, observing Slip's glance, says: "No sense all of us watching it."

which time Sach photographs the gangsters while Slip keeps them at a distance by twirling a rope.

William Beaudine obviously went to some pains to make the production a handsome one. He chose to photograph the poker raid sequence from atop a building, so the siren-blaring police cars are effective.

BOWERY BUCKAROOS

Released November 22, 1947, by Monogram. Produced by Jan Grippo. Directed by William Beaudine. Scenario by Tim Ryan, Edmond Seward and Jerry Warner. Photographed by Marcel Le Picard. Edited by William Austin. Art direction by David Milton. Musical direction by Edward Kay. Set decorations by Raymond Boltz. Assistant direction by Frank Fox. Songs: "Louie the Lout," by Eddie Maxwell; "Two Gun Tillie," lyrics by Eddie Maxwell, music by Edward Kay. Sound by John Carter. Special effects by Augie Lohman. *66 minutes.*

Terrence Aloysius "Slip" Mahoney, Leo Gorcey; *Horace Debussy "Sach" Jones,* Huntz Hall; *Bobby,* Bobby Jordan; *Gabe,* Gabriel Dell; *Whitey,* Billy Benedict; *Chuck,* David Gorcey; *Catherine Briggs,* Julie Gibson; *Louie Dumbrowski,* Bernard Gorcey; *Blackjack McCoy,* Jack Norman (Norman Willis); *Kate Barlow,* Minerva Urecal; *Luke Barlow,* Russell Simpson; *Chief Hi-Octane,* Chief Yowlachie; *Indian Joe,* Iron Eyes Cody; *Ramona,* Rose Turich; *Rufe,* Sherman Sanders; *Moose,* Billy Wilkerson; *Jose,* Jack O'Shea (Shea); *Spike,* Bud Osborne; *Saloon girl,* Cathy Carter.

Sach can't understand why Louie gets fidgety when a Western sheriff comes looking for Louie the Lout. Louie then tells the boys that he is Louie the Lout, who twenty years earlier had left the West to escape a murder charge. The boys set out to clear Louie. Things don't go well for them when they reach Hangman's Hollow; a map painted on Sach's back washes off, and they can't find Catherine Briggs, who is entitled to a gold mine left by her murdered father. Gabe, however, gets in well with Blackjack and his mob when he poses as a gambler, and is able to promote Slip as a sharpshooter. They use this to advantage to get Blackjack into a trap, and coerce him to confess to the slaying of Catherine's father. Catherine learns of her bequest, and Louie arrives with the original copy of the map for a happy ending . . . until Sach wakes up from the dream he had.

The *Bowery Buckaroos* writers did their homework on satirizing Westerns and came up with a good spoof of the horse opera.

The boys are seen to good advantage. Slip gets a chance to stop the film when he cautiously crosses a street and straddles into a saloon. Gabe gets to be an actor who plays an actor; he has a memorable moment in which he introduces Slip as the unparalleled sharpshooter "Dead Eye" Dan McGuirk, whose reputation he seeks to prove by throwing a deck of cards—the ace of spades of which already has a hole shot through it—into the air, and having Slip claim credit when the ace comes down neatly pierced.

Considering that there are no lines that stand out as being extremely funny, one wouldn't think that there would have been any conflicts over who spoke them. But there were. Julie Gibson, who played Catherine Briggs, recalled that Leo ordered that the camera be stopped mid-take to have some dialogue rewritten so that he would have the funniest lines.

However, she could rest assured that she would get to sing her song "Two Gun Tillie" without interruption. Likewise, the song "Louie the Lout" was one that only Bernard Gorcey could sing.

ANGELS' ALLEY

Released March 21, 1948, by Monogram. Produced by Jan Grippo. Directed by William Beaudine. Scenario by Edmond Seward, Tim Ryan and Gerald Schnitzer. Photographed by Marcel Le Picard. Edited by William Austin. Editing supervised by Otho Lovering. Art direction by David Milton. Musical direction by Edward Kay. Set decorations by Raymond Boltz, Jr. Production supervised by Glenn Cook. Assistant direction by Wesley Barry. Camera operated by Edward Kearns. Sound by Franklin Hansen. Script clerk, Ilona Vas. Grip, Harry Lewis. Costumes by Lorraine MacLean and Richard Bacheler. Still photographs by Talmadge Morrison. *67 minutes.*

Terrence Aloysius "Slip" Mahoney, Leo Gorcey; *Horace Debussy "Sach" Jones,* Huntz Hall; *Whitey,* Billy Benedict; *Chuck,* David Gorcey; *Jimmy,* Frankie Darro; *Tony "Piggy" Lucarno;* Nestor Paiva; *Ricky Moreno,* Gabriel Dell; *Daisy Harris,* Rosemary La Planche; *Josie O'Neill,* Geneva Gray; *Father O'Hanlon,* Nelson Leigh; *Boomer O'Neill,* Tommie Menzies; *Mrs. Mamie Mahoney,* Mary Gordon; *Harry "Jag" Harmon,* Bennie Bartlett; *Andrew T. Miller,* Buddy Gorman; *Willis,* John Eldredge; *Jocky Burns,* Dick Paxton; *Attorney Felix Crowe,* Robert Emmett Keane; *Judge,* John H. Elliott; *Mike,* Wade Crosby; *Bits,* Dewey Robinson, William Ruhl, Meyer Grace.

Slip hopes that his cousin Jimmy will be a good addition to the family while he stays with the Mahoneys, but since Jimmy is a recently released convict, his only job offer comes from an auto thief, Tony Lucarno. When Slip learns that Jimmy is working for Lucarno, ostensibly an honest businessman, he enlists the boys' aid to rescue him. However, when Slip is caught inside a warehouse while trying to prevent Jimmy from being found committing a second offense, he pleads guilty to robbery, protecting Jimmy, who wasn't caught. Slip is given a jail term that stands until a priest declares responsibility for him. Jimmy, impressed by Slip's not talking, quits car stealing and gives Slip details about Lucarno's set-up. Lucarno, also impressed by Slip's ethics, hires Slip to steal cars. The car stealing ring is exposed when Slip and the boys lead the police to Lucarno's hide-out garage.

Angels' Alley degenerates the Slip Mahoney character by presenting him as a self-sacrificer. Here he is trying to hide the guilt of his cousin Jimmy, and tries to take Jimmy's rap to save his poor mother's heart. He doesn't stop to think that his mother might mind if *he* went to jail. The Slip Mahoney we've grown to know wouldn't be so irrational as to do what the Slip Mahoney here does: He places others ahead of himself.

Angels' Alley is refreshing in one respect: it has a wholesome aura. This is due in part to Slip's mother, played by veteran actress Mary Gordon, who always

Leo, Mary Gordon, Frankie Darro. Mary Gordon plays Slip's mother, who is a substitute for Louie, who is not in Angels' alley.

achieved excellence in her Eastside Kids appearances as Muggs's mother. She makes the Mahoney home, a shabby apartment, a nice place for Slip to have as his base. It also becomes a place his friends visit. In one scene, the Mahoney's dinner is interrupted by the other boys, who one by one burst in with news about crooked Jimmy. Mrs. Mahoney invites them to eat, but they look to the moments when her back is turned so that they can relate their information to Slip.

Angels' Alley looks better when it is viewed as a humdrum hoodlum melodrama that just happens to cast the Bowery Boys. Films like this were ground out by the hundreds in Hollywood's lesser studios. Since very few people want to see even a small sampling of these films, *Angels' Alley* can be taken as a typical example that can be endured because it casts the Bowery Boys.

The Bowery Boys writers took one liberty with the established formula that others wouldn't have taken, though. They ended the film with a line calling attention to the fact that the film was indeed a film. Slip claims credit for rounding up the auto thieves, and afterward, Sach, mad that his heroics weren't mentioned, says to Slip, "This is the last time I make a movie with you!"

JINX MONEY

Released June 27, 1948, by Monogram. Produced by Jan Grippo. Directed by William Beaudine. Scenario by Edmond Seward, Tim Ryan and Gerald Schnitzer. Suggested by the story by Jerome T. Gollard. Photographed by Marcel Le Picard. Edited by William Austin. Art direction by David Milton. Musical direction Edward J. Kay. Set decorations by Raymond Boltz, Jr. Production supervised by Glenn Cook. Assistant direction by Wesley Barry. First camera operator, William Marguiles. Script clerk, Ilona Vas. Grip, Harry Lewis. Sound by Tom Lambert. Costumes by Richard Bachler. Still photographs by Bud Grayhill. *6121 ft. 68 minutes.*

Terrence Aloysius "Slip" Mahoney, Leo Gorcey; *Horace Debussy "Sach" Jones,* Huntz Hall; *White,* Billy Benedict; *Chuck,* David Gorcey; *Butch,* Bennie Bartlett; *Lippy Harris,* Sheldon Leonard; *Gabe, reporter,* Gabriel Dell; *Capt. James Q. Broaderik,* Donald MacBride; *Candy McGill,* Betty Caldwell; *Lullaby Kane,* John Eldredge; *Benny the Meatball,* Ben Weldon; *Tipper,* Lucien Littlefield; *Louie Dumbrowski,* Bernard Gorcey; *Augie Pollack,* Benny Baker; *Jack "Cold Deck" Shapiro,* Ralph Dunn; *Virginia,* Wanda McKay; *Officer Rooney,* Tom Kennedy; *Sergeant Ryan,* William Ruhl; *Bank president,* Stanley Andrews; *Tax man,* George Eldredge; *Meek man,* William H. Vedder; *Bank president,* Mike Pat Donovan.

A gambler wins $50,000 in a card game with gangsters. However, when he turns up dead, the gangsters compete with each other to get the money. Slip and Sach find the money in a gutter near where the man was killed, and earmark three-fourths of it to charity. The boys become involved with the police when a man sitting in Louie's Sweet Shop is found dead at the counter. Capt. Broaderik is assigned to investigate. He learns from Sach that "an umbrella with a hand" dropped a tablet into the deceased man's drink. When the boys try to hide the money in their club, a gunman demands that they turn it over. He is killed mysteriously. Sach again sees "the umbrella with a hand." Slip is tricked by Candy into meeting gangster Lippy Harris. Harris forces Slip to call Sach and order him to bring Harris the money. When Sach arrives with the story of his bundle being stolen, Broaderik arrives too. Upon opening Harris's closets, Sach and Broaderik find two more corpses, deceased associates of Harris who would have received a share of the loot. As Broaderik tries to make sense of what has happened, the man carrying the

Frankie Darro, Leo Gorcey and Huntz hall, looking collectively three hundred years old. If there is one film they should look aged in, it is this one, their most mature to date. They might be tired from the shortest production schedule yet—eight days—which resulted in the use of shoddy backscreen projection for the car scenes.

Slip, Sach, Chuck, Butch (Bennie Bartlett) and Whitey meet the hold-up man whose murder will be the second they are involved in.

umbrella shows up and demands the money. (Sach still has it on his person.) He is revealed to be an old police informer.

Jinx Money's scriptwriters obviously started with a fully developed gangster story before the boys were written into it. This makes the film more subtle than its counterparts, and the boys don't carry the burden of the story. They are seen only in scenes for which adolescents are appropriate, and Slip and Sach have some mannerisms that they otherwise wouldn't exhibit.

The boys (all five) have some funny moments aside from the plot. Whitey rigs up an electrical deterrent for anyone who would try to steal the money from the combination-safe in the boys' clubroom. This is the first mechanical ingenuity the boys have shown since they were the Eastside Kids. (This is also the first time they've had a clubroom since those days.)

Slip gets droolingly romantic when he meets Candy. Although she is in league with Harris, he thinks that she has something else in mind when she offers to take him to her apartment. Some wonderful close-ups show Slip fondling his hat as he bashfully accepts her offer.

Louie's character is more developed, too. At fade-out, the boys pay off their charity pledges, and exalt in having $12,000 left over. A tax man comes in and takes that amount as the boys' obligation to Uncle Sam. They console themselves by the thought that they are not in debt. Louie reminds them that they owe the sweetshop proprietor $3.80. In a surprise final gag, the boys are seen tumbling out of Louie's. Louie comes out victoriously rubbing his hands.

Jinx Money has a split personality: it shows the boys engaging in teen-agers' activities, but it also has a plot too intricate for children to understand.

SMUGGLERS' COVE

Released October 24, 1948, by Monogram. Produced by Jan Grippo. Directed by William Beaudine. Scenario by Edmond Seward and Tim Ryan. Based on the *Bluebook Magazine* story "Smuggler's Cove," by Talbert Josselyn. Photographed by Marcel Le Picard. Edited by William Austin. Editing supervised by Otho Lovering. Art direction by David Milton. Musical direction by Edward J. Kay. Set decorations by Raymond Boltz, Jr. Assistant direction by William Calihan. Sound by Earl Sitar. *5973 ft. 66 minutes.*

Terrence "Slip" Mahoney, Leo Gorcey; *Horace Debussy "Sach" Jones,* Huntz Hall; *Whitey,* Billy Benedict; *Chuck,* David Gorcey; *Butch,* Bennie Bartlett; *Gabe Moreno, private eye,* Gabriel Dell; *Count Petrov Bons,* Martin Kosleck; *Terrence Mahoney Esq.,* Paul Harvey; *Teresa Mahoney,* Amelita Ward; *Digger,* Eddie Gribbon; *Sandra Hasso,* Jacqueline Dalya; *Captain Drum,* Gene Stutenroth; *Doctor Latka,* Leonid Snegoff; *Franz Leiber,* John Bleifer; *Karl,* Andre Pola; *Ryan, building foreman,* William Ruhl; *Attorney Williams,* Emmett Vogan; *Messenger,* Buddy Gorman; *Building manager,* George Meader.

While Slip and Sach are working as janitors, Slip accepts a telegram informing him that Terrence Mahoney Esquire has inherited an old estate. Confusing himself for Mahoney Esquire, Slip takes the boys to the Long Island mansion, where they are greeted by Digger, the caretaker. Digger works for Count Petrov, who runs a smuggling operation from a remote section of the house. The boys discover Petrov when they investigate the area behind a swinging panel. Gabe, working as a detective, comes to the house and finds an underground cove that connects to a subterranean labyrinth. His presence alerts the real owners, who have come to the house for a rest, and who, after clearing up the misunderstandings with Slip, join forces with the boys to rout the smuggler and his mob. All of this causes a rise in Mahoney Esquire's blood pressure, which prompts him to give Slip the house.

Despite a limited plot, *Smugglers' Cove* unfolds beautifully and makes the most of every situation. The plot takes focus throughout. Like most films of its type, it has secret panels, paintings that swing in from their frames, and peepholes in the portraits, but it is a credit to the film that it doesn't stress these things, showing them only in passing.

Smugglers' Cove is infinitely superior to most "B" films, and no doubt this is due to its being made to look like a sharp "B" espionage flick. The film uses the kids only when it has decent material for them. In no other film of this period are they on screen for as little time as they are in *Smugglers' Cove*. What the film has instead are fantastic scenes showing Petrov (Martin Kosleck) and company at work. Kosleck was Hollywood's perfect Nazi, doing lucrative business throughout the Second World War, often playing Hitler's man Goebbels. Roles dried up after Germany surrendered, but he doesn't seem disheartened by being cast in this Monogram film. Instead, he gives a superlative performance (as the cruel and cunning Petrov) which holds the audience's interest during the long spells of the boys' absence.

Paul Harvey puts in a good performance as the harried houseowner, and Gabe is in good form, especially when he goes into a dance to elude Digger the caretaker, who would have him go no further than the front door. In keeping with the attention to minor players, it is a supporting character, Paul Harvey's, who subdues the meanies in the free-for-all.

Smugglers' Cove is a stylish film, and production values are good. The sets are so spacious that when Slip falls back on a Henry VIII proportioned bed, his body occupies only a small fraction of the center of the frame. Backdrops of a ship seen through a window and of a seacoast against the cove are very good, making the film look more expensive than it is. Underground tunnels add authenticity, although the Eastside Kids/Bowery Boys fan will recognize them from other films in the series.

Sach (in the upper corner), behind Amelita Ward, watches Paul Harvey get ready to clobber Gene Stutenroth. Slip pokes Eddie Gribbon to no avail.

Sach re-enects the murder he and Slip witnessed. Chuck, Butch and Whitey are alarmed.

Sach and Slip shake hands with Officer Gabe Moreno.

TROUBLE MAKERS

Released December 10, 1948, by Monogram. Produced by Jan Grippo. Directed by Reginald LeBorg. Scenario by Edmond Seward, Tim Ryan and Gerald Schnitzer. Story by Gerald Schnitzer. Photographed by Marcel Le Picard. Edited by William Austin. Musical direction by Edward J. Kay. Set decorations by Raymond Boltz Jr. Production managed by Allan K. Wood. Assistant direction by Gene Anderson. Sound by Frank McWhorter. Camera operated by Bill Marguiles. Script supervised by Mary Chaffee. Makeup by Webb Overlander. Grip, George Booker. Still photographs by Al St. Hilaire. *6207 ft. 69 minutes.*

Terrence Aloysius "Slip" Mahoney, Leo Gorcey; *Horace Debussy "Sach" Jones,* Huntz Hall; *Whitey,* Billy Benedict; *Chuck,* David Gorcey; *Butch,* Bennie Bartlett; *Officer Gabe Moreno,* Gabriel Dell; *Ann Prescott,* Helen Parrish; *Silky Thomas,* John Ridgely; *Hatchet Moran,* Lionel Stander; *Feathers,* Frankie Darro; *André Schmidlapp,* Fritz Feld; *Louie Dumbrowski,* Bernard Gorcey; *Captain Madison,* Cliff Clark; *Jones, cop,* William Ruhl; *Morgue keeper,* David Hoffman; *Lefty,* John Indrisano; *Needles the tailor,* Charles La Torre; *Doorman,* Charles Coleman; *Sandy, first newsboy,* Buddy Gorman; *Second newsboy,* Kenneth Lundy; *Gimpy, henchman,* Pat Moran; *Sam,* Herman Cantor; *Fat bellboy,* Maynard Holmes; *Gorcey's stunt double,* Frankie Darro; *Hall's stunt double,* Carey Loftin.

With Lionel Stander of the fog-horn voice.

While looking through a telescope, the boys witness a murder in the nearby El Royale Hotel, but they don't see the killer's face. The boys have their friend Officer Gabe Moreno accompany them to the hotel, but when they arrive there is no evidence of a murder having been committed anywhere in the room, which belongs to Silky Thomas. The boys learn from a newspaper photo that the victim was Doc Prescott, so Slip and Sach go to the morgue to learn more. At the morgue they meet the man's daughter, Ann Prescott, and they tell her what they saw. As she runs the El Royale, she arranges to have them hired as bellboys so that they can investigate. They are able to learn a great deal when an ex-con, Hatchet Moran, mistakes Sach for an old friend, Chopper McGee, and lets him in on what he and Silky Thomas plan to do. The boys tell what they have learned to Gabe. Gabe then investigates on his own, which stirs panic in Silky's henchman Feathers, who frames Gabe for neglecting his assigned duties; Gabe is suspended. Slip puts some pieces together, and accuses Silky of murdering Prescott for his share of the hotel. Silky and his henchmen try to kill Slip and Sach, but they and the other boys trap the thugs in hampers positioned under the outlet of a laundry chute.

Trouble Makers is a banquet of mystery and slapstick. The film often combines laughs and suspense, and the comedy is integrated into the film in such a way that it contributes to the tone. Hotel manager André Schmidlapp (master comedian Fritz Feld) has a hard time training Slip and Sach, as they don't submit well to the military-like drills the bellboys are put through. He tells them that he would not have them were it not for Miss Prescott's insisting that they be hired. "I would not hire you to sharpen pencils."

Gabe is made good use of, as no other cop would leave his beat to see what the boys had found. Huntz is close to being Leo's equal in the film, closer than he has been in any film since *Bowery Champs* (1944).

The murder concept is handled well. Since the boys witness the murder without anyone knowing that they are watching, this gives them an edge, as the murderer and the other people involved don't know that they should put road-blocks in the boys' way. The murder itself, photographed in an iris, is well presented, simulating the view from the telescope.

FIGHTING FOOLS

Released April 17, 1949, by Monogram. Produced by Jan Grippo. Directed by Reginald LeBorg. Scenario by Edmond Seward, Gerald Schnitzer and Bert Lawrence. Photographed by William Sickner. Edited by William Austin. Art direction by David Milton. Musical direction by Edward Kay. Set decorations by Raymond Boltz, Jr. Production managed by Allan K. Wood. Assistant direction by Mel Shyer and Ed Morey, Jr. Sound by Earl Sitar. Camera operated by John Martin. Script supervised by Ilona Vas. Makeup by Charles Huber. Grip, Harry Lewis. Gaffer, Lloyd Garnell. Still photographs by Al St. Hilaire. *5763 ft. 69 minutes.*

Terrence Aloysius "Slip" Mahoney, Leo Gorcey; *Horace Debussy "Sach" Jones,* Huntz Hall; *Whitey,* Billy Benedict; *Chuck,* David Gorcey; *Butch,* Bennie Bartlett; *Gabe Moreno, reporter,* Gabriel Dell; *Johnny Higgins,* Frankie Darro; *Blinky Harris,* Lyle Talbot; *Louie Dumbrowski,* Bernard Gorcey; *Boomer Higgins,* Teddy Infuhr; *Mrs. Higgins,* Dorothy Vaughan; *Bunny Talbot,* Evelynne Eaton; *Goon,* Frank Moran; *Joey Prince,* Bill Cartledge; *Marty,* Anthony Warde; *Beef,* Ralph Peters; *Rosemeyer, arena guard,* Tom Kennedy; *Lefty Conlin,* Ben Welden; *Highball,* Eddie Gribbon; *Needles,* Marty Mason; *Editor,* Paul Maxey; *Jimmy Higgins,* Robert Walcott; *Lug,* Meyer Grace; *Tough customer,* Frank Hagney; *Dave Dorgan,* Bert Hanlon; *Dynamite Carson,* Bert Conway; *Call boy,* Bud Gorman; *Young man in sweetshop,* Roland Dupree; *Boxing commissioner,* Stanley Andrews; *Fighter in gym,* Johnny Duncan; *Sam "Bill" Radar, announcer,* Sam Hayes; *Pete, bartender,* Mike Pat Donovan; *Fighters,* Joe Gray, Larry Anzalone, Johnny Kern, Al Bayne; *Fight announcer,* Jack Mower; *Referees,* Charlie Sullivan, Jimmy O'Gatty, Gene Delmont, John Indrisano; *Fighters (montage),* Sammy LaMarr, Benny Goldberg; *Handler,* Eddie Rio; *Knockdown timekeeper,* Carl Sklover; *Ad lib bit,* Joe Greb.

The boys are concessionaires at a boxing ring who promote Bowery athletes, including Jimmy Higgins. When he is killed in a match, they get his older brother Johnny to leave his drunkard existence to be matched in some bouts. When Johnny's first opponent (Joey Prince) throws the fight after fifty seconds, the stewards conduct an inquiry into whether the fight was rigged; Prince says it was, and that Johnny had accepted money from the fight-fixers. It is a lie, but Johnny is suspended. The gangsters then strong-arm Slip (acting as Johnny's manager) and Johnny into a deal; the gangsters will clear Johnny of the charges made by Prince, and Johnny will take a dive in the next fight. Slip and Johnny agree to the arrangement knowing that they won't go through with it. However, the gamblers have Johnny's younger brother Boomer kidnapped to assure that Johnny keeps his promise. Johnny puts up a good fight while Sach searches for Boomer. When Sach arrives at the ring with the lad, Johnny knocks out his opponent, turning the tables on the gangsters who were responsible for the death of his brother. They are then arrested.

Sports plots were a staple of the series, but *Fighting Fools* has more than a sports plot. It has a heart, especially when Slip convinces Louie to loan him the sweetshop loft as a

The celebrations never stopped at Louie's Sweetshop, proprietored by Louie Dumbrowski (in white coat; look down, you'll see him!).

Dell, Gorcey, Frankie Darro.

Ben Weldon, Bill Cartledge, Frankie Darro, Huntz and Leo. In this scene their characters face the wrath of boxing commissioner Stanley Andrews.

training place for Johnny. If Louie had a child, Slip suggests, "and he had a chance to become the lightweight champ of the world, would you deprive him of that?" Louie is moved by this. Slip vividly describes the imaginary progeny, and asks, "You love your son, don't you?" "I'm crazy about him," the fervent Louie answers.* Slip now needs only to ask to receive. The tactic has worked.

Slapstick comedy is at a minimum. When it is included, it is as part of the plot. Such is the case when Sach puts a frankfurter on the carpet outside the kidnapper's door, knocks on the door, gets one of the child's abductors to come out, and moves the wiener by string. The kidnapper is distracted by this, and Sach tip-toes into the kidnappers' den while the crook is too bewildered to notice.

Sports plots were a staple of Hollywood as well of the Bowery Boys series. This version neither belittles the form nor expands its boundaries. *Fighting Fools* is an interesting combination of a well-honed sports story and hearty Bowery drama.

*These lines have a deeper meaning if you recall that Louie and Slip were in real-life father and son.

HOLD THAT BABY!

Released June 26, 1949, by Monogram. Produced by Jan Grippo. Directed by Reginald LeBorg. Scenario by Charles R. Marion and Gerald Schnitzer. Photographed by William Sickner. Edited by William Austin. Editing supervised by Otho Lovering. Art direction by David Milton. Musical direction by Edward Kay. Set decorations by Raymond Boltz, Jr. Production managed by Allan K. Wood. Assistant direction by William Calihan. Sound by Tom Lambert. Camera operated by John Martin. Script supervised by Ilona Vas. Makeup by Charles Huber. Grip, Harry Lewis. Gaffer, Lloyd Garnell. Still photographs by Eddie Jones. *5763 ft. 64 minutes.*

Terrence Aloysius "Slip" Mahoney, Leo Gorcey; *Horace Debussy "Sach" Jones,* Huntz Hall; *Whitey,* Billy Benedict; *Chuck,* David Gorcey; *Butch,* Bennie Bartlett; *Gabe Moreno, washer salesman,* Gabriel Dell; *Louie Dumbrowski,* Bernard Gorcey; *Cherry Nose Mason,* John Kellogg; *Bananas,* Frankie Darro; *Hope Andrews,* Florence Auer; *Faith Andrews,* Ida Moore; *Laura Andrews,* Anabel Shaw; *Gypsy Moran,* Max Marx; *Burton the cop,* Edward Gargan; *Joe the Crooner,* Meyer Grace; *Jonathan Andrews III,* Jody Dunn; *Dr. Foster,* Emmett Vogan; *First policeman,* William Ruhl; *John Winston, executor,* Pierre Watkin; *Dr. Hans Heinrich,* Torben Meyer; *Dr. Hugo Schiller,* Fred Nurney; *Cynthia, mannequin,* Francis Irvin; *Sanitarium receptionist,* Lin Mayberry; *First patient,* William J. O'Brien; *Second Patient,* Danny Beck; *Nurse,* Cay Forrester; *Second policeman,* Herbert Patterson; *Customer,* John O'Connor; *Black baby,*

Harold Noflin; *Shoeshine boy,* Roy Aversa; *Newsboy,* Buddy Gorman; *Third patient,* Robert Cherry; *Fourth patient,* Angi O. Poulos; *Jonathan Andrews (still picture),* Henry Mowbray.

The boys are operators of a laundromat who find a baby in the linen. The infant is Jonathan Andrews III, heir to a large fortune. His mother has abandoned the baby so that her aunts cannot cheat her or her baby of their inheritances. The aunts have the mother, Laura, committed to a mental ward, but the boys discover who the baby is from a newspaper and learn where Laura is. Slip and Sach visit her, tell her that the baby is safe, and help her escape. The aunts want to keep Laura and the baby from attending the reading of their brother's will, so they enlist gangsters to keep the boys, Laura and the baby captive. Slip and Sach escape with Laura and the baby, attend the reading, and see that justice is done. The aunts and the gangsters are arrested.

Hold That Baby! steered away from the comedy-melodrama emphasis that the recent films had had, and adopted one of straight comedy. The plot is concerned with gangsters and evil old ladies, but the focus is on the boys' comedy.

The ladies are played by Ida Moore and Florence Auer, who extract their characters from the two homocidal maniacs who offer poisoned elderberry wine to lonely elderly gentlemen in *Arsenic and Old Lace*.

It is due to the actions of the aunts that Slip and Sach visit the sanitarium, the setting of the best scene. Slip registers Sach as a patient. This ruse will let them roam the facilities while they do their detective work. Slip prepares entrance forms for Sach to sign. Sach carefully puts down an "X." This disturbs Slip, who whispers to his pal, "Don't sign your *right* name." Sach erases it and replaces it with an "O." Huntz Hall does his first superb solo scene as Sach when he wanders through a medical supply room. It is a toy shop in his eyes, and he takes the playthings he wants.

The production is honed to the style of short comedies. The fight scene, which erupts when Slip, Sach and Laura try get to the will-reading, is full of gags. Sach pulls a gun and has everyone back away. He pulls the trigger. A B-A-N-G flag emanates from the barrel.

Sidelight: *Hold that Baby!* gave Leo and Huntz a chance to practice the duties of parenthood. While *Hold That Baby!* was being shot and released, the wives of both were pregnant.

ANGELS IN DISGUISE

Released September 25, 1949, by Monogram. Produced by Jan Grippo. Directed by Jean Yarbrough. Scenario by Charles R. Marion, Gerald Schnitzer and Bert Lawrence. Photographed by Marcel Le Picard. Edited by William Austin. Art direction by David Milton. Musical direction by Edward Kay. Set decorations by Raymond Boltz, Jr. Editing supervised by Otho Lovering. Production managed by Allan K. Wood. Sound by Ben Remington. Camera operated by William Marguiles. Assistant direction by William Calihan. Script supervised by Ilona Vas. Grip, Harry Lewis. Gaffer, Lloyd Garnell. Still photographs by Ed Jones. *5688 ft. 63 minutes.*

Terrence Aloysius "Slip" Mahoney, Leo Gorcey; *Horace Debussy "Sach" Jones,* Huntz Hall; *Whitey the Whip,* Billy Benedict; *Chuck the Chiller,* David Gorcey; *Butch the Butcher,* Bennie Bartlett; *"Big Louie" Dumbrowski,* Bernard Gorcey; *Lt. Gabe Moreno,* Gabriel Dell; *Mr. Carver,* Edward Ryan; *Angles Carson,* Mickey Knox; *Vickie Darwell,* Jean Dean; *Miami,* Richard Benedict; *Johnny Mutton,* Joseph Turkel; *Jim Cobb, publisher,* Ray Walker; *Roger T. Harrison,* William Forrest; *Bertie Spangler,* Pepe Hern; *Millie,* Marie Blake; *Martin Lovell,* Rory Mallinson; *Johnson, foreman,*

Joseph Turkel, Edward Ryan, David Gorcey, Billy Benedict, Bennie Bartlett, Huntz Hall, Bernard and Leo Gorcey, Richard Benedict, Mickey Knox.

Roy Gordon; *Nurse,* Jane Adams; *Hodges,* Don Harvey; *Bookkeeper,* Tristram Coffin; *Watchman,* Lee Phelps; *Officer,* Jack Mower; *Morgue attendant,* William J. O'Brien; *Man,* Carl Sklover; *Whelan,* Herbert Patterson; *Newswriter,* John Morgan; *Nurse,* Dorothy Abbott; *Malone,* Tom Monroe; *Technical; pool sequences,* Harold Baker; *Rewrite man,* Jack Gargan; *First detective,* Peter Virgo; *Pretty nurse,* Doretta Johnson; *Male nurse,* Wade Crosby.

Lying bleeding in a gutter, Slip tells how he and Sach got beat up . . . They had been copy boys for a newspaper who learned that their best friend, Lt. Gabe Moreno, had been wounded in a shoot-out that claimed another cop. They found out that the Loop Gang, the most notorious criminals in the city, were responsible. The five boys joined their ranks to aid the police in catching them red-handed, but their leader, Carver, caught on and substituted his plans. The newspaper's cartoonist, who put clues in his strips to alert the Loop Gang about traps, came to their robbery site and pointed out that Slip and Sach were the snitchers. The gangsters tried to even the score while fending off cops before being defeated by the law.

"As you can plainly see," Slip says in his opening bit of narration, "I didn't get that puss [face] in no beauty parlor." He refers to the blood and bruises. He has injuries certainly suffered in a fight. "That mess of skin and bones lying over there is my bosom companion Horace Debussy Jones. To tell you the truth, I think he looks better that way."

Angels in Disguise is a spoof of detective films in which the outcome is already partially known. Slip and Sach will wind up in that gutter. Our knowledge of this is played on in some of this dialogue. In one scene, Gabe tells the boys to be careful: "I don't want you guys to wind up with busted heads." We know that they will.

Slip's commentaries come every two to eight minutes. He tells us what we need to know about the plot, but in his own way. Unfortunately, the film doesn't offer much more than the narration. Because the narration is so obtrusive, the straight material suffers. Good comedy-drama needs to develop by means of scenes. Information must be conveyed in incidences, things the audience is witness to. Narration, if used as a substitute for story development (as is the case here), shortchanges the viewer by presenting only ready-made impressions.

In this age when television programs repeat the same formulas week after week, it can be appreciated that Grippo and Yarbrough decided to throw everybody off-track. However, when Gorcey isn't narrating and the detective music isn't playing, the film can be as dead as the corpses in the film's morgue scene.

Slip's being in the arms of Vickie (Jean Dean) earns the ire of the insidious Mr. Carver (Edward Ryan).

MASTER MINDS

Released November 20, 1949, by Monogram. Produced by Jan Grippo. Directed by Jean Yarbrough. Scenario by Charles R. Marion. Additional dialogue by Bert Lawrence. Photographed by Marcel Le Picard. Edited by William Austin. Art direction by David Milton. Musical direction by Edward Kay. Set decorations by Raymond Boltz, Jr. Production managed by Allan K. Wood. Assistant direction by William Calihan. Sound by Dean Spencer. Camera operated by Bill Marguiles. Script supervised by Ilona Vas. Makeup by Jack P. Pierce. Grip, Harry Lewis. Gaffer, Lloyd Garnell. Still photographs by Ed Jones. *5742 ft. 64 minutes.*

Terrence Aloysius "Slip" Mahoney, Leo Gorcey; *Horace Debussy "Ali Ben Sachmo" Jones,* Huntz Hall; *Whitey,* Billy Benedict; *Butch,* Bennie Bartlett; *Chuck,* David Gorcey; *Gabe Moreno,* Gabriel Dell; *Louie Dumbrowski,* Bernard Gorcey; *Dr. Druzik,* Alan Napier; *Atlas,* Glenn Strange; *Otto,* William Yetter; *Benny,* Kit Guard; *Hugo,* Skelton Knaggs; *Nancy Marlowe,* Jane Adams; *Juggler,* Whitey Roberts; *Constable Isiah Hoskins,* Harry Tyler; *Mrs. Hoskins,* Minerva Urecal; *Mike Barton,* Chester Clute; *Woman,* Anna Chandler; *Henchman,* Stanley Blystone; *Young man,* Robert Coogan; *Father,* Pat Goldin; *Hoskins boy,* Tim Connor; *Second Hoskins boy,* Kent O'Dell.

When Sach gets a toothache, he is able to predict things. Slip and Gabe put him into a carnival sideshow, where Sach becomes so popular that word of his mental capacities reaches Dr. Druzik. Druzik, who wants to transplant a gifted brain into his ape man, kidnaps Sach and takes him to his haunted house hideout. A transfer of brains takes place electronically. The monster, now bearing Sach's voice

Whitey, Slip, Gabe, Chuck and Butch surround "Ali Ben Sachmo."

and personality, escapes and leads Slip and the boys back to the house. When the electrical impulses wear off, Sach and the monster revert to their original states. The boys have to flee the monster and find the real Sach. Gabe comes to the house too, and, with the other boys, is captured. Druzik's attempts to finalize his experiment are halted for good by the arrival of Louie, dressed as a "haunted" knight, and the local constable, who has been aroused by the goings on.

Master Minds took the mad-scientist-in-a-haunted-house formula and took it one step further by having the experiment actually take place.

The experiment results in a monster with Sach's brain that scares the boys, even though he is playful and harmless, and has Sach's funny walk and nonsensical humor. When Louie hears the familiar Sach voice, and then looks up and sees a monster, he goes into hysterics and drops a glass. The other boys' reactions are similar, and Slip only begrudgingly agrees to follow the monster to the house—and only because he wants to find Sach.

The boys' loyalties are divided. Which are they to follow, the monster who talks like Sach or the Sach who acts like a monster? They choose the one that looks like Sach, even though he attacks them on every possible occasion.

Louie, like Gabe and the boys, is drawn to the house. He is initially reluctant, but motivated by the desire to recoup the money the boys owe him, he goes into the underground passage that leads him into the house. Therefore, all of the Bowery boys principals are involved.

Production sideline: Huntz Hall in real life has an ability to predict events. He says: "All my life I've been able to predict what was going to happen. And most of the time I've been able to avoid the mishaps I knew would be encountered." He contends that he will never ignore a premonition, recalling a time when he only barely escaped death after ignoring a vision. It had come to him in October 1971. He mentally saw his body twisted amid twisted steel. Just then, his phone rang; it was his wife, who reported that she needed to be picked up. He ignored his premonition and set out for her. His car was demolished en route by a high-speed car. He was in a coma for three days. "I'm grateful to have survived that accident," he says, "and I'll never disregard my premonitions again."

BLONDE DYNAMITE

Released February 12, 1950, by Monogram. Produced by Jan Grippo, Directed by William Beaudine. Scenario by Charles R. Marion. Photographed by Marcel Le Picard. Edited by William Austin. Editing supervised by Otho Lovering. Art direction by David Milton. Musical direction by Edward Kay. Production managed by Allan K. Wood. Set decorations by Raymond Boltz, Jr. Sound by Dean Spencer. Script supervised by Ilona Vas. *5992 ft. 66 minutes.*

Terrence Aloysius "Slip" Mahoney, Leo Gorcey; *Horace Debussy "Sach" Jones,* Huntz Hall; *Whitey (Witmore),* Billy Benedict; *Chuck (Cedric),* David Gorcey; *Butch (Bartholemew),* Buddy Gorman; *Louie Dumbrowski,* Bernard Gorcey; *Gabe Moreno, banker,* Gabriel Dell; *Joan Marshall,*

Gorman and Karen Randle, Adele Jergens and Leo, Lynn Davies and Benedict, Beverlee Crane and David Gorcey.

Adele Jergens; *Champ Falon*, Harry Lewis; *John Lero "Zero" Pacchile*, Murray Alper; *Sarah Dumbrowski*, Jody Gilbert; *Professor*, John Harmon; *Samson*, Michael Ross; *Tom, cop*, Tom Kennedy; *Verna*, Lynn Davies; *Bunny*, Beverlee Crane; *Tracy*, Karen Randle; *Mr. Jennings*, Stanley Andrews; *First dowager*, Constance Purdy; *Second dowager*, Florence Auer; *Solicitor*, Robert Emmett Keane.

Slip, Sach, Butch, Chuck and Whitey turn Louie's Sweet Shop into an escort bureau when Louie leaves them in charge while on vacation. Their main clients are a group of girls who want to keep the boys busy while gangsters dig a tunnel from the bureau to a nearby bank. Sach is left in charge of the bureau, but the gangsters get him to cooperate. The gangsters have a bank-vault combination obtained from bank-employee Gabe, but Gabe (blackmailed into giving it to them) has supplied a phony. No longer worried that he will be held responsible for the bank's cash shortage, Gabe goes to the police to report what he did. He needn't have; due to Sach's bumbling misdirection, the bank robbers drill into the police station.

At times, *Blonde Dynamite* looks as though it caters to the adolescent male fantasy that women could be so crazy about young lads that they would pay to be with them. Fortunately, screenwriter Charles R. Marion apparently foresaw such a fault and wrote in some scenes showing that the escort business can have its downside. In one scene, a winsome Whitey and noisy Sach are on assignment with two staunch (and portly) society matrons. The foursome attends the opera, where the boys can't sit still in the box seat, and where a clash develops between the uncouth boys and the refined women. Whitey is more excited by his companion getting the prize in a box of Cracker-Jacks than by anything performed by the musicians.

Chuck and Butch don't fare any better on their date, which isn't one in any real sense of the word. They have been dispatched to meet a gathering of women. What they don't know is that the women are taking a self-defense course. Chuck and Butch become the tackling dummies for the self-defense students.

There is nothing special about *Blonde Dynamite*, however, making it a mystery as to why it was shot in eleven days, as opposed to the usual seven to eight. It's hard to see what the extra time was spent on.

LUCKY LOSERS

Released May 14, 1950, by Monogram. Produced by Jan Grippo. Directed by William Beaudine. Scenario by Charles R. Marion. Additional dialogue by Bert Lawrence. Photographed by Marcel Le Picard. Edited by William Austin. Editing supervised by Otho Lovering. Art direction by David Milton. Musical direction by Edward J. Kay. Production managed by Allan K. Wood. Set decorations by Raymond Boltz, Jr. Sound by John Kean. Script supervised by Ilona Vas. *6249 ft. 69 minutes.*

Terrence Aloysius "Slip" Mahoney, Leo Gorcey; *Horace Debussy "Sach" Jones*, Huntz Hall; *Whitey*, Billy Benedict; *Chuck*, David Gorcey; *Butch*, Buddy Gorman; *Gabe Moreno, newscaster*, Gabriel Dell; *Louie Dumbrowski*, Bernard Gorcey; *Bruce McDermott*, Lyle Talbot; *Margo (alias Countess)*, Hillary Brooke; *Wellington Jefferson "Buffer" McGee*, Harry Tyler; *John "Chick" Martin*, Harry Cheshire; *Carol Thurston*, Wendy Waldron; *Johnny Angelo*, Joseph Turkel; *David J. Thurston*, Selmer Jackson; *Bartender*, Frank Jenks; *Tom Whitney*, Douglas Evans; *Andrew Stone III*, Glen Vernon; *First conventioner*, Dick Elliott; *Second conventioner*, Chester Clute.

Our two heroes work in a Wall Street brokerage firm owned by David J. Thurston. When Thurston reportedly commits suicide, television reporter Gabe tries to look into other causes of death. Dice that Slip finds on Thurston's desk lead him to conclude that Thurston was in trouble with the High Hat Club, a gambling house. The boys become expert croupiers under the tutelage of Buffer McGee, and become employed by the High Hat Club. They learn that their boss, Bruce McDermott, had syndicate connections with Thurston. Gabe reports this on his television program and is beat up. Gabe goes on the air from his hospital bed and reports that "Chick," a man high in social circles, has been giving protection to gangsters like McDermott, and is responsible for Thurston's death. Tom Whitney of the District Attorney's Office turns for help to Gabe, who refers him to the boys. The boys tell Whitney what they know, then he sets a trap for "Chick," who turns out to be John Martin, a civic leader who was ostensibly Thurston's friend.

The film starts off amusingly, with the boys working in the stock market. Sach, reading ticker tapes, delivers such lines as, "American elevator, going up and down and sideways." The focus then changes to David Thurston. His murder will change the rhythm of the film.

Slip and Sach organize the rest of the boys, and all take lessons in the technique of cards and dice use. (Their progress is traced through a very lengthy montage, which shows the boys at various levels of expertise.) Slip and Sach pay a visit to the nightclub which has been their destination all along: the High Hat Club. They are dressed well, deceptively attired as gentlemen, but a problem still exists: how to get into the gambling room. It is guarded. But leave it to Slip to come up with a solution. A conventioneer's lapel button will guarantee admittance, so Slip sets his eyes on the many out-of-towners. He engages a sloshed conventioneer and pretends to be loaded himself. As a victim of drink, Slip is able to ask for a lapel button and receive it.

The film never regains the zest it has in these innocent moments, and it loses its focus entirely.

One would think that Jan Grippo (who produced) and William Beaudine (who directed) would have learned from another film of theirs that shared this one's problem. Yet, *Lucky Losers* is *News Hounds* all over again.

TRIPLE TROUBLE

Released August 13, 1950, by Monogram. Produced by Jan Grippo. Directed by Jean Yarbrough. Scenario by Charles R. Marion. Additional dialogue by Bert Lawrence. Photographed by Marcel Le Picard. Edited by William Austin. Editing supervised by Otho Lovering. Art direction by David Milton. Musical direction by Edward Kay. Produc-

tion managed by Allan K. Wood. Set decorations by Raymond Boltz, Jr. Sound by Tom Lambert. Script supervised by Ilona Vas. *5984 ft. 66 minutes.*

Terrence Aloysius "Slip" Mahoney (23322), Leo Gorcey; *Horace Debussy "Sach" Jones (23323),* Huntz Hall; *Whitey,* Billy Benedict; *Chuck,* David Gorcey; *Butch,* Buddy Gorman; *Gabe Moreno,* Gabriel Dell; *Louie Dumbrowski,* Bernard Gorcey; *Skeets O'Neil,* Richard Benedict; *Bat Armstrong,* Pat Collins; *Ma Armstrong,* Effie Lairch; *"Pretty Boy" Gleason,* Paul Dubov; *Benny the Blood,* Joseph Turkel; *Squirrely Davis,* George Chandler; *Hobo Barton,* Eddie Gribbon; *Shirley O'Brien,* Lyn Thomas; *Judge,* Jonathan Hale; *Warden Burnside,* Joseph Crehan; *Ma's henchmen,* Eddie Foster, Frank Marlowe; *Murphy,* Edward Gargan; *Convict,* Tom Kennedy; *Guard,* Lyle Talbot.

While coming home from a masquerade party at midnight, the boys try to stop a warehouse robbery and are themselves accused by the police of robbing it. While on bail and awaiting trial, Whitey recognizes a voice on his short-wave radio as being that of a prisoner the boys heard on a radio broadcast. The voice mentions a locality that is later robbed. Slip realizes that he could find out who committed the robbery that the boys are accused of if he

could investigate from behind prison bars. Therefore, Slip accepts the charges and he and Sach are sent to prison. In prison, they meet Bat Armstrong, the prisoner who has been making short-wave broadcasts to let his comrades know ripe robbery locales. The boys set a trap by mentioning that Louie has a large amount in his safe. Bat instructs his comrades and they rob Louie, but when it is reported to Bat that the net was only $75, Bat figures out that Slip and Sach betrayed him. He decides to take them with him when he breaks out so that he can do them in. A radio message is made to his comrades instructing them to help him escape, but Whitey receives and decodes it. Whitey, Chuck and Butch disguise themselves as Armstrong's mob and catch Armstrong after he, Slip and Sach have exited prison gates.

Triple Trouble is a pessimistic film. Over and over, it delivers the message that men can be sucked into circumstances beyond their control. Slip and Sach stage a fight in the prison yard so as to see the warden (to report the break-out plan) without letting the other prisoners know that that is their intention. Instead of getting an escort to the warden, they get a warning that fighting could land them in solitary confinement.

Slip and Sach try to get to Bat Armstrong's radio. They are caught roaming about administration halls without authorization. This time they *are* sent to solitary confinement.

Louie suffers throughout. In his words, "this has taken ten years off my life." On three occasions (after hearing the radio message that his store will be robbed; after his store *is* robbed; and after hearing that Bat will break jail and take Slip and Sach as hostages) Louie becomes so anguished that he runs into the street screaming about what has happened. Not only does Louie not get police help, or even a kind ear, but the policeman on the beat warns him that he can be hauled to jail for disturbing the police.

Fatalistic comedy can work if the pessimism is delicately blended with the comedy, as in the Laurel and Hardy manner. In *Triple Trouble*, it isn't.

BLUES BUSTERS

Released October 29, 1950, by Monogram. Produced by Jan Grippo. Directed by William Beaudine. Scenario by Charles R. Marion. Additional dialogue by Bert Lawrence. Photographed by Marcel Le Picard. Edited by William Austin. Art direction by David Milton. Musical direction by Edward Kay. Production managed by Allan K. Wood. Assistant direction by William Calihan. Sound by Tom Lambert. Set decorations by Raymond Boltz, Jr. Script supervised by Ilona Vas. Songs performed by Sach: "Wasn't It You?" (Ben Raleigh, Bernie Wayne), "Bluebirds Keep

Singing in the Rain" (Johnny Lange, Elliott Daniel), "Let's Have a Heart to Heart Talk" (Billy Austin, Eddie Brandt, Paul Sanders) and "You Walked By" (Raleigh, Wayne). Songs performed by Lola: "Better Be Looking Out for Love" (Ralph Wolfe, Johnny Lange) and "Joshua Fit the Battle of Jericho" (traditional). Slip mangles "Dixie" (Albert Pike). Production title: *Bowery Thrush. 67 minutes.*

Terrence Aloysius "Slip" Mahoney, Leo Gorcey; *Horace Debussy "Sach" Jones, the Bowery Thrush,* Huntz Hall; *Whitey,* Billy Benedict; *Chuck,* David Gorcey; *Butch,* Bennie Bartlett; *Gabe Moreno, song plugger,* Gabriel Dell; *Louie Dumbrowski,* Bernard Gorcey; *Lola Stanton,* Adele Jergens; *Rick Martin,* Craig Stevens; *Sally Dolan,* Phyllis Coates; *Teddy Davis,* William Vincent; *Bimbo,* Paul Bryar; *Joe Ricco,* Matty King; *Dubbing Hall's voice,* John Lorenz; *Dubbing Jergens' voice,* Gloria Wood.

Sach's tonsillectomy leaves him with a good singing voice. Louie's is converted into the Bowery Palace nightclub so that Sach can be brought to the attention of the public and Louie can make some needed cash. Rival club owner Rick Martin recognizes Sach's profitability and has his singer, Lola, trick Sach into signing a contract. A dancer at the Bowery Palace, Sally, arranges to have Rick kiss her in view of Lola. Lola, feeling betrayed, goes to the boys and tells them that she had led Sach to believe he was signing an autograph, not a contract, so the boys get Sach back. But the boys' dreams of paying Louie's debts are short-lived; Sach loses his singing voice after a visit to the doctor.

Blues Busters is engrossing in that it shows us all the facets of show business, and for presenting Mr. Gorcey and Mr. Hall in new roles, which are adult roles. Slip is tuxedoed for the most part. He acts as master of ceremonies at Louie's, and delivers straight-role lines, such as: "Eat a little, drink a little—enjoy yourselves—until you get your checks." He is a different person, without many violent mannerisms.

When Rick Martin tells the new Slip that he has Sach's contract, and shows him the legal and binding contract, Slip accepts this. He doesn't throw Martin out, as he might have had this situation occurred in another film.

Sach (usually called Horace here) changes too. He gets antagonistic when irked. When Rick Martin censures Sach for being late to rehearsal, he screams back, "So what? So fire me! Give me my autograph back."

The supporting players are showcased more than usual. The plot is resolved when Sally (the dancer, also Slip's girlfriend) goes to Rick's apartment to be seen accepting a contract (and a kiss) from Rick. The ruse works, of course, as Sally's honest motives are more than an even match for Rick's professional infidelity.

When Horace's (Sach's) voice fails, Terrence's (Slip's) remark about it is one that compares the devastation on the

stage to the devastation Hollywood was experiencing at the time. His line is: "Dis is the worst thing dat's happened since television."

Gabriel Dell again has a thankless role, as a songplugger. His role is one contrived to fit him into the plot (the show biz plot), just as his other recent roles had. (The most conspicuous examples of this are his being cast as a lawyer in *Triple Trouble*, the criminal justice story; a banker in *Blonde Dynamite*, a bank robbery story; a cop, private eye or reporter in four films in which the boys conduct investigations.) This time there was a difference: This role was his last.

Production sideline: As it would happen, Huntz was once considered to have a good singing voice. However, that was during the Depression, and one sumer Huntz had to accept a job selling peanuts at Madison Square Garden. When the season was over, he was left with the hawker's voice he would have for the rest of his life.

Buddy, Leo, Bernard, Adele Jergens, Billy, David.

The girl on the right (Virginial Hewitt) is a spy. Horrors!

BOWERY BATTALION

Released January 24, 1951, by Monogram. Produced by Jan Grippo. Directed by William Beaudine. Scenario by Charles R. Marion. Additional dialogue by Bert Lawrence. Photographed by Marcel Le Picard. Edited by William Austin. Art direction by David Milton. Musical direction by Edward Kay. Production supervised by Allan K. Wood. Assistant direction by William Calihan. Sound by Tom Lambert. Set decorations by Raymond Boltz, Jr. Script supervised by Ilona Vas. *6173 ft. 69 minutes.*

Terrence Aloysius "Slip" Mahoney, Leo Gorcey; *Horace Debussy "Sach" Jones,* Huntz Hall; *Whitey,* Billy Benedict; *Chuck,* David Gorcey; *Butch,* Buddy Gorman; *Louie Dumbrowski,* Bernard Gorcey; *Sergeant Frisbie,* Donald MacBride; *Marsha Davis,* Virginia Hewitt; *Commanding Officer Hatfield,* Russell Hicks; *Colonel Masters,* Selmer Jackson; *Decker,* John Bleifer; *Conroy,* Al Eben; *Recruiting officers,* Frank Jenks, Michael Ross; *Waiter in officer's mess,* Emil Sitka; *Branson,* Harry Lauter.

Slip, Sach, Whitey, Butch and Chuck are privates in the Army who are assigned to guard Louie, who is being used to bait spies. Louie is kidnapped under their noses, but the boys get on his trail, and round up the spies.

Armed services comedies were relatively safe investments for studios—Martin and Lewis's *At War With the Army* proved that the same year—so naturally a service comedy was a shoo-in for the first Bowery Boys film made under new circumstances. Gabe was gone, and in the reorganization that followed his departure, the three "background" boys (Whitey, Butch, Chuck) were promoted to the stature of Slip and Sach. Drama was subdued, and comedy (pure comedy) carried this film and the subsequent films. Naturally, a situation was required which exuded comic possibilities. The Army setting was just the thing; it provided ample opportunity for satire, sight-gags, slapstick, and sassy comebacks.

As superior officer, Louie endeavors to win the boys over to the "new" him. As he puts it, "I want to make the boys as proud of me as I am of them." This is relieving, as Louie had been so frustrated after the boys left for duty that he couldn't function, and at one point cried, "I can't stand another day without them swindling me."

There is one beautifully photographed, well-executed sequence: a gem of a scene in which the members of Company H (five of whom are our boys) go through physically exerting manuevers. Most of the recruits do fine, but not the undisciplined five. Guess who ends up "practicing for the Olympics" in the mud? Sach.

Despite the slight nature of the last half, at least one loose end is not wrapped up. It involves some WACS whom the boys make dates with during an encounter on the grounds. Throughout the next hours the boys look forward to the date. After their leave is cancelled (for manuevers) the girls are shown waiting for the boys at 4th and Main. They vow revenge for being "stood up." Yet we never see them again! No revenge is ever delivered.

Michael Ross and Frank Jenks would like to have Slip in the Army. But they don't tell him that this is what they're after.

GHOST CHASERS

Released April 29, 1951, by Monogram. Produced by Jan Grippo. Directed by William Beaudine. Scenario by Charles R. Marion. Additional dialogue by Bert Lawrence. Photographed by Marcel Le Picard. Edited by William Austin. Art direction by David Milton. Musical direction by Edward Kay. Production managed by Allan K. Wood. Assistant direction by Wesley Bary. Set decorations by Raymond Boltz, Jr. Sound by Tom Lambert. Set continuity by Mary Chaffee. *69 minutes.*

Terrence Aloysius "Slip" Mahoney, Leo Gorcey; *Horace Debussy "Sach" Jones,* Huntz Hall; *Witmore "Whitey" Williams,* Billy Benedict; *Chuck,* David Gorcey; *Butch,* Buddy Gorman; *Louie Dumbrowski,* Bernard Gorcey; *Edgar Alden Franklin Smith,* Lloyd Corrigan; *Cynthia,* Jan Kayne; *Margo the Medium,* Lela Bliss; *Dr. Basil Granville,* Philip Van Zandt; *Jack Eagan,* Robert Coogan; *Gus,* Michael Ross; *Leonardi,* Donald Lawton; *Dr. Siegfried,* Hal Gerard; *Professor Krantz,* Marshall Bradford; *Mrs. Parelli,* Argentina Brunnetti; *Mrs. Mahoney,* Doris Kemper; *Madame Zola,* Belle Mitchell; *First reporter,* Paul Bryar; *Second reporter,* Pat Gleason; *Photographer,* Bob Peoples,; *Girl,* Marjorie Eaton; *Lady at seance,* Bess Flowers.

Slip becomes interested in communication with spirits when a spiritualist moves into his neighborhood and offers to put local women in contact with the deceased—for a price. When Slip exposes her as a fake, she reveals that she's working for Margo the Medium, an eminent spiritualist whose show had made Sach and Whitey believe in ghosts. The boys visit Margo's place to investigate, although ostensibly to let Louie talk to his late uncle. The ghost of Edgar Smith befriends Sach, and helps him investigate on his own. Slip, Whitey, Butch and Chuck are caught snooping, and are put in a room slowly filling with rising water, but Edgar saves them by using a special chalk that draws an outlet for the water. The boys then rout the quacks.

Working merely from the title *Ghost Chasers* or from the idea of a "séance" film, Monogram writers could have written a gangster film disguised as a ghost story. However, Charles R. Marion and Bert Lawrence added extra elements to assure that *Ghosts Chasers* emerged as a notch above the norm. The inclusion of Edgar the Ghost adds a touch of the supernatural, and *Ghost Chasers* is thus a good combination of comedy and fantasy.

Sach was given his best showcase to date. No doubt the fantasy theme increased his prominence. Early in the film, Whitey remarks, "He's a believer." "Sure," says Sach, "I believe in anything." Thus it is natural that Edgar the Ghost would make himself visible and audible only to Sach. Sach insists to the others that Edgar exists, though, and Whitey tells Slip, "You've got to stop beating this guy

LEO **GORCEY** The **BOWERY BOYS** **GHOST CHASERS** with **HUNTZ HALL** LLOYD CORRIGAN · LELA BLISS MONOGRAM A JAN GRIPPO Production Directed by WILLIAM BEAUDINE

Marshall Bradford, Lela Bliss, Philip Van Zandt and Hal Gerard have just frozen Leo and Buddy Gorman by hypnotic suggestion.

Huntz as a characteristic Sach, with Lloyd Corrigan, a superb and justly busy character actor.

on the head." Sach is so dim-witted, it seems, that when the other boys are hypnotized, Sach is not affected. "Gad zook," remarks Edgar when he finds out, "I knew you were too smart to have intelligence."

The other four Bowery Boys (Slip, Whitey, Butch and Chuck) aren't as prominent as Sach. They are seen mostly in mechanical material: trying to escape an enclosed chamber filling with water, being carried while immobile, ineptly exploring the house, etc.

Nevertheless, Slip is the leader of the Bowery Boys, and he abuses Sach. In a *To Have and Have Not* takeoff, Slip tells Sach, "If you want anything, just whistle." Sach asks, "How do you whistle?" Answer: "Just pucker your lips— and I'll bash them in."

Ghost Chasers is unique among Bowery boys films. It has a ghost character we can take to our hearts. This allows for clever touches, such as Edgar's helping to extricate the boys from dilemmas with "magic chalk," graphite which forms doorways along lines traced by the stick. The magic chalk also tells us not to take the plot seriously. As it is, the subduing of the culprits comes about as the result of improbable turns. Perhaps as a test of the audience's acceptance, Edgar turns to the camera at several points and talks directly to the viewer. At fade out, while Sach is being mobbed by the other boys for insisting that Edgar is real, Edgar says to the camera, "It's plain that his young companions don't believe in ghosts. Dost thou?"

114

LET'S GO NAVY!

Released July 29, 1951, by Monogram. Produced by Jan Grippo. Directed by William Beaudine. Scenario by Max Adams. Additional dialogue by Bert Lawrence. Photographed by Marcel Le Picard. Edited by William Austin. Art direction by David Milton. Musical direction by Edward Kay. Production managed by Allan K. Wood. Assistant direction by William Calihan. Sound by William Lynch. Set decorations by Otto Siegel. Technical advice by Lt. Robert M. Garick, USNR. Script continuity by Ilona Vas. *6149 ft. 68 minutes.*

Terrence Aloysius "Slip" Mahoney (alias "Dalton B. Dalton"), Leo Gorcey; *Horace Debussy "Sach" Jones (alias "Hobenocker"),* Huntz Hall; *Whitey ("Schwartz"),* Billy Benedict; *Chuck ("Merriweather"),* David Gorcey; *Butch ("Stevenson"),* Buddy Gorman; *Louie Dumbrowski,* Bernard Gorcey; *Mervin Longnecker,* Allen Jenkins; *Princess Papoola,* Charlita; *Commander Tannen,* Paul Harvey; *Joe,* Tom Neal; *Red,* Richard Benedict; *Sgt. Mulloy,* Emory Parnell; *Lt. Smith,* Douglas Evans; *Shell game operator,* Frank Jenks; *Donovan, cop,* Tom Kennedy; *Kitten,* Dorothy Ford; *Dalton B. Dalton,* Harry Lauter; *Horatio Hobenocker,* Dave Willock; *Nuramo,* Peter Mamakos; *Lt. Bradley,* Ray Walker; *Captain,* Jonathan Hale; *Policeman,* Paul Bryar; *Merriweather,* Richard Monahan; *Stevenson,* William Lechner; *Harry Schwartz,* George Offerman, Jr.; *Detective Snyder,* Mike Lally; *Lt. Moss,* Russ Conway; *Petty Officer Grompkin,* Harry Strang; *Sailor,* William Vincent; *Storekeeper,* Lee Graham; *Disbursing officer,* Pat Gleason; *Third officer,* George Eldredge; *First aide,* William Hudson; *Second aide,* Bob Peoples; *Officer,* John Close; *Postman,* Emil Sitka; *Fat sailor,* Ray Dawe; *Recruiting officer,* Ray Walker; *Sailor with Nuramo tattoo,* Murray Alper; *First sailor,* Jimmy Cross; *Second sailor,* Bill Chandler; *Third Sailor,* Don Gordon; *Fourth sailor,* Neyle Morrow; *Fifth sailor,* Joey Ray.

Sixteen hundred dollars raised in the Bowery for charity and entrusted to the boys is stolen by two men in sailor suits. To vindicate themselves, the boys try to find the crooks, and so join the Navy, enlisting under assumed names so as not to be obligated to serve their terms. After a year on the seas, the boys haven't found the crooks, but with $2000 Sach wins gambling they are able to make restitution. Back in New York, the same men rob them again, but the crooks are subdued by the boys' captain. Having exposed the robbers as imposters, the boys go to the Navy office to be commended, but through a bureaucratic mistake are re-enlisted.

Let's Go Navy! is a good combination of comedy and fantasy. It is the first time the boys leave the United States, but not the last, as future series' producer Ben Schwalb and future series' director-writer Edward Bernds knew a good thing when they saw it. Bernds explains that getting the

Butch, Whitey, Slip and Chuck are aghast when they discover that Sach has taken refuge in a cannon barrel that is about to be fired.

boys to foreign locales could be tricky business since the plot had to be believable.

In *Let's Go Navy!,* it is. He further explained that fantasy elements had to be presented in such a way that they weren't silly. Here it's scripted that a parrot (Davy) aids Sach against a slight-of-hand shell-game operator. The operator scrambles three identical cups. Sach is supposed to decide under which cup a ball is hidden. Sach's eyes aren't as quick as the game operator's hands, but Davy's eyes are. Thus Davy wins $2000 for Sach. The script idea is an acceptable one.

According to *The Motion Picture Herald*, the preview audience, expecting a prestigious picture, started laughing thirty seconds into the film.

A selection of reviews shows how strongly the film kept a hold on viewers:

From *The Motion Picture Herald*: "Any resemblance betwen this and any other Bowery Boys picture is purely geneological. It is far funnier, faster and more fruitful as to audience reaction than anything the Leo Gorcey-Huntz Hall duo has furnished their following."

Hollywood Reporter: "Jan Grippo offers the best in the group's long and successful career."

Variety: " . . . a very funny picture, unquestionably the best Bowery Boys film yet produced. Jan Grippo leaves the series after 23 pix with a superior credit."

Jan Grippo left as the result of a personal tragedy: his wife had died. The aforementioned Mr. Schwalb would take over as producer in a little more than a year, and the aforementioned Mr. Bernds would be brought in by him.

CRAZY OVER HORSES

Released November 18, 1951, by Monogram. Produced by Jerry Thomas. Directed by William Beaudine. Scenario by Tim Ryan. Photographed by Marcel Le Picard. Edited by William Austin. Art direction by David Milton. Musical direction by Edward Kay. (Opening credit music: Overture to *William Tell*, by Rossini.) Production supervised by Allan K. Wood. Assistant direction by William Calihan. Sound by Tom Lambert. Set decorations by Robert Priestley. Costumes by Sidney Mintz. Script supervised by Ilona Vas. British release title: *Win, Place and Show*. 5819 ft. 65 minutes.

Terrence Aloysius "Slip" Mahoney, Leo Gorcey; *Horace Debussy "Sach" Jones*, Huntz Hall; *Whitey*, Billy Benedict; *Chuck*, David Condon (Gorcey)*; *Butch*, Bennie Bartlett; *Louis Xavier Dumbrowski*, Bernard Gorcey; *Terry Flynn*, Gloria Saunders; *Duke*, Ted de Corsia; *Weepin' Willie*, Allen Jenkins; *Mr. Flynn*, Tim Ryan; *J.T. Randal*, Russell Hicks; *Mazie*, Peggy Wynne; *Swifty*, Michael Ross; *Uniformed security guard*, Bob Peoples; *Charlie*, Perc Landers; *Groom*, Leo "Ukie" Sherin; *Crap-shooting stable attendant*, Robert "Smoki" Whitfield; *Announcer*, Sam Balter; *Evans*, Ray Page; *Pinkerton man*, Darr Smith; *Elderly man*, Wilbur Mack; *Elderly woman*, Gertrude Astor; *Jockeys*, Bill Cartledge, Whitey Hughes, Delmar Thomas, Bernard Pludow; *Silent man*, Ben Frommer

*David Gorcey acted under his mother's maiden name, "Condon," until 1956.

Louie is mad when the boys bring him a horse as repayment of a debt owed by stable-owner Flynn. But Slip thinks the horse, My Girl, is a thoroughbred. The horse had been left at Flynn's by gamblers, who now want her back so they can use her in a switch. Flynn gives them Louie's address, but the boys won't sell their share of My Girl. The gamblers switch My Girl with a poor horse, Tarzana, but the boys switch them back. The boys enter their horse against Tarzana in a race. The boys' horse wins, and the gamblers lose a great deal in bets. The head gambler tries to shoot his comrades for inept handling, but before he can fire the gun, the boys leads the police in to arrest them.

Crazy Over Horses is consistent and even, a good comedy. The continuity is integrated into the story, every scene logically building upon the previous one.

Sach takes advantages of a few chances to tell off Slip. When Slip, bashfully trying to hide his thoroughbred expertise, tells Flynn's daughter Terry, "Oh, I used to be an exercise boy," Sach says, "You could do with a little exercise now." When Slip has had enough, he throws Sach out of his life. Sach, in tears, says, "When you get in trouble, don't call on me for more."

Crazy Over Horses was written solely by Tim Ryan, the comic who plays Flynn. A vaudevillian who performed all over the United States with his wife Irene (visible throughout the U.S. later as Granny in "The Beverly Hillbillies"), Ryan knew comedy. He did something to the Bowery Boys formula (on this film) that had only been done once before: He avoided ending the story with a confrontation between the good guys and the bad. What's more, there is no fight anywhere in the film.

HOLD THAT LINE

Released March 23, 1952, by Monogram. Produced by Jerry Thomas. Directed by William Beaudine. Scenario by Tim Ryan and Charles R. Marion. Photographed by Marcel Le Picard. Edited by William Austin. Art direction by Martin Obzina. Musical direction by Edward Kay. Production managed by Allan K. Wood. Assistant direction by Edward Morey Jr. 5749 ft. 64 minutes.

Terrence Aloysius "Slip" Mahoney, Leo Gorcey; *Horace Debussy "Sach/Hurricane" Jones*, Huntz Hall; *Chuck*, David Condon; *Butch*, Bennie Bartlett*; *Junior*, Gil Stratton Jr.; *Morris Dumbrowski*, Bernard Gorcey; *Louie Dumbrowski*, Bernard Gorcey; *Biff Wallace*, John Bromfield; *Dean Forrester*, Taylor Holmes; *Candy Callin*, Veda Ann Borg; *Harold Lane*, Bob Nichols; *Katie Wayne*, Mona Knox;

LEO GORCEY and the BOWERY BOYS in CRAZY OVER HORSES

Leo GORCEY and THE BOWERY BOYS in

HOLD THAT LINE

featuring Huntz Hall

with
JOHN BROMFIELD
MONA KNOX
VEDA ANN BORG
TAYLOR HOLMES

A JERRY THOMAS PRODUCTION

DIRECTED BY   SCREENPLAY BY   ADDITIONAL DIALOGUE

The boys are sent to Ivy University by two trustees who are anxious to see what effect the boys will have on the students. While the students dismiss the boys as silly, Sach develops a vitamin mixture in Chemistry that turns him into a star athlete. Stalwart football hero Biff Wallace has Sach kidnapped before a game in order to aid gamblers, but after injuries take him out of the game his school spirit haunts him and he tells Slip where to find Sach. Sach is rescued, and returns to the game, but his new batch of vitamins is a failure. Slip takes to the field and scores the winning touchdown.

Hold That Line transported the five Bowery remedials to an atmosphere where they're comically out of place. They wouldn't want to be like the people that they meet at college, however. Certainly they don't look favorably on the pretentious football star or the snooty newspaper editor they meet.

When newspaper editor Harold Lane introduces athletic hotshot Biff Wallace to the boys, Slip immediately asks what Biff's racket is. "Why, he's an All-American," replies the baffled Lane. "Well, we're *all* Americans," says Slip, "but what did he do after that?"

The boys arrive at the dean's office wearing raccoon coats and playing ukeleles. Once in class, Sach amazes the math professor with his quick answers. He then shows Slip that his answer was arrived at thanks to an adding machine under his feet.

On the football field, Sach makes remarks about football terms he's never heard before, such as "coach" ("How 's your brother Pullman?"), "scrubs" ("What do you think we are, janitors?") and "hike" ("Fine time to go for a walk"). However, his strange powers acquired from his Chemistry test tubes suddenly amaze everyone.

Louie arrives at college for the big football game. He is a source of encouragement for the disheartened players. When the boys realize that abducted Sach won't be playing, Louie convinces the other boys to do their best on the playing field. (The football field was that of Los Angeles City College, where all of the film's outdoor scenes were shot. The college was conveniently located near Monogram Studios, about a half-mile away.)

There is a good special effect. After Dean Forrester drinks Slip's hastily made batch of Sach's vitamin, the dean shrinks to miniature size.

The film ends on a bang, thanks to an excellent job by director Beaudine in framing the closing gag. Sach announces that he has invented a new formula, and proceeds to drink it. The camera peers through an outside window into the lab. Sach jumps out the window and disappears from view, and all that the viewer sees are the open-mouthed expressions of the boys, as the soundtrack reveals a strange buzzing noise. Sach is flying!

Penny, Gloria Withers; *Mr. Billingsley,* Francis Pierlot; *Mr. Stanhope,* Pierre Watkin; *Professor Grog,* Byron Foulger; *Coach Rowland,* Paul Bryar; *Assistant coach,* Bob Peoples; *Football announcer,* Tom Hanlon; *Mike Donelli,* George Lewis; *Big Dave,* Al Eben; *Professor Wintz,* Ted Stanhope; *Professor Hovel,* Percival Vivian; *Murphy,* Tom Kennedy; *Police sergeant,* Bert Davidson; *Miss Whitsett,* Marjorie Eaton; *Girl student,* Jean Dean; *Boy student,* Steve Wayne; *First player,* Ted Jordan; *Second player,* George Sanders; *Girl,* Marvelle Andre.

*Misbilled as "David Bartlett" in credits.

HERE COME THE MARINES

Released June 29, 1952, by Monogram. Produced by Jerry Thomas. Directed by William Beaudine. Scenario by Tim Ryan, Charles R. Marion and Jack Crutcher. Photographed by Marcel Le Picard. Edited by William Austin. Art direction by Martin Obzina. Musical direction by Edward Kay. Production managed by Allan K. Wood. Assistant direction by Andrew McLaglen. Sound by Charles Cooper. Set continuity by Robert Priestley. Wardrobe by Frank Beetson. Script supervised by Ilona Vas. Production title: *Bowery Leathernecks.* British release title: *Tell It to the Marines.* 5924 ft. 66 minutes.

Terrence Aloysius "Slip" Mahoney, Leo Gorcey; *Horace Debussy "Sach/Hardhead" Jones, Jr.,* Huntz Hall; *Chuck,* David Condon; *Butch,* Bennie Bartlett; *Junior,* Gil Stratton, Jr.; *Louie Dumbrowski,* Bernard Gorcey; *Colonel Tom*

The boys face trouble when the Mata Hari of the film—Lulu Mae (Myrna Dell)—is discovered in their barracks. Sach, Butch, Slip, Junior (Gil Stratton, Jr.) and Chuck try to persuade her to leave.

Brown, Hanley Stafford; *Captain Miller,* Arthur Space; *Lulu Mae,* Myrna Dell; *Jolly Joe Johnson,* Paul Maxey; *Corporal Stacy,* Murray Alper; *Sheriff Benson,* Tim Ryan; *Major Desmond, CIA,* William Newell; *Captain Harlow, CIA,* Riley Hill; *Secretary,* Lisa Wilson; *Colonel Evans,* James Flavin; *Cook,* Robert Coogan; *Marine,* Leo "Ukie" Sherin; *Croupier,* Sammy Finn; *Dealer,* Buck Russell; *Doctor,* Stanley Blystone; *Marine,* Chad Mallory; *Sgt. Lane,* Perc Launders; *Corporal Mitchell,* Alan Jeffory; *Captain Graham,* Bob Cudlip; *Medic,* Bob Peoples; *Hoodlums,* William Vincent, Jack Wilson; *Salesman,* Dick Paxton; *Girl,* Barbara Grey; *Hoodlum,* Courtland Shepard; *Postman,* William Bailey; *Stickman,* Paul Bradley.

Slip is drafted into the Marines; and the other boys get their notices shortly thereafter. On his first day in camp, Sach impersonates a doctor and cooks a terrible soup in the camp kitchen. Colonel Brown is about to reprove Sach for this, but then he learns that Sach is the son of his old war buddy, and makes him a sergeant. Sach is put in charge of Slip, Butch, Chuck and Junior. While on drill, the boys find a dead Marine with a playing card near him; Slip pockets the card. The card is the same type used at Jolly Joe Johnson's gambling house. The boys investigate his club with two intelligence officers. Johnson suspects that the boys are wise to him, so he sends Lulu Mae to their barracks to get them into trouble. The boys discover her, and force her to let them into the gambling house at night. They find clues, but Johnson and his cronies find them snooping. They are in a tight spot, but the Marine intelligence officers, who haven't stopped watching the place, come to their rescue and arrest the murderers.

The problem with *Here Come the Marines* is its tone—or, rather, its monotone. It only has one mood. The problem is that Sach gets to play sergeant too much. It would have been a good one-time gag, but dragged out to the length of the picture, the idea gets thin and grating.

What's more, the film shows Sach getting ahead by being annoying. When he cooks a terrible soup—and it turns out to be a formula that will melt any known metal—he is promoted to "Sergeant Jones."

When he runs amuck in the boys' barracks with a dud missile—which turns out to be not a defective missile—he is cited for "heroism" and is promoted to "Staff Sergeant Jones."

When Sach camouflages a foxhole so well that his pal the colonel falls into it, Sach is promoted by that very same colonel to "Technical Sergeant Jones."

As Slip puts it, "If Sach can just figure out how to break a couple of the colonel's ribs, the colonel ought to make a captain out of him." That sums up our feelings for Sach.

Production values are abysmally low. The fight scene is two-and-a-half minutes long and is shown in three shots.

Gil Stratton, Jr. (appearing as Junior in his second and last Bowery Boys entry) tells how he got into the series:

"Jerry Thomas asked me how I'd like to be a Bowery Boy. I said, 'I wouldn't. Why?' 'Because you need the money, that's why.'

"I hid as much as I could. When a line came up that was my line, they'd ask, 'What are you going to do?' 'Give it to Leo or Huntz.' They loved it. I tried to be as invisible as possible."

FEUDIN' FOOLS

Released September 21, 1952, by Monogram. Produced by Jerry Thomas. Directed by William Beaudine. Scenario by Bert Lawrence and Tim Ryan. Photographed by Marcel Le Picard. Edited by William Austin. Art direction by David Milton. Musical direction by Edward Kay. Production supervised by Allan K. Wood. Sound by Charles Cooper. Special effects by Ray Mercer. *5631 ft. 63 minutes.*

Terrence Aloysius "Slip" Mahoney, Leo Gorcey; *Horace Debussy "Sach" Jones,* Huntz Hall; *Butch,* Bennie Bartlett; *Chuck,* David Condon; *Louie Dumbrowski,* Bernard Gorcey; *Ellie Mae Smith,* Anne Kimbell; *Tiny Smith,* Dorothy Ford; *Luke Smith,* Paul Wexler; *Clem Smith,* Oliver Blake; *Caleb Smith,* Bob Easton; *Yancy Smith,* O.Z. Whitehead; *Big Jim,* Lyle Talbot; *Pinky,* Leo "Ukie" Sherin; *Corky,* Benny Baker; *Grandpa Smith,* Russell Simpson; *Traps,* Fuzzy Knight; *Mr. Thompson,* Arthur Space; *Private detectives,* Bob Bray, Bob Keyes.

Sach inherits a farm in Hogliver Hollow, Kentucky, and the boys journey to it. On their first day in the country, the boys learn that they they have to use discretion in saying the name "Jones" because the neighboring Smiths are having a feud with the Joneses. The Smiths come in handy when bank robbers arrive at the Joneses' door asking for the dressing of wounds they suffered when the police shot at them. The boys address the robbers as "Jones" and the ever-ready Smiths shoot at them.

The potential here was slim at the start: A comedian or comedians just don't have much to do in a Country/Old South setting. It is a credit to the Bowery Boys that they carried it off better than Abbott and Costello did in their painful-to-watch *Comin' Round the Mountain,* released the same year.

The best moments are at Louie's, where the familiar elements add a homespun touch to the unwelcome story. After this, the film never regains what zest it had. There is a protracted dinner sequence gathering the Smiths and the Mahoney clan. Afterwards, Sach does some milking and chicken feeding for comic effect, but this scene, a highlight, would have been a throwaway scene in another film.

There is a technical joke at the end which is rather creative. Slip has remarked that in money matters he is "Mr. Jones," after which the Smiths take aim. Slip runs, but the Smiths still fire. Sach looks into the camera and says, "He got it right in—" The words "The End" are

Paul Wexler, Bob Easton, O.Z. Whitehead and Oliver Blake—as the feudin' Smiths—take aim, as Sach plugs his ears and Anne Kimbell and Dorothy Ford look on.

superimposed over his face. Sach nods to indicate that those words refer to where Slip got hit.

The film appears to have been made to test the hillbilly trade. (The "What the Motion Picture Did for Me" section of *The Motion Picture Herald*, in which theater owners sent in their opinions of films, indicate that the boys were immensely popular with rural folk.) When Louie arrives mid-picture, the Smiths confuse him for a "revenuer," catering to the ever-popular notion that hillbillies don't pay taxes on their moonshine whiskey sales.

NO HOLDS BARRED

Released November 23, 1952, by Monogram. Produced by Jerry Thomas. Directed by William Beaudine. Scenario by Tim Ryan, Jack Crutcher and Bert Lawrence. Photographed by Ernest Miller. Edited by William Austin. Art direction by David Milton. Musical direction by Edward Kay. Production supervised by Allan K. Wood. Assistant direction by Austen Jewell. Sound by Charles Cooper. Set decorations by Robert Priestley. Script supervised by Ilona Vas. Wardrobe by Frank Beetson. Special effects by Ray Mercer. 5888 *ft.* 65 *minutes.*

Terrence Aloysius "Slip" Mahoney, Leo Gorcey; *Horace Debussy "Sach/Hammerhead/Steel Fingers/Iron Elbow/Terrible Toes" Jones,* Huntz Hall; *Chuck,* David Condon; *Butch,* Bennie Bartlett; *Louie Dumbrowski,* Bernard Gorcey; *Pete Taylor,* Leonard Penn; *Rhonda Nelson,* Marjorie Reynolds; *Himself,* Hombre Montana; *Mike the Mauler,* Henry Kulky; *Barney,* Murray Alper; *Gertie Smith,* Barbara Grey; *Betty,* Lisa Wilson; *Stickup man,* Nick Stewart; *Himself,* Ted Christy; *Challenger (himself),* Pat Fraley; *Himself,* "Brother" Frank Jares; *Sam,* Leo "Ukie" Sherin; *Referee*

Benny Baker, Sach, Leo "Ukie" Sherin, Slip and Louie prepare for an operation on Lyle Talbot.

121

"Your hat, sir?"
"Coitenly it's his hat."

Henry Kulky, David, Huntz, Bennie, Leo.

(himself), John Indrisano; Himself, Count John Maximillian Smith; Referee (himself), Mike Ruby; Mr. Hunter, Tim Ryan; Mildred, Sandra Gould; First mug, Bob Cudlip; Second mug, Mort Mills; Max, Ray Walker; Pete, Bill Page; Dr. Howard, George Eldredge; Arena messenger, Meyer Grace; Announcer, Jimmy Cross.

Sach's cranium hardens bizarrely so that it can withstand any pain. Slip enters him in a wrestling match and hires a trainer. Before the match, Sach's condition subsides, but the power moves to his fingers. From then on, Sach's powers move to a different part of his body before each match and he wins effortlessly. Taylor, the manager of one of Sach's opponents (Hombre Montana), tries to get a rematch, but Slip makes unreasonable demands. Taylor has Sach's next opponent injured, and offers his client as a substitute; the boys reluctantly accept. Taylor, to find out where Sach's powers are, has the boys kidnapped by some cronies, but none of them can find any phenomenal powers in Sach. The boys escape to the ring, where Sach takes a beating before defeating Montana with the power in his derriére.

No Holds Barred is a pure fantasy film. Unlike films such as *Francis* (1949), which start with a fantasy premise and then play the situations as they would really evolve, *No Holds Barred* is fantasy in every respect. Even in the ring, things happen that would never happen in real life.

Throughout, the film re-presents the improbable thesis that Sach's powers can change place before each bout, without fail. And each time Slip is battered when Sach finds the new spot. Slip is always on the receiving end when Sach finds his powers by flexing his elbows, flicking his fingers, stretching his legs. In the last scene, the film breaks the boundary between film and theater auditorium. Sach's new powers are in a place that can't be mentioned on film. Trying to come up with a nickname comparable to "Iron Elbow," "Terrible Toes" and "Steel Finger," Slip is about to suggest a new name several times, only to be vetoed by Sach before he emits a syllable. Finally, Sach says, "You say it and we're out of pictures."

JALOPY

Released February 15, 1953, by Allied Artists. Produced by Ben Schwalb. Directed by William Beaudine. Screenplay by Tim Ryan, Jack Crutcher and Edmond Seward, Jr. Additional dialogue by Bert Lawrence. Story by Tim Ryan and Jack Crutcher. Photographed by Harry Neumann. Edited by William Austin. Art direction by David Milton. Musical direction by Marlin Skiles. Production supervised by Allan K. Wood. Assistant direction by Austen Jewell. Sound by Charles Cooper. Set decorations by Robert Priestley. Script supervised by Ilona Vas. Wardrobe by Frank Beetson. *5558 ft. 62 minutes.*

Terrence Aloysius "Slip" Mahoney, Leo Gorcey; *Horace Debussy "Sach" Jones,* Huntz Hall; *Chuck,* David Condon; *Butch,* Bennie Bartlett; *Louie Dumbrowski,* Bernard Gorcey; *Skid Wilson,* Robert Lowery*; *Bobbie Lane,* Jane Easton; *Prof. Bosgood Elrod,* Leon Belasco; *Tony Lango,* Richard Benedict; *Red Baker,* Murray Alper; *Race announcer,* Tom Hanlon; *"Invented" girl,* Mona Knox; *Party guest,* Conrad Brooks; *Jalopy drivers,* Robert Rose, George Dockstader, George Barrows, Fred Lamont, Teddy Mangean, Bud Wolfe, Carey Loftin, Louis Tomei, Dude Criswell, Dick Crockett, Pete Kellett, Carl Saxe.

*Billed "Bob Lowry" in credits.

Slip enters the Bowery Boys' car in an auto race hoping to net enough money so that Louie can pay his bills, but he comes in last. A new fuel formula developed by Sach is his answer. The boys test it at the track, and it makes the car go around the lap in eleven seconds. Gambler Skid Wilson tries to get the formula but to no avail. A batch that Sach creates before the big race turns out defective, so Slip must start racing before Sach has arrived with a good batch. Sach arrives during the race, and puts the formula into the car, but the new batch causes the car to go backwards. Slip changes direction, and goes on to win, driving backwards.

Jalopy was a turning point in the series. The influence of Ben Schwalb, who took over as producer on this film, is easy to see. The gangster characters are now played for buffoons, and so are the boys. Schwalb elected to instill into the series a purer form of comedy, as he felt that a policy of piling laughs upon laughs would create comedies that were made as they were supposed to be made.

It was a smart move on his part to transform the Bowery Boys into buffoons, as they were obviously getting older, and audiences might tire of grown men who appeared to be retreating into adolescence. Turning the lead characters into mistake-prone ones also increased their appeal to children, who might be more appreciative than their elders of men in their thirties who acted like children.

The changes were prompted by Leo and Huntz. "The

Jalopy, *like all of the Bowery Boys films, was a Gorcey family get-together: Bernard, Leo and David are in the forefront. The family resemblance is apparent in this still.*

Gorcey, Jane Easton, Hall.

boys wanted a change from the directors they had been using," recalls assistant director Austen Jewell. "They felt that maybe someone new directing could bring some fresh ideas, new ways of doing the same kind of comedy they had been doing for years."

Whatever the reason, audiences didn't appreciate this initial entry under the new policy. *Consumer Reports* magazine indicates that public opinion of *Jalopy* was "poor to fair," a condemnation bestowed on few of their pictures.

Under the new policy, the plot isn't *divorced from* the comedy, but *works with* the comedy. The business of Sach standing on the running board while the car is in motion, pouring into the tank the stuff that will make the car go backwards, is *both* funny *and* part of the plot.

An old comedy staple, the running gag, is worked well into the film. Early in the film, Sach's scientific activity sets off an explosion. Chemical fumes cloud the sweetshop doorway. When they clear, Skid's girlfriend Bobbie is standing in Louie's doorway. The boys think Sach has invented her. The idea is repeated in the middle of the picture. Yet another variation of the idea is presented in the moments before fade-out, when Slip, Sach and Sach's professor friend deliberately spill Sach's "girl" formula onto Louie's floor as so to create dates for themselves. All three men leave with their "inventions," and the bottle is left with Louie. Louie tries it, but it doesn't work for him.

Not many viewers have the patience to watch a thirty-lap race presented in the time that it takes to go thirty laps, yet this is how the film treats its races. The second race is about a quarter-hour long, and is comprised of scenes of Slip and Sach shot against back-screen projection, and of leftover shots from *The Roar of the Crowd*, released by Allied Artists in Technicolor that same year. *The Roar of the Crowd* and *Jalopy* both used Ascot Raceway in Gardena, Ca., for background, had Tom Hanlon as the announcer, and were directed by William Beaudine.

LOOSE IN LONDON

Released May 24, 1953, by Allied Artists. Produced by Ben Schwalb. Directed by Edward Bernds. Scenario by Elwood Ullman and Edward Bernds. Photographed by Harry Neumann. Edited by John C. Fuller. Art direction by David Milton. Musical direction by Marlin Skiles. Assistant direction by Austen Jewell. Sound by Charles Cooper. Production supervised by Allan K. Wood. Editing supervised by Lester A. Sansom. Makeup by Eddie Polo. Set decorations by Charles Steenson. Script supervised by Ilona Vas. Special effects by Ray Mercer. Production title: *Bowery Knights*. 5616 ft. 62.5 minutes.

Terrence Aloysius "Slip" Mahoney, Leo Gorcey; *Horace Debussy "Sach" Jones*, Huntz Hall; *Chuck Anderson*, David Condon; *Butch Williams*, Bennie Bartlett; *Louie Dumbrowski*, Bernard Gorcey; *Sir Percy, Earl of Walsingham*, Walter Kingsford; *Sir Edgar Whipsnade*, Walter Kingsford; *Aunt Agatha*, Norma Varden; *Lady Marcia*, Angela Greene; *Reggie*, William Cottrell; *Herbert*, Rex Evans; *Hoskins, butler*, James Logan; *J. Allison Higby, solicitor*, Alex Fraser; *Taxi driver*, Clyde Cook; *Tall girl*, Joan Shawlee; *Steward*, James Fairfax; *Sir Talbot Edgecomb*, Wilbur Mack; *Bly*, Charles Keane; *Skinny man*, Teddy Mangean; *Lady Hightower*, Gertrude Astor; *Ames*, Matthew Boulton; *Pierre*, Charles Wagenheim.

Lawyers determine that Sach is a relative of a dying British earl, Sir Percy. He is given a first-class ticket on a steamship to Britain, which the boys exchange for four modest-class tickets. Louie accidentally passes out on liquor in their stateroom closet, so he goes with them too. On their first day in England, the boys earn the scorn of the other members of the family when Sach convinces the Earl that he should consume ice cream instead of his prescriptions. The relatives, who had tampered with the earl's medicine and are now worried about his health improving, plot to kill the earl. The boys expose the plot and the scheming heirs. Sir Percy decides to make Sach his principal heir, but a moment before he signs the papers, a messenger arrives to inform them that Sach and Sir Percy aren't related.

Loose in London is a very funny film, offering slapstick, puns, slapstick, outrageous situations, plus more slapstick. It's easy to understand why there was so much slapstick; not only were there two skilled comedy writers at the helm (one of whom directed), there was the society setting, which was an ideal one for "the puncturing of dignity" (which is how slapstick was defined by Mack Sennett). We are never let down. At one point where the film fades to a droll art auction, we feel that we have been betrayed. But shortly thereafter the film catches us by surprise when Slip unintentionally tears off a girl's skirt! Decorum doesn't remain intact long.

Loose in London has many of the elements which were soon to become standards in the series. In the opening scene, a lawyer comes to Louie's Sweetshop looking for Sach after discovering his lineage. This was soon to become the standard way of getting plots started. Sight gags abound: Sach getting mad at a stuffed, trophied fox, who comes to life and bites his nose; Sach munching on a monocle that he has mistaken for a cracker.

No one connected with *Loose in London* wanted audiences to notice undue similarities between it and *Boys of the City*, both of which have a dungeon scene. *Boys of the City* was now in full view of the public, as the Eastside Kids films had just been released to television. In the Los Angeles area they played in prime time Sunday evenings, 6:30 to 7:30 p.m.

This was Ben Schwalb's second Bowery Boys film as producer, although he was backed up by 30 years' experience in motion pictures. He recalls, "I was with the

Louie, Sach and Slip surround Sir Percy (Walter Kingsford), as the evil plotters—Rex Evans, James Logan, John Dodsworth, Angela Greene and William Cottrell—lurk in the background.

company and I was a producer, so of course they had to consider me. It was a lucrative assignment; they assigned it to me. Very simple."

He knew that Jan Grippo had been the producer and had given it up. "I guess he had made enough money, and they were not easy pictures to make. Leo and Huntz were difficult, and finally his [Grippo's] wife died, and he decided to give it up."

Edward Bernds, for whom *Loose in London* marked his first Bowery Boys film (he wrote and directed), echoes Schwalb's memories of working with Gorcey and Hall. He recalls that when it was announced that he would be their new director, the publicity man asked him, "Are you going to direct it or referee it?" He further explains:

"The last day of every picture was always an ordeal. Huntz and Leo were their most obnoxious and obstructive the last day; it's as if they knew they were going to be finished anyway, that they wouldn't be blamed for going overschedule if they loused something up at the beginning or middle of a picture. So the last day was always tough. On *Loose in London*, we had what should have been an easy

Gorcey, Hall, Rex Evans.

last day, but the boys refused to buckle down and loused up rehearsals. I never hit an actor in my life, but I think I came pretty close that day. But Ben Schwalb calmed me down, he said it always happened, that I should keep my cool, that we'd finish the picture somehow. We did, but it took ten tough hours to finish what should have taken seven or eight easy hours' work."

Assistant director Austen Jewell admits that there were delays, but has a different perspective. "The reason why there were delays in the schedule is that they were in their way professionals. You'd always feel it could be done better, or that a scene wasn't as funny as the last, so a real effort was made to eject everything they possibly could, to go-round the stock of ideas that had no relation to the story. So the schedule fouled up, and on the last day of shooting you had to do—not eight or ten pages—but seventeen pages."

It was Schwalb who decided to commission Bernds, as well as Bernds' frequent co-writer, Elwood Ullman. "I think the three of us were a very successful team," Schwalb says. The next films bear him out.

Production sidelight: *Loose in London* was originally planned in 1950 for release in Summer 1951, although the title then was *Knights of the Square Table.* Coincidentally, Edward Bernds had directed a Three Stooges short called *Squareheads of the Round Table* while at Columbia in 1948.

CLIPPED WINGS

Released August 14, 1953, by Allied Artists. Produced by Ben Schwalb. Directed by Edward Bernds. Screenplay by Charles R. Marion and Elwood Ullman. Story by Charles R. Marion. Photographed by Harry Neumann. Edited by Bruce B. Pierce. Art direction by David Milton. Musical direction by Marlin Skiles. Production managed by Allan K. Wood. Assistant direction by Richard Mayberry. Editing supervised by Lester A. Sansom. Sound by Frank McWhorter. Wardrobe by Smoke Kring. Set dressings by Bob Priestley. Dialogue direction by Tim Ryan. Makeup by Norman Pringle. Script supervised by Ilona Vas. Special effects by Ray Mercer. *5781 ft. 65 minutes.*

Terrence Aloysius "Slip" Mahoney, Leo Gorcey; *Horace Debussy "Sach" Jones,* Huntz Hall; *Chuck,* David Condon; *Butch,* Bennie Bartlett; *Louie Dumbrowski,* Bernard Gorcey; *Lt. Dave Moreno,* Todd Karns; *Dorene Thompson,* June Vincent; *Colonel Davenport,* Fay Roope; *Eckler,* Philip Van Zandt; *Sgt. Anderson,* Renie Riano; *Mildred,* Mary Treen; *Cralia Dupree,* Frank Richards; *Anders,* Michael Ross; *Sgt. Riley,* Elaine Riley; *Hilda,* Jeanne Dean; *Allison,* Anne Kimbell; *Sgt. Broski,* Henry Kulky; *Colonel Blair,* Lyle Talbot; *Sgt. Whitney,* Ray Walker; *Federal man,* Arthur Space; *AP,* Lou Nova; *Rookie watching Slip mop,* Conrad Brooks.

Slip and Sach go to Air Force headquarters to find out why their friend Dave Moreno has been held for treason. Mistaking directions to the visitors ward, they go to the enlistment office and unwittingly join up. Because a female cadet is named H. Jones, Sach is assigned to the WAF barracks. The boys manage to see Dave, but he tells them that he doesn't want help, not disclosing that he is being used to bait spies. Slip and Sach do some investigating, but must make a hasty retreat in an airplane when chased. Sach flies them miles away, and by sheer good fortune lands them at the spies' hideout. They rout the agents.

Clipped Wings is the Bowery Boys at their funniest. Leo and Huntz are the prime focus; the other boys disappear for 20 minutes at a time. This is not in itself unusual. What is unusual is that Slip and Sach are separated. They are assigned to different barracks, and face their first days in camp without the other. The material is good, so the characters survive the experiment.

Slip's character is redefined in *Clipped Wings.* At the same time, his relationship with Sach changes. This new relationship is probed in the film. In the opening scene, Slip is the same Slip we've always known. He yells at Sach for taking correspondence flying lessons, and then wisely—acting as if he has more experience—tells Sach that with the course "You'll get your wings, but after your first flight those wings will be sprouting from your shoulder blades."

Yet, a few scenes later when the boys are taking their Air Force admittance tests, Slip tries to pound square pegs into round holes, just as Sach does. They are both morons!

However, Leo Gorcey was a highly skilled comedian, and is delightful as a buffoon.

The airplane sequence shows that Sach's mail-order flight lessons weren't too helpful. The airplane gets out of control, and tension mounts inside the cockpit. Sach opens his flying handbook and finds a chapter entitled "How to Face Death in the Air." Slip asks that he turn the page. Sach turns page after page, but the title of each chapter is "How to Face Death in the Air." Slip asks, "Who wrote that book? An undertaker?" As Sach learns, the last chapter is entitled, "Now That You're Dead."

The boys' mature friend is named Dave Moreno, whose last name is the same as Gabe Moreno, played in earlier years by Gabriel Dell. In the two-and-a-half years since Dell left the series, this was the first role to be written for which he would have been ideally cast. Dell says today that he wanted to leave the series earlier, but "I had nowhere else to go." Huntz says, "I don't blame him for leaving. Leo and I were getting the whole deal." This is especially borne out in *Clipped Wings.*

Slip covers Sach's mouth, lest he tell Lou Nova what Slip had been thinking.

Director Edward Bernds, Leo, Huntz. Leo and Huntz are dressed as Dr. Hockenlopper and Mrs. Abernathy.

PRIVATE EYES

Released December 6, 1953, by Allied Artists. Produced by Ben Schwalb. Directed by Edward Bernds. Scenario by Elwood Ullman and Edward Bernds. Photographed by Carl Gutherie. Edited by Lester A. Sansom. Art direction by David Milton. Musical direction by Marlin Skiles. Production managed by Allan K. Wood. Sound by Charles Cooper. Set decorations by Charles Steenson. Assistant direction by Austen Jewell. Continuity by Ted Schlitz. Wardrobe by Smoke Kring. Makeup by Norman Pringle. Production title: *Bowery Bloodhounds. 5801 ft. 64 minutes.*

Terrence Aloysius "Slip" Mahoney, Leo Gorcey; *Horace Debussy "Sach" Jones,* Huntz Hall; *Chuck,* David Condon; *Butch,* Bennie Bartlett; *Louie Dumbrowski,* Bernard Gorcey; *Herbie,* Rudy Lee; *Myra Hagen,* Joyce Holden; *Professor Damon,* Robert Osterloh; *John Graham,* William Forrest; *Chico,* Peter Mamakos; *Karl,* Myron Healey; *Andy, cop,* Tim Ryan; *Oskar,* Lou Lubin; *Wheelchair patient,* Emil Sitka; *Soapy,* William Phillips; *Al,* Gil Perkins; *Aggie, nurse,* Edith Leslie; *Eddie the Detective,* Chick Chandler; *Bit,* Lee Van Cleef.

After being punched in the nose by juvenile pal Herbie, Sach acquires mind-reading ability. Slip puts this peculiarity to work by opening the Eagle Eye Detective Agency. Their first client is a beautiful blonde, Myra, who is trying to sever her underworld relations with a mink-coat ring, and leaves the boys an envelope which would expose the gang if the contents were revealed to the authorities. The mob attempts to retrieve the envelope, but Sach has locked it in the safe and has lost the combination. Having abducted young Herbie, the gangsters are able to blackmail Slip and Sach while Herbie and Myra are held hostage in a sanitarium. Learning of the location, Slip and Sach don disguises and infiltrate the hideout, rout the mob, and expose an insurance man who had pretended to help them.

Private Eyes is the fastest-paced entry in the Bowery Boys series and one of the funniest. Transcending its meager budget, the film is consistently brisk and does not let up for a moment, allowing Gorcey and Hall to romp freely. Much of the credit must be given to director Edward Bernds, who lets the boys perform without too much plot interference.

In the office of the Eagle Eye Detective Agency, the boys begin to play with atmosphere. Sach predicts that—in the tradition of Robert Mitchum and Humphrey Bogart movies—a beautiful blonde will enter the room. Of course, Myra appears through the door a split-second later.

The manila envelope she leaves behind furnishes the groundwork for another gag that explores Sach's thought processes. He places the papers in a safe, and then asks Slip where he should put the combination. Slip tells him to set it in a "safe place." With Sach's logic, that means putting it in the safe, regardless that he will be unable to open it afterward.

The film picks up speed during the sanitarium scene. Slip dons a disguise as myopic Viennese physician "Dr. Hockenlopper," borrowing from bearded character actor Sig Ruman. Sach puts on convincing drag as rich, old "Mrs. Abernathy." When their ruse is discovered, the boys are forced to elude their assailants through the sanitarium halls, with many amusing escapades along the way. Finally, they lure each member of the ring into a huge mineral bath.

It is during this sequence that *Private Eyes* attains the atmosphere of a Columbia two-reeler, particularly those starring the short-subject department breadwinners, the Three Stooges. Director Bernds and writer Elwood Ullman, both of whom worked for the Stooges, contribute to the result. Ullman also wrote for Buster Keaton, Charley Chase, Andy Clyde, Abbott and Costello, and Martin and Lewis.

Present in the cast is Emil Sitka, fall guy in dozens of Three Stooges comedies, here cast as a wheelchair-bound patient who is continually knocked out of his chair by the chasing procession. This role was based on one in a Stooges short, *Monkey Businessmen* (1946), in which former silent-comedian Snub Pollard had the part.

Although Bernds found Gorcey and Hall very unco-operative at times, he allowed them some say in the material they performed. "They didn't improvise or ad-lib during a scene," says Bernds. "That's amateur stuff."

"But," continues Bernds, "The boys would hash a scene over in discussion or rehearsal, making changes or objections to dialogue, and things like that. I tried to be patient, even if they threw out pet lines I had written. They had been Dead End Kids, Eastside Kids and Bowery Boys for a long time and they knew their characters well. And

Desk-bound and liking it!

sometimes I had to admit that their stuff was better than mine, and unless I felt it downright bad for the picture, I tried to be reasonable and flexible. When I did put my foot down, they usually backed off. I never had a really serious mutiny with them, although after one picture Huntz said he would never work with me again." He did, however.

PARIS PLAYBOYS

Released March 7, 1954, by Allied Artists. Produced by Ben Schwalb. Directed by William Beaudine. Scenario by Elwood Ullman and Edward Bernds. Photographed by Harry Neumann. Edited by John C. Fuller. Editing supervised by Lester A. Sansom. Art direction by David Milton. Musical direction by Marlin Skiles. Production managed by Allan K. Wood. Assistant direction by Edward Morey, Jr. Sound by Ray Mercer. Set decorations by Robert Priestley. Wardrobe by Smoke Kring. Set continuity by John Franco. *5602 ft. 65 minutes.*

Terrence Aloysius "Slip" Mahoney, Leo Gorcey; *Horace Debussy "Sach" Jones,* Huntz Hall; *Prof. Maurice Gaston Le Beau,* Huntz Hall; *Chuck,* David Condon; *Butch,* Bennie Bartlett; *Louie Dumbrowski,* Bernard Gorcey; *Mimi Du-Boise,* Veola Vonn; *Gaspard,* Steven Geray; *Vidal,* John E. Wengraf; *Marcel,* Fritz Feld; *Celeste,* Marianne Lynn; *Pierre,* Alphonse Martell; *Cambon,* Gordon Clark.

French professors mistake Sach for a French scientist. After the mistake is cleared up, the professors, amazed at Sach's resemblance to the missing Professor Le Beau, send Slip and Sach to Paris; Louie goes too. The professors have Sach impersonate Le Beau, and hope his presence will bring the real professor out of hiding. As it turns out, Le Beau returns, just at a time when Sach has perfected a rocket formula. Spies try to steal it, but Le Beau, Sach and Slip

Slip reads to John E. Wengraf and Steven Gerey a formula Sach will mix up. "And top the whole thing off with Routine 11."

A nocturnal sequence in which Sach's life is threatened is reworked from a scene in Loose in London.

rout them. Sach is honored for inventing the chemical solution that Le Beau had worked on for years.

Paris Playboys is a labored non-comedy. Shot on a set that looks like the one used for *Loose in London*, and resembling that picture in other ways, it is no more than a dull procession of misunderstandings.

Once Slip, Sach and Louie make it to France, mechanical gags take over. Slip's tie twirls, Sach's lips motorize, and Louie's ears emit steam when the three consume "Le Beau's regular," a cocktail that the waiter at the sidewalk cafe prefers to serve only to "the professor." At Le Beau's residence, a grooming session ends with Louie sliding on his stomach directly to the camera. This jest, which might have been funny, doesn't work because there aren't nuances that build to it.

Chuck and Butch are out of the picture once America is left behind. Edward Bernds explains from the writer's side: "David Gorcey and Bennie Bartlett were excess baggage and they knew it. I tried to give the boys things to do, but it just didn't work. They were there, I suppose, as symbols of the big gang Leo had in the Eastside Kids pictures. Bernard Gorcey was a different matter. He was a feisty little man who really wanted good lines and good scenes. He'd ask Ben Schwalb, Elwood [Ullman] or me to write more of him into the scripts, and we'd try to do it. Leo Gorcey wasn't very kind to his father. He'd say, 'Pop, don't chew up the scenery.' On a couple of occasions I'd tell Leo, 'I'll tell him when. He's doing fine.' Dave and Bennie were patient, did their work. Leo and Huntz would rib them, make cracks about their excess baggage roles."

THE BOWERY BOYS MEET THE MONSTERS

Released June 6, 1954, by Allied Artists. Produced by Ben Schwalb. Directed by Edward Bernds. Scenario by Elwood Ullman and Edward Bernds. Photographed by Harry Neumann. Edited by William Austin. Art direction by David Milton. Musical direction by Marlin Skiles. Production supervised by Allan K. Wood. Assistant direction by Edward Morey, Jr. Sound by Ralph Butler. Special effects by Augie Lohman. Set decorations by Joseph Kish. Hair-dressings by Mary Smith. Wardrobe by Bert Henrickson. Set continuity by John L. Banse. *5882 ft. 65.5 minutes.*

Terrence Aloysius "Slip" Mahoney, Leo Gorcey; *Horace Debussy "Sach" Jones,* Huntz Hall; *Chuck,* David Condon; *Butch,* Bennie Bartlett; *Louie Dumbrowski,* Bernard Gorcey; *Dr. Derek Gravesend,* John Dehner; *Anton Gravesend,* Lloyd Corrigan; *Grissom, butler,* Paul Wexler; *Amelia Gravesend,* Ellen Corby; *Francine Gravesend,* Laura Mason; *Gorog, robot,* Norman Bishop; *Cosmos, gorilla,* Steve Calvert; *Herbie Wilkins,* Rudy Lee; *Officer Martin,* Paul Bryar; *Officer O'Meara,* Pat Flaherty; *Skippy Biano,* Jack Diamond.

Slip and Sach think a vacant lot would be an ideal baseball field for the local kids. It is owned by the Gravesends, a family of mad scientists. Slip and Sach visit them and are detained by the Gravesends, who want the pair for their experiments. When the boys don't return to Louie's, Louie, Butch and Chuck go to the Gravesend house, but are captured. Sach is strapped to an operating table so that his brain can be transferred to a gorilla or a robot, depending on which Gravesend—Derek or Anton—gets his way. Slip is sought by Anton as a back-up "brain donor" for his robot, and by Amelia, who wants to feed him to her man-eating plant. Francine, a vampiress, wants Sach. Slip discovers that the robot will follow his orders, and instructs it to subdue its masters. Slip then frees Sach, Louie and the boys.

The Bowery Boys Meet the Monsters has a funny script and the best supporting cast in the series' history. It is replete with puns, horror house clichés and talent.

The supporting actors were of such calibre that they motivated Gorcey and Hal to give better, more enthusiastic performances. "When the boys worked with real pro actors," recalls director Edward Bernds, "they performed like pros. The scenes with that goony family went like clockwork. The boys had to keep up with some very good people, and they did; they were good and they behaved themselves."

When Slip and Sach first meet the Gravesend clan, Sach observes:

"It's raining cats and dogs out there."
"Isn't that nice," Amelia answers. "I just
love cats and dogs."

The Gravesends offer Sach a pickle, and he offers his suggestion for making pickles prettier. "When you plant the seeds, turn the skin inside out, so that instead of having warts, they'll have dimples." The mad scientists then know that they have the perfect subject for their experiments.

One scene, which occurs before the boys arrive at the house, shows the scientists at their diabolical pinnacle. Derek has determined that the ideal brain for his gorilla, "and the one that will most snugly fit into his cranial cavity," is one with a brain potential "between plus five and plus seven." Anton (Lloyd Corrigan, Edgar of *Ghost Chasers*), always skeptical of anything his brother does, declares, "A creature with a brain that small wouldn't have sense enough to come out of the rain." Cut then to Slip and Sach in front of the house, Sach standing in the rain!

The scientists' sister, the woman who made the comments about liking cats and dogs, is Amelia (Ellen Corby, an Oscar nominee for 1948's *I Remember Mama,* winner of an Emmy for her Grandma Walton role in television's "The Waltons"). She is very funny when she slyly tries to garnish Slip for her "pet," the man-eating plant. When she holds Louie at gunpoint, she says, "It would be a pity to shoot you Mr. Dumbrowski. You're under the legal size."

There is yet another Gravesend: Francine. A vampiress, her first line is, "Young men coming, how interesting." When the brothers decide to use Slip and Sach for their experiments, she says, "It's no fair. Why should they have them both?" Her fangs only show when she tries to seduce Sach. Sach, who has just been untied from the operating

Laura Mason, Gorcey, Hall.

No, it's not Bela or Boris. It's Sach.

table by Francine, tells her that he'd like to do something for her sometime. "You will," she says softly, "sooner than you think." Sach does his motor-lips.

Gorcey's malaprops reached their highest mark in this film. In a telephone conversation with Derek, he says:

"Hello . . . I have a little matter I would like to disgust [discuss] with you. It refrains [pertains] to some kids here in the Bowery. You see, I'm what you might call a benfracturer [benefactor] of humanity, and being that this matter is highly contagious [comprehensive] I'd like it if me and my accomplice [colleague], Mr. Jones, could come out tonight and prevaricate [prevail] about it in person. But tell me, are you going to coagulate [cooperate] with us, or ain't you?"

The *Motion Picture Herald* review of this film is interesting, as it contains perceptive observations on what allows a series to continue. The reviewer pointed out that a single episode may seem more enjoyable than it is, because the enjoyment is partially based on pleasant memories of previous films, and that these memories cushion jolting elements. It's possible that the reviewer wrote his panning review merely to express these views. He started it thus: "The safeguards that build around a series of pictures—the audience's favorable disposition towards it, the readiness to forgive a letdown in any quarter, the cushioning reservoir of pleasant memories—are subject to quite a strain in this item in the longest running series now making the round."

Such reviews didn't hurt business for *The Bowery Boys Meet the Monsters.* With a title that suggested that it was a send-up of the Abbot and Costello "Meet" pictures, *The Bowery Boys Meet the Monsters* was the series' highest gross, according to Ben Schwalb. Edward Bernds attributes this to the title (a descriptive title) and the concept.

Both Anton (Lloyd Corrigan, left) and Derek (John Dehner, right) want Sach's brain. Butler Grissom has a suggestion: "50-50."

JUNGLE GENTS

Released September 5, 1954, by Allied Artists. Produced by Ben Schwalb. Directed by Edward Bernds. Scenario by Elwood Ullman and Edward Bernds. Photographed by Harry Neumann. Edited by Sam Fields. Art direction by David Milton. Musical direction by Marlin Skiles. Production supervised by Allan K. Wood. Assistant direction by Austen Jewell. Sound by Ralph Butler. Editing supervised by Lester A. Sansom. Set continuity by John Banse. Hairdressings by Maudlee MacDougall. Makeup by Eddie Polo. Wardrobe by Bert Henrickson. Special effects by Augie Lohman. *5673 ft. 64 minutes.*

Terrence Aloysius "Slip" Mahoney, Leo Gorcey; *Horace Debussy "Sach" Jones,* Huntz Hall; *Chuck,* David Condon; *Butch,* Bennie Bartlett; *Louie Dumbrowski,* Bernard Gorcey; *Grimshaw,* Patrick O'Moore; *Dr. Goebel,* Rudolph Anders; *Anatta,* Laurette Luez; *Dan Shanks,* Harry Cording; *Trader Holmes,* Eric Snowden; *Malaka,* Woody Strode; *Rangori, witch doctor,* Joel Fluellen; *Fats Lomax,* Murray Alper; *Captain Daly,* Emory Parnell; *Tarzan type,* Jett Norman (Clint Walker); *Painter on boat,* Emil Sitka; *Omotawa,* Roy Glenn, Sr.; *Harmes,* John Harmon; *Officer Cady,* Pat Flaherty.

The boys go to Africa, where diamonds are smelled out by Sach (whose sinus medication heightens this sense). With the other boys, he exposes a fake spirit scaring the natives.

Shot indoors on what were once "Bomba, the Jungle Boy" sets, *Jungle Gents* suffers from being forced, and from confining the Bowery Boys to cramped surroundings with limited possibilities. The first part is funny, filled with gags and inspiration, but at the half-time mark, the boys are made captive—and so are the laughs. An enormous quantity of time is wasted while Sach tries to catch a cold (so that the natives will release the boys, as he is no good to the natives with a congested snoz), dresses as a witchdoctor, and tries to remember which words will make the tribesmen bend down once he has supplanted the witchdoctor.

The film contains what possibly ranks as the worst scene in the series: Sach's attempted suicide.

The implication that Sach would consider suicide betrays our notions of him. Sach lives too much within himself to want to do such a self-destructive thing. Furthermore, *Jungle Gents* has it that Sach wants to commit suicide because the *others* are angry with him for accidentally burning their map. This is certainly not the Sach we've known.

The real Sach is the one who glides through the opening scene with wisecracks. He chastises Louie when Louie's store is visited by the police, cracking, "I told you not to sell root beer floats to minors!" When he searches for the diamonds, he puts a woman's hand to his nose, smells her ring, then snubs the man she's with for giving her a ring made of glass!

Sach isn't the only one who looks dumb. Slip, Louie, their tour guide and their safari crew also have some explaining to do: why do they hack through a trail of brush when there are open fields within feet of them? Every time the safari stops to pause and look at the animals, the animals are roaming on open land. (The answer to the question is that the shots of the boys hacking through the brush were made in Hollywood, and no one bothered to ask whether they would make sense when intercut with the animal shots filmed in Africa.)

Africa was an inappropriate setting for comedians whose stock-in-trade was interacting with people and belittling them. There *are* some funny moments, however. On the trail, Slip says, "There ain't a hostile native within five hundred miles of here." A bamboo spear instantly harpoons a tree. "Someone just broke the world record," observes Sach . . . . In an exchange explaining years of banter, Slip asks Sach, "Why do you ask me those stupid questions?" "So I can hear your stupid answers," Sach remarks.

Life *magazine pin-up girl Lauretta Luez speaks her one line of (dicernible) dialogue: "Kiss. Kiss. Kiss."*

BOWERY TO BAGDAD

Released January 2, 1955, by Allied Artists (Released October 1954, in Britain). Produced by Ben Schwalb. Directed by Edward Bernds. Scenario by Elwood Ullman and Edward Bernds. Photographed by Harry Neumann. Edited by John C. Fuller. Editing supervised by Lester A. Sansom. Art direction by David Milton. Musical direction by Marlin Skiles. Production managed by Allan K. Wood. Assistant direction by Edward Morey, Jr. Sound by Ralph Butler. Set decorations by Joseph Kish. Special effects by Augie Lohman. Wardrobe by Bert Henrickson. Makeup by Eddie Polo. Hairdressings by Mary Smith. Released in 1.85:1 (scope) aspect ratio. *64 minutes.*

Terrence Aloysius "Slip" Mahoney, Leo Gorcey; *Horace Debussy "Sach" Jones,* Huntz Hall; *Chuck,* David Condon; *Butch,* Bennie Bartlett; *Louie Dumbrowski,* Bernard Gorcey; *Velma (alias Cindy Lou Calhoun),* Joan Shawlee; *Genie,* Eric Blore; *Duke Dolan,* Robert Bice; *Gus,* Richard Wessel; *Canarsie,* Rayford Barnes; *Tiny,* Michael Ross; *Selim,* Rick Vallin; *Abdul,* Paul Marion; *Claire,* Jean Willes; *Caliph,* Charlie Lung; *Man,* Leon Burbank.

The story of Aladdin's Lamp begins in the Dark Ages, when the magic lamp belonging to the Caliph of Baghdad is stolen. Its history is a long one, leading to . . . New York of the present day, where Sach buys it. Underworld figures see the boys using it, and snatch it. They discover that the genie won't grant them wishes without the approval of Slip and Sach. The gangsters send out girls to lure the twosome to the gangsters' penthouse. The boys flee from the gangsters, and get away from them with the help of the genie. However, when the genie blinks them to Baghdad to get them to safety, the boys are confronted by the Caliph of Baghdad, who claims possession of the lamp. Slip and Sach are returned to New York without a genie.

Bowery to Bagdad has more scenes taking place in the sweetshop than usual for films of this period. In one that is an excellent sample of the boys' comedy, Slip asks for a cup of coffee. Sach is willing to oblige, handing Slip a mug of dark liquid. Slip sips the contents and spits them out vengefully. It was a cup of paint, "with turpentine in it!"

Producer Ben Schwalb relished his work on the series. In a 1955 interview, he said:

"There is a peculiar chemistry that keeps a motion picture series going for years. In the case of the Bowery Boys, I guess that it's just that the public likes the boys, and that the formula has been continually changed so that the series is kept interesting and different."

Writer Elwood Ullman recalls that personalities could conflict on the set. He didn't participate in the shouting matches, however. "I was a writer, that's it. When I had nothing else to do I looked at what was going on. I didn't

Surprise! Rick Vallin (of Ghosts on the Loose*) returns (left).*

She's a delight for every man's eyes. That's how the coming attractions trailer described Joan Shawlee (formerly Joan Fulton).

try to make changes on the set. After ten, twenty minutes, I left. I wasn't wanted on the set." On writing: "I racked my brains out for three weeks up, maybe five weeks, maybe six, an average of a month (and then I hoped I did another)."

Ullman sums up his Bowery boys experience thusly: "It was ordinary studio routine. We did one picture and then (we hoped) we did another."

Amanda Blake of TV's long-running "Gunsmoke" series "enjoys" the attentions of Slip and Sach. Gavin Gordon (second from left) and Dayton Lumis are not bemused. Ronald Keith is the lad. The set design has the same floor plan as those in Loose in London *and* Paris Playboys.

HIGH SOCIETY

Released April 17, 1955, by Allied Artists. Produced by Ben Schwalb. Directed by William Beaudine. Screenplay by Bert Lawrence and Jerome S. Gottler. Story by Elwood Ullman and Edward Bernds. Photographed by Harry Neumann. Edited by John C. Fuller. Editing supervised by Lester A. Sansom. Art direction by David Milton. Musical direction by Marlin Skiles. Assistant direction by Austen Jewell. Sound by Ralph Butler. Production managed by Allan K. Wood. Set decorations by Joseph Kish. Wardrobe by Bert Henrikson. Makeup by Eddie Polo. Set continuity by Gloria Morgan. Special effects by Ray Mercer. Released in 1.85:1 (scope) aspect ratio. *5513 ft. 61 minutes.*

Terrence Aloysius "Slip" Mahoney, Leo Gorcey; *Horace Debussy "Sach" Jones,* Huntz Hall; *Chuck,* David Condon; *Butch,* Bennie Bartlett; *Louie Dumbrowski,* Bernard Gorcey; *Terwillinger III (Master Twig),* Ronald Keith; *H. Stuyvesant Jones,* Dayton Lummis; *Clarissa,* Amanda Blake; *Frisbie, butler,* Gavin Gordon; *Attorney Sam Cosgrove,* Addison Richards; *Marten,* Kem Dibbs; *Henry Baldwin,* Paul Harvey; *Palumbo, pianist,* Dave Barry.

While Slip and Sach are working in an auto garage, Sach is told that he is heir to the fortune of the late Terwillinger Debussy Jones. Stuyvesant Jones invites the two to the

Jones's mansion for a weekend of paper signing. The rightful heir is the youngster Terwillinger III (called Twig), who the boys and Louie side with after learning that Sach's birth certificate was doctored by Stuyvesant. When the bank representative arrives to sign papers with Sach, Stuyvesant and two scheming cousins show Sach a gun they can use against him, and Sach delays signing as long as he can. Meanwhile, Slip, Louie and Twig try to save Sach from the schemers. Sach exposes the ruse to the bank man, and the relatives put a gun to him to get him to cooperate. Slip, Louie and Twig then break into the crooks' nest and rout the schemers.

High Society opens on a bright note. A sign informs us that we're at the Bowery Garage, operated by "Terence Mahoney, General Manager, General Superintendant, General Treasurer" and "Horace Debussy Jones, General Help." Sach is not proficient at handling cars. One repaired auto is doomed for destruction when Sach can't determine what lever-position will put the car in gear for driving out: "D" is for Day Driving, "N" is for Night driving, "L" is for Long distance driving, and " 'R' . . . right straight ahead!"

The posh surroundings at the mansion don't inhibit Mahoney and Jones. They tell young Twig that he'll have to relinquish the master bedroom to Sach. As Twig is not so easily dissuaded, Slip and Sach go into Edward G. Robinson and James Cagney impersonations.

High Society was the only Bowery boys picture to be nominated for an Academy Award (for Best Original Story). Edward Bernds explains:

"Elwood [Ullman] and I wrote the story, not the screenplay, for *High Society*. Some other writers wrote the screenplay. Elwood and I were busy on something else, and Huntz pressured Ben to use some friends of his to write the screenplay. Meanwhile, M.G.M. had made the multi-million dollar star-studded picture with the same title. I don't know if they knew there was another *High Society* floating around. When the Motion Picture Academy sends out ballots, they list only the title and studio, and ignore the writers' names. The Academy voters thought they were voting for the M.G.M. blockbuster and paid no attention that it was Allied Artists, not M.G.M. I knew it was a mistake immediately and I wanted to correct it with the Academy. I undertook the step to call the president of Allied Artists (Elwood wanted the mistake to stand), and he agreed that there was no advantage and no dignity in letting the mistake stand. So I sent the Academy a telegram, and they sent Elwood and me a letter thanking us for getting the Academy out of an embarrassing situation. If we hadn't withdrawn, *High Society* might conceivably have won; the Original Story-only category is a tricky one—there aren't many entries. Most original screen stories are screenplayed by the same writers who write the story. It was a kind of fluke Elwood and I didn't screenplay *High Society* like the other ones we did. The Academy sent us the Academy nomination plaques. I still have mine hanging in my office. Sometimes when I show it to people, I explain it was a mistake. Sometimes I don't."

SPY CHASERS

Released July 31, 1955, by Allied Artists. Produced by Ben Schwalb. Directed by Edward Bernds. Scenario by Bert Lawrence and Jerome S. Gottler. Photographed by Harry Neumann. Edited by John C. Fuller. Editing supervised by Lester A. Sansom. Art direction by David Milton. Musical direction by Marlin Skiles. Production supervised by Allan K. Wood. Assistant direction by Edward Morey, Jr. Set decorations by Joseph Kish. Sound by Ralph Butler. Special effects by Ray Mercer. Wardrobe by Bert Henrickson. Makeup by Bob Dawn. Hairdressings by Mary Westmoreland. Set continuity by Mary Chaffee. Released in 1.85:1 (scope) aspect ratio. *61 minutes.*

Terrence Aloysius "Slip" Mahoney, Leo Gorcey; *Horace Debussy "Sach" Jones,* Huntz Hall; *Chuck,* David Condon; *Butch,* Bennie Bartlett; *Louie Dumbrowski,* Bernard Gorcey; *Colonel Alex Baxis,* Leon Askin; *Lady Zelda,* Veola Vonn; *King Rako,* Sig Rumann; *Princess Ann,* Lisa Davis; *George,* Frank Richards; *Michael,* Paul Burke; *Boris,* Richard Benedict; *Little girl,* Linda Bennett; *Nick,* Mel Welles; *Phony courier,* John Bleifer.

Slip, Sach, Butch and Chuck come to the aid of Princess Ann of Truania and her father, the exiled king, when the royal pair asks Truanian-born Louie to stash a diacritical half-coin (the other half of which will be delivered when it is safe for the king to return to his country). Slip and Sach distrust the king's right-hand man (Colonel Baxis) and Ann's lady-in-waiting (Zelda), and their suspicions turn out to be right, as the two are traitors who intend to use their knowledge of the half-coin to send the king back at an inopportune time. The villains' plans are overheard by Ann, who is kidnapped. Slip and Sach trace Colonel Baxis to a sleazy café where they find the bound-and-gagged princess. The princess accompanies the boys back to Louie's Sweet Shop, where Louie, Chuck and Butch have tied up a coin courier. The princess identifies the courier as the genuine courier. Slip and Sach confront the Colonel and Zelda, whom they subdue, much to the appreciation of the king.

Spy Chasers is prime Bowery Boys comedy. Its beauty lies in the integration of funny sequences into a well-structured plot. From the opening scene, in which Sach mirthfully interrupts the princess's discussion of her plight and also Slip's keen observations, to the climactic fight, in which Sach becomes the heavy's combat compatriot through Zelda's hypnotic suggestions, *Spy Chasers* provides non-stop laughs.

Said Ben Schwalb in 1955, "Experienced people help give a picture value. I also make sure that there is no quality of sameness in any of the films. The heavies and the leading ladies are always different people in each picture. This adds variety." These words seem especially appropriate to *Spy Chasers*, as it has excellent production values and a superb cast, with Sig Ruman, Leon Askin and Veola Vonn giving outstanding performances.

The following Ben Schwalb quote is also appropriate, although it applies well to all of the Bowery Boys films: "Leo and Huntz have an instinctive feeling about dialogue and scenes. They live their parts before the camera and they know just what will play for a laugh and what will not."

Slip tells his Bowery Fort, "We're working for a king now," before drilling them.

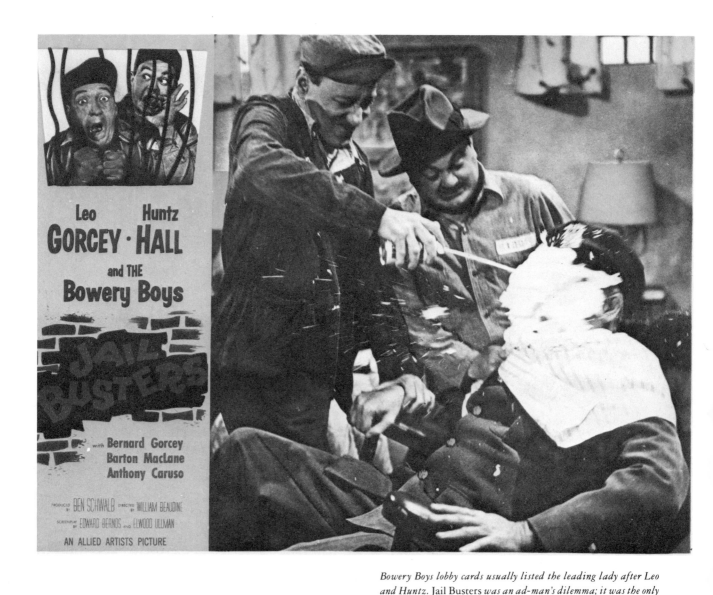

Bowery Boys lobby cards usually listed the leading lady after Leo and Huntz. Jail Busters was an ad-man's dilemma; it was the only film in the series with an all-male cast.

JAIL BUSTERS

Released September 18, 1955, by Allied Artists. Produced by Ben Schwalb. Directed by William Beaudine. Scenario by Elwood Ullman. Photographed by Carl Gutherie. Edited by William Austin. Editing supervised by Lester A. Sansom. Art direction by David Milton. Musical direction by Marlin Skiles. Production supervised by Allan K. Wood. Sound by Ralph Butler. Set decorations by Joseph Kish. Sound effects edited by Charles Schelling. Wardrobe by Bert Henrickson. Makeup by Emile LaVigne. Set continuity by Richard Chaffee. Special effects by Ray Mercer. Production title: *Doing Time.* 5503 ft. 61 minutes.

Terrence Aloysius "Slip" Mahoney (41326), Leo Gorcey; *Horace Debussy "Sach" Jones (41328),* Huntz Hall; *Butch Williams (41327),* Bennie Bartlett; *Charles "Chuck" Ander-* *son,* David Condon; *Louie Dumbrowski,* Bernard Gorcey; *Warden B.W. Oswald,* Percy Helton; *Guard Jenkins,* Barton MacLane; *Ed Lannigan,* Anthony Caruso; *Gus,* Murray Alper; *Big Greenie,* Michael Ross; *Dr. Fernando F. Fordyce,* Fritz Feld; *Cy Bowman,* Lyle Talbot; *Marty,* Henry Kulky; *Mug photographer,* Emil Sitka; *Tomcyk,* John Harmon; *Hank (12784),* Henry Tyler.

After newspaper employee Chuck suffers a beating while undercover in prison, the boys decide to get themselves sent up. Chuck's editor, Cy Bowman, desperate for funds, is more than pleased to assist them in enacting a robbery for which they will receive a bogus conviction. Once behind prison gates, the boys discover that the short stay they expected (to investigage Chuck's beating) has been extended since Bowman did not return the jewelry they stole. The boys uncover the story to which Chuck was assigned–that inmates such as Ed Lannigan have been paying off guards so that they can lead the "life of Riley." The boys expose the scam and capture the participants, then turn them over to the warden.

The prison scenes put the boys through the standard convict paces. When they have their mug shots taken by the photographer, the lens explodes when the shutter is exposed to Sach. The boys are not helpful when they are made into kitchen personnel; Sach interprets the order "wash the lettuce" to mean scrubbing each leaf in soapy water and then hanging it up to dry.

The boys are assigned more activities than their fellow prisoners. They are the only inmates in their psychiatry session. The prison psychologist feels the strain. When the doc is told by the warden over the intercom that Mahoney, Jones and Williams will visit him again, the psychiatrist scurries about the room on a balloon-popping rampage.

Ben Schwalb said in 1955: "A comedy should be tailored for your principals. In the case of the Bowery Boys, the writers we use have a knowledge of how these films are made. This is extremely important. It's not easy to write comedy and to think up fresh situations."

DIG THAT URANIUM

Released January 8, 1956, by Allied Artists. Produced by Ben Schwalb. Directed by Edward Bernds. Scenario by Elwood Ullman and Bert Lawrence. Photographed by Harry Neumann. Edited by William Austin. Editing supervised by Lester A. Sansom. Art direction by David Milton. Musical direction by Marlin Skiles.

Terrence Aloysius "Slip Mahoney, Leo Gorcey; *Horace Debussy "Sach" Jones,* Huntz Hall; *Chuck,* David Condon; *Butch,* Bennie Bartlett; *Louie Dumbrowski,* Bernard Gorcey; *Hank "Mac" McGinty,* Raymond Hatton; *Ron Haskell,* Harry Lauter; *Jeanette,* Mary Beth Hughes; *Joe Hody,* Myron Healey; *Frank Loomis,* Richard Powers; *Indian,* Paul Fierro; *Chief,* Francis McDonald; *Olaf, mechanic,* Frank Jenks; *Tex,* Don Harvey; *Shifty Robinson,* Carl "Alfalfa" Switzer; FLASHBACK SCENE: *Lone*

Percy Helton—who only two years later assumed a regular role in the Bowery Boys series as Mike Clancy—is confronted by Slip, Butch and Sach. Helton plays Warden B.W. Oswald. When asked what his initials stand for, he answers, "Bread and water."

The Lone Disarrangers, Slip and Sach, demand a strong drink: milk. The shaky bartender, Louie, obliges. Slip remarks, after Louie has poorly poured it, "Next time try gettin' some in the glass."

Disarrangers, Leo Gorcey, Huntz Hall; *Pecos Pete,* Myron Healey; *Idaho Ike,* Richard Powers; *Saloon girl,* Mary Beth Hughes; *Bartender,* Bernard Gorcey; *Customers,* David Condon, Bennie Bartlett.

The boys discover that the uranium mine they bought isn't the route-to-wealth they thought it would be. Badmen, wary of these Panther Pass newcomers, and whose suspicions of the boys having uranium is incorrectly confirmed by a misunderstanding, pursue their mineral claim. When the badmen try to kill the boys, they escape by car, and lead the badmen on a chase, during which the boys trick the villains into driving off a cliff.

The villains are typecast in the best tradition of Saturday-matinee Westerns. They spout such lines as "When I plug 'em, they stay plugged." They play poker, and Louie joins them for a game. Although the crooks have rigged the game by exchanging cards under the

table, Louie upsets the outcome by calling with four aces. He had intercepted the cards under the table without knowing that the aces were to be passed. (Shemp Howard had been led into just such a game in the Three Stooges short *Out West* (1947), also directed by Edward Bernds.) Naturally, black hats are appropriate for these varmints, particularly when they appear in Sach's dream of the Old West.

The dream scene is one of the best in the series. Slip and Sach are the Lone Disarrangers. Slip considers himself more adept than Sach, and tells a nemesis, "You have to forgive my sideclick." Sach may not be adept at gunplay, but he is adept at comebacks. When a villain remarks, "You aren't going to shoot us in cold blood?" Sach responds, "No, we're going to take you out in the sun and warm you up first." As this is Sach's dream, he can put Slip in his place and get away with it. Example: Sach fires two gunshots into the floor; Slip's response is "I'm going to count my toes later and they better all be there," to which Sach coolly says, "If you find eight, you're lucky."

Authenticity was achieved by shooting at oft—used Iverson's Ranch in the San Fernando Valley. Director Bernds worked out the climactic chase between the villains' jeep and the boys' jalopy to utilize the set's possibilities, but had to revamp the routine when the crew was losing light. "I had to tell the stunt drivers to ad-lib and make the near-misses as hairy as they dared. They did a great job. I have a sneaky feeling that their improvised routine may have been better than the one I so carefully planned."

Dig That Uranium marks the last celluloid appearances of Bernard Gorcey and Bennie Bartlett. Austen Jewell (the assistant director) has some words which may serve as eulogies.

First, on Bernard: "Leo's father was quite a comedian; I thought he was one of the funniest character people of his time. He was quite an influence on Leo and David, and I always looked forward to working with him because he was an old-time comic with just perfect timing.

"Sometimes on a very short schedule you don't have time to direct comedies as they should be directed, but he came up with very innovative ideas."

Mr. Jewell recalls that Leo may have spoken berating words to his father, but: "I think Leo said some things he really didn't mean, but I'm sure he respected his father. Surely he respected him as a craftsman, because he created so much more than he's given credit for, and he advised Leo to carry on."

On Bennie (and David too): "If you're going to have a gang, so to speak, you need not two people—two people are not a gang—you need two, three, four other people. Naturally, Leo and Huntz being the stars of the show, they had the most lines, so the other fellows were there primarily for reaction shots. They had to be someone to play off of. There would have been something lacking without them."

Raymond Hatton, who was a stalwart of the Western, having played in the "Three Musquiteers" westerns of the Thirties (featuring John Wayne), tests Sach's grip.

CRASHING LAS VEGAS

Released April 22, 1956, by Allied Artists. Produced by Ben Schwalb. Directed by Jean Yarbrough. Scenario by Jack Townley. Photographed by Harry Neumann. Edited by George White. Art directon by David Milton. Musical direction by Marlin Skiles. Production managed by Allan K. Wood. Assistant direction by Edward Morey, Jr. Special effects by Ray Mercer. Sound by Joe, Donaldson. Set decorations by Joseph Kish. Wardrobe by Bert Henrikson. Makeup by Emile LaVigne. *5593 ft. 62 minutes.*

Terrence Aloysius "Slip" Mahoney, Leo Gorcey; *Horace Debussy "Sach" Jones,* Huntz Hall; *Chuck,* David Condon; *Myron,* Jimmy Murphy; *Carol LaRue,* Mary Castle; *Sam,* Nicky Blair; *Oggy,* Mort Mills; *Tony Murlock,* Don Haggerty; *Mrs. Kelly,* Doris Kemper; *Wiley,* Jack Rice; *"Live Like a King" host,* Bob Hopkins; *Joe Crumb,* John Bleifer; *Man in seat 87,* Emil Sitka; *First policeman,* Dick Foote; *Second policeman,* Don Marlowe; *Bellboy,* Jack Grinnage; *Police sergeant,* Terry Frost; *Woman,* Minerva Urecal; *Croupier,* Frank Scannell; *Floor manager,* Joey Ray; *Waiter,* Jack Chefe; *Guard,* Frank Hagney; *Elevator operator,* Speer Martin; *Usher,* Jimmy Brandt; *Waiter,* Cosmo Sardo; *Bit,* Alfred Tonkel.

In Crashing Las Vegas, *Sach struts about in sun glasses and loud clothes. He is smug and gets annoying. Mary Castle, once groomed to replace Rita Hayworth (should Hayworth cause trouble) looks at a semi-sober Leo.*

Sach is able to predict numbers after receiving an electric shock. The boys go to Las Vegas after he wins them a hotel stay on a game show. Gangsters, aware that Sach wins money on every roulette spin, blackmail him into giving them his money after making Sach believe that he killed a man, but the other boys expose the hoax.

Crashing Las Vegas tries to spoof television game shows and gambling systems. It succeeds at doing the first, but the Las Vegas footage is comprised of just standard "B" film plottage.

The coming-attractions trailer advertised the film thusly: "The Bowery Boys are bustin' out all over with a blonde, a bankroll, and a blue-chip brawl." All clichés. That about describes the last part.

Crashing Las Vegas was the first Bowery Boys film since the fifties began without Bernard Gorcey (Louie); a "Mrs. Kelly," the landlady, takes his place. The death of Bernard drove Leo to the bottle. Says Edward Bernds, "There was a time when I thought Leo was a better actor with a few drinks in him, but it caught up with him as it always will. If you look at *Dig That Uranium,* you can see his eyes are bloodshot, his face bloated, his lines slurred." We have never noticed insobriety in *Dig That Uranium,* but it's obvious that he was drunk during shooting of *Crashing Las Vegas,* particularly during a roulette table sequence in which he bobs up and down while Sach and the gamblers' moll talk.

As it is, *Crashing Las Vegas* is Sach's film. He is the central character. It is he who gets the power and romances the girl.

This was Leo Gorcey's last Bowery Boys film.

PRIMER FOR 1956–1958

Huntz Hall and Stanley Clements with Jane Nigh.

STANLEY CLEMENTS: Stanley Clements was chosen as Leo Gorcey's replacement. Edward Bernds said, "Stan was a fine actor—I know, I worked with him on several pictures—but it just didn't work. I saw part of one of his pictures (where he was replacing Leo) on television the other day and it just didn't work. The whole thing was rather sad." Jane Nigh (who co-starred with Clements) called Stanley Clements "a nice man, a fine actor."

Ben Schwalb supports Stan as having been the right man for the part, and contends to this day that he made the right decision in hiring Stan. "Ed [Bernds] never voiced that objection to me, and I happen to disagree with him. Stan wasn't the same as Leo; no two persons are alike. He didn't have the aggressiveness Leo had. I would say that Leo played it better than 'Stash' Clements did, but I would not call him inappropriate. And if Stan had been there a couple of years like Leo, he might have developed his own way. He had made several pictures for

me at Allied Artists, and I knew his work. He was not under contract to Allied Artists. I contracted him as I needed him. I think he was as well cast as anyone who replaces someone else."

Huntz and Stan did develop a suitable chemistry. In some situations Stan was equal to Leo as a cohort and foil to Huntz. In *Hold That Hypnotist*, Sach explains to "Duke" (Stan) that their treasure hunt is futile; Sach has discovered that his source of information was ultimately derived from a comic book. Duke chuckles heartily, sharing Sach's good humor. Neither seems upset over the efforts they went through before discovering the mistake, and Duke doesn't hit Sach impulsively as Slip would have. When Sach feels relieved, Duke reaches for a heavy tool. Sach reminds him, "You promised not to lay a hand on me." "But I said nothing about a pick," Duke rages.

COPY CHARACTERS: In each of the first three Stanley Clements films, there was a supporting character which drew upon an existing personality. In *Fighting Trouble*, the villain was named "Frankie Arbo," a transparent attempt to summon up viewers' recollections of Frankie Darro. The villain in *Hot Shots* could have been Cary Grant's stand-in. As for *Hold That Hypnotist*, Jane Nigh (the leading lady) herself has stated that the creative minds told her to play the role as it would be played by Marilyn Monroe or Jayne Mansfield.

MRS. KELLY: Introduced in *Crashing Las Vegas*, Mrs. Kelly was the boys' landlady. She filled the same function as Louie. She appeared in the first three Stanley Clements-Huntz Hall pictures, then disappeared.

MIKE CLANCY'S CAFÉ: This became the boys' new "home base." It first appeared in the fourth Clements-Hall picture. Its interior decor was that of Louie's Sweet Shop. The proprietor was first played by Percy Helton, who was replaced after one picture by Dick Elliott.

DUKE COVELESKE AS A "MEDIATOR": Stanley Clements filled a function that Leo Gorcey didn't; since his character was believable, Duke could be sure that what he said would be taken as fact. In *Looking for Danger*, it is Duke who serves as the flashback narrator. He was a "mediator." In *In the Money*, he interprets the action for the audience. He says of Sach, who has opted not to take the other boys with him across the Atlantic, "It's oblivious he doesn't want us to go with him, and that makes me want to go all the more."

HUNTZ'S NEW CHARACTER: The character of Sach became something else when he no longer had an unquestionable leader to play off. He had to direct his jokes and ideas to the audience. He was also called upon to convey certain plot points that previously he wouldn't have understood. In *Fighting Trouble*, the boys are trying to keep a Chicago gangster in their apartment by making him think that the New York police have surrounded him, doing so by rigging the radio so that it will receive a bogus broadcast. Before this, we saw Chuck with a microphone, promising to hook up the appropriate gadget. However, during Chuck's "interruption broadcast," the New Sach comments to Duke, "Chuck sure sounds good, doesn't he?" just to *make sure* we've got the message.

Finally, Huntz Hall himself disliked the new arrangement: "The series ended when Bernard Gorcey died. Leo quit the series after that, saying he couldn't work with anyone else playing his father's part." (On the one picture Leo did without his father, he accomplished the

impossible. He was the highest paid actor in Hollywood that year, on an hourly basis. And for that he played half the picture while drunk.) "So I did seven pictures without him with Stanley Clements because I had a contract and it had to be fulfilled. After those seven pictures it was over, *it didn't work*. It just wasn't the same. They had me playing Leo's part and my part. Playing the leader of the gang—and it didn't work."

Adele Jergens is back.

FIGHTING TROUBLE

Released September 16, 1956, by Allied Artists. Produced by Ben Schwalb. Directed by George Blair. Scenario by Elwood Ullman. Photographed by Harry Neumann. Edited by William Austin. Original musical score by Buddy Bregman. Art direction by David Milton. Production managed by Allan K. Wood. Sound by Ralph Butler. Assistant direction by Don Torpin. Music edited by Jill Campbell. Sound edited by Charles Schelling. Set direction by Joseph Kish. Set continuity by Richard Chaffee. Wardrobe by Bert Henrikson. Makeup by Emile LaVigne. Construction supervised by Jimmy West. Property direction by Ted Mossman. Production title: *Chasing Trouble. 61 minutes.*

Horace Debussy "Sach" Jones, Huntz Hall; *Stanislaus "Duke" Coveleske,* Stanley Clements; *Chuck Anderson,* David Gorcey; *Danny,* Danny Welton; *Mae Randall,* Adele Jergens; *Frankie Arbo,* Thomas B. Henry; *Chips Conroy,* William Boyett; *"Handsome Hal" Lomax,* Joseph Downing; *Ray Vance,* Tim Ryan; *Mrs. Kelly,* Queenie Smith; *Bates,* John Bleifer; *Dolly Tate,* Laurie Mitchell; *Smoggy Smith,* Charles Williams; *McBride,* Clegg Hoty; *Evans,* Michael Ross; *Max Kling,* Benny Burt; *Vic Sarmini,* Rick Vallin; *Hawaiian girl,* Ann Griffith.

Sach and Duke attempt to photograph notorious gangster Frankie Arbo for the *New York Morning Blade*, and they succeed. But Sach exposes the negative, thereby making futile all of the efforts they had gone through to pose as interior decorators to take the pictures. Now more than ever desiring to shoot a picture for a newspaper payoff, the boys smuggle a camera into the backroom of Arbo's nightclub. Sach disguises as one of Arbo's connections, a Chicago-based, pill-popping hoodlum named "Handsome Hal" Lomax, and attends a meeting Arbo holds at which he distributes counterfeit money. Police arrive and take the gangsters into captivity.

Fighting Trouble moves on flimsy material. In the opening scenes, Bowery Boy Danny says he needs $200 to replace his boss's missing cash register reserve. Sach and Duke have nothing to do with this, and Danny has no reason to believe he will be turned over to the police. On this hangs 60 minutes of plot.

Sach's ineptitude is annoying. He ruins one roll of Frankie Arbo photo negatives, and then, at the end, doesn't improve upon himself when he exposes another.

When Sach is introduced (this, the first time he is on the Bowery without Slip), he is a boastful Sach, one with an inflated ego, with no reason to be so proud of a camera accessory he invented: a lens attachment that finds the subject on its own, via radar, snaking its tubular body as it changes direction.

The film tries to throw us off-track: Sach is about to be implicated, exposed as a Lomax-imposter, when Lomax's girlfriend is asked to identify her beau. She chooses Sach. Sach is saved from a beating because the femme had had enough of the real Hal's cheating. And also, the plot has it that Danny gets hired by the nightclub, thus allowing the boys to get their information. This is too convenient to be believable.

The funniest scene in the film is the interior decorating scene. Sach and Duke don disguises. Sach lives up to his beard and costume. Duke says of him to Arbo's moll (played by Adele Jergens), "Don't bother him, he's temperamental." The apartment is in shambles after Sach's wholesale ravage in the name of "art."

HOT SHOTS

Released December 23, 1956, by Allied Artists. Produced by Ben Schwalb. Directed by Jean Yarbrough. Screenplay by Jack Townley and Elwood Ullman. Story by Jack Townley. Photographed by Harry Neumann. Edited by Neil Brunnenkant. Art direction by David Milton. Musical direction by Marlin Skiles. Production managed by Allan K. Wood. Assistant direction by Dan Torpin. Sound by Ralph Butler. Sound edited by Charles Schelling. Set direction by Joseph Kish. *5527 ft. 61 minutes.*

This posed shot is funnier than anything in the entire film.

Horace DeBussy "Sach" Jones, Huntz Hall; *Stanislaus "Duke" Coveleske,* Stanley Clements; *Chuck,* David Gorcey; *Myron,* Jimmy Murphy; *Joey Munroe,* Phil Phillips; *Mrs. Kelly,* Queenie Smith; *George Slater,* Mark Dana; *Connie Forbes,* Joi Lansing; *Palmer M. Morley,* Robert Shayne; *Karl,* Henry Rowland; *Tony,* Dennis Moore; *Mrs. B. L. Taylor,* Isabel Randolph; *Henry, bartender,* Frank Marlowe; *Bit man,* Joe Kirk; *Captain W. K. Wells,* Ray Walker.

Sach and Duke acquaint themselves with television executives after an eight-year-old TV star prankishly steals the boys' car. The executives think the boys know how to handle the star, Joey Munroe, so Sach and Duke are hired by the television network to be the child's confidants. They are assigned the titles of 34th and 35th Vice-Presidents. When Joey's uncle and manager kidnap the child for ransom, Duke and Sach come to his rescue.

Hot Shots uses a television-style script with no integrated comedy, replete with cheap sentiment and clichés. There are only two funny scenes. One has Sach, Duke, Chuck and Myron preparing for a party. Sach says that the "R.S.V.P." on the invitation stands for "Rye, Scotch, Vodka and Pumpernickel." Duke corrects him in that the initials mean "Real Stupid Vice-President." Duke calls off a number of foods, and the boys hold up appropriate utensils. "Right," Duke responds every time. When he calls out "peas," they hold up knives. "Right."

The other scene has the boys in their spacious office (it's about the size of an office-building floor). They turn on a fan which blows papers all over and causes a secretary's skirt to fly up. It's a sad commentary on the film that one of its two funny scenes gets its laughs from something mechanical rather than from people.

The writers had the audacity to introduce Joey Munroe, played by Phil Phillips. He exhibits an unbearably precocious nature, reminiscent of young Robert Blake as whiny "Mickey" in the last M.G.M. "Our Gang" shorts. It's hard to understand why the boys feel sorry for him, not only because he accuses them of being kidnappers after he had stolen their car, but because he is everything they weren't as kids.

The boys once again crash high society, this time in a misfired dinner-party sequence. What there is in the way of humor is strained, such as the old dollar-bill-in-the-egg gag, where a real egg is substituted for the one that the performer of a magic trick (Sach) thinks is an empty shell containing a greenback. The result is that the yolk ends up on a distinguished man's noggin.

It is interesting that *Hot Shots* takes aim at the television industry, since the film seems more like a television show in direction, script and production than a film. The writers' forced attempts to justify a fight ending are transparent, as is the bad-uncle-turned-kidnapper twist.

HOLD THAT HYPNOTIST

Released February 24, 1957, by Allied Artists. Produced by Ben Schwalb. Directed by Austen Jewell. Scenario by Dan Pepper. Photographed by Harry Neumann. Edited by George White. Art direction by David Milton. Musical direction by Marlin Skiles. Production managed by Allan K. Wood. Sound by Ralph Butler. Sound edited by Charles Schelling. Assistant direction by Edward Morey, Jr. Set direction by Joseph Kish. Wardrobe by Bert Henrikson. Set continuity by Richard M. Chaffee. Makeup by Emile LaVigne. Construction by James West. *61 minutes.*

Horace Debussy "Sach" Jones, Huntz Hall; *Stanislaus "Duke" Coveleske,* Stanley Clements; *Chuck,* David Gorcey; *Myron,* Jimmy Murphy; *Cleo Daniels,* Jane Nigh; *Dr.*

Mel Wells, Huntz, Jane Nigh.

Simon Noble, Robert Foulk; *Mrs. Kelly,* Queenie Smith; *Jake Morgan,* James Flavin; *Gale,* Murray Alper; *Book clerk,* Dick Elliott; *Maid,* Mary Treen; FLASHBACK SCENE: *Algy Winkle,* Huntz Hall; *Blackbeard,* Mel Welles; *Bartender,* Stanley Clements; *Wench,* Jane Nigh; *Customers,* David Gorcey, Jimmy Murphy.

The boys want to expose hypnotist Dr. Noble as a "quack." Noble regresses Sach to the year 1682 when Sach lived a previous life as Algy Winkle, a tax collector who wins a treasure map from Blackbeard the Pirate. The boys learn that the treasure was never claimed, so they have Noble put Sach into another trance so they can learn the location of the missing chest. When Sach discloses the location, Nobel and his business partner Morgan draw their guns. Sach is put into a trance in which he keeps the boys hostage (Sach is told that he is Horatio guarding a bridge). The boys break the spell (with the help of Noble's former secretary, Cleo), and Sach, Duke and the boys set out for the treasure. They arrive at the Hudson Cove spot hours later, but stumble onto the cache first. They fight Noble and Morgan, push them into a mud pool, and then set out for New York. However, their dreams of the easy life are shattered: Sach learns that his "memories" of a previous life were inspired by a comic book, and police identify the "treasure" as loot never recovered from a jewelry store robbery for which the thieves were sent to jail.

Hold That Hypnotist was an improvement over its two predecessors. At the helm was director Austen Jewell, who had been an assistant director on most of the episodes made during the last four years. Both *Fighting Trouble* and *Hot Shots* were directed by men who had not worked with the Bowery Boys before. This was Austen Jewell's first film as a director, though.

Hold That Hypnotist was, however, written by a man who had no previous connection to the Bowery Boys. He was Dan Pepper, whose script nonetheless gives the reins to Huntz Hall, as it rightfully should.

According to leading lady Jane Nigh, Huntz was "very excited that he was going to be the lead." He had a contract guaranteeing that he would be the lead, and flaunted it to his comrades on the set.

The plot of *Hold That Hypnotist* was based on the then-popular (allegedly) true story of a girl (Virginia Tighe, whose identity was protected by the psuedonym of Ruth Simmons) who had undergone hypnosis (under the supervision of Dr. Morey Bernstein) and revealed that she lived a previous life as an Irish girl named Bridey Murphy. Bridey's story was told in a best-selling book, which is satirized in *Hold That Hypnotist* as Nobel's *The Previous Life of Sally Klingle.* Bowery Boys films were often based on contemporary issues—that is, if we are to believe the *Motion Picture Herald,* which in its review of *Spy Chasers* said, "The Bowery Boys are shunted into as many headline-conscious screenplays as are available." Could this mean that corrupt prisons and embezzlement of inheritances were prevalent in that

Myron (Jimmy Murphy), Chuck and Duke look on as Doctor Noble (Robert Foulk) hypnotizes Sach.

period, as depicted in *Jail Busters* and *High Society*?

One off-the-course bit shows how facetious Sach often is. In the midst of their research, Sach reads from a book that Duke has before him. However, he reads it upside-down. Duke wants to know why. Sach answers, "That's what comes from working in a printing shop."

Both Huntz Hall and Stanley Clements perform with enthusiasm. Director Austen Jewell recalls why: "Stan, one of the most cooperative people, realized the problem I had because I had never directed them before. Huntz was also cooperative, as he was one of the people who asked for me, made it possible for me to get the job. It was not a problem of getting them to work, but of allowing them to get all they could onto the screen."

SPOOK CHASERS

Released June 2, 1957, by Allied Artists. Produced by Ben Schwalb. Directed by George Blair. Scenario by Elwood Ullman. Photographed by Harry Neumann. Edited by Neil Brunnenkant. Art direction by David Milton. Musical direction by Marlin Skiles. Production managed by Allan K. Wood. Sound by Ralph Butler. Music edited by Eve Newman. Sound edited by Charles Schelling. Set decorations by Robert J. Mills. First assistant director, Austen Jewell. Second assistant director, Lindsley Parsons, Jr. Dialogue direction by Bert Lawrence. Construction by Jimmy West. Property mas-

For Spook Chasers, *Allied Artists assigned a still photographer who had not learned the fine art of framing a photograph.*

ter, Sam Gordon. Special effects by Augie Lohman. Wardrobe by Bert Henrikson and Irene Caine. Makeup by Emile LaVigne. Hairdressings by Alice Monte. *5502 ft. 62 minutes.*

Horace Debussy "Sach" Jones, Huntz Hall; *Stanislaus "Duke" Coveleske,* Stanley Clements; *Chuck,* David Gorcey; *Myron,* Jimmy Murphy; *Blinky,* Eddie LeRoy; *Mike Clancy,* Percy Helton; *Dolly Owens,* Darlene Fields; *Harry Shelby,* Bill Henry; *Snap Sizzolo,* Peter Mamakos; *Ziggie,* Ben Welden; *Ernie,* Robert Christopher; *Lt. Harris,* Robert Shayne; *Doctor Moss,* Pierre Watkin; *First doll,* Audrey Conti; *Second doll,* Anne Fleming; *Photographer,* Bill Cassidy.

The boys go with café owner Mike Clancy to a mountain house that he has bought to help him rest his nerves. The house that he bought sight-unseen turns out to be a run-down farmhouse, but the boys find money stashed away on the property. The real-estate agent (Shelby) becomes aroused when the boys pay off the amount due on the house in a large cash payment. Gangsters who knew the former house-owner are also interested. Shelby has his secretary (Dolly) invite Sach on a date, during which she gets him drunk and makes him reveal where the boys got the money. Sach, Duke, Mike and the boys then spend a ghost-infested night in the house. The boys discover secret passages and use them to track down the ghosts, who turn out to be Shelby and Dolly. The boys also find the gangsters in the house. The boys subdue them and turn them over to the police.

Film buffs enchanted with the great gags which have been used time and time again in classic comedies should enjoy *Spook Chasers.* Writer Elwood Ullman has often stated that the best way to get sure-fire laughs was to put a comedian in an eerie setting. Apparently the Spring of 1957 was a slow period for humor, because *Spook Chasers* dusts off all of the old ghost jokes and more.

After the boys realize that Mike has been sold a lemon of a house, the boys console Mike and themselves by taking steps to freshen up the place. Blinky starts varnishing a table, while Duke eats a sandwich and drinks coffee. The coffee cup and the cup containing varnish are sure to get mixed up, and they do. Blinky dips his brush in the coffee, and Duke gets a mouthful of varnish. When that mix-up is cleared, Blinky mistakes the sandwich for his brush and. . . well, you know what happens.

The spooky night, during which the villains try to scare the boys out of the house, furnished the writer with an excuse to use all the old spook gags. There's the old Mack Sennett moving bed, which slides into the wall with Blinky in it. A spook-sheeted baddie takes Blinky's place in the bed. Sach, who shares Blinky's room, then enacts the "ghost-in-the-bed/thinking-that-it's-your-buddy" gag.

Rounding out the tally of standard "house" jokes is the famous "painting-the-cuckoo-when-it-comes-out-of-the-clock" bit. Sach is saddled with the responsibility of doing this gag, which is so mechanical and time-worn that he becomes indistinguishable from those who had done it before.

But what can you say about a film in which a ghost pops up near the end of the film, floats through walls, then leaves without an explanation ever being delivered?

LOOKING FOR DANGER

Released October 6, 1957, by Allied Artists. Produced by Ben Schwalb. Directed by Austen Jewell. Scenario by Elwood Ullman and Edward Bernds. Photographed by Harry Neumann. Edited by Neil Brunnenkant. Art direction by David Milton. Musical direction by Marlin Skiles. Production managed by Allan K. Wood. Sound by Ralph Butler. Wardrobe by Bert Henrikson. Makeup by Emile LaVigne. *62 minutes.*

Horace Debussy "Sach" Jones ("Haupman von Schnaubel"), Huntz Hall; *Stanislaus "Duke" Coveleske ("Schultz"),* Stanley Clements; *Chuck,* David Gorcey; *Myron,* Jimmy Murphy; *Blinky,* Eddie LeRoy; *Shareen ("The Hawk"),* Lili Kardell; *Colonel Ahmed Tabari,* Richard Avonde; *Sultan Sidi Omar,* Michael Granger; *Hassan,* Peter Mamakos; *Wolff,* Otto Reichow; *Mike Clancy,* Dick Elliott; *Lester Bradfield,* John Harmon; *Zarida,* Joan Bradshaw; *Sgt. Watson,* Harry Strang; *Major Harper DSS,* Paul Bryar; *Mustapha,* George Khoury; *Wetzel,* Henry Rowland; *Sari,* Jane Burgess; *Waiter,* Michael Vallon.

Duke tells an officer of the War Department how the boys lost a pot during World War II. . . . Sach and Duke were sent on a mission to locate "The Hawk," a member of a North African underground organization. Disguised as Nazi officers, they came into the capital city of Raz-Mamuth to encounter sultan Sidi-Omar, an ally of the Axis. Sidi-Omar tells the boys that he knows they are Americans, and the twosome accept a message from Sidi-Omar. Sach shows it to one of Sidi-Omar's dancing girls, Shareen, who reveals that she is The Hawk. She and the boys try to telegraph the Americans, but are discovered doing so and are imprisoned. Chuck, Myron and Blinky, dressed as Germans, free the boys, and all five round up the Sultan. . . . Duke also reports that the Hawk arranged for the Americans to defeat the Nazis in an important battle. But Duke has said nothing about the pot.

Sach, posing as a Nazi officer, tries to impress Hassan (Peter Mamakos) and Sultan Sidi-Omar (Michael Granger).

For *Looking For Danger,* the series junked the format it had been using and traded up to a fresh format featuring betrayal and suspense. In addition to the knives, daggers and fear, *Looking For Danger* offers a woman who can be trusted; a new Sach; and a kidding look at 1957 modern jazz (1957 modern jazz in WWII?). This should tip off the viewer that Duke's recollections are fabricated. At the end of the film, it turns out that Duke's story is discredited, as the pot—the loss of which his story purports to explain—turns out not to be lost, but serving a function at Mike's beanery.

Few of the old Bowery Boys details are here. Sach wields a saber when approached by the sultan; as a fight seems inevitable, Sach doesn't hide under the table. Instead, he encourages the black-hearted, saber-bearing sultan, challenging, "Come on, they don't call me the fighting coward for nothing."

Unlike the women in the Gorcey films, the woman here can be trusted. When Duke and his pal learn that the ally they were sent to find (i.e., "The Hawk") is a woman, Sach's remark is one that reveals how phenomenal this is: "I've read plenty of spy stories and I've never heard of a beautiful spy being on our side."

One of the Bowery Boys' standard gags was reshaped and given a new twist. It is the "routine" bit. After Chuck, Myron and Blinky (dressed as Nazis) have released Sach and Duke, they have Sach and Duke pretend to be prisoners. When one of the sultan's men asks what Sach and Duke are allegedy being marched off for, Myron answers, "The prisoners are wanted for *routine* questioning." The sultan's man asks, "What routine?" "Routine 21." And the fight starts.

Though *Looking For Danger* is a good film, director Austen Jewell concedes that it could have been better. "I made suggestions [just before shooting] and was politely refused. Ben [Schwalb] ran a very tight ship. He was a very pleasant man, very kind, yet the plots were thought out, and he knew from many, many years of experience what would go with them and what wouldn't."

UP IN SMOKE

Released December 22, 1957, by Allied Artists. Produced by Richard Heermance. Directed by William Beaudine. Screenplay by Jack Townley. Story by Elwood Ullman and Bert Lawrence. Photographed by Harry Neumann. Edited by William Austin. Art direction by David Milton. Musical direction by Marlin Skiles. Production managed by Allan K. Wood. Assistant direction by Jesse Corallo, Jr. Sound by Frank McKenzie. Set decorations by Joseph Kish. Music edited by Carl D. Kuhlman. Sound edited by Del Harris. *61 minutes.*

Sach, Mike Clancy (Dick Elliott), the girl with ulterior motives (Judy Bamber) and Duke.

Horace Debussy "Sach" Jones, Huntz Hall; *Stanislaus "Duke" Coveleske,* Stanley Clements; *Chuck,* David Gorcey; *Blinky,* Eddie LeRoy; *Mr. Bub, the Devil,* Byron Foulger; *Mike Clancy,* Dick Elliott; *Mabel,* Judy Bamber; *Tony,* Ric Roman; *Sam,* Ralph Sanford; *Al,* Joe Devlin; *Policeman,* James Flavin; *Friendly Frank, used car dealer,* Earle Hodgins; *Desk sergeant,* John Mitchum; *Police clerk,* Jack Mulhall; *Dr. Bluzak,* Fritz Feld; *Druggist,* Wilbur Mack; *Bernie,* Benny Rubin.

Sach sells his soul to the devil in exchange for horseracing tips, which he'll use to replenish the charity funds that he lost. The underworld learns of his prophetic connections, but Sach inadvertently sees to it that the gamblers never get the name of a winning horse. On the last day of Sach's deal, Sach substitutes himself for the jockey of the horse that will win. Sach tries to make it lose, but the horse is the first across the finish line. Since Sach rode the horse, it is disqualified, and this violates Sach's contract with the devil. The devil is discredited by his superiors and is forced to work at Mike's Lunchroom. Sach helps the devil by suggesting that the gamblers be his next customers.

Repetition characterizes *Up in Smoke.* The film cuts from the lunchroom to the bookmaking office, and back, and rarely breaks the pattern. One exception occurs when Sach, after a run-in with the police, lands in a psychiatrist's office.

Sach gets the psychiatrist to reveal what's in the back of his mind. The psychiatrist says, "I see myself on the subway platform."

"That's nothing, " says Sach, "That's just your subway conscious mind."

Byron Foulger as the Devil is the only refreshing element. His dry humor is wonderful ("Sometimes I just hate myself," he says gleefully). But even he doesn't know when to stop. He responds to Sach's remark, "For two cents I'd jump in the East River," by duly depositing two pennies on the lunchroom counter.

New producer Richard Heermance kept sets sparse, and writers Elwood Ullman and Bert Lawrence simply updated the old 16th century story of Faust.

Up in Smoke was almost not made. Ben Schwalb, who had been producing the series, quit ("I quit the series. I didn't want any more of it," he said recently), and the studio hadn't wanted to find a replacement. However, Richard Heermance was hired to make two more films.

Ben Schwalb explains: "Heermance made two more, and I think that was to finish Huntz's contract. Instead of paying him off for doing nothing, they made two more pictures."

Fortunately the next picture turned out to be an acceptable cap to the series.

The Devil (Byron Foulger) assures Sach that he makes many deals like the one that he made with Sach. "You don't suppose all the successes of the world got there on their own, do you?"

IN THE MONEY

Released February 16, 1958, by Allied Artists. Produced by Richard Heermance. Directed by William Beaudine. Screenplay by Al Martin and Elwood Ullman. Story by Al Martin. Photographed by Harry Neumann. Edited by Neil Brunnenkant. Art direction by David Milton. Musical direction by Marlin Skiles. Production managed by Allan K. Wood. Assistant direction by Jesse Corallo, Jr. Set decorations by Joseph Kish. Wardrobe by Sidney Mintz. Music edited by Carl D. Kuhlman. Sound edited by Del Harris. Sound by Phil Mitchell. Makeup by Emile LaVigne. Production title: *On the Make. 61 minutes.*

Horace Debussy "Sach" Jones, Huntz Hall; *Stanislaus "Duke" Coveleske,* Stanley Clements; *Chuck,* David Gorcey; *Blinky,* Eddie LeRoy; *Mike Cummings,* John Dodsworth; *Babs DeWitt,* Patricia Donahue; *John Clarke,* Leonard Penn; *Inspector Herbert Saunders,* Paul Cavanagh; *Inspector White,* Leslie Denison; *Mike Clancy,* Dick Elliott; *Dr. Rufus B. Smedley,* Owen McGiveney; *Dowager in hotel room,* Norma Varden; *Bellboy,* Ashley Cowan;

"*I know my* right, *and this is it."*

Sach is hired to cross the Atlantic as the escort of a pedigree poodle, not knowing that her coat conceals a cache of diamonds. His employers book passage on the same ship, and watch Sach like a hawk. Also on board are detectives from Scotland Yard, and the boys, who have stowed away to keep Sach out of trouble. In London, the boys discover Sach's part in the smuggling when they take the dog to a veterinarian. The veterinarian reveals to the Scotland Yard detectives that the diamonds are concealed in the dog's coat. The detectives meet the boys at their hotel, where both parties encounter the dog's owners. When the dog eludes all, everyone tries to find her. When she is found, the boys aid the police in apprehending the culprits, and thereby avoid being arrested themselves.

This final outing of the Bowery Boys series should be treated as more than the unpretentious, albeit pleasant, comedy that it is. It incorporates many of the old touches, and captures the charisma of the lead players. *In the Money* can be looked at as a satisfactory wrap-up of the series' twelve-year output.

In the Money has the favorite characterizations, chases, improbable gags, a straightforward plot and a favorable locale. Sach is enjoyable as the dupe who thinks that the dog owners have good intentions. They told him that they're afraid of "dognappers," and he has no reason not to believe them. The boys are all in on one gag when they open the door to their hotel room and a cloud of London fog cascades out.

The finale in the hotel halls combines the slick pace and the flair for action we've come to expect. One problem exists though: the suave villains are built up to be so clever, and their plan so perfect (a good cut-away sequence shows a diamond-filled cut of carpet being placed on the dog's body), and their crime so nominal, that one feels sorry for them when they're caught, especially since Sach nets them through no fault of his own.

David Gorcey, Eddie LeRoy, Stanley Clements and Huntz Hall seem ready to take bows in this still representing the last scene of the last Bowery Boys film.

BIOGRAPHIES

Explanation of biography credits:

Studio follows title; abbreviations are used for the most common names. Year is included in parenthesis. The only technical credit is that of director, indicated by "D:" Cast credits include only major players; initials or parenthetical character name indicates actor's position in cast.

Studio abbreviations:

MGM	=	Metro-Goldwyn-Mayer
20CF	=	Twentieth Century-Fox
WB	=	Warner Brothers
Para.	=	Paramount
RKO	=	Radio-Keith-Orpheum
Gold.	=	Samuel Goldwyn
Col.	=	Columbia
Uni.	=	Universal
AIP	=	American-International
BV	=	Buena Vista (Disney)
FBO	=	Film Booking Office
Rep.	=	Republic
AA	=	Allied Artists
Mono.	=	Monogram
Lip.	=	Lippert
SG	=	Screen Guild
FC	=	Film Classics
E-L	=	Eagle-Lion
PRC	=	Producers Releasing Corporation
DCA	=	Distribution Corp. America

LEO GORCEY

The most vehement of the original Dead End Kids, and leader of the Eastside Kids and the Bowery Boys for 16 years, Leo Bernard Gorcey was the prototype of the wise young punk. The shortest of the gang at 5'6", Gorcey was also the oldest, born June 3, 1917, in New York's Washington Heights district.

As "Spit" in *Dead End*, Gorcey created a pugilistic guttersnipe who would dispute anything just for the sport of it. Later, in the Eastside Kids and Bowery Boys, he softened his disposition somewhat and became the leader of his pack of misfits, always ready to clean up his neighborhood of wrongdoers, but "allerigic" to actual work. Along with catch phrases such as "Dis is moida," "Can you pitcha dat?" and "Age before beauty," he mangled the English language with his monstrous malaprops and Bowery pronunciation.

Leo was the second of the three sons born to Bernard and Josephine Gorcey; Fred (born in 1915) was the oldest and David (1921) was the youngest. He also had a half-sister, Audrey by a later marriage of his mother.

Gorcey's father had earned a reputation as a successful actor through his role as Papa Isaac Cohen in *Abie's Irish Rose*, the longest running Broadway show until *Tobacco Road*. However, despite being president of his high school drama class, Leo wanted to be a plumber, not an actor.

When casting calls went out for the Broadway production *Dead End* in 1935, his father insisted that Leo try out for a role. Leo didn't want to leave his job as apprentice in his Uncle Rob's plumbing shop where he was earning $6 a week, but when he was temporarily fired, he visited his brother at the rehearsal hall and landed a role in *Dead End*, but not as "Spit." Accompanied by younger brother David, Gorcey played one of a rival gang, the "Second Avenue Boys." Leo eventually replaced Charles Duncan as "Spit," and was soon singled out by critics as the most convincing of the boys. His salary soon went from $35 to $50, and upward.

When he went to Hollywood with the rest of the kids in 1937, their exploits received much press. They raced around Hollywood in their newly acquired jalopies with little or no regard for the law. By age 21, Gorcey had reportedly received 18 citations for various traffic offenses, including speeding. According to his autobiography, Gorcey fixed it with bailiffs so his first 25 charges did not culminate in court appearances. Despite his reputation, Gorcey attended church and wrote poems and short stories.

Most of Gorcey's notoriety and publicity came through his marital adventures, which rivaled Mickey Rooney's in public attention. "I married them all," he once said.

His first wife was a 17-year-old dancer, Catherine "Kay" Marvis, whom he married in Yuma, Arizona, on May 16, 1939, and honeymooned with near Boulder Dam. She is visible in several Eastside Kids films, including *Kid Dynamite* and *Block Busters*, in which she had credited roles. Leo was to recall that she was "about as intellectual as a retarded turtle." The Gorcey marriage lasted five years. On February 24, 1945, Kay married Groucho Marx, with whom Leo had worked on radio's "Pabst Blue Ribbon Town." When Leo found he was required to pay alimony despite Groucho's earning more money than he, he complained to the comedian in person. Groucho, however, refused to become involved in his wife's personal affairs. In 1951, she would divorce Groucho, having netted a bundle from her 12-year stint as a comedian's wife. She never remarried.

Honeymooning with Kay.

"Edward G. Robinson helps bandage the hand of Leo Gorcey after an exciting "Abandon Ship" sequence in which Gorcey was injured on the set of Destroyer *at Columbia Studios." —Caption written by Columbia for still # D-116-P-41.*

The second Mrs. Gorcey was 26-year-old Evalene Bankston, whom Leo married on October 24, 1945, and later found to be his most unbridled wife. She refused to accept the religion of the high-paid Bowery Boys star, and created a silence when she felt they had nothing to talk about. She filed for divorce in the third year of their marriage, on February 29, 1948. Figuring that evidence of her husband's cheating habits would increase her alimony and share of the settlement, she hired two detectives to search the Gorcey home at 4616 Longridge Avenue in Sherman Oaks. Upon entering, they found Leo greatly disturbed. Since the Gorceys weren't on speaking terms, Mr. Gorcey expressed his anger by drawing his gun and firing three shots at Mrs. Gorcey. Luckily, the shots were errant. Leo was arrested for assault with a deadly weapon, but the charge was dropped. Leo countersued for illegal entry and won $35,000 from his ex-wife and her sleuths. The amount she paid deeply cut into her $50,000 divorce settlement.

Gorcey waited another year before his third wedding, this time to actress Amelita Ward. When Leo married her in Ensenada, Mexico, on February 12, 1949, she had just recently been leading lady in the Bowery Boys film *Smuggler's Cove*, and had also appeared in two Eastside Kids vehicles (*Clancy Street Boys* and *Come Out Fighting*). She bore Leo his first children: Leo Jr., born in 1949, and Jan, a daughter named after Leo's agent-producer, Jan Grippo, in 1951. However, after seven years of marriage, it was Gorcey who filed for divorce, in February, 1956, citing affairs she had with at least three men: a cowboy, a dentist and a doctor. In the divorce settlement, Leo won custody of the children and the Calabassas home at 23629 Long Valley Road. Lita was the recipient of a piece of property the Gorceys owned in the North.

By this time, Gorcey had a severe drinking problem. This was not helped by the death of his father in an auto accident. Everywhere Leo looked on the set, he saw apparitions of his father. Realizing that his health depended upon his leaving Hollywood, he sought recluse on his ranch in Los Molinos, Ca., 100 miles north of Sacramento in Tehama County. In the same year, 1956, he married his fourth wife, his children's governess, Brandy. For the first time in his life, he had the opportunity to relax, and on his Brandy Lee Ranch, he raised Hereford cattle, chickens and pigs. He increased his family size up there: At the turn of the decade, he welcomed into the world his second daughter, Brandy Jo. He was well equipped to leave the screen: he made $12,500 on his last eight days of shooting, not including the $10,000 he collected as his 15 percent of the profits on his last film, *Crashing Las Vegas*.

However, by the early Sixties, the acting bug bit him again, and he was soon advertising in trade magazines with photographs of his slightly aged self in a variety of

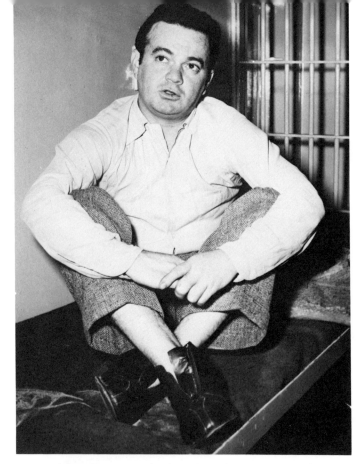

Leo in a police station after being dragged in for taking a few potshots at his estranged wife in 1948.

Huntz Hall, Richard Lamparski (of "Whatever Became of . . ." book series fame), and Leo Gorcey. The aging Leo looked like Edward G. Robinson, and Huntz had adapted his clean-shaven facial features for serious Broadway work, when this reunion photo was shot, 1968.

costumes. In 1964, it was announced that Leo and Huntz Hall would form Four Winds Productions in order to produce a film in which they would star. There were talks of negotiations with Milton Berle, Hal Collins and Buddy Arnold for a script originally written by Berle for himself and Mickey Rooney.

After divorcing Brandy (1962), Gorcey published his memoirs, *An Original Dead End Kid Presents: Dead End Yells, Wedding Bells, Cockle Shells and Dizzy Spells*, in 1967. He also married for what he hoped would be the last time, to Mary Gannon, in February, 1968. It was the last, for he died June 2, 1969, an hour before his fifty-second birthday, of a liver ailment, in an Oakland hospital.

In addition to his timeless work with the kids, he tallied up strong non-series credits during his Hollywood years. He did his first solo work, a bit in Republic's *Portia on Trial* (1937), while preparing for the film version of *Dead End*. The following year he was loaned out to M.G.M. for a featured role as Joan Crawford's brother in *Mannequin*. He more or less sticks to his established character, particularly in a scene in which he complains about the hot dogs and sauerkraut his family has to live on. When informed by his mother that many boys would be happy to have the food, he replies, "Tell me who and I'll give 'em mine."

At his home lot, Warner Brothers, he had two similar bits, in *Invisible Stripes* (1939) and *Out of the Fog* (1941), as a warehouse foreman and a short order cook/bartender, respectively. From 1940 to 1942, he had roles in five features made for M.G.M.'s "B" picture department while committed to Monogram. One of these films, *Born to Sing* (1942), a let's-put-on-a-show type, features a musical finale directed by Busby Berkeley.

In 1941, Gorcey worked in a Republic musical with Jane Frazee, bearing the unusual title *Angels With Broken Wings*. Although the part was another supporting job, the role was a harbinger of later Eastside Kids and Bowery Boys characterizations of Gorcey. His lines include, "Dames! When I see what dey can do to a nice, hardworkin, truckdriver,. . . I get disillusioned," and, to Billy Gilbert, "Greetings Gate" (long a catch phrase of Bob Hope's radio show). The same year he had a shot in an "A" picture, Paramount's *Road to Zanzibar*, as a boy who briefly speaks to Bing Crosby. However, his part is excised from most television prints in circulation.

During the war years, Gorcey played opposite one of his idols, Edward G. Robinson, in *Destroyer* (1943), a Columbia release. In the film, Gorcey is used extensively. Whenever someone is needed to walk across the screen or do a chore, it's usually Leo. During this time, he also found employment in radio, throwing barbs at Groucho Marx on "Pabst Blue Ribbon Town."

He had a part in an insignificant Paramount "B" whodunit, *Midnight Manhunt* (1945), and three years later had his last solo role for fifteen years. In Stanley

Kramer's *So This is New York*, his role is almost autobiographical. The film (completed March 8, 1948) is loaded with references to his shooting of his second wife. Other characters say that he has a "murderous streak" and a jail record. He is so realistic in a scene where he gets drunk that one could fall asleep watching him.

Seven years after his retirement, Gorcey advertised himself in the trade papers. Stanley Kramer, whom Leo had worked for fifteen years earlier, cast him in his comedy extravaganza *It's a Mad, Mad, Mad, Mad World*. Leo plays a cab driver who delivers Sid Caesar and Edie Adams to a San Diego department store.

Two years later, Gorcey was reunited with Huntz Hall in a country-western opus, *Second Fiddle to a Steel Guitar*, in which the duo, as comic stagehands, steal what there is of the picture. The two also did a cameo with a myriad of other stars in *The Phynx* (1969), a disaster which has yet to see general release.

Portia on Trial (Rep. 1937). D: George Nicholls, Jr. Frieda Inescort, Walter Abel, Heather Angel, Neil Hamilton, Ruth Donnelly, Barbara Pepper

Mannequin (MGM 1938). D: Frank Borzage. Joan Crawford, Spencer Tracy, Alan Curtis, Ralph Morgan, (CLIFFORD CASSIDY), Elisabeth Risdon.

Invisible Stripes (WB 1939). D: Lloyd Bacon. George Raft, Jane Bryan, William Holden, Humprey Bogart, Flora Robson, Paul Kelly, (JIMMY).

Gallant Sons (MGM 1940). D: George B. Seitz. Jackie Cooper, Bonita Granville, (DOC REARDON), June Preisser, William Tracy, Tommy Kelly.

Out of the Fog (WB 1941). D: Anatole Litvak. Ida Lupino, John Garfield, Thomas Mitchell, Eddie Albert, George Tobias, John Qualen, (EDDIE), Bernard Gorcey.

Road to Zanzibar (Para. 1941). D: Victor Schertzinger. Bing Crosby, Bob Hope, Dorothy Lamour, Una Merkel, Eric Blore, Joan Marsh, (BOY).

Angels With Broken Wings (REP. 1941). D: Bernard Vorhaus. Binnie Barnes, Gilbert Roland, (PUNCHY DORSEY), Mary Lee, Jane Frazee, Billy Gilbert.

Down in San Diego (MGM 1942). D: Robert B. Sinclair. Dan Dailey, Jr., Bonita Granville, Ray McDonald, (LG), Stanley Clements, Henry O'Neill.

Born to Sing (MGM 1942). D: Edward Ludwig. Virginia Weidler, Ray McDonald, (SNAP COLLINS), Rags Ragland, Douglas MacPhail, Sheldon Leonard.

Sunday Punch (MGM 1942). D: David Miller. William Lundigan, Jean Rogers, Dan Dailey, Jr., Guy Kibbee, J. Carroll Naish, (BIFF).

Maisie Gets Her Man (MGM 1942). D: Roy Del Ruth. Ann Sothern, Red Skelton, Allen Jenkins, Donald Meek, Lloyd Corrigan, (CECIL).

Destroyer (Col. 1943). D: William B. Seiter. Edward G. Robinson, Glenn Ford, Marguerite Chapman, Edgar Buchanan, (SARECKY), Regis Toomey.

Midnight Manhunt (Para. 1945). D: William Thomas. William Gargan, Ann Savage, (CLUTCH), Don Beddoe, Paul Hurst, Charles Halton.

So This Is New York (UA 1948). D: Richard O. Fleischer. Henry Morgan, Rudy Vallee, Hugh Herbert, Virginia Grey, Dona Drake, (SID MERTZER).

It's a Mad, Mad, Mad, Mad World (UA 1963). D: Stanley Kramer. Spencer Tracy, Milton Berle, Sid Caesar, Buddy Hackett, Ethel Merman, Mickey Rooney, Jonathan Winters, Phil Silvers, (FIRST CABBIE), 40 cameos.

Second Fiddle to a Steel Guitar (Marathon 1965). D: Victor Duncan. Arnold Stang, (STAGEHAND), Huntz Hall, Minnie Pearl, Homer and Jethro, Bill Monroe, Lefty Frizzell.

The Phynx (WB 1970). D: Lee H. Katzin. A. Michael Miller, Ray Chippeway, Dennis Larden, Lonny Stevens, Joan Blondell, (CAMEO APPEARANCE).

HUNTZ HALL

"We couldn't step out of character when the whistle blew. I've been slugged at least 25 times by guys who wanted to find out if I'm as tough as I make out. I've had more black eyes than a prize fighter." Huntz Hall said this in 1944. The line shows how the tough guy image has been confused with the Sach Jones we all have inside us waiting to escape. He represents a magnification of the ignoramus in many people. With his upturned baseball cap, huge bowtie, crooked nose and blank expression, Hall appeared in a total of 81 features and serials with the gang, more than any other individual actor.

Huntz's father was an air conditioning repairman. He apparently did well in controlling the temperature of his own home because he and his wife had 16 children. Henry Richard, rechristened "Huntz" by a brother because his nose made him look German, was the fourteenth.

Shortly after his birth on August 15, 1919, he made his stage debut in his hometown of New York. He was one year old; the play was *Thunder on the Left.* Following his graduation from St. Stephen's grammar school, Hall entered the famed Professional Children's School. During this time, Huntz was a boy soprano with the Madison Square Quintette, which performed at the Roxy Theatre, and appeared in an experimental 1932 television broadcast. When he subjected his voice to peanut hawking at a circus in Madison Square Garden, he lost his gift. He found radio work on "Bobby Benson's Adventures" (with Billy Halop), "The Life of Jimmy Braddock" and Arch Oboler's "Rich Kid."

While still at the Professional Children's School, Hall heard about casting auditions for *Dead End.* "I went down to try out for *Dead End* and I tried out for Spit. I was going to my class from Professional Children's

School and a man comes down the street called Martin Gabel and he looked at me and said, 'You've been down to try out for *Dead End?*' And I said, 'Yeah, but I lost it.' He said, 'Come back again and I'll put you in a taxi, send you back.' So he takes me back and they were all sitting in the green room, and I walk in with Martin Gabel, and Sidney Kingsley was rehearsing them and all of a sudden there was a kid doing 'Hey, look at me fellas, I got a machine gun, De De De Dey De Dey De Dey,' and Kingsley said 'READ THE LINE, READ THE LINE,' and the kid said, 'Hey look at me, I got a machine gun, Tee-dee Tee-dee Tee-dee Tee-dee.' So Kingsley turned to me. He said, 'Can you do a machine gun?' 'Look at me, I got a machine gun, Y ha Hea Hea Hea.' That's how I got in *Dead End*, with all the training, the tap dancing, singing lessons."

Huntz still hasn't forgotten his roots. When he told this story, 40 years later, he paused to mention that Gabel gave him a dollar for the taxi, which he bypassed in favor of the subway. Even after achieving fame, he fondly remembered the ninety-five cents taxi fare he pocketed.

Like the other kids, Huntz was quickly taken by the Hollywood lifestyle. In 1940, he eloped with 18-year-old dancer Elsie May Anderson to Yuma, Arizona. (Yuma was a popular place for Hollywood celebrities to get married.)

His scant solo roles were uneventful. In *Private Buckaroo* (1942), he has only two short scenes, playing a dead-pan corporal who teaches Harry James to blow a bugle (!). Nevertheless, his years at Universal were a key period for him in learning the art of comedy. He picked up a few pointers from Shemp Howard, and spent time on the sets of the studio's W.C. Fields vehicles watching

the "Great Man" in action.

At this time. Huntz Hall met Bela Lugosi. Lugosi approached him and said, *"Huntz Hall*, I hearrr you're going to work for Mono-grrram." It was so.

Contrary to his insipid screen image, Huntz could be incisive. "I picked the baseball cap because it was the national pastime and the game was played all over the world. I just turned it up in front." Here he is using the same logic advertising professionals are paid multi-digit thousands of dollars a year to apply to products. He analyzed the situation and opted for the choice that would benefit him most.

Huntz was also devoting time to a favorite pursuit: girls. His attention to stenographers, secretaries and salesgirls in the films reflected his real life flirtatiousness. Jane Nigh recalls, "He asked me for a date about 1943, but I wouldn't go out with him because he had *such* a bad reputation," In Doug McClelland's *The Golden Age of "B" Movies*, Evelyn Ankers recalls an incident that occurred during a day's shooting of *Hit the Road*: "I thought I was the last one to leave the set, but on my way out I bumped into 'little tough guy' Huntz Hall (acne and all). He put his arms around me and tried to force me to kiss him. I responded as my daddy taught me to—I let him have it with my knee right between the legs. He fell to the ground yelling bloody murder and I took off." He also took up an interest in Shakespeare, which is observable in the films. (He ad-libbed "parting is such sweet sorrow " from time to time.)

Huntz and Elsie Mae were divorced April 8, 1944. He served in the Army until he received an honorable discharge for bad eyesight, Returning to movie making, Huntz made three 1945 solo appearances—all of which had him playing military personnel. The first two, *Bring On the Girls* and *Wonder Man*, cast him as a sailor. In the latter (shot in Technicolor), his back is seen for a considerable amount of time wrapped around a pretty civilian. Only after his identity is revealed do we see another side: a persona that punches Danny Kaye in the jaw.

His third 1945 non-series role outshines these; Louis Milestone's *A Walk in the Sun* has been hailed as one of the most realistic portraits of men in war ever filmed. Hall plays Carraway, one of a platoon of men marching on a suicidal mission through Italy. He reminisces to another soldier about the bands represented in his sister's record collection, and argues that the human body, and not the leaf, is the most complicated form on earth. He was recognized for his work in the film by the New York Theatre Critics Circle, who presented him with the coveted Blue Ribbon Award.

On October 29, 1948, Hall and a producer-friend heard noises outside Huntz's newly acquired residence at 1775 North Sycamore in Los Angeles, and phoned the police. When the cops arrived, they found no prowlers. What they did find was $200 worth of marijuana buried in four cans in Hall's backyard. Six months later, Hall was exonerated by a hung jury. It was never disclosed how the contraband got there.

Today Huntz is a good boy. In 1973, he served on Princess Grace [Kelly] of Monaco's Council on Drug Abuse.

During the trial proceedings, Huntz eloped to Mexico City with showgirl Leslie Wright, in December 1948, with another wedding, a more formal one, the next February in Las Vegas. (He had been engaged to another showgirl, Doris Sands of New York, in 1946.) He had his first son, Leslie Richard, on September 22, 1949, two weeks after Leo Gorcey had his first son. A second boy, Gary, followed shortly.

Because of his percentage deal with the Bowery Boys pictures, Huntz was doing well financially. In a November 1954 interview, Huntz commented, "I could retire in three years and Leo could retire today." He expressed one disadvantage to being a celebrity: "When we go on tour, little kids kick me in the leg." While this would suggest that Hall didn't like kids, he raised his own children beautifully. His son Gary graduated with honors from Yale.

He had been a proud father all along, and cast and crew members of the Bowery Boys production company could expect to see Huntz's sons on the set one day on every picture.

In the early Fifties, Huntz teamed with Gabe Dell to form the "Hall and Dell" nightclub duo to perform when he wasn't filming. This stage partnership cost each a wife. On May 14, 1953, Leslie Hall and Barbara Dell sued the pair for divorce, claiming that they thought more of their nightclub act than they did of their wives. In addition to her $600 a month alimony and $100 a month child support, Mrs. Hall received 5 percent of Huntz's gross income.

Hall's reign as a bachelor got him into more trouble with the law. On April Fool's Day, 1954, Hall allegedly roughed up the apartment building manager at 1111 Larabee Street when the manager tried to quiet a noisy party at which Huntz was a guest. Living at 8818 Appian Way at the time, Huntz was charged with disturbing the peace, fined $50, and placed on probation.

Another police run-in occurred February 1, 1959, when he was hauled in on a drunk driving charge. Giving his address as 8949 Sunset Blvd., the former Bowery Boy was described in newspaper accounts as "belligerent and mad at everyone."

Huntz has always been funny with cars and finances. Jane Nigh recalls that before *Hold That Hypnotist* started filming, he went to Las Vegas and won some money, part of which he used to buy a $10,000 Cadillac. In 1976, *Who's Who in Hollywood* reported that he was buying a new Rolls-Royce every year with money he made in offshore oil. A little over a year later, when other Hollywood luminaries were pulling up to a Hollywood film convention in expensive vehicles, Hall pulled up

A grizzled character pose from Gentle Giant.

Broadcasting nonetheless turned out to be Huntz's career base during the Sixties. In 1960, Allied Artists sold the Bowery Boys to television syndication, bestowing on Huntz his 10 percent cut of the profits when he most needed it. He appeared on "The Jerry Lester Show" and "The Tonight Show," but made his video acting debut on a two-part special of the show "Flipper." Broadcast September 24 and October 1, 1966, the episode, "Disaster in the Everglades," allowed Huntz to play a serious role once again. Television ads depicted a grubby-looking Huntz trudging through the swamplands. This led to work as an acting coach on both "Flipper" and its counterpart series, "Gentle Ben." The latter had grown out of the film *Gentle Giant*, which cast Huntz as the comic sidekick to villainous Ralph Meeker.

The Seventies brought more television employment. He served as dialogue coach on the TV-movie *Lost Island* (1971), and had a role in another TV job, *Escape*, the same year. In September of that year, he was cast as comic hoodlum Dutch in CBS's "The Chicago Teddy Bears," a comedy gangster spoof starring Dean Jones, which lasted three months in a Thursday night 8:00 slot. In the mid-Seventies he was seen in occasional roles on the Saturday-morning live-action show "The Ghost Busters." Starring Forrest Tucker and Larry Storch, the CBS series was produced and directed for Filmation by one-time Little Tough Guy Norman Abbott.

On the big screen, Huntz only received bit parts in a couple of features, including Gabriel Dell's *Manchu Eagle Murder Caper Mystery*. Then in 1977, director Ken Russell cast Huntz as movie mogul Jesse Lasky in *Valentino*. Huntz says he's in debt to Russell for giving him the chance to do what he wanted to do: "act." The film received lackluster reviews, but Huntz was warmly received. After that, he accepted the script for *The Super Duper Service Station*, which made it to the R-rated screen as *Gas Pump Girls*. His billing reads "Huntz Hall as Uncle Joe," the character being the owner of a small gas station who has a heart attack, thus forcing his resourceful niece to take over operations. And the film points out with its camera angles that she has her "resources" in all the right places!

Huntz spent much of the late Seventies on the New York stage and performing with veteran actors. E.G. Marshall and Dennis O'Keefe were on the same program with him when he did a production of Neil Simon's *The Odd Couple*. *The Sunshine Boys*, also from Simon, is on his credits, garnered on the Southern California dinner theater circuit with Marvin Kaplan, with whom he had worked on TV's "The Chicago Teddy Bears." Also to his name: *Born Yesterday, The Streets of New York* and *Norman, Is That You?*

In 1982, Huntz appeared on what could be described as an "adult Saturday Night Live." This made-for-cable special entitled "Channel Zero" utilized the talents of Chevy Chase, Laraine Newman and Martin Mull,

behind the wheel of a beat-up Volkswagen. (Huntz finds it necessary to borrow cars when he attends public events. He is besieged by fans who have obtained his address through D.M.V. records. Consequently, he moves from apartment to apartment every three months.)

Huntz was uninvolved with motion pictures for some time after the Bowery Boys expired. The Sixties saw a parade of unfulfilled projects planned by Hall. In 1964 the Gorcey-Hall partnership was formed for a film to be produced for their Four Winds Productions by Ben Melzer. The following year saw the proposal for a film to star Huntz and Basil Rathbone, to be based on *Dr. Jekyll and Mr. Hyde*. The proposed title? *Dr. Rock and Mr. Roll*. Hall-initiated television projects included a rumored "Bowery Boys Cartoon Series" in which he and Leo would provide their own voices, and a Seventies' program to be called "The Ghetto Boys," obviously to be influenced by the work he was most associated with.

among others, and featured Huntz in a scene spoofing long-distance telephone commercials.

Residing with his third wife, Leah, in Hollywood, Hall is a proud family man. His son Gary became an Episcopal priest. In 1978, Huntz was presented with the National Film Award for Outstanding Contributions and Achievements in the Film Industry on behalf of the National Film Society.

And how is Huntz? If that fortune he could retire on in 1957 isn't enough, he struck it rich in offshore oil. He still does dinner theater work and television commercials. Huntz apparently is living the way he always has; leaving each new day open for adventure. And isn't that what life is all about?

The Return of Dr. X (WB 1939). D: Vincent Sherman. Wayne Morris, Rosemary Lane, Humphrey Bogart, Dennis Morgan, John Litel, (PINK).

Zis Boom Bah (Mon. 1941). D: William Nigh. Grace Hayes, Peter Lind Hayes, Mary Healey, (SKEETS SKILLHORN), Jan Wiley, Benny Rubin.

Private Buckaroo (Uni. 1942). D: Edward E. Cline. Andrews Sisters, Dick Foran, Harry James and His Music Makers, Joe E. Lewis, Jennifer Holt, Shemp Howard, (CORPORAL ANEMIC).

Junior Army (Col. 1942). D: Lew Landers. Billy Halop, Freddie Bartholemew, (BUSHY THOMAS), Bobby Jordan, Bernard Punsly, Boyd Davis, William Blees.

Bring On the Girls (Para. 1945). D: Sidney Lanfield. Eddie Bracken, Veronica Lake, Sonny Tufts, Marjorie Reynolds, Grant Mitchell, (SAILOR).

Wonder Man (Gold.-UA 1945). D: H. Bruce Humberstone. Danny Kaye, Virginia Mayo, Vera-Ellen, S.Z. Sakall, Donald Woods, (MIKE, A SAILOR).

A Walk in the Sun (20CF 1945). D: Lewis Milestone. Dana Andrews, Richard Conte, John Ireland, Lloyd Bridges, Sterling Holloway, (CARRAWAY).

Second Fiddle to a Steel Guitar (Marathon 1965). D: Victor Duncan. Arnold Stang, Leo Gorcey, (STAGEHAND), Minnie Pearl, Homer and Jethro.

Gentle Giant (Para. 1967). D; James Neilson. Dennis Weaver, Vera Miles, Clint Howard, Ralph Meeker, (DINK SMITH), Charles Martin.

Huntz on the Mike Douglas Show.

The Phynx (WB 1970). D: Lee H. Katzin. A. Michael Miller, Ray Chippeway, Dennis Larden, Lonny Stevens, Joan Blondell, (CAMEO APPEARANCE).

Escape (Para.-TV 1971). D: John Llewellyn Moxey. Christopher George, William Windom, Marilyn Mason, Avery Schreiber, Gloria Grahame, (GILBERT).

Herbie Rides Again (BV 1974). D: Robert Stevenson. Helen Hayes, Ken Berry, Stefanie Powers, Keenan Wynn, John McIntyre, (CAR JOUST JUDGE), Ivor Barry.

Manchu Eagle Murder Caper Mystery (UA 1975). D: Dean Hargrove. Gabriel Dell, Will Geer, Joyce Van Patten, Anjanette Comer, Vincent Gardenia, (DEPUTY ROY).

Won Ton Ton, the Dog Who Saved Hollywood (Para. 1976). D: Michael Winner. Bruce Dern, Madeline Kahn, Art Carney, Phil Silvers, Teri Garr, (MOVING MAN).

Valentino (UA 1977). D: Ken Russell. Rudolf Nureyev, Leslie Caron, Michelle Phillips, Carol Kane, Felicity Kendall, (JESSE LASKY), Seymour Cassel.

Gas Pump Girls (Far West 1979). D: Joel Bender. Kirsten Baker, Dennis Bowen, (UNCLE JOE), Sandy Johnson, Mike Mazurki, Joe E. Ross.

The Escape Artist (Orion 1982). D: Caleb Deschanel. Raul Julia, Griffin O'Neal, Desi Arnaz, Teri Garr, Joan Hackett, Gabriel Dell, (TURNKEY).

Gabe Dell draws to fire in Framed *(1975).*

GABRIEL DELL

The most successful of all the kids in his work away from the gang, Gabriel Dell did not learn the niceties of his trade until after he had worked on Broadway and appeared on screen 40 times. The most eclectic of the boys in his role variations, Gabe could play a club member, a cheap hoodlum or the boys' more mature friend.

However, he was only the third oldest of the original six Dead End Kids, born October 4, 1919, in Brooklyn (later given as 1930 in Barbados), as Gabriel Marcel Del Vecchio. His father, an Italian immigrant, hoped that his son would follow in his footsteps and become a doctor. Gabe had other ideas: He had the performing bug. He made a deal with his dad: If he made good marks in English, drama classes and class plays, his father would sponsor him in a good theatrical school. Gabe was soon enrolled in the Professional Children's School.

Singing in the choir at St. Paul's Church as a boy and then working on a kid show at station WWBC in New York, Gabe seemed destined for an entertainment career.

He almost made his stage debut a few years before *Dead End* when he and his sister were slated for roles in *The Good Earth*, with Alla Nazimova and Claude Rains. However, due to an infantile paralysis epidemic in Philadelphia, where the debut was to take place, no child performers were permitted to appear on stage.

By the time he was cast in *Dead End*, Gabe had changed his last name to Dell (though he never legally acquired the monicker). In Hollywood, Gabe scampered back and forth between Warners, Universal and Monogram, but never worked apart from the boys.

During World War II, Dell became a member of the Merchant Marine, in which he served as Lieutenant (j.g.)

for three and a half years. In Dell's words, "I went 'to save democracy.' " Returning to Monogram and the new Bowery Boys, Gabe found his characterization of mature Gabe Moreno to be outside the structure of the gang.

He left the series for good in 1950, winning a role in the Broadway musical revue *Tickets Please*. He also formed a nightclub partnership with Huntz Hall that resulted in the breakup of both men's marriages. Gabe's wife Barbara and Mrs. Hall jointly divorced them May 14, 1953, citing the act as an alienating factor.

Deciding that he should finally learn his trade the correct way, Gabe spent three years at the Actor's Studio, worked in industrial shows, and took classes in ballet and modern dance. He studied mime under Etienne Decroux, the man who taught Marcel Marceau. Marrying ballerina Viola Essen (who had appeared in Ben Hecht's *The Spectre of the Rose* in 1946), he had a son, Beau Del Vecchio, in 1956.

Gabe landed a role in Fred Finklehoffe's comedy-musical *Ankles Aweigh*, starring Betty and Jean Kean, in 1955. Cast as a sailor, Gabe joined in on numbers such as "Walk Like a Sailor" and "Here's to Dear Old Us."

Television beckoned Dell in the late Fifties when he joined the stock company of NBC's "The Steve Allen Show." Joining Don Knotts, Louis Nye, Tom Poston, Bill Dana, Pat Harrington, Dayton Allen and Skitch Henderson, Gabe was a member of what was considered to be the best TV stock company of all-time. Gabe was often called upon to do his Bela Lugosi imitation, which always brought down the house. When the Allen show ended in 1959, Dell stayed on in the (surprise!) "New Steve Allen Show," which lasted a year.

Back on the New York stage, Gabe took the role of

By Wonder
Walter Bard

Boris Adzinidzinadze in a 1959 revival of Cole Porter's *Can Can*. From 1961 to 1964, Dell was able to secure roles in several on- and off-Broadway shows, a combination of musicals, dramas and comedies, as well as flops and successes. They included: *The Automobile Graveyard, Fortuna* (in the title role), *Man Out Loud, Girl Quiet/Spanish Armada, Wonderful Town, Oklahoma, Marathon '33* and *Anyone Can Whistle*.

Surprisingly, Gabe did not make his first film appearance away from the boys until 1960, when he went to Puerto Rico to appear in a low-budget pseudo-comedy called *Caribe* (it was released two years later as *When the Girls Take Over*). In 1963, he went into a recording studio for A.A. Records and supplied all the voices for "Famous Monsters Speak," with dialogue written by Cherney Berg. On one side, Gabe plays a reporter at a press conference at which actual, taped recordings of Frankenstein's monster are played. Gabe also supplies voices for Dr. Frankenstein and the beast. On side two, he gets to use his vampire dialect in a similar story about Dracula. This disc is still a popular seller around Halloween.

Returning to Broadway in 1964, Dell won the role that was a turning point for him. He assayed the title character in Lorraine Hansberry's *The Sign in Sidney Brustein's Window*, which ran for some 99 performances and got Gabe some recognition as a serious dramatic actor.

It was at this time that he learned a lesson. In *Sign* he was billed above the title for the first time. When he first gazed at the marquee, he was ecstatic: "This was it; this was what it was all about. Then two days later, it was gone." He realized then that he would have to keep improving on himself.

He followed this up with another hit, replacing Alan Arkin in the role of Harry Berlin in the long-running comedy show *Luv*. Off-Broadway, he played in *Chocolates* (1967) and the following year was third-billed in *Something Different*.

A second son, Gabriel Jr., was born in 1967, to third wife Allyson Daniell (the daughter of character actor Henry Daniell). His son could see him come into the living room via television. He appeared on "The Naked City," "Ben Casey," "Mannix" and "Then Came Bronson." He finished off the decade with another success, as "The Contestant" in Elaine May's *Adaption*.

In the last two decades, Gabe has developed some strong convictions, He is a teetotaler. (Wise, considering that three of his five *Dead End* colleagues were lost to alcohol.) He is also fighting the war against drugs, thinking of actor friends he has seen defeated by dope, when their careers were at a low ebb. "I'm convinced that's how a person gets hooked. A sense of unproductivity and unworthiness takes over and then they try to make something happen to them."

Gabe's philosophy is that of Zen. As a follower of this Eastern religion, he shuns materialism, and lives a life that isn't dependent on man-made conveniences. The Zen convictions are ones he accepted once mature. He had been born into a Jewish family.

The Seventies found Gabe gravitating toward more film and television roles. His Broadway performances were limited to the flop *Fun City* (1972), *Where Do We Go From Here?* (1974) and *Lamppost Reunion* (1975). He continued with television shots, in "The Name of the Game," "McCloud," "Banyon" and "Sanford and Son."

In June 1972, ABC cast Gabe as bartender Harry Grant, the proprietor of "The Corner Bar" in the mature summer replacement series of that name. When the show reappeared the next season, Dell was replaced.

Gabe was captured on celluloid several times during the Seventies. His image changed from one appearance to another. In *Who is Harry Kellerman and Why Is He Saying Those Terrible Things About Me?*, he plays a greying man who has a yen for girls. Gabe excuses himself from a conversation with Dustin Hoffman because he has "a foreign shipment" coming in. When Hoffman asks him if by "shipment" he means "European Stewardesses," Gabe answers with a subtle "Yeah." In *Framed* (1975) he plays a mob-hired assassin friend of Joe Don Baker, and has a sense of humor. He takes on a disguise with a Southern accent, fedora hat and mustache, as he and Baker try to exploit political graft.

Later in 1975, Dell co-authored a screenplay with Dean Hargrove called *The Manchu Eagle Murder Caper Mystery*, in which Gabriel Dell, for the first time in films, was the full-fledged star. He is a private eye in a spoof of Forties detective films. Huntz Hall has a supporting role as a police deputy.

In the wake of the mid-Seventies TV private eye boom, CBS cast Gabe in a 1976 pilot, "Risko," essaying Joe Risko, a more up-to-date gumshoe. The next year he had another chance for television success in Norman Lear's "A Year at the Top." Gabe played Frederick Hanover, the Devil's son, and the plot was based on the old concoction of souls being sold to the Devil for material success. Mickey Rooney starred, but the series did not make it past six episodes.

In 1979, Gabe was involved in a revival of *Luv*, at Mickey Rooney's dinner playhouse in the Long Beach-docked Queen Mary. His counterpart was none other than Huntz Hall. The two were billed in newspaper ads as "The Bowery Boys." Gabe has continued to act, but recently he has moved behind the scenes as well, as a director at some small theaters and playhouses. Considering his varied experience in just about every aspect of performing, Dell seems an excellent choice to coach actors in getting the best performance possible.

When the Girls Take Over (Trans-Oceanic 1962). D: Russell Hayden. Robert Lowery, Marvin Miller, Jackie Coogan, Jimmy Ellison, (HENDERSON).

Fifty-Five Days in Peking (AA 1963). D: Nicholas Ray. Charlton Heston, Ava Gardner, David Niven, Flora Robson, John Ireland, (REPORTEDLY HAS A BIT ROLE, THOUGH NOT IN CAST LIST).

Gabe Dell (left), with Bob Berand, in a 1969 Mark Taper Forum production of Adaptions.

Who is Harry Kellerman and Why Is He Saying Those Terrible Things About Me? (National General 1971). D: Ulu Grosbard. Dustin Hoffman, Barbara Harris, Jack Warden, David Burns, Dom DeLuise, (SID).

Earthquake (Uni. 1974). D: Mark Robson. Charlton Heston, Ava Gardner, George Kennedy, Richard Roundtree, Lorne Greene, (MILES' MANAGER).

Framed (Para. 1975). D: Phil Karlson. Joe Don Baker, Conny Van Dyke, (VINCE GREESON), John Marley, Brock Peters, Roy Jenson.

Manchu Eagle Murder Caper Mystery (UA 1975). D: Dean Hargrove. (MALCOLM), Will Geer, Joyce Van Patten, Anjanette Comer, Jackie Coogan, Vincent Gardenia, Huntz Hall.

300 Year Weekend (Worldvision Enterprises 1977). D: Victor Stoloff. William Devane, Michael Tolan, Sharon Laughlin, Roy Cooper, (GD), Mel Dowd.

The Escape Artist (Orion 1982). D: Caleb Deschanel. Raul Julia, Griffin O'Neal, Desi Arnaz, Teri Garr, Joan Hackett, (UNCLE BURKE), Huntz Hall.

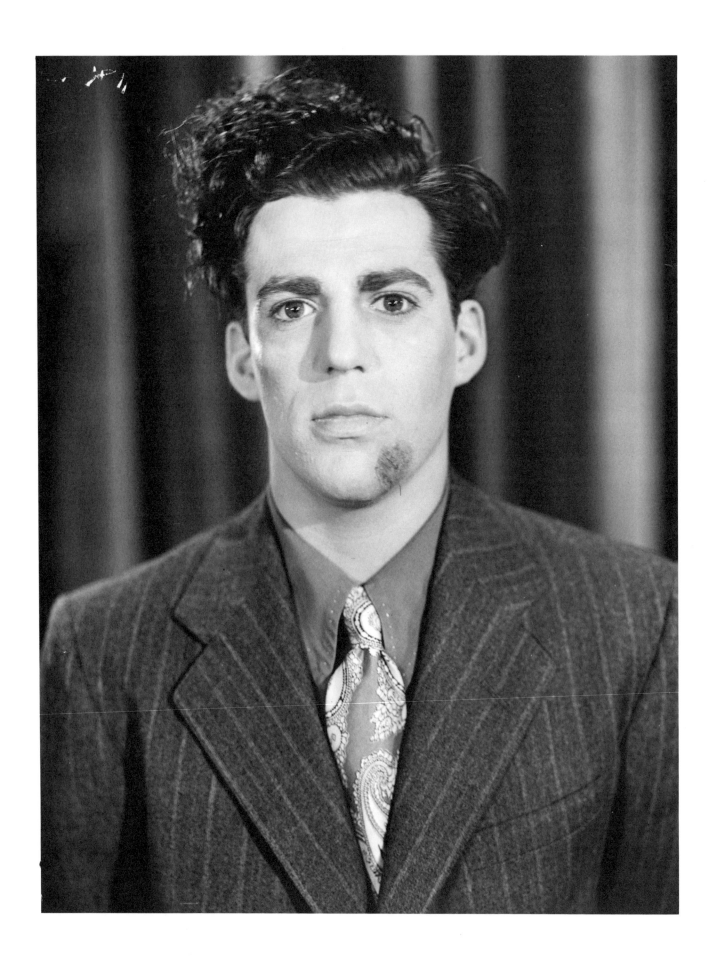

BILLY HALOP

A professional actor from age six, Billy Halop never fulfilled his goal to become a respected film star, like idol Paul Muni, away from the shadow of the Dead End Kids. Billy was the original leader and heartthrob of the group, despite his appearing in little over a dozen films with the kids.

William Halop was born into a show business family in Brooklyn, on May 11, 1920. His mother Lucille was a dancer. In 1926 he made his professional performing debut with his younger sister Florence when a small radio station requested children from his private school for roles in a broadcast.

This led to a prepubescent career over the airwaves, appearing with Florence on children's shows such as "The Children's Hour" and "Let's Pretend." For a while he played the title role in "Skippy," and could be heard on the serial "Home Sweet Home." His greatest radio fame as a youth was in the title role as a juvenile cowboy on CBS's "Bobby Benson's Adventures," which ran from 1932 to 1936, sponsored by Heckers H-O Cereal. He toured the country with Colonel W.T. Johnson's rodeo portraying Bobby Benson for eager kiddies.

By the time he won his *Dead End* role, Halop was earning about $750 a week for his radio roles. His previous experience entitled him to more money than the others and a private dressing room, factors that eventually fueled friction between himself and the other five Dead Enders.

Furthermore, Billy did not want to be typecast as a Dead End Kid and saw his future as a featured performer on his own. In 1939, Warners gave him a couple of non-series roles to test his mettle as an actor. In *Dust Be My Destiny*, Halop played the older brother of Bobby Jordan, friends of drifter John Garfield.

A bigger break came in *You Can't Get Away With Murder*, which gave him equal screen time with star Humphrey Bogart. Billy is a young hood whose emulation of tough Bogie lands him in the federal pen after the two pull a job. At the end, Bogart guns his young companion down in a freight car to keep him from talking. Halop then gasps for life until he can betray Bogart.

He had a few subsequent roles in the early Forties, but nothing to break a new career open by. In 1943, he entered the military service, leaving his film career dormant. A sergeant in the Signal Corps, Billy was stationed in the Special Services and performed in productions for troops in Europe. However, when the war ended, Halop had to face the realities of a returning veteran. He suddenly found film roles hard to come by, and had to be satisfied with playing the leader in PRC's *Gas House Kids* (1946).

In May 1946, Billy travelled to Las Vegas to marry 23-year-old New York actress Helen Tupper. But his first marriage was destined for disaster, and the two were divorced January 14 of the following year. Billy was apparently unready for life with his first mate, for he testified that she refused to keep house or cook during their marriage.

The movie industry once again looked promising for Billy, when 20th Century-Fox cast him in *Dangerous Years*, a 1947 juvenile delinquency drama. For the first time, Billy realized his dream of being the first-billed star without the guise of the Dead End Kids. Ironically, the film is remembered today because it was Marilyn Monroe's film debut, not for Halop's performance.

This break did not lead to better things for Billy, and the anguish he suffered from lack of work led to a

DEK-L16
C.S.B.63

Jordan, Halop, Gorcey, Hall, Dell.

With Helen Parrish in Little Tough Guy.

drinking problem, a nervous breakdown and a suicide attempt. On February 14, 1948, Billy married Barbara Hoon, who was eight years his elder, in Palm Springs.

Unable to secure constant work in films, Halop decided to explore the infant medium of television. His first role came in the CBS drama "Racket Squad" in 1952, and over the next three years he was seen in "playhouse" type productions such as "Footlights Theater," "Favorite Story" and "Robert Montgomery Presents."

Los Angeles police locked Billy up at his own request on a drunk charge in June of 1954. Billy called the police and told them he had taken eight sleeping pills, which turned out to be a falsehood. Claiming that his wife had left him, he received a five-day suspended sentence.

He recovered and received a role in *Air Strike* (1955), which cast later Bowery Boy Stanley Clements (who, like Halop, had a small part) and Billy together for the only time. In 1957, he did a TV spot in CBS's "Telephone Time."

His ten-year marriage to Barbara finally came to an end when they separated March 5, 1958. They divorced, childless, in January of the following year.

No longer getting acting roles with regularity, Billy began working as an electric dryer salesman for the Leonard Appliance Company of Los Angeles. He excelled in this, received recognition in the field, and was once named Most Creative Salesman in the U.S. by the National Association of Manufacturers.

On December 17, 1960, he married his "first love," Suzanne Roe, a multiple sclerosis victim. Leaving his job as head chef at Ted's Rancho in Malibu, Halop wanted to seek a medical degree, but was discouraged by friends because of his age. Instead, he became a Registered Nurse at St. John's Hospital.

Still active in film and television, he was seen on two episodes of "The Adventures of Ozzie and Harriet" in 1963, as well as on "Perry Mason" and "The FBI." A few bit parts in movies followed.

Things were not working out with his marriage, and in 1967 he divorced Suzanne and moved into a trailer court. His future lay in television, and in 1969, the first steady acting part came his way since the Dead End Kids days. NBC cast him in its hour-long dramatic series "Bracken's World," which used the movie industry as its background. Billy had a small but repeating role as Pat, the studio projectionist. Debuting September 1969, the show ran through 41 episodes before its January 1971 demise.

Passing the time with a part as a judge in an "Adam-12" episode, Billy found another steady part on one of television's most memorable series, "All in the Family." He played Bert Munson, a taxi driver, who hung out at Kelsey's Bar, frequented by Carroll O'Connor's Archie Bunker. It is only fitting that Billy should end up as a tough character from the streets of New York.

Some time after a part in the TV movie *Phantom of Hollywood*, which takes place on the M.G.M. back-lot, Halop fell victim to two coronaries. He died in his sleep of a heart attack on November 9, 1976, leaving his mother, brother Joel and sister Florence.

Dust Be My Destiny (WB 1939). D: Lewis Seiler. John Garfield, Priscilla Lane, Alan Hale, Frank McHugh, John Litel, (HANK GLINN), Bobby Jordan.

You Can't Get Away With Murder (WB 1939). D: Lewis Seiler. Humphrey Bogart, (JOHNNIE STONE), Gale Page, John Litel, Henry Travers, Harold Huber.

Tom Brown's Schooldays (RKO 1940). D: Robert Stevenson. Jimmy Lydon, Cedric Hardwicke, Freddie Bartholemew, Gale Storm, Josephine Hutchinson, (FLASHMAN).

Blues in the Night (WB 1941). D: Anatole Litvak. Priscilla Lane, Richard Whorf, Betty Field, Lloyd Nolan, Jack Carson, (PEPE).

Sky Raiders (Uni. serial 1941). D: Ford Beebe and Ray Taylor. Donald Woods, (TIM BRYANT), Robert Armstrong, Kathryn Adams, Edward Ciannelli, Bill Cody, Jr.

Junior Army (Col.1942). D: Lew Landers. (JIMMIE FLETCHER), Freddie Bartholemew, Huntz Hall, Bobby Jordan, Bernard Punsly, Boyd Davis, William Blees.

Gas House Kids (PRC 1946). D: Sam Newfield. (TONY ALBERTINI), Robert Lowery, Teala Loring, Carl Switzer, Rex Downing, Hope Landon.

Dangerous Years (20CF 1947). D: Arthur Person. (DANNY JONES), Ann E. Todd, Jerome Cowan, Anabel Shaw, Scotty Beckett, Darryl Hickman.

Too Late for Tears (UA 1949). D: Byron Haskin. Lizabeth Scott, Don DeFore, Dan Duryea, Arthur Kennedy, Kristine Miller, (BOAT ATTENDANT).

Challenge of the Range (Col. 1949). D: Ray Nazarro. Charles Starrett, Smiley Burnette, Paul Raymond, (REB MATSON), Steve Darrell, Henry Hall.

Air Strike (Lip. 1955). D: Cy Roth. Gloria Jean, Richard Denning, Don Haggerty, Bill Hudson, Alan Wells, (BH).

For Love or Money (Uni. 1963). D: Michael Gordon. Kirk Douglas, Mitzi Gaynor, Thelma Ritter, Julie Newman, Gig Young, (ELEVATOR OPERATOR).

A Global Affair (MGM 1964). D: Jack Arnold. Bob Hope, Yvonne DeCarlo, Robert Sterling, John McGiver, Lilo Pulver, Michele Mercier.

Mr. Buddwing (MGM 1965). D: Delbert Mann. James Garner, Jean Simmons, Suzanne Pleshette, Angela Lansbury, Katherine Ross, (SECOND CABBIE).

Fitzwilly (UA 1967). D: Delbert Mann. Dick Van Dyke, Barbara Feldon, Edith Evans, John McGiver, John Fielder, (LUIGI).

Phantom of Hollywood (MGM-TV 1974). D: Gene Levitt. Skye Aubrey, Jack Cassidy, Jackie Coogan, Broderick Crawford, Peter Lawford, (STUDIO ENGINEER).

BOBBY JORDAN

"Bobby Jordan must not have had a guardian angel."
—Leo Gorcey, in his autobiography

The youngest of the original Dead End Kids, Bobby Jordan also led the most tragic life of them all, falling victim to his child star status. The young smart aleck of the Dead Enders, he became the innocent "good" boy of the Eastside Kids, and was one of three Dead Enders who appeared in all four film series.

The son of a New York merchant, Robert Jordan made his debut in life on April Fool's Day, 1923. Four-and-a-half years later, he was working in a Christmas carol film. At age six, he won a radio serial role. With varied skills, including the ability to tap dance and play the saxophone, Bobby entered talent contests around Harrison, New York. At one point, he modeled junior boys clothing. Through the Professional Children's School, Bobby made his stage debut in the 1930 production of *The Would-Be Gentleman*, as a page. Among the other students of the school at that time was Eddie Bracken, who played a slave.

Though the youngest, Bobby was the first of the boys to work in motion pictures, with a 1933 role in a Universal short subject. Bobby appeared in *Dead End* for the entire first season and the beginning of the second, but left in mid-November, 1936, returning in time to join the other boys on their trip to Hollywood.

During his Warner Brothers tenure, Jordan had a memorable role as the aggravating nephew of gangster-gone-straight Edward G. Robinson in the hilarious *A Slight Case of Murder* (1938). He kept busy during the 1938-39 season, working on loan-out, and at the home

studio in solo appearances. In 1940's *Young Tom Edison*, he played a would-be bully skeptical of the experiments of Mickey Rooney in the title role.

After a role in the serial *Adventures of the Flying Cadets* in 1943, he entered the military as a foot soldier in the 97th Infantry. Back in civilian life in 1945, he was involved in an elevator accident which forced the removal of his right kneecap.

His former equals Gorcey and Hall were the clear-cut stars of the new Bowery Boys series, and Bobby was forced to take a back seat. After eight episodes, he left, ending any hopes for a steady career. He had married Lee, who was ten years older, in 1946, and in 1949 the couple had a son, Robert Carl.

He then became a bartender, which was the worst thing in the world considering that he was an alcoholic.

During the next decade, to support his family, Bobby was forced to work as a door-to-door photograph salesman and a roughneck for a Coalinga oil driller. In 1956 he had a bit part in a bit film, *The Man Is Armed*, which spelled the end of his film career.

In 1957, he and his wife divorced, with her retaining custody of eight-year-old Robert Jr. In May 1958, he was cited for being $612 behind in alimony. His wife was awarded a total of $1137 in alimony and child support. Newspapers couldn't help pointing out that he once lived in a $150,000 mansion and made $1500 a week.

On August 25, 1965, Bobby entered the Veterans Hospital in Sawtelle, California, for treatment of cirrhosis of the liver, hastened by his heavy drinking. Shortly after 8:00 A.M., September 10, Bobby Jordan succumbed to the disease. He was 42.

A Slight Case of Murder (WB 1938). D: Lloyd Bacon. Edward G. Robinson, Jane Bryan, Allen Jenkins, Ruth Donnelly, John Litel, (DOUGLAS FAIRBANKS RO-SENBLOOM).

Reformatory (Col. 1938). D: Lewis D. Collins. Jack Holt, (PINKEY LEONARD), Charlotte Wynters, Grant Mitchell, Tommy Bupp, Frankie Darro.

My Bill (WB 1938). D: John Farrow. Kay Francis, Bonita Granville, Anita Louise, Dickie Moore, John Litel, (REGINAL COLBROOK).

Off the Record (WB 1939). D: James Flood. Pat O'Brien, Joan Blondell, (MICKEY FALLON), Alan Baxter, William Davidson, Morgan Conway.

Dust Be My Destiny (WB 1939). D: Lloyd Bacon. John Garfield, Priscilla Lane, Alan Hale, Frank McHugh, Billy Halop, (JIMMY GLINN).

Young Tom Edison (MGM 1940). D: Norman Taurog. Mickey Rooney, Fay Bainter, George Bancroft, Virginia Weidler, Eugene Pallette, (JOE DINGLE).

Military Academy (Col. 1940). D: Ross Lederman. Tommy Kelly, (DICK HALL), David Holt, Jackie Searl, Don Beddoe, Jimmy Butler.

Junior Army (Col. 1942). D: Lew Landers. Billy Halop, Freddie Bartholemew, Huntz Hall, (COWBOY), Bernard Punsly.

The Adventures of the Flying Cadets (Uni. serial 1943). D: Ray Taylor and Lewis D. Collins. Johnny Downs, (JINX ROBERTS), Jennifer Holt, Ward Wood, Billy Benedict, Eduardo Ciannelli.

The Treasure of Monte Cristo (SG 1949). D: William Berke. Glenn Langan, Adele Jergens, Steve Brodie, (ITALIAN FRIEND), Michael Whalen, Margia Dean.

The Man Is Armed (Rep. 1956). D: Franklin Adreon. Dane Clark, William Talman, May Wynn, Robert Horton, Barton MacLane, Fred Wayne.

Bobby Jordan gave Edward G. Robinson more trouble than he could handle in A Slight Case of Murder *(1938).*

Bobby Jordan, 1958, arrested for failing to pay his wife alimony.

BERNARD PUNSLY

The "quiet" Dead End Kid never had the motion picture aspirations of his five mates. He left the screen in 1943, and resurfaced—as a practicing M.D.

Bernard Punsly (often misspelled "Punsley") was born on July 11, 1922. Little did Mrs. Punsly's doctor know that he was delivering a prospective internist. Young Bernard had no show business experience when he was cast in the play *Dead End*. As pudgy "Milty," he was the "new" member of the gang. When the kids went into movies, Bernard remained in the background as the least visible kid at Warner Brothers and Universal.

While the other boys were out raising havoc in Hollywood, the studious Bernard was home reading books. He was not—nor did he want to be—the tough guy people saw on screen. "Sure, I can dish it out and I can take it," he once explained, "but most people don't understand I'm only tough when I'm acting."

Apparently Bernard never wanted to be an actor. He explains, "When you're fifteen years old, the whole show business idea seems, on the surface, like the thing to do. I just came face to face with the realities of it all."

Bernard's lack of filmic ambition resulted in a lack of non-series roles. His only known part away from the gang—other than in the unclassifiable semi-gang picture *Junior Army* with Halop, Hall and Jordan—was in Paramount's *The Big Broadcast of 1938*, in a scene featuring W.C. Fields. Bernard is a caddy who must put up with Fields' antics when he comes to a golf course to play a few aborted rounds.

After completing the second-to-last Universal picture, Bernard entered the service via the Army Medical Corps. This furnished him with the training for his life's career. Upon his discharge, Bernard entered the University of Georgia, and after years of work in medical school, became a certified M.D.

He says he doesn't watch his old films. "My kids will, but to me they're like looking at snapshots of when I was younger. Don't get the wrong impression: I had fun doing those films at the time. I just grew out of that scene."

Once known as Milty, Fats, Hunky, Ouch and Ape, he can now be paged as Dr. Bernard Punsly. His office, located in the Del Amo Mall in Torrance, California, is about 30 miles from where he once romped before motion picture cameras. Asked whether his medical cronies know about his former career as a Dead End Kid, he answered, "If they do, they're very discreet."

BERNARD PUNSLY, M.D.

DIPLOMATE OF THE AMERICAN BOARD
OF INTERNAL MEDICINE

SUITE 208
21320 HAWTHORNE BLVD.   PHONE FRONTIER 0 Edited
TORRANCE, CALIF. 90503   DAY OR NIGHT

188

DAVID GORCEY

Playing in the shadow of brother Leo and father Bernard for 20 years (he appeared in 60 series films, more than anyone except Huntz), David Gorcey, who used the last name Condon during those years when his brother and father were well-known, wrestled futilely with show business as a career. To his credit, he was not "infected" by performing, and has managed nicely in the unglamourous world of the priesthood.

Born on February 6, 1921, in Washington Heights, David was the last of the Jewish-Catholic Gorcey couple's three sons. He was slightly taller and not quite as pudgy as Leo, but had the same thick, jet-black hair.

It was David who arranged for Leo to get his *Dead End* role. David was set to play one of the Second Avenue Boys, but Leo hadn't auditioned for a part. However, Leo was fired from his plumbing job on the day of the dress rehearsal, so Leo went to the theater to visit David. The boy David was to play opposite fainted before he was to go onstage. David didn't want to jeopardise his part, so he coaxed his brother into playing the other part. Leo was discovered to be an "imposter," but since he was so good, he was asked to assume the part. Had David not helped his brother, Leo would never have gone on to play "Spit" and Slip Mahoney.

Leo was to repay the favor later when he insisted that Monogram give David a Bowery Boys role as part of Leo's deal to play Slip Mahoney.

He was offered a chance to follow Leo's Hollywood success with his role as a Universal Little Tough Guy, but ended up in the Monogram fold behind his more accomplished brother. He left the Eastside Kids (1942) after a brief stint, presumably for military duty, but returned in 1946 when the Bowery Boys were organized, and remained faithful to the series, appearing in every film made during the 12-year span except the debut film.

Like father Bernard, he sought out a few non-series roles to supplement his credits (and income). His final solo part was his funniest, in *Abbott and Costello in the Foreign Legion* (1950). He plays a newsboy hawking papers in the middle of the Sahara Desert. When Lou Costello asks him why he is peddling his wares in such a remote location, David snaps, "Can I help it if they gave me a bad corner?"

He was married to Dorthea during the Forties, and in 1946, she gave birth to David Jr. On September 16, 1951, she filed for divorce, complaining, "He stays out nights."

At the time of the divorce, David worked in a gas station in Sherman Oaks. Second jobs were not uncommon in the Gorcey family; Bernard owned a printing shop on Santa Monica Blvd., west of La Cienega, and Leo sold real estate in the San Fernando Valley.

Today, the survivor of the acting Gorceys is the Reverend David Gorcey, a Los Angeles-based clergyman who specializes in helping kids. He has been involved in drug dissuasion programs aimed at troubled youngsters. It is fitting that an ex-Dead End Kid turned his attention to the plights of underprivileged youths.

Prairie Moon (Rep. 1938). D: Ralph Staub. Gene Autry, Smiley Burnette, Champion, Shirley Dean, Tommy Ryan, (CITY KID), Walter Tetley.

Juvenile Court (Col. 1938). D: Ross Lederman. Paul Kelly, Rita Hayworth, Frankie Darro, Hally Chester, Don LaToree, (PIGHEAD).

Little Tough Guys in Society (Uni. 1938). D: Erle C. Kenton. Frankie Thomas, Harris Berger, Hally Chester, Charles Duncan, (YAP), William Benedict, Mischa Auer, Mary Boland, Edward Everett Horton, Helen Parrish, Jackie Searl.

Newsboys' Home (Uni. 1939). D: Harold Young. Jackie Cooper, Edmund Lowe, Wendy Barrie, Samuel S. Hinds, Edward Norris, Elisha Cook, Jr., William Benedict, (YAP), Charles Duncan, Harris Berger, Hally Chester, Irving Pichel.

Code of the Streets (Uni. 1939). D: Harold Young. Harry Carey, Frankie Thomas, Harris Berger, Hally Chester, (YAP), Charles Duncan, William Benedict, James McCallion, Leon Ames, Juanita Quigley, Paul Fix, El Brendel.

Sergeant Madden (MGM 1939). D: Josef von Sternberg. Wallace Berry, Tom Brown, Alan Curtis, Laraine Day, Fay Holden, (PUNCHY), Etta McDaniel.

City For Conquest (WB 1940). D: Anatole Litvak. James Cagney, Ann Sheridan, Arthur Kennedy, Donald Crisp, Frank Craven, (FORSYTHE BOY).

Blues in the Night (WB 1941). D: Anatole Litvak. Priscilla Lane, Richard Whorf, Betty Field, Lloyd Nolan, Jack Carson, Elia Kazan.

Tuxedo Junction (Rep. 1941). D: Frank McDonald. Weaver Brothers and Elviry, Thurston Hall, Frankie Darro, Sally Payne, Clayton Moore, Billy Benedict.

French Key (Rep. 1946). D: Walter Colmes. Albert Dekker, Mike Mazurki, Evelyn Ankers, John Eldredge, Frank Fenton, Richard Arlen.

Killer McCoy (MGM 1947). D: Roy Rowland. Mickey Rooney, Brian Donlevy, Ann Blyth, James Dunn, Tom Tully, (TRAINER ASSISTANT).

The Babe Ruth Story (AA 1948). D: Roy Del Ruth. William Bendix, Claire Trevor, Charles Bickford, Sam Levene, William Frawley, (FOURTH NEWSBOY).

Abbott and Costello in the Foreign Legion (Uni. 1950) D: Charles Lamont. Bud Abbott, Lou Costello, Patricia Medina, Walter Slezak, Douglass Dumbrille, (DESERT NEWSBOY).

"SUNSHINE SAMMY" MORRISON

Ernest Frederick "Sunshine Sammy" Morrison is almost a walking book of show business history. Before playing Scruno, the only black member in the entire 20-year history of the series, Morrison was *the original* Our Gang kid, a juvenile sidekick to Harold Lloyd, a vaudeville star, dancer and band leader.

Born in 1912 in New Orleans, Morrison was the son of a chef for a rich Louisiana family. The Doheny family, visiting in New Orleans, liked Mr. Morrison's work and persuaded him to work for them out west. One of the frequent visitors to the Doheny's Los Angeles mansion was John T. Osborne, head of his own film studio and father of child star Baby Marie Osborne. The elder Morrison was invited to Osborne's studio, and soon came in handy when a film crew needed a black baby.

"So they asked my father," recalls the junior Morrison. "'Bring a baby out here tomorrow,' and he said, 'Okay.' He didn't take me, he took the neighbor's kid. For some reason, every time they put the camera on, he raised hell. They couldn't get anything out of him. So somebody says, 'Joe, you got a kid. Bring yours out here tomorrow. He can't be any worse than this one.' So I happened to be just the opposite, because I didn't cry and my eyes were open. They got what they wanted, and someone says, 'Joe, we should call this kid Sunshine because he didn't cry all day today.' My dad added Sammy behind the Sunshine, and took the name and copyrighted it."

After some minor work at the Osborne studios, Ernie went to Mack Sennett studios for a brief uncontracted stint, in which he did no work. Finally, in 1919, he wound up at the Rolin studio in the Bradbury mansion in downtown Los Angeles. The young head of the company, Hal Roach, was busy with his two star comedians: Harold Lloyd and Snub Pollard.

When Sunshine Sammy's undeniable charisma was discovered, he was placed prominently in films showcasing each of the comedians. He appeared with Lloyd in *Haunted Spooks* and *Get Out and Get Under*, in both cases almost out-doing the legendary comedian with his youthful antics. He was billed equally with Pollard during the 1920-21 season when the pair appeared together in a series of one-reelers as a comic team, overriding age and color barriers. The next time Ernie saw Snub was when the latter performed in bit parts at Monogram.

When Roach moved his studio to Culver City, Morrison went with him, continuing to work with comics such as Jimmy Parrott, Billy Engle and George Rowe. In 1921, Roach awarded Sunshine Sammy his own series, but only one film, *The Pickaninny*, was produced. The idea was aborted by Roach, who finally brought to fruition his plan for a kids series—Our Gang. Already possessing a contract providing a 10 percent profit share, unheard of in those days, Morrison, the first one chosen for the gang, knew he was a valuable commodity.

After 28 Our Gang films, Morrison left in 1924 to

Best Wishes
& Thanks For Everything
For
"Sunshine Sammy"
1981

"Sunshine Sammy" shows his prize to George Rowe in this shot, circa 1921.

*"Sunshine Sammy," with Allen "Farina" Hoskins and goats, in an
early Our Gang comedy.*

pursue a career in vaudeville, at first capitalizing on his Our Gang fame and then polishing his various talents as an entertainer. For the next 16 years, he pounded the boards, spending most of his time in New York. In those days it was possible to play theaters in the New York vicinity continually for 52 weeks a year.

Morrison has many fond memories of his vaudeville years. With his partner Sleepy Williams, he was constantly active on the circuit. He shared bills with Jack Benny and Abbott and Costello, and resided in the same entertainers' hotel as Count Basie when the latter was writing his famous songs.

Morrison was one of the fortunate child actors who recognized the moral values of his experiences. On the subject of popular silent film idol Wallace Reid, whose death was induced by a Hollywood-fed narcotics habit, he says:

"I wondered, being a kid; I was trying to find out why he died. I tried at the studio, and I being a little kid, they shrugged me off. Finally, one actor pulled me over and said, 'Ernie, I understand you're trying to find out what happened to Wallace.' He set me down, and ran it down to me, what it [morphine] would do to you, tear you up inside, so forth. I was a kid; I was satisfied he told me.

"Years later, I was with some guys. They took me up to a big palatial place. They had bunks in there, for guys in there who could smoke hop. You could get anything on a drug line you wanted. I walked in there and see these guys tying up their damn arms, putting on rubber, snorting coke. What that actor told me that day came back. MAN, I BROKE THE DOOR DOWN GETTING OUT OF THERE."

In regard to an 11-day jail sentence incurred when a woman claimed that he had fathered her child, he states, "I decided, no way was I going to do anything where they could put me in a place where I couldn't come out when *I wanted to get out.*

"They'd say, 'Jail is made for people,' and I'd say, 'Some people. Not for me.'"

In the late Thirties, Morrison and his partner went to Australia for a year, and when they returned, Ernie found that the movies beckoned him again. Included were *I Can't Give You Anything But Love, Baby*, in which he and Jeni LaGon sing the title song. (He had previously done some musical soundies.) Sam Katzman, a former theatrical producer with whom he had worked, also wanted him to fill out the cast of the Eastside Kids.

From the start, he had to draw upon his own New York experiences for his role as Scruno. "The first script I ever got," he recalls, "I said, 'No way.' So I went to Sam, I told him, 'Look, now I grew up in New York, and I know how a black guy with white kids down on the Eastside is going to act and talk. This damn script is all wrong.' He said, 'Okay, you take the script and read it, then you do it the way you think it ought to be done.' One day the director—he hadn't been with us before—

wanted me to read these lines, and I said, 'I can't read them like that.' Sam came on the set, and the director said, 'Sammy won't work.' Sam said, 'There must be something wrong if *he* won't work.' Sam directed it, I said it like I thought it should be said, and he said, 'Cut! Cut! *That's a good scene.*' And Sam said, 'Any time he doesn't want to do it, let him alone, and you'll get something.'"

Morrison spent three years with the Eastside Kids, and often went on promotional tours with Huntz Hall and Bobby Jordan up and down the coast of California. However, two factors terminated his work with the gang.

When one of the Step Brothers, a stage and film dance team who were friends of Sammy's, had to take leave, Morrison was asked to fill in. A couple of film appearances followed, and Morrison was almost awarded a contract at 20th Century-Fox when he was called for war duty.

When he got out of the service after a two-year stint, he was offered a part in the Bowery Boys, whose films were being produced by Morrison's agent Jan Grippo. He declined the offer: "I didn't like the set-up."

Morrison eventually wound up working in the aircraft industry in the Los Angeles area. He worked at several plants making parts for aircraft, and spent 17 years at a Compton company, inspecting the quality of factory parts. For some 30 years, he was not involved in show business in any way.

Now living just a stone's throw away from the site of the old Hal Roach studio where the Our Gang series and some of the Eastside Kids films were shot, Morrison has recently set out to conquer television. He has done bits on "Good Times" and "The Jeffersons," as well as appearing in the pilot of a "Jeffersons" spin-off which was to be based on the maid character, Florence.

"Sunshine Sammy" in Boys of the City.

"Sunshine Sammy" Morrison being accosted by autograph seekers
at the Sons of the Desert convention, Los Angeles, 1980.

Gang War (Million Dollar 1939). D: ? Ralph Cooper, Gladys Snyder, Reggie Fenderson, Lawrence Criner, Monte Hawley.

I Can't Give You Anything But Love, Baby (Uni. 1940). D: Albert S. Rogell. Broderick Crawford, Peggy Moran, Johnny Downs, Warren Hymer, John Sutton, (JOE, THE BUTLER).

Fugitive From a Prison Gang (Col. 1940). D: Lewis D. Collins. Jack Holt, Marian Marsh, Robert Barrat, Philip Terry, Dennis Moore.

The Ape Man (Mon. 1943). D: William Beaudine. Bela Lugosi, Louise Currie, Wallace Ford, Henry Hall, Minerva Urecal, (COPY BOY).

Greenwich Village (20CF 1944). D: Walter Lang. Don Ameche, Carmen Miranda, William Bendix, Vivian Blaine, Felix Bressart, Step Brothers, (ONE OF THE STEP BROTHERS).

Shine on Harvest Moon (WB 1944). D: David Butler. Ann Sheridan, Jack Carson, Dennis Morgan, Irene Manning, S.Z. Sakall, Step Brothers, (ONE OF THE STEP BROTHERS).

"Our Gang" comedies with Sunshine Sammy" (all produced by Hal Roach and released by Pathe):

1922: *Our Gang, Fire Fighters, Young Sherlocks, One Terrible Day, A Quiet Street, Saturday Morning.*

1923: *The Big Show, The Cobbler, The Champeen, Boys to Board, A Pleasant Journey, Giants vs. Yanks, Back Stage, Dogs of War, Lodge Night, Fast Company, Stage Fright, July Days, Sunday Calm, No Noise, Derby Day.*

1924: *Tire Trouble, Big Business, The Buccaneers, Seein' Things, Commencement Day, It's a Bear, Cradle Robbers.*

STANLEY CLEMENTS

Between his stints with the Eastside Kids and the Bowery Boys, Stanley Clements built up a sizeable reputation as a teenage hoodlum in many major Hollywood productions. It is for this that he should be remembered, not for his questionable casting as Leo Gorcey's successor.

Of Polish descent, Stanley was born in Long Island on July 16, 1926. When he was three, his mother, Anna, remarried to building wrecker Ignatius Adroncik and the family moved to Brooklyn, He was the youngest of four boys, following Benny (1914), Joey (1920) and Walter (1924). He also had two sisters: Anna Jr. and Jennie.

Attending P.S. 49 in Brooklyn, Clements picked up the nickname Stash, a Polish translation of Stanley. It was there that Stan realized that his ambition was to be a performer. After touring in vaudeville for two years, Clements joined "Major Bowes' Amateur Hour" on tour before returning to Brooklyn because he was homesick.

In 1941, he signed a contract with 20th Century-Fox. A year earlier, he had been singing in subways for handouts, before police stopped him. His second film role, as Cesar Romero's juvenile pal in the gangster comedy *Tall, Dark and Handsome*, cemented his place in Hollywood.

According to his 1942 20th Century-Fox studio biography (if studio bios are to be believed), Stan liked horses, veal cutlets and the Brooklyn Dodgers. His favorite author was said to be Horatio Alger.

After a brief stint in the Eastside Kids, Stanley found that he was in demand for prime roles in Hollywood "A" features. In George Stevens' *The More the Merrier* (1943), he is a lad who suspects Joel McCrea of being a Japanese spy. He rose even further to receive fifth-billing in Leo McCarey's classic *Going My Way* (1944), as the leader of a bunch of kids whom a priest (Bing Crosby) tries to win over. He was showcased in *Salty O'Rourke* (1945), playing a smart aleck jockey who gives up his life at the end so that leads Alan Ladd and Gail Russell can live happily ever after.

Stanley served in the U.S. Army from 1944 to 1946, during which time he wed actress Gloria Grahame (in 1945). When they divorced in 1948, she was just making a name for herself with roles in *It's a Wonderful Life* and *Crossfire*. Several years afterward she won an Academy Award for Best Supporting Actress in *The Bad and the Beautiful* (1952).

Stan kept busy in the late Forties and early Fifties, mostly in *film noir* type pictures. At Monogram/Allied Artists, he starred in an action series produced by future Bowery Boys budgeter Ben Schwalb.

Clements' second marriage came in December 1951, when he and Polish immigrant Maria Walek tied the knot. She had been in the country a year and a half.

When he was announced as the new "brains" of the Bowery Boys in April 1956, he had already flirted with the series via his associations with Schwalb and director Edward Bernds (*White Lightning* and *Hot News*, both

Stanley Clements in Salty O'Rourke *(1945)*

1953), in addition to his experiences as an Eastsider.

After the Bowery Boys breakup, Clements again sought roles, though they did not come as readily as before. In 1958 he co-wrote the screenplay for *The Devil's Partner*, which was produced the same year, but not released until 1961. After larger roles in a couple of low-budget films, he did a cameo in *It's a Mad, Mad, Mad, Mad World*, as one of Spencer Tracy's fellow detectives. (Unfortunately, most of his appearance—which is spread over five scenes—is not seen on television, since the film was shot in Cinemascope, and Clements was photographed in that part of the widescreen frame which was cropped at the sides.)

In 1964, Stan and Maria adopted her eight-year-old nephew Sylvester from Poland. "We couldn't have children of our own," explained Stan, "so we wanted Sylvester very badly." The boy was the first child adopted from a country behind the Iron Curtain under a proxy adoption law.

"We were afraid it would never come true. I wanted to give him the chance and education I never got."

Clements continued to reside in the L.A. area until he succumbed to emphesema on October 16, 1981. He was fifty-five.

Accent On Love (20CF 1941). D: Ray McCarey. George Montgomery, Osa Massen, J. Carroll Naish, Cobina Wright Jr., (SC), Minerva Urecal.

Tall, Dark and Handsome (20CF 1941). D: H. Bruce Humberstone. Cesar Romero, Virginia Gilmore, Milton Berle, Charlotte Greenwood, (HARRY). Sheldon Leonard.

Down in San Diego (MGM 1941). D: Robert B. Sinclair. Dan Dailey, Jr., Bonita Granville, Ray McDonald, Leo Gorcey, (SC), Henry O'Neill.

I Wake Up Screaming (20CF 1942). D: H. Bruce Humberstone. Betty Grable, Victor Mature, Carol Landis, Laird Cregar, William Gargan, (NEWSBOY).

Right to the Heart (20CF 1942). D: Eugene Forde. Joseph Allen, Jr., Brenda Joyce, Cobina Wright, Jr., (STASH), Don DeFore, Hugh Beaumont.

On the Sunny Side (20CF 1942). D: Harold Schuster. Jane Darwell, (TOM SANDERS), Katharine Alexander, Donald Douglas, Freddie Mercer, Ann Todd.

They Got Me Covered (Gold.-RKO 1943). D: David Butler. Bob Hope, Dorothy Lamour, Lenore Aubert, Otto Preminger, Edward Ciannelli, (COPY BOY).

Stan and fiancée Maria Welek just before their 1951 wedding.

The More the Merrier (Col. 1943). D: George Stevens. Jean Arthur, Joel McCrea, Charles Coburn, Richard Gaines, Bruce Bennett, (MORTON RODAKIEWICZ).

Sweet Rosie O'Grady (20C 1943). D: Irving Cummings. Betty Grable, Robert Young, Adolphe Menjou, Reginald Gardiner, Virginia Grey, (DANNY).

Thank Your Lucky Stars (WB 1943). D: David Butler. Eddie Cantor, Joan Leslie, Dennis Morgan, Edward Everett Horton, S.Z. Sakall, (BOY).

The Girl in the Case (Col. 1944). D: William Berke. Edmund Lowe, Janis Carter, Robert Williams, Richard Hale, (TUFFY), Carole Mathews.

Going My Way (Para. 1944). D: Leo McCarey. Bing Crosby, Rise Stevens, Barry Fitzgerald, Frank McHugh, (TONY SCAPONI), Jean Heather.

See My Lawyer (Uni. 1945). D: Eddie Cline. Ole Olsen, Chic Johnson, Alan Curtis, Grace McDonald, Noah Beery, Jr., (WILLIE).

Salty O'Rourke (Para. 1945). D: Raoul Walsh. Alan Ladd, Gail Russell, (TIMOTHY CATE), William Demarest, Bruce Cabot, Spring Byington.

Variety Girl (Para. 1947). D: George Marshall. Mary Hatcher, Olga San Juan, DeForrest Kelley, William Demarest, Frank Faylen, (A PARAMOUNT ACTOR IN PRODUCTION NUMBER).

Big Town Scandal (Para. 1948). D: William C. Thomas. Philip Reed, Hillary Brooke, (SC), Carl Switzer, Darryl Hickman, Tommy Bond.

Hazard (Para. 1948). D: George Marshall. Paulette Goddard, Macdonald Carey, Fred Clark, (JOE, BELL-HOP), Frank Faylen, Maxie Rosenbloom.

The Babe Ruth Story (AA 1948). D: Roy Del Ruth. William Bendix, Claire Trevor, Charles Bickford, Sam Levene, William Frawley, (MESSENGER).

Winner Take All (Mono. 1948). D: Reginald LeBorg. Joe Kirkwood, Jr., Leon Errol, Elyse Knox, William Frawley, (SC), John Shelton.

Racing Luck (Col. 1948). D: William Berke. Gloria Henry, (BOOTS WARREN), David Bruce, Paula Raymond, Harry Cheshire, Dooley Wilson.

Canon City (E-L 1948). D: Crane Wilbur. Scott Brady, Jeff Corey, Whit Bissell, (NEW), DeForrest Kelley, Ralph Byrd.

Bad Boy (AA 1949). D: Kurt Neumann. Lloyd Nolan, Jane Wyatt, Audie Murphy, James Gleason, (BITSY), Martha Vickers.

Mr. Soft Touch (Col. 1949). D: Gordon Douglas and Henry Levin. Glenn Ford, Evelyn Keyes, John Ireland, Beulah Bondi, Percy Kilbride, (ARNBY SWEENEY).

Johnny Holiday (UA 1949). D: Willis Goldbeck. William Bendix, Allen Martin, Jr., (EDDIE DUGAN), Jack Hagen, Herbert Newcomb, George Cisar.

Red Light (UA 1950). D: Roy Del Ruth. George Raft, Virginia Mayo, Gene Lockhart, Barton MacLane, Harry Morgan.

Military Academy (Col. 1950). D: Ross Lederman. (STASH), Myron Welton, Gene Collins, Leon Tyler, James Millican, James Seay.

Destination Murder (RKO 1950). D: Edward L. Cahn. Joyce MacKenzie, Hurd Hatfield, (JACKIE WALES), Albert Dekker, Myrna Dell, James Flavin.

Pride of Maryland (Rep. 1951). D: Philip Ford. (FRANKIE), Peggy Stewart, Frankie Darro, Joe Sawyer, Robert Barrat, Harry Shannon.

Boots Malone (Col. 1952). D: William Dieterle. William Holden, Johnny Stewart, (STASH CLEMENTS), Basil Ruysdael, Carl Benton Reid, Ed Begley.

Jet Job (Mono. 1952). D: William Beaudine. (JOE KOVAK), Elena Verdugo, John Litel, Bob Nichols, Tom Powers, Dave Willock.

Army Bound (Mono 1952). D: Paul Landres. (FRANK CERMAK), Karen Sharpe, Steve Brodie, Harry Hayden, Lela Bliss, Gil Stratton, Jr., Danny Welton.

Off Limits (Para. 1953). D: George Marshall, Bob Hope, Mickey Rooney, Marilyn Maxwell, Eddie Mayehoff, (BULLETS BRADLEY), Jack Dempsey.

White Lightning (AA 1953). D: Edward L. Bernds. (MIKE), Steve Brodie, Gloria Blondell, Barbara Bestar, Lyle Talbot, Frank Jenks.

Hot News (AA 1953). D: Edward Bernds. (SC), Gloria Henry, Ted de Corsia, Veda Ann Borg, Mario Siletti, Scotty Beckett.

The Rocket Man (20CF 1954). D: Oscar Rudolph. Charles Coburn, Spring Byington, Anne Francis, John Agar, George Winslow, Emory Parnell.

Mad At the World (Filmakers 1955). D: Harry Essex. Frank Lovejoy, Keefe Brasselle, Cathy O'Donnell, Karen Sharpe, (PETE), Paul Dubov.

Robbers' Roost (UA 1955). D: Sidney Salkow. George Montgomery, Richard Boone, Sylvia Findley, Bruce Bennett, Warren Stevens, Peter Graves.

Wiretappers (Continental 1956). D: Dick Ross. Bill Williams, Georgia Lee, Douglas Kennedy, Phil Tead, (SC), Ric Roman.

A Nice Little Bank That Should Be Robbed (20CF 1958). D: Henry Levin. Tom Ewell, Mickey Rooney, Mickey Shaughnessy, Dina Merrill, Madge Kennedy, (FITZ).

Sniper's Ridge (20CF 1961). D: John Bushelman. Jack Ging, (CORPORAL PUMPHREY), John Goddard, Douglas Henderson, Gabe Castle, Allan Marvin.

Saintly Sinners (UA 1962). D: Jean Yarbrough. Don Beddoe, Paul Bryar, (SLIM), Ellen Corby, Ron Haggerty, Erin O'Donnell.

It's a Mad, Mad, Mad, Mad World (UA 1963). D: Stanley Kramer. Spencer Tracy, Milton Berle, Mickey Rooney, Jonathan Winters, Dorothy Provine, (DETECTIVE), 40 cameos.

Tammy and the Doctor (Uni. 1963). D: Harry Kellar. Sandra Dee, Peter Fonda, Macdonald Carey, Beulah Bondi, Margaret Lindsay, (WALLY DAY).

That Darn Cat (BV 1965). D: Robert Stevenson. Hayley Mills, Dean Jones, Dorothy Provine, Neville Brand, Ed Wynn, Roddy McDowell.

Panic in the City (Commonwealth United Entertainment 1968). D: Eddie Davis. Nehemiah Persoff, Anne Jeffreys, Howard Duff, Stephen McNally, Dennis Hopper.

The Timber Tramps (Howco International-Arizona General 1975). D: Tay Garnett and Chuck D. Keen. Leon Ames, Claude Akins, Joseph Cotton, Cesar Romero, Rosey Greer, (SC).

Hot Lead and Cold Feet (BV 1978). D: Robert Butler. Jim Dale, Karen Valentine, Don Knotts, Jack Elam, Darren McGavin.

BILLY BENEDICT

In *Master Minds*, as the boys are about to enter a secret cavern, Slip says to Whitey, "You go first, you're the oldest." As it happened, the blond-haired actor who played the bucolic Whitey, Billy Benedict, *was* the oldest, born April 16, 1917, in Haskell, Oklahoma. He is one of the most prolific Hollywood bit players of all time. Besides his 36 films with the Dead End Kids/Little Tough Guys, Eastside Kids and Bowery Boys, Billy appeared in over 90 features and serials over a 40-year span. He built a reputation as the pre-eminent newsboy and messenger boy in motion picture history.

While and after being raised in Tulsa, Oklahoma, William Benedict had a colorful and varied series of jobs. He worked in a bank, but quit because he was required to comb his hair. He also sold newspapers in Denver, worked in a Kansas wheatfield, and was a plumber's helper (as was Leo Gorcey), in Portland, Oregon. Bitten by the acting bug, Billy studied dancing and appeared in school plays.

At age 17, he phoned a 20th Century-Fox casting director long distance and then hitchhiked to the West Coast. He won a contract with the studio, and his first role, in *$10 Raise*, set the precedent: He played an office boy.

He polished his bit-playing so that in his brief appearances he left a memorable impression. In Howard Hawks' *Bringing Up Baby* (1938), he plays Cary Grant's caddy, who is mortified along with Grant at the golf course antics of Katharine Hepburn.

One of five boys chosen to play Universal's Little Tough Guys, Billy continued to free-lance in bit parts. In *My Little Chickadee* (1940), he is a bashful country boy whose schoolroom is taken over by Mae West. Opposite Laurel and Hardy in *Great Guns* (1941) during an Army corral scene, he professes his knowledge of horses. "I've been buckin' broncs since I been knee-high to a cy-ote!"

In addition to his other work, Benedict is remembered by serial fans for his work in several 12-chapter cliffhangers. His most memorable part is as the sidekick of Billy Batson, the boy who turns into a superhero in *The Adventures of Captain Marvel* (1941).

Billy could still make an impression with his bit parts during the Forties. In George Stevens' *Talk of the Town* (1942), he is a messenger boy whose backfiring scooter upsets the serenity of professor Ronald Colman. He is one of the townspeople involved in the innocent lynching of three men in *The Ox-Bow Incident* (1943). He is beautifully seen with a lump in his throat at the film's end. As a Western Union boy in *Without Reservations* (1946), he gets a chance to snub a newsboy, even though he would return to that occupation in future films.

A member of the Monogram gang from 1943 to 1951, Billy remains one of the best-remembered components of the series. More or less replacing "Sunshine Sammy" Morrison as the second comic of the Eastsiders, Billy became Whitey, comic counterpart to Huntz Hall's Sach, in the Bowery Boys, with whom he had special comic interactions in the films.

Billy Benedict, as a buck private, in Great Guns.

When he left the series, Billy took fewer and fewer acting parts. He became an assistant in making miniature sets for Hollywood motion pictures. He returned to film acting from time to time, and in 1969 played a news vendor in *Hello Dolly*. Prophetically, this was the same year he was married, for the first time, to a girl named Dolly.

In the Seventies, Billy tried his hand at television acting. He had his first regular series role since the Bowery Boys when he was cast in CBS' drama "The Blue Knight" in 1975. He played Toby, an informer for George Kennedy's Bumper Morgan, the title character. In 1976 he had a part in the miniseries "The Moneychangers," starring Kirk Douglas.

$10 Raise (20CF 1935). D: George Marshall. Edward Everett Horton, Karen Morley, (OFFICE BOY).

The Doubting Thomas (20CF 1935). D: David Butler. Will Rogers, Billie Burke, (CADDY).

College Scandal (Para. 1935).D: Elliott Nugent. Arline Judge, Kent Taylor, (PENWORTHY PARKER).

The Silk Hat Kid (20CF 1935).D: Bruce Humberstone. Lew Ayres, Mae Clarke, (UNCLE SAM).

Way Down East (20CF 1935).D: Henry King. Rochelle Hudson, Henry Fonda, (AMOS).

Show Them No Mercy (20CF 1935).D: George Marshall. Rochelle Hudson, Cesar Romero, (WILLIE).

Your Uncle Dudley (20CF 1935).D: Eugene Forde. Edward Everett Horton, Lois Wilson, (CYRIL CHURCH).

Three Kids and a Queen (Uni. 1935).D: Edward Ludwig. May Robson, Frankie Darro, (FLASH).

The Country Doctor (20CF 1936).D: Henry King. Jean Hersholt, June Lang, (THE GAWKER).

Meet Nero Wolfe (Col. 1936).D: Herbert Biberman. Edward Arnold, Lionel Stander.

Ramona (20CF 1936).D: Henry King. Loretta Young, Don Ameche, (JOSEPH HYAR).

Adventure in Manhattan (Col. 1936).D: Edward Ludwig. Joel McCrea, Jean Arthur.

The Witness Chair (RKO 1936).D: George Nicholls, Jr. Ann Harding, Walter Abel, (BENNY RYAN).

M'Liss (RKO 1936).D: George Nicholls, Jr., Ann Shirley, John Beal.

They Wanted to Marry (RKO 1936).D: Lew Landers. Betty Furness, Gordon Jones.

Libeled Lady (MGM 1936).D: Jack Conway. Jean Harlow, William Powell, (JOHNNY).

Tim Tyler's Luck (Uni. serial 1937).D: Ford Beebe and Wyndham Gittens. Frankie Thomas, Frances Robinson.

That I May Live (20CF 1937).D: Allan Dwan. Rochelle Hudson, Robert Kent.

The Last Gangster (MGM 1937).D: Edward Ludwig. Edward G. Robinson, Rosa Stradner, (OFFICE BOY).

Laughing at Trouble (20CF 1937).D: Frank R. Strayer. Jane Darwell, John Carradine.

Love in a Bungalow (Uni. 1937).D: Ray McCarey. Nan Grey, Kent Taylor, (TELEGRAPH BOY).

Walking Down Broadway (20CF 1938).D: Norman Foster. Claire Trevor, Phyllis Brooks.

Hold That Co-Ed (20CF 1938).D: George Marshall. John Barrymore, George Murphy, (SYLVESTER).

Bringing Up Baby (RKO 1938).D: Howard Hawks. Cary Grant, Katharine Hepburn, (DAVID'S CADDY).

King of the Newsboys (Rep. 1938).D: Bernard Vorhaus. Lew Ayres, Helen Mack, (SQUIMPY).

Young Fugitives (Uni. 1938).D: John Rawlins. Harry Davenport, Robert Wilcox, (JUDD).

Little Tough Guys in Society (Uni. 1938).D: Erle C. Kenton. Frankie Thomas, David Gorcey, (TROUBLE).

Newsboys' Home (Uni. 1939).D: Harold Young. Jackie Cooper, Little Tough Guys, (TROUBLE).

Code of the Streets (Uni. 1939).D: Harold Young. Frankie Thomas, Little Tough Guys, (TROUBLE).

Man of Conquest (Rep. 1939).D: George Nicholls, Jr., Richard Dix, Gail Patrick, (FIEFIST).

Legion of the Lawless (RKO 1940).D: David Howard. George O'Brien, Virginia Vale.

The Bowery Boy (Rep. 1940).D: William Morgan. Jimmy Lydon, Dennis O'Keefe.

Melody Ranch (Rep. 1940).D: Joseph Santley. Gene Autry, Jimmy Durante, Ann Miller, (SLIM).

My Little Chickadee (Uni. 1940).D: Eddie Cline. W.C. Fields, Mae West, (LEM).

Citadel of Crime (Rep. 1941).D: George Sherman. Robert Armstrong, Frank Albertson.

The Man Who Lost Himself (Uni. 1941).D: Edward Ludwig. Brian Aherne, Kay Francis.

Adventures of Captain Marvel (Col. serial 1942).D: William Witney and John English. Tom Tyler, Junior Coghlan, (MURPH).

The Mad Doctor (Para. 1941).D: Tim Whelan. Basil Rathbone, Ellen Drew.

The Great Mr. Nobody (WB 1941).D: Ben Stoloff. Eddie Albert, Joan Leslie.

Tuxedo Junction (Rep. 1941).D: Frank McDonald. Weaver Brothers and Elviry, Frankie Darro.

Time Out for Rhythm (Col. 1941).D: Sidney Salkow. Ann Miller, Rudy Vallee.

Confessions of Boston Blackie (Col. 1941).D: Edward Dmytryk. Chester Morris, Harriet Hilliard, (ICE CREAM MAN).

Great Guns (20CF 1941).D: Monty Banks. Stan Laurel, Oliver Hardy, (RECRUIT AT CORRAL).

Home in Wyomin' (Rep. 1942).D: William Morgan. Gene Autry, Smiley Burnette, (RECEPTIONIST).

Talk of the Town (Col. 1942).D: George Stevens. Cary Grant, Jean Arthur, (WESTERN UNION BOY).

On the Sunny Side (20CF 1942).D: Harold Schuster. Jane Darwell, Stanley Clements, (MESSENGER BOY).

Get Hep to Love (Uni. 1942).D: Charles Lamont. Gloria Jean, Donald O'Connor, (SODA JERK).

Perils of Nyoka (Col. serial 1942).D: William Witney. Kay Aldridge, Clayton Moore, (RED).

Second Chorus (Para. 1942).D: H.C. Potter. Fred Astaire, Paulette Goddard, (DOOR MAN).

Lady in a Jam (Uni. 1942).D: Gregory LaCava. Irene Dunne, Patric Knowles, (BARKER).

Rings On Her Fingers (20CF 1942).D: Rouben Mamoulian. Henry Fonda, Gene Tierney, (NEWSBOY).

Mrs. Wiggs of the Cabbage Patch (Para. 1942).D: Ralph Murphy. Fay Bainter, Carolyn Lee, (OPERA HOUSE USHER).

Heart of the Golden West (Rep. 1942).D: Joseph Kane. Roy Rogers, Gabby Hayes, (MESSENGER BOY).

Wildcat (Para. 1943).D: Frank McDonald. Richard Arlen, Arline Judge, (BUD SMITHERS).

Aerial Gunner (Para. 1943).D: William H. Pine. Chester Morris, Richard Arlen, (PRIVATE ARLEN).

Whispering Footsteps (Rep. 1943).D: Howard Bretherton. John Hubbard, Rita Quigley, (JERRY MURPHY).

Adventures of the Flying Cadets (Uni. serial 1943).D: Ray Taylor and Lewis D. Collins. Johnny Downs, Bobby Jordan, (ZOMBIE PARKER).

The Ox-Bow Incident (20CF 1943).D: William Wellman. Henry Fonda, Dana Andrews, (GREENE).

Nobody's Darling (Rep. 1943).D: Anthony Mann. Mary Lee, Gladys George, (SAMMY).

Moonlight in Vermont (Uni. 1943).D: Edward Lilley. Gloria Jean, Ray Malone, (ABEL).

Goodnight Sweetheart (Rep. 1944).D: Joseph Santley. Robert Livingston, Ruth Terry, (BELLBOY).

The Merry Monohans (Uni. 1944).D: Charles Lamont. Donald O'Connor, Peggy Moran, (MESSENGER).

They Live in Fear (Col. 1944).D: Josef Berne. Otto Kruger, Cliff Severn.

That's My Baby (Rep. 1944).D: William Berke. Richard Arlen, Ellen Drew.

Follow the Boys (Uni. 1944).D: Edward Sutherland. George Raft, Vera Zorina, (JOE, A SOLDIER).

Brenda Starr, Reporter (Col. serial 1945).D: Wallace Fox. Joan Woodbury, Kane Richmond, (PESKY).

Hollywood and Vine (PRC 1945).D: Alexis Thurn-Taxis. James Ellison, Wanda McKay, (JOE, A NEWSBOY).

Road to Utopia (Para. 1945).D: Hal Walker. Bob Hope, Bing Crosby, (NEWSBOY).

The Story of G.I. Joe (UA 1945).D: William Wellman. Burgess Meredith, Robert Mitchum, (WHITEY).

A Boy, a Girl and a Dog (F C 1945).D: Herbert Kline. Jerry Hunter, Sharyn Moffett, (MESSENGER BOY).

One More Tomorrow (WB 1946).D: Peter Godfrey. Ann Sheridan, Dennis Morgan.

Do You Love Me? (20CF 1946).D: Gregory Ratoff. Maureen O'Hara, Dick Haymes, (WESTERN UNION BOY).

Never Say Goodbye (WB 1946).D: James V. Kern. Errol Flynn, Eleanor Parker, (MESSENGER BOY).

The Kid From Brooklyn (Gold.-RKO 1946).D: Norman Z. McLeod. Danny Kaye, Virginia Mayo, (NEWSBOY).

Without Reservations (RKO 1946).D: Mervyn LeRoy. Claudette Colbert, John Wayne, (WESTERN UNION BOY).

The Hucksters (MGM 1947).D: Jack Conway. Clark Gable, Deborah Kerr, (BELLBOY).

Fun On a Week-End (UA 1947).D: Andrew Stone. Eddie Bracken, Priscilla Lane.

The Pilgrim Lady (Rep. 1947).D: Lesley Selander. Lynne Roberts, Warren Douglas.

Secret Service Investigator (Rep. 1948).D: R. G. Springsteen. Lynne Roberts, Lloyd Bridges, (COUNTER MAN).

The Magnetic Monster (UA 1953).D: Curt Siodmak. Richard Carlson, King Donovan, (ALBERT).

Bride of the Monster (DCA 1956).D: Edward D. Wood, Jr. Bela Lugosi, Tor Johnson, (NEWSBOY).

Rally 'Round the Flag, Boys! (Para. 1958).D: Leo McCarey. Paul Newman, Joanne Woodward, (BELLBOY).

Last Train From Gun Hill (Para. 1959).D: John Sturges. Kirk Douglas, Anthony Quinn, (SMALL MAN).

Lover Come Back (Uni. 1961).D: Anthony Mann. Doris Day, Rock Hudson, (SECOND MUSICIAN IN ELEVATOR).

The Hallelujah Trail (UA 1965).D: John Sturges. Burt Lancaster, Lee Remick, (SIMPSON, A MINER).

Zebra in the Kitchen (MGM 1965).D: Ivan Tors. Jay North, Martin Milner, (MAN IN TOY STORE).

What Am I Bid? (E erson 1967).D: Gene Nash. LeRoy Van Dyke, Kristin Nelson, (CLEM).

Big Daddy (United Film Organization 1969).D: Carl K. Hittleman. Victor Buono, Joan Blondell.

Hello Dolly (20CF 1969).D: Gene Kelly. Barbra Streisand, Walter Matthau, (NEWS VENDOR).

The Sting (Uni. 1973).D: George Roy Hill. Paul Newman, Robert Redford.

Homebodies (Avco Embassy 1974).D: Larry Yust. Frances Fuller, Ian Wolfe, (WATCHMAN).

Farewell My Lovely (Avco Embassy 1976).D: Dick Richards. Robert Mitchum, Charlotte Rampling.

Won Ton Ton, the Dog Who Saved Hollywood (Para. 1976).D: Michael Winner. Bruce Dern, Madeline Kahn, (MAN ON BUS).

BENNIE BARTLETT

A promising child actor and musical prodigy in the Thirties, Bennie Bartlett became one of the most familiar of the "other" Bowery Boys. Having appeared in two 1943 Eastside Kids entries, he returned in 1948, and during the next eight years was a mainstay in 24 Bowery Boys films as Butch Williams.

Freckle-faced, redheaded Benjamin Bartlett was born to Mr. and Mrs. F.A. Bartlett in Independence, Kansas, on August 16, 1927. Quickly showing a musical ability, young Bennie became a child piano prodigy. He made his film debut at age eight as a specialty in RKO's *Millions in the Air* (1935). The following year he was featured in an episode of Ted Husing's *Star Reporter in Hollywood* for Paramount, performing his own original composition entitled "Old Fashioned Mill."

This led to a contract with Paramount in 1936, and he was soon playing opposite the studio's hottest properties in feature films. He was fifth-billed under Fred Mac-Murray and Joan Bennett in *Thirteen Hours By Air,* about an airplane crash and the occupants involved. He also had a featured part in *The Texas Rangers.* Acknowledged

as a leading child actor in the short subject "Lucky Starlets," with Baby LeRoy, David Holt, Billy Lee and Virginia Weidler, he was cast in the elaborate production *Maid of Salem* (1937), starring Claudette Colbert. On loan to 20th Century-Fox, he was showcased as a spoiled rich boy brought down to earth by Shirley Temple in *Just Around the Corner* (1938).

Bartlett was cast with Jackie Cooper in the first Henry Aldrich saga, *What a Life* (1939). Bennie's character is named Butch Williams—the very same name he was given while a Bowery Boy. Among his 1939 output was *The Great Man Votes,* which gave him a chance at a big role opposite the legendary John Barrymore.

By the early Forties, he was faced with the problems of a child star reaching pubescence. His Eastside appearances were made while free-lancing. The next time he was heard from—after the war—he was playing Orvie in the 1947 *Gas House Kids* films. This led the way to his replacing Bobby Jordan in the Bowery Boys.

When he left the Bowery Boys in late 1955, he disappeared from the Hollywood scene.

Millions in the Air (RKO 1935). D: Ray McCarey. John Howard, Wendy Barrie, Willie Howard, George Barbier, Benny Baker, (KID PIANIST).

Sky Parade (Para. 1936). D: Otho Lovering. Jimmie Allen, William Gargan, Katherine DeMille, Kent Taylor, Grant Withers, (JIMMIE ALLEN, AGE 9).

Timothy's Quest (Para. 1936). D: Charles Barton. Dick Moore, Eleanor Whitney, Tom Keene, Virginia Weidler, Elizabeth Patterson, Sally Martin.

Thirteen Hours by Air (Para. 1936). D: Mitchell Leisen. Fred MacMurray, Joan Bennett, ZaSu Pitts, John Howard, (WALDEMAR), Grace Bradley.

The Princess Comes Across (Para. 1936). D: William K. Howard. Carole Lombard, Fred MacMurray, Alison Skipworth, Douglass Dumbrille, William Frawley, Sig Ruman.

The Texas Rangers (Para. 1936). D: King Vidor. Fred MacMurray, Jack Oakie, Jean Parker, Lloyd Nolan, Edward Ellis, (DAVID).

Maid of Salem (Para. 1937). D: Frank Lloyd. Claudette Colbert, Fred MacMurray, Louise Dresser, Gale Sondergaard, Bonita Granville, (TIMOTHY CLARKE).

Exclusive (Para. 1937). D: Alexander Hall. Fred MacMurray, Frances Farmer, Charlie Ruggles, Lloyd Nolan, Fay Holden, Ralph Morgan.

Time Out for Romance (20CF 1937). D: Mal St. Clair. Claire Trevor, Michael Whalen, Joan Davis, Chick Chandler, Douglas Fowley, (ORVILLE HEALY).

Danger—Love At Work (20CF 1937). D: Otto Preminger. Ann Sothern, Jack Haley, Mary Boland, John Carradine, Edward Everett Horton, (JUNIOR PEMBERTON).

Let Them Live (Uni. 1937). D: Harold Young. John Howard, Nan Grey, Edward Ellis, Judith Barrett, Rob-

Bulldog Drummond's Revenge (Para. 1937). D: Louis King. John Barrymore, John Howard, Louise Campbell, Reginald Denny, E.E. Clive, (CABIN BOY).

Penrod and His Twin Brother (WB 1938). D: William McGann. Billy Mauch, Bobby Mauch, Frank Craven, Spring Byington, Charles Halton, (CHUCK).

Just Around the Corner (20CF 1928). D: Irving Cummings. Shirley Temple, Joan Davis, Charles Farrell, Amanda Duff, Bill Robinson, (MILTON RAMSBY).

Gang Bullets (Mono. 1938). D: Lambert Hillyer. Anne Nagel, Robert Kent, Charles Trowbridge, Morgan Wallace, J. Farrell MacDonald, John T. Murray.

Sons of the Legion (Para. 1938). D: James Hogan. Donald O'Connor, Billy Lee, Billy Cook, Evelyn Keyes, Elizabeth Patterson, (RED O'FLAHERTY).

Jesse James (20CF 1939). D: Henry King. Tyrone Power, Henry Fonda, Nancy Kelly, Randolph Scott, Henry Hull, Brian Donlevy.

The Family Next door (Uni. 1939). D: Joseph Santley. Hugh Herbert, Joy Hodges, Eddie Quillan, Ruth Donnelly, Juanita Quigley, (RUFUS).

Honeymoon in Bali (Para. 1939). D: Edward H. Griffith. Fred MacMurray, Madeleine Carroll, Allan Jones, Osa Massen, Helen Broderick, (MESSENGER BOY).

What a Life (Para. 1939). D: Ted Reed. Jackie Cooper, Betty Field, John Howard, Janis Logan, Vaughan Glaser, (BUTCH WILLIAMS).

Our Neighbors the Carters (Para. 1939). D: Ralph Murphy. Fay Bainter, Frank Craven, Edmund Lowe, Genevieve Tobin, Scotty Beckett, (JUNIOR CARTER).

The Great Man Votes (RKO 1939). D: Garson Kanin. John Barrymore, Peter Holden, Virginia Weidler, Katharine Alexander, Donald MacBride, (DAVE McCARTHY).

Alias the Deacon (Uni. 1940). D: Christy Cabanne. Bob Burns, Mischa Auer, Peggy Moran, Dennis O'Keefe, Virginia Brissac, (WILLIE CLARK).

Let's Make Music (RKO 1940). D: Leslie Goodwins. Bob Crosby, Jean Rogers, Elisabeth Risdon, Joseph Buloff, (TOMMY), Louis Jean Heydt.

Tillie the Toiler (Col. 1941). D: Sidney Salkow. Kay Harris, William Tracy, George Watts, Daphne Pollard, Jack Arnold, Marjorie Reynolds.

Meet John Doe (Col. 1941). D: Frank Capra. Gary Cooper, Barbara Stanwyck, Edward Arnold, Walter Brennan, James Gleason, Spring Byington.

Code of the Outlaw (Rep. 1942). D: John English. Bob Steele, Tom Tyler, Rufe Davis, Welden Heyburn, Melinda Leighton, (TIM).

Henry Aldrich, Editor (Para. 1942). D: Hugh Bennett. Jimmy Lydon, Charles Smith, John Litel, Olive Blackeney, Rita Quigley, (TUBBY JONES.)

He Hired the Boss (20CF 1943). D: Thomas Z. Loring. Stuart Erwin, Evelyn Venable, Thurston Hall, Vivian Blaine, William T. Orr, (JIMMY).

Nobody's Darling (Rep. 1943). D: Anthony Mann. Mary Lee, Gladys George, Louis Calhern, Jackie Moran, (THE DEACON), Lee Patrick.

Follow the Band (Uni. 1943). D: Jean Yarbrough. Eddie Quillan, Mary Beth Hughes, Leon Errol, Anne Rooney, Samuel S. Hinds, (COOTIE).

Her Adventurous Night (Uni. 1946). D: John Rawlins. Dennis O'Keefe, Helen Walker, Scotty Beckett, Fuzzy Knight, Tom Powers, (HORACE).

The Adventures of Don Coyote (UA 1946). D: Reginald LeBorg. Frances Rafferty, Richard Martin, Marc Cramer, Val Carlo, (BB), Frank Fenton.

Gas House Kids Go West (PRC 1947). D: William Beaudine. Carl Switzer, Tommy Bond, (ORVIE), Rudy Wissler, Chili Williams, John Sheldon.

Gas House Kids in Hollywood (E-L 1947). D: Edward L. Cahn. Carl Switzer, Tommy Bond, (ORVIE), Rudy Wissler, James Burke, Jan Bryant.

Heart of Virginia (Rep.1948). D: R.G. Springsteen. Janet Martin, Robert Lowery, Frankie Darro, Paul Hurst, Sam McDaniel, (BREEZY TRENT).

Cheaper By the Dozen (20CF 1950). D: Walter Lang. Clifton Webb, Myrna Loy, Jeanne Crain, Mildred Natwick, Edgar Buchanan, (JOE SCALES).

Girls of Pleasure Island (Para. 1953). D: F. Hugh Herbert and Alvin Ganzer. Leo Genn, Don Taylor, Gene Barry, Elsa Lanchester, Audrey Dalton, (SAILOR).

BERNARD GORCEY

A fine actor in his own right, Bernard Gorcey has become familiar to audiences as Louie Dumbrowski, the short-tempered, short-statured sweetshop proprietor who had to put up with the antics of the Bowery Boys in his establishment.

The father of Leo and David, he first experienced life in 1888, Russian-born of Swiss and Jewish descent. He and his Irish wife, Josephine Condon, came to the United States where they found work in vaudeville. A square-shaped, tiny man, 4' 10", Gorcey worked as a dialect comedian in shows such as *Katinka*, *Wildflower* and *Rose-Marie*.

On May 23, 1922, the Broadway production of Anne Nichols' *Abie's Irish Rose* opened at the Fulton Theater, deemed to certain failure by critics because of its lack of lofty subject matter. The plot revolved around the marriage of an Irish girl to the son of a hard-line Jewish family. Gorcey was the comic relief, as Isaac Cohen, dedicated to breaking up his relative's marriage yet succumbing to such un-kosher temptations as ham and wine. However, his biggest concern was to stay on the good side of his imposing wife.

Despite the predicted failure, *Abie* fooled everybody by playing for five-and-a-half years, a record for that time and some years afterward. Bernard continued in the role of Isaac Cohen for three and a half years and was in the play for the October 1927 closing. He was also seen in other roles during the run of *Abie*.

The Song of the Flame, opening in December 1925, featured the talents of Oscar Hammerstein and George Gershwin, and included Bernard as a comic Russian. He next played a Japanese merchant, George Washington Goto, in the Shuberts' *Cherry Blossoms* of March 1927. These roles showed his abilities in various dialects.

Fresh on the heels of *Abie*, Paramount acquired the rights for a motion picture version of the play. Bernard was one of the few stage performers imported for the film, and when it was released in April 1928, Mordaunt Hall of the *New York Times* stated that Bernard contributed "most of the fun."

At this time, Bernard was working on radio in "Popeye," but he soon returned to Broadway. All of Gorcey's stage roles in the Thirties were comic Jewish parts, in the manner of Isaac Cohen. Between 1930 and 1932, he appeared in *Pressing Business*, *The Joy of Living*, *Wonder Boy* and *Keeping Expenses Down*.

For a long spell, Bernard had deserted his family (the result of his wife's being unfaithful to him during his time away on the road), but returned home in 1935. He had started a family in 1915 when son Fred was born; he was 26, his wife was 14. Anxious to make up for his absence, he approached son David and encouraged him to try out for a role in *Dead End*. David won a role. He was accompanied at the rehearsal by brother Leo, and both ended up having roles as Second Avenue Boys.

Returning to the New York stage in 1935, Bernard was again cast in Jewish roles for *The Creeping Fire* and *Satellite*. Ten years after it closed, *Abie's Irish Rose* was revived in April 1937, and Bernard's Isaac was again singled out as the funniest character.

When Charlie Chaplin was concocting his first all-talking film, *The Great Dictator* (released 1940), he created a Jewish ghetto where the lowly barber that he plays practices. Chaplin and Gorcey (as Mr. Mann) are members of a Jewish league who are served puddings, one of which contains a coin which will determine who will go on a dangerous mission. A two-shot shows both of them together during the funny eating sequence.

Bernard Gorcey in Abie's Irish Rose *as Isaac Cohen, who frowns on Abie, the Jew who married a Catholic. The "in-joke" about Bernard playing this role is that he himself was a Jew married to a Catholic. This photograph was shot for the 1928 film.*

Staying in Hollywood where his two sons were already working, Bernard had a role in *Out of the Fog* (1941) as a waterfront gambler in the establishment served by waiter Leo Gorcey. At Monogram, he did some one-scene bits in two Bela Lugosi vehicles, which led to regular comedy bit parts in Eastside Kids films.

In October 1944, he ventured back to Broadway for the show *Horses Are Like That*, a Runyonesque racetrack saga.

With the Bowery Boys series debut, Bernard was back to a small part in *Live Wires* before settling in as Louie Dumbrowski for the next ten years. Though he possessed a very short fuse, Louie continually gave in to the smooth talking of Slip, after which he found himself bouncing all over the globe on various expeditions, with a cash register full of IOUs from unpaid-for sodas.

During his work with the Bowery Boys, Gorcey supplemented his income by operating a print shop on Santa Monica Blvd. in West Los Angeles. He also found work in other films, including a large part as a cigar manufacturer in Louis Milestone's *No Minor Vices* (1948). He also did some television work, such as playing an auction assistant in an "I Married Joan" episode.

On August 31, 1955, just after completing work on *Dig That Uranium*, Gorcey's auto collided with a bus at the corner of 4th and LaBrea in Los Angeles. Gorcey was kept alive in a hospital for a week and a half before he succumbed to the injuries on September 11.

Abie's Irish Rose (Para. 1928). D: Victor Fleming. Charles Rogers, Nancy Carroll, Jean Hersholt, J. Farrell MacDonald, (ISAAC COHEN), Ida Kramer, Nick Cogley.

The Great Dictator (UA 1940). D: Charles Chaplin. Charlie Chaplin, Paulette Goddard, Jack Oakie, Reginald Gardiner, Billy Gilbert, Maurice Moskovitch, (MR. MANN), Emma Dunn.

Out of the Fog (WB 1941). D: Anatole Litvak. John Garfield, Ida Lupino, Thomas Mitchell, Eddie Albert, George Tobias, (SAM PEPPER).

Footlight Fever (RKO 1941). D: Irving Reis. Alan Mowbray, Donald MacBride, Elisabeth Risdon, Lee Bonnell, Elyse Knox.

So Ends Our Night (UA 1941). D: John Cromwell. Frederic March, Margaret Sullavan, Frances Dee, Glenn Ford, Anna Sten, Eric von Stroheim.

Joan of Paris (RKO 1942). D: Robert Stevenson. Paul Henried, Michele Morgan, Thomas Mitchell, Laird Cregar, May Robson, Alan Ladd.

Charlie Chaplin and Bernard Gorcey with Paulette Goddard in
The Great Dictator *(1940).*

THE OTHERS

Black Dragons (Mono. 1942). D: William Nigh. Bela Lugosi, Joan Barclay, Clayton Moore, George Pembroke, Robert Frazier, (CABBIE).

Bowery at Midnight (Mono. 1942). D: Wallace Fox. Bela Lugosi, John Archer, Wanda McKay, Tom Neal, Vince Barnett, (TAILOR).

A Desperate Chance for Ellery Queen (Col. 1942). D: James Hogan. William Gargan, Margaret Lindsay, Charlie Grapewin, John Litel, Lillian Bond, James Burke.

The Unknown Guest (Mono. 1943). D: Kurt Neumann. Victor Jory, Pamela Blake, Harry Hayden, Emory Parnell, Nora Cecil, Veda Ann Borg.

French Key (Rep. 1946). D: Walter Colmes. Albert Dekker, Mike Mazurki, Evelyn Ankers, John Eldredge, Frank Fenton, Richard Arlen.

The High Wall (MGM 1947). D: Curtis Bernhardt. Robert Taylor, Audrey Totter, Herbert Mitchell, Dorothy Patrick, H.B. Warner, (HIRSCH).

No Minor Vices (MGM 1948). D: Louis Milestone. Dana Andrews, Lili Palmer, Louis Jourdan, Jane Wyatt, (MR. ZITZFLEISCH), Norman Lloyd.

The Doctor and the Girl (MGM 1949). D: Curtis Bernhardt. Glenn Ford, Charles Coburn, Gloria DeHaven, Janet Leigh, Warner Anderson, (PATIENT).

The Set-Up (RKO 1949). D: Robert Weiss. Robert Ryan, Audrey Totter, George Tobias, Alan Baxter, Wallace Ford, Percy Helton, (TOBACCO MAN).

Pickup (COL. 1951). D: Hugo Haas. Hugo Haas, Beverly Michaels, Allan Nixon, Howard Chamberlain, Jo Carroll Dennison, (JOE).

Journey Into Light (20CF 1951). D: Stuart Heisler. Sterling Hayden, Viveca Lindfors, Thomas Mitchell, H.B. Warner, Ludwig Donath.

Chicago Calling (UA 1951). D: John Reinhardt. Dan Duryea, Mary Anderson, Gordon Gebart, Ross Elliott.

BUDDY GORMAN

A veteran of 19 Eastside Kids and Bowery Boys films, Gorman was a diminutive lad with a squeaky voice and wavy hair. He temporarily replaced Bennie Bartlett as Butch in 1950-51, having done various bits in previous Bowery Boys films. Other roles were newsboy-oriented.

Film include: *Whistling in Brooklyn* (MGM 1943), *Higher and Higher* (RKO 1943), *Meet Me in St. Louis* (MGM 1944), *Since You Went Away* (Selznick-UA 1944), *Wife Wanted* (Mono. 1946), *The Jolson Story* (Col. 1946), *Thoroughbreds* (Rep. 1946), *Her Husband's Affairs* (Col. 1947), *The Babe Ruth Story* (AA 1948), *It's a Great Feeling* (WB 1949), *A Modern Marriage* (Mono. 1950).

BOBBY STONE

Initially a nemesis, Stone became a member of the Eastside Kids midway during his 1941 to 1944 12-appearance pact. Finding parts in a couple of other films in the Thirties and Forties (as a tropical native and a Mexican, among other roles), Stone resurfaced in the Sixties working for his old producer, Sam Katzman. Bobby served as production coordinator and unit production manager on all of Katzman's Four-Leaf Productions releases, which included exploitation films and a couple Elvis Presley vehicles. He finally attained associate producer status in 1970 when Sam put him in charge of *How to Succeed With Sex*, an X-rated gem directed by Bert I. Gordon, the man responsible for *Amazing Colossal Man*.

Robert Stone passed away in the Seventies.

Films as actor include: *Gangster's Boy* (Mono. 1938), *Streets of New York* (Mono. 1939), *South of Pago Pago* (UA 1940), *Down Argentine Way* (20CF 1940), *Hop Harrigan* (Col. serial 1946), *Train to Alcatraz* (Rep. 1948), *Kissin' Cousins* (MGM 1964).

Films as production coordinator, unit production manager or associate producer: *Get Yourself a College Girl* (MGM 1964), *Your Cheatin' Heart* (MGM 1964), *Harum Scarum* (MGM 1965), *When the Boys Meet the Girls* (MGM 1965), *Hold On* (MGM 1966), *The Fastest Guitar Alive* (MGM 1967), *Hot Rods to Hell* (MGM 1967), *The Love-In* (Col. 1967), *Riot On Sunset Strip* (AIP 1967), *For Singles Only* (Col. 1968), *A Time to Sing* (MGM 1968), *Angel Angel Down We Go* (AIP 1969), *How to Succeed With Sex* (Medford Film Corp. 1970).

DONALD HAINES

Skinny in the first seven Eastside Kids got his start in the Our Gang comedies where his blond, freckled complexion was put to good use as an all-purpose kid. His feature film work included a pair of Jackie Cooper vehicles in which Donald was featured, and *Boys' Town*, which cast him as Alabama. After his stint with the kids, Haines went off to serve his country in World War II. He didn't return.

Our Gang films (Produced by Hal Roach and released by MGM): *Shivering Sherlocks, The First Seven Years, Teacher's Pet, Schools Out,* 1930: *Helping Grandma, Love Business, Little Daddy, Bargain Days, Big Ears,* 1931; *Readin' and Writin', Free Eats, Choo Choo, Birthday Blues, A Lad an' a Lamp,* 1932; *Fish Hooky,* 1933.

Feature films: *Skippy* (MGM 1931), *When a Feller Needs a Friend* (MGM 1932), *No Greater Glory* (Col. 1934), *Kid Millions* (Gold-UA 1934), *Little Man What Now?* (Uni. 1934), *Straight from the Heart* (Uni. 1935), *A Tale of Two Cities* (MGM 1935), *Little Miss Nobody* (20CF 1936), *Love and Kisses* (20CF 1937), *Boys' Town* (MGM 1938), *Kidnapped* (20CF 1938), *Three Comrades* (MGM 1938), *Sergeant Madden* (MGM 1939), *Never Say Die* (Para. 1939), *Seventeen* (Para. 1940), *Prison Camp* (Col. 1940), *Men of Boys' Town* (MGM 1941).

DAVE DURAND

The muscular Eastside Kid (six films), who also appeared in *Angels With Dirty Faces* and *Keep 'Em Slugging,* is the third Eastside Kid to have appeared in Our Gang films. Like "Sunshine Sammy" Morrison and Donald Haines, Durand served his juvenile-group acting apprenticeship in two of Hal Roach's comedies. Durand became known as a scene-stealing child actor in silents and a number of sound classics, working with the likes of Wallace Beery, Bette Davis, Edward G. Robinson and Maurice Chevalier. In 1940, he replaced Noah Beery, Jr., in the lead of Columbia's two-reel series *The Glove Singers.* Durand is now living in a rest home outside of Chicago.

Our Gang films (Roach-Pathe): *Sundown Limited, Uncle Tom's Uncle* (1925).

Feature films: *Tropic Madness* (FBO 1928), *Innocents of Paris* (Para. 1929), *Song of Love* (Col. 1929), *Jazz Cinderella* (Chesterfield 1930), *Ladies Love Brutes* (Para. 1930), *Bad Sister* (Uni. 1931), *A Rich Man's Folly* (Para. 1931), *Silver Dollar* (WB 1932), *Jennie Gerhardt* (Para. 1933), *Life of Jimmy Dolan* (WB 1933), *Cradle Song* (Para.

Dave Durand salutes in Naval Academy *(1941).*

1933), *Viva Villa* (MGM 1934), *As the Earth Turns* (WB 1934), *Wednesday's Child* (RKO 1934), *The Band Plays On* (MGM 1934), *Little Men* (RKO 1935), *Streets of New York* (Mono. 1939), *Boys' Reformatory* (Mono. 1939), *Scouts to the Rescue* (Uni. serial 1939), *Golden Gloves* (Para. 1940), *Ghost Breakers* (Para. 1940), *The Tulsa Kid* (Rep. 1941), *Naval Academy* (Col. 1941).

JIMMY STRAND

Prominent in six Eastside Kids films, Strand's few other credits on screen include Monogram's *Are These Our Parents?* (1944) and Paramount's *Salty O'Rourke* (1945), as a jockey pal of Stanley Clements.

JIMMY MURPHY

Myron in the five latter-day Bowery Boys films, Jimmy had a role in the classic *Mr. Roberts* and later provided the voice of a raccoon in Disney's *The Gnome Mobile.* Among his more interesting roles is as a hot-headed western youth killed by a cowboy-vampire in *Curse of the Undead.*

According to Allied Artists publicity, he was discovered parking cars at a prominent Hollywood restaurant, and was quickly shuttled into his Bowery Boy role.

Features include: *Mr. Roberts* (WB 1955), *The Delicate Delinquent* (Para. 1957), *Curse of the Undead* (Uni. 1959), *Born to Be Loved* (Uni. 1959), *Platinum High School* (MGM 1960), *California* (AIP 1963), *Wall of Noise* (WB 1963), *Follow Me Boys* (BV 1966), *Out of Sight* (Uni. 1966), *The Gnome Mobile* (BV 1967), *The Good Guys and the Bad Guys* (WB 1969).

FRANKIE BURKE

Reknowned for his resemblance to James Cagney (whose character he played as a boy in *Angels With Dirty Faces*), the late Frankie Burke graced three Dead End Kids films and played an Eastsider in the first two pictures. Unfortunately, he couldn't parlay the Cagney-lookalike status into a film career.

Features include: *Women in the Wind* (WB 1939), *Pride of the Bluegrass* (WB 1939), *You Can't Get Away With Murder* (WB 1939), *Prison Camp* (Col. 1940), *The Quarterback* (Para. 1940), *Ride Kelly Ride* (20 CF 1941), *Shadow of the Thin Man* (MGM 1941).

HALLY CHESTER

One of the original Little Tough Guys, Chester worked with the Dead End Kids once at Warners, and in five features and two serials at Universal. He was also an original Eastside Kid and made two appearances with the Monogram gang. Born March 6, 1921, in Brooklyn, the Bernard Punsly look-alike trained on the New York stage and temporarily crashed Hollywood as an actor. After a series of personal appearance tours from 1941 to 1944, Chester returned to the movie capital and found his true calling in films: as a producer. Getting his feet wet with a series of musical shorts in 1944, Hal E. Chester (as he was now known) initiated a comedy feature series based on Ham Fisher's "Joe Palooka" comic strip, at Monogram. It starred Joe Kirkwood, Jr., and Leon Errol as Joe and Knobby Walsh. Graduating to more prestigious films, Chester was named vice-president of the short-lived Mutual Films Corporation in 1952. In 1956, Chester and his wife Virginia moved to England, where he continued to produce films through the late Sixties. Returning to the U.S., he made *The Secret War of Harry Frigg*, starring Paul Newman. The famous actors who worked under this former Little Tough Guy and Eastside Kid are an impressive lot: Constance Bennett, Charles Coburn, William Bendix, Mickey Rooney, Dana Andrews, Terry-Thomas and Yul Brynner. He and his wife produced three sons: Timothy (1949), Stephen (1954-1978) and Mark (1959).

Features as an actor include: *Juvenile Court* (Col. 1938), *Little Tough Guys in Society* (Uni. 1938), *Newsboys' Home* (Uni. 1939), *Code of the Streets* (Uni. 1939), *When Tomorrow Comes* (Uni. 1939).

Features as a producer include: 10 "Joe Palooka" films (Mono. 1946-1951), *Smart Women* (AA 1948), *Underworld Story* (UA 1950), *The Highwayman* (AA 1951), *Models Inc.* (Mutual 1952), *The Beast From 20,000 Fathoms* (WB 1953) (co-produced with Jack Dietz), *Crashout* (Filmakers 1955) (also screenplay), *The Weapon* (Alliance 1956) (also director), *The Bold and the Brave* (RKO 1956), *The Haunted* (British 1957), *Curse of the Demon* (Col.-British 1957), *School for Scoundrels* (Continental-British 1960), *Hide and Seek* (Uni.-British 1964), *The Secret War of Harry Frigg* (Uni. 1968), *The Double Man* (WB 1968), *Take a Girl Like You* (Col.-British 1970).

HARRIS BERGER

The blond-haired leader of the original Eastside Kids was also in four features and a serial with the Universal bunch and one film with the Warners crew. In October 1935, while the play *Dead End* was getting underway, Berger was working in *Achilles Had a Heel* on Broadway. As for *Dead End*, he replaced Huntz Hall as Dippy when the latter left for Hollywood, and in February 1938 had a stage role in *Sunup to Sundown*. After a bit part in *Angels With Dirty Faces*, he handled the Hall role in the "Lux Radio Theater" version. Berger succumbed to a heart attack in the late Seventies.

Films include: *Little Tough Guys in Society* (Uni. 1938), *Newsboys' Home* (Uni. 1939), *Code of the Streets* (Uni. 1939), *Oh Johnny, How You Can Love* (Uni. 1940), *City for Conquest* (WB 1940).

EDDIE LeROY

Bespectacled Blinky of the last four Bowery Boys films did the majority of his performing in other mediums. His only two other film roles were in *The Vicious Circle* (UA 1948) and *The Happy Years* (MGM 1950). LeRoy made his performing debut at a very early age playing nightclubs, where he literally had to be sneaked in because he was underage. Over the years, he made live appearances in New York, Las Vegas and London. But perhaps his biggest role was on TV in his scene-stealing performance as Andy Griffith's sidekick Ben in the U.S. Steel Hour's live telecast of *No Time For Sergeants* (1955), which preceded stage and film versions.

He was a regular on "The Milton Berle Show" in the early Fifties, and it was this that indirectly led to his Bowery Boys role. Huntz Hall had made several guest appearances, during which his comedy was stifled by the scene-stealing Berle. LeRoy helped Hall practice to overcome this, and when Hall recognized LeRoy years later auditioning for the Bowery Boy role, he immediately had him hired.

LeRoy also appeared on "The Red Skelton Show," "Varsity Varieties" and "The Patti Page Show," and in recent years has moved out of the spots and into roles as producer, director, writer, and even occasionally host, for television, radio, records and film. He is currently working for Sonny Fox Productions, which produced "The Golden Age of Television" for PBS.

EUGENE FRANCIS

The debonair, English-accented Algy Wilkes in four early Eastside Kids films later worked in the TV series "Calliope" and is now living in the New York area.

JOHNNY DUNCAN

Duncan left a distinctive impression; twice a wayward rich boy, Duncan was cast in his remaining two Eastside Kids films as a rival club's member and as an Eastside club member who was a talented jockey. He can fleetingly be seen in *Fighting Fools* in a bit part. That same year, 1949, he essayed the role he is most known for: Robin, the Boy Wonder, in the serial "Batman." He reportedly later ran afoul of a gang in Las Vegas and is currently somewhere in that gambling town.

Feature films include: *Call of the Canyon* (Rep. 1942), *Campus Rhythm* (Mono. 1943), *Mystery of the 13th Guest* (Mono. 1943), *Jive Junction* (PRC 1943), *Teenage* (JDK-Continental 1944), *Trail of San Antone* (Rep. 1947), *Street Corner* (Wilshire-Viro 1948), *Batman* (Col. serial 1949), *Highway Dragnet* (AA 1954).

MENDE KOENIG

The three-time 1945 Eastside Kid also played the part of a leader of a gang of urchins who help Gloria Jean overcome crooks in *River Gang* (1945). He is now deceased.

GIL STRATTON JR.

Twice a Bowery Boy, Stratton was the original Bud Hooper in Broadway's *Best Foot Forward* (1941). Working on radio as a curtain boy on CBS' "The First Nighter" and as Billy Green in the network's "Those Websters," Stratton made his film debut with a bang in 1943. He was third billed under Mickey Rooney and Judy Garland in MGM's *Girl Crazy*. After his Bowery Boys 1952 stint, his film work increased in stature: he played

Gil Stratton (center right), with Judy Garland, in his film debut, Girl Crazy (1943).

Cookie in *Stalag 17* and bike-gang member Mousie in *The Wild One*. He was tapped by CBS to play the lead in the series "That's My Boy" in 1954, in the part Jerry Lewis had created in the Martin & Lewis film of the same name. In April 1954, he got the job he really wanted, that of a sportscaster, on Los Angeles CBS outlet KNXT (2). KNXT retained him for twenty years, after which he brought his play-by-play abilities to L.A. Aztecs soccer games, and early subscription TV broadcasts of L.A. Kings hockey. Stratton returned to the evening newscast fold on KTLA (5) and KTTV (11), and frequently did the baseball pre-game show, "Dodger Dugout," for the latter station. In 1984 he retired, but he owns a radio station in Hawaii. He resides with wife Dee Arlen, herself a former actress.

Feature films: *Girl Crazy* (MGM 1943), *Kilroy Was Here* (Mono. 1947), *Dangerous Years* (20CF 1947), *Half-Past Midnight* (20CF 1948), *Mr. Belvedere Goes to College* (20CF 1949), *Hot Road* (Mono. 1950), *Battle Zone* (AA 1952), *Army Bound* (Mono. 1952), *Stalag 17* (Para. 1953), *The Wild One* (Col. 1954), *A Bundle of Joy* (RKO 1956).

NORMAN ABBOTT

Ape in *Keep 'Em Slugging*, Norman was Bud Abbott's nephew, and chances are it was this connection that spiraled him into this role. After working as dialogue director (including a chore on Abbott and Costello's

Africa Screams), Abbott has become a respected television director. Perhaps his most famous work is "Get Smart" and the Jack Benny specials of the Sixties and early Seventies. He was also responsible for "Ghost Busters," on which Huntz Hall infrequently appeared.

SAM EDWARDS

One of the Eastside Kids in the original film, Edwards appeared in many "B" films and even had a decent part as Birdwell in the Academy Award-winning *Twelve O'Clock High*.

Features include: *Rubber Racketeers* (Mono. 1942), *Captain Midnight* (Col. serial 1942), *The Street With No Name* (UA 1948), *Twelve O'Clock High* (20CF 1949), *The Sun Sets at Dawn* (E-L 1950), *Operation Pacific* (WB 1951), *Gang Busters* (Visual Drama Inc. 1955), *Between Heaven and Hell* (20CF 1956), *Revolt in the Big House* (AA 1958).

EDDIE BRIAN

A bit player in *Angels With Dirty Faces* and a member of the original Eastside Kids, Brian also worked in Hal Roach's *Captain Fury* (1939) and a couple of westerns. He reappeared in CBS's "Concerning Miss Marlowe" in 1954, playing a featured role.

DICK CHANDLEE

A kid in *Clancy Street Boys* and in the cast of *Keep 'Em Slugging*, Chandlee was in *Tom Brown's Schooldays* (1940), with Billy Halop, and Bob Hope's *Nothing But the Truth* (1941).

BILL BATES

The sleepy organ player in *Ghosts on the Loose* had a bit part in Alfred Hitchcock's *Shadow of a Doubt* (1943).

WILLIAM FRAMBES

The homespun Homer in the original Bowery Boys entry, *Live Wires*, found his biggest role as Dead-Pan Hackett in the popular wartime escapist film *Janie* and its sequel. He also worked with both Laurel and Hardy and Abbott and Costello.

Feature films: *Janie* (20CF 1944), *Circumstantial Evidence* (20CF 1945), *State Fair* (20CF 1945), *Junior Miss* (20CF 1945), *Nothing But Trouble* (MGM 1945), *Let's Go Steady* (Col. 1945), *Abbott and Costello in Holly-wood* (MGM 1945), *Bringing Up Father* (Mono. 1946), *Centennial Summer* (20CF 1946), *Janie Gets Married* (20CF 1946), *The Shocking Miss Pilgrim* (20CF 1947).

DANNY WELTON

Formerly Myron Welton, Danny worked with Stanley Clements in two pictures, *Military Academy* (Col. 1950) and *Army Bound* (AA 1952). Interestingly, there was a Danny Welton (perhaps the same man) who was a harmonica player and made recordings for Dot Records. His last known film role was as a drunk in *Terrified* (Crown Int. 1963).

KENNETH LUNDY

The kid in *Junior G-Men* had many newsboy roles and a part in Paramount's *The Major and the Minor* (1942).

EDDIE MILLS

A one-picture appearance in *Clancy Street Boys* was about all he did, but he did have one subsequent role others would have killed for, a part opposite Charlie Chaplin in the comedian's latter-day *Monsieur Verdoux* (1946). He participated in much slapstick in that ahead-of-its-time film.

FRANKIE THOMAS

Briefly a Dead End Kid in *Angels Wash Their Faces*, Frankie Thomas worked with the gang in *On Dress Parade* and was the leader of the Little Tough Guys in two features. He is best known for his role as the student president of *Boys' Town* (1938) and as Nancy Drew's boyfriend in the Warner Brothers series of 1938-39.

Thomas then packed his bags for New York. He found that the Broadway stage offered him lead roles. He played a mature school student, as remembered by a past teacher, who in the present is about to be inaugurated President, in *Remember the Day*, which became a Claudette Colbert movie in 1942.

FRANKIE DARRO

Though never an actual member of the gang, Darro had key roles in four Bowery Boys films, three times cast as an ex-Bowery Boy who went astray. Darro also was involved in several series and films that were precursors to the Dead End/Eastside/Bowery faction (see "Forerunners, Imitators and Offspring" chapter). Born i

Chicago in 1917, Darro (né Johnson) came from a circus-aerialist family and started working in silent films at age six. He became a juvenile action star in silent and sound serials, and became typecast as the ultimate Hollywood jockey, playing horse riders in dozens of films, including *Broadway Bill*, *Charlie Chan at the Race Track*, *The Ex-Mrs. Bradford*, *Saratoga* and *Heart of Virginia*. In later years he became a regular on TV's "The Red Skelton Show."

[There has been some confusion in recent years concerning the famed director Sidney Lumet (*Twelve Angry Men*, *Long Day's Journey Into Night*, *Serpico*, *Network*) having been a Dead End Kid. His only connection is that he played one of the "little kids" in the original stage version of *Dead End*.]

SIDNEY MILLER

The spectacled buddy of the Eastsiders in *Mr. Wise Guy* also had a featured role in *Boys' Town*. He had also played a juvenile inmate in Warners' *Mayor of Hell* (1933), which influenced both *Crime School* and *Hell's Kitchen*. He has more recently been a director of film and television, but in 1970 returned to the acting trade to enact Adolph Hitler in Jerry Lewis's *Which Way to the Front?*

Other kids who only appeared in one film, such as Bill Lawrence, Bill Chaney, Jack Edwards and Al Stone, have disappeared without a trace. In the case of Stone (the obnoxious Herbie in *Million Dollar Kid*), this is just as well.

VIOLENCE....

...the violence of hardpressed youth...of hungry hearts and hungry stomachs...guarding the street crumbs that gave them life!

JACKIE COOPER in A UNIVERSAL PICTURE

NEWSBOYS' HOME

with

EDMUND LOWE

Wendy BARRIE · Edward NORRIS
Samuel S. HINDS · Elisha COOK, Jr.
and

THE LITTLE TOUGH GUYS

Directed by HAROLD YOUNG · Associate Producer KEN GOLDSMITH
Screenplay by GORDON KAHN
Original story by Gordon Kahn and Charles Grayson

UNIVERSAL PICTURES

FOR RELEASE
DECEMBER 23RD

This ad from an exhibitors' magazine makes an unusual claim. It promises "three times normal run." Its detractors would say it delivered.

220

FORERUNNERS, IMITATORS
AND OFFSPRING

"'11-Year-Old Boy Convicted, Guilty of Murder in the Second Degree.' Suppose a man kills because his wife is unfaithful, it's: 'temporary insanity;' but an 11-year-old: 'just a savage.'"

—Spencer Tracy
as Father Flanagan
in *Boys Town* (1938),
written by Dore Schary

The Dead End Kids were not the first juvenile delinquents to appear on screen. However, they were the first to develop characterizations. As it became apparent that they were successful, it was not surprising to see producers attempting to duplicate the success of the boys by creating their own bunches of kids who talked out of one side of their mouths and paraded through run-down streets. However, more often than not, they lacked one essential: the charm of Leo Gorcey, Huntz Hall and the rest of their mob.

The name "Bowery Boys" dates all the way back to the title of a 1914 Mack Sennett comedy featuring the Keystone Kiddies. This bunch was more a forerunner to Our Gang than the Dead Enders, though. The title was used again in Republic's *The Bowery Boy* (1940), with Jimmy Lydon and Billy Benedict, but without any mob of toughs.

(The name "Bowery Boys—divorced from film—goes back even further. In the 1850s, one of the mobs that terrorized New York was named The Bowery Boys. There was also a group of young toughs who idolized them, called "the Little Bowery Boys." This group of

young toughs should be considered to have had no influence on the film group—these ten-year-olds committed murder!

(It should be pointed out that one of the groups that rivaled the real-life Bowery Boys—in sacking and burning the city of New York during the Draft Riots of 1863 (considered among the worst calamities in the history of the United States), in cracking skulls, and in beating up the police captain—was the "Five Pointers," which was the name of the Eastside Kids' rival gang in *Block Busters*.)

In his 1931 MGM talkie *Sidewalks of New York*, Buster Keaton is plagued by group of venemous pre-teens labeled "Eastside Kids" in a newspaper headline within the film.

But the first recognizable harbinger to the Dead Enders came in 1933 at Warner Brothers. At a time when other studios were churning out polished fluff, director William Wellman created a harsh Depression film entitled *Wild Boys of the Road*, featuring a bunch of youths who take to a hobo lifestyle of crime and nomadic wandering. The leader of the group was 16-year-old Frankie Darro, a film actor since the Twenties, who was the most important forerunner to the Dead End Kids. In another 1933 Warner Brothers production, starring James Cagney, Darro led a group of reform school inmates whose ranks included Sidney Miller and Our Gang graduate "Farina" Hoskins. The film, *Mayor of Hell*, was the blueprint for both *Crime School* and *Hell's Kitchen*.

By 1935, Darro had a series of his own, for Maurice Conn's Ambassador Pictures. The nine low-budget ac-

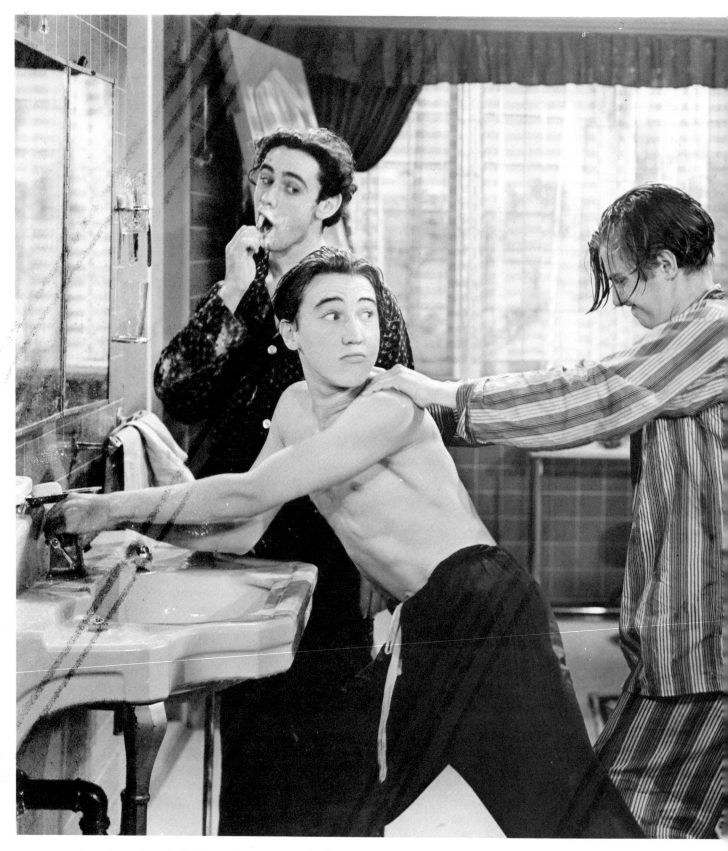

"Little Tough Guys in Society": left to right, David Gorcey, Hally Chester, Charles Duncan, William Benedict.

tion films, which continued through 1937, had titles which reflected their attitudes: *Men of Action, Born to Fight, Tough to Handle, Anything for a Thrill, Young Dynamite.*

After leaving Ambassador in 1937, Darro was signed by Monogram, a studio which had just re-formed after two years of dormancy. The studio put him through three films, starting with *Wanted By the Police*, which were in the style of the Ambassador series. But with the fourth, *Irish Luck* (1939), the format was revised, with black comic Mantan Moreland joining Frankie to form a light comedy action team that survived through eight more films, until 1941. Though not "gang" pictures, these Darro films may have had an influence on the structure of those of the Eastside Kids.

"*Dead End* without clothes; *Dead End* without any makeup," read the ads for *Boys of the Streets* (1938), the first of three Monogram films featuring former Our Ganger and MGM star Jackie Cooper. *Gangster's Boy* (1938) and *Streets of New York* (1939) had similar influences. The presence of future Eastside Kids Bobby Stone and Dave Durand also tie these films to the series.

The first group of kids intentionally patterned after the Dead End Kids was the group Universal created to pick up where *Little Tough Guy* left off. David Gorcey and Hally Chester had rounded out the gang in *that* film, and they were two of the Little Tough Guys, who made three pictures on their own before merging with Universal's edition of the Dead End Kids to form "The Dead End Kids and Little Tough Guys" (Universal believed in simple titles). With David hired as Yap and Hally as Murphy, the studio added two actors who had been in stage editions of *Dead End*: Charles Duncan (the original Spit) as Monk and Harris Berger (Hall's replacement as Dippy) as Sailor. Rounding out the quintet was William Benedict—on vacation from newsboy roles—as Trouble.

Little Tough Guys in Society (1938) was the debut of this new line-up. Since none of the five (in Universal's opinion) had leadership qualities, Frankie Thomas was imported from Warners to play a straight character: Danny. *Little Tough Guys in Society* was, for the most part, a comedy, with an anticipated confrontation between the uncouth boys and a spoiled rich brat (Jackie Searl, from *Little Tough Guy*). The cast of Mary Boland, Mischa Auer and Edward Everett Horton reflected the comedy accent, as did the direction of former Mack Sennett employee Erle C. Kenton.

The second two pictures were more serious, directed by Harold Young. *Newsboys' Home* (1939) saw Jackie Cooper (as Rifle Edwards) replacing Thomas, with Edmund Lowe and Wendy Barrie as operators of a newspaper sponsoring a boys' home. *Code of the Streets* (1939) had the boys attempting to prove a man innocent of murder, under the leadership of Thomas as Bob Lewis. The year 1938 was the year of MGM's *Boys'*

Town, which dealt with juvenile delinquency from a more positive outlook. Meanwhile, Frankie Darro, away from Monogram, was busy in two Columbia attempts to probe into adolescent crime: *Juvenile Court* happened to boast the presence of Little Tough Guys David Gorcey and Hally Chester, while *Reformatory* did it one better by featuring real Dead Ender Bobby Jordan.

For all the slum problems on the Bowery, there were hard times elsewhere too, a fact emphasized in the all-black gang, The Harlem Tuff Kids, in films meant for the all-black theaters which sprang up in the 1930s to show the all-black films which proliferated at the time. Introduced in the Million Dollar Productions' *Reform School* (1939) with Louise Beavers, the group consisted of Eugene Jackson (Pineapple in the Our Gang silents), Deforrest Covan, Eddie Lynn and Bob Simmons. Two years later, Jackson, Covan and Lynn were joined by Freddie Baker and Paul White for *Take My Life*, a starring vehicle for Goldseal. The plot sounded like it had been concocted by Eastside Kids writers: One of the gang is framed for murder, and after he is vindicated, the kids join the Army.

RKO's *Boy Slaves* (1939) was a stern indictment of the exploitation of working youth, and featured nicknames such as Knuckles, Pee Wee and Atlas. The film took place in a country setting, as did *Tuxedo Junction* (1941), a Republic vehicle starring the homespun-humorous Weaver Brothers and Elviry. In this one, Frankie Darro was the leader of a bunch of city boys who help the Weavers pick their crops

One of the strangest films in the category of imitations is Columbia's *Junior Army* (1942), which featured four Dead End Kids: Billy Halop, Huntz Hall, Bobby Jordan and Bernard Punsly. It is interesting in that it is the only film these four actors made at that studio. It is also interesting in that it is better than any of the films they made at Universal and any of the Monogram Eastside Kids films made up through 1942.

During the war years, while the Eastside Kids were cleaning up their act, exploitation films began to zero in on such problems as wayward girls, teenage pregnancy and even venereal disease, in titles such as *Where Are Your Children?, Are These Our Parents?, Teenage* and the infamous *Mom and Dad*.

In 1946, Sam Katzman, having just lost Leo Gorcey, Huntz Hall and the rest to the Bowery Boys, once again "cashed in" with a new series, *The Teen Agers*. In an ad placed for exhibitors, Monogram promoted, "Booming juke boxes, zooming record sales and jammed dance floors prove SWING'S THE THING! That's why this swell new series has been so amazingly successful!" For each film, two contemporary bands, similar in stature to Mike Riley's Orchestra in *Kid Dynamite*, were slated. Titles for the series' 1946 schedule included *High School Hero, Freddie Steps Out* and *Junior Prom*, and later ones included *Sarge Goes to College, Vacation Days* and *Campus Sleuth*. Frankie Darro (that name again) appeared, two years before the first of his four Bowery Boys films. The male stars were Freddie Stewart, Warren Mills and Jackie Moran. Female leads were June Preisser, Ann Rooney and Noel Neill, one of whom played a blonde who makes All-American in one of the outlandish screenplays.

Another blatant attempt to copy the Bowery Boys was made by Monogram's rival, Producers Releasing Corporation (PRC), whose structure was so similar to Monogram's that they changed their name to Eagle-Lion at around the same time that the better Monogram releases were going out under the "Allied Artists" label. In October 1946, they released *Gas House Kids*, directed by their all-purpose megaphone man, Sam Newfield. This new gang was led by—of all people—Billy Halop, just returned from the war and unable to get parts "Not Suited for a Former Dead End Kid." He is the leader of a mob made up of another "former," former Our Gang male lead Carl "Alfalfa" Switzer, along with Rex Downing, David Reed and Rocco Lanza.

Halop was gone by the time of *Gas House Kids Go West* (1947), deciding not to stick around and get typed again. Switzer moved up to take over leader honors as Alfalfa, with former Our Gang villain Tommy Bond as Chimp. For authenticity, PRC imported Bowery director William Beaudine and former Eastsider Bennie Bartlett as Orvie. Rudy Wissler and Ray Dolciame rounded out the gang. Switzer, Bond, Bartlett and Wissler were back in *Gas House Kids in Hollywood* (1947), directed by Edward L. Cahn, which put the cap on the series. Bartlett used these films as his ticket back to the Monogram fold.

During the late Forties, the only other collective mobs were those headed by Stanley Clements, from *Going My Way* (1944, with the aforementioned Switzer) to *Mr. Soft Touch* (1949). But the final blatant copy of the Dead End Kids came in *Military Academy* (Columbia 1950), featuring "Stanley Clements and the Tenth Avenue Gang." Backing up Clements' Stash were Myron Welton, Gene Collins and Leon Tyler.

The new juvenile delinquents of the Fifties were a far different breed from the original urchins from *Dead End*. The youths of the Cold War age were middle-class kids who rebelled for the sake of rebellion, unlike the Dead End Kids who had to fight to survive. A harmless 1950 Monogram film titled *Hot Rod* displayed the vast differences between the kids of that age and the rebels of the Depression era. Material objects such as cars were staples of teen life; In the days of the Dead End Kids, the kids could barely afford a rollerskate.

Yet even today, the influence of the Dead End Kids and Bowery Boys is still felt. Some have cited that Slip and Sach were reincarnated in the characters of "Fonzie" and "Ralph Malph" in the long-running, top-rated "Happy Days" TV series, premiered in 1974. As recently as 1979, a Lorimar-produced television series broadcast on CBS, "Flatbush," featured a group of New York do-gooders with strange nomenclatures ("Socks" was the Sach-like character) and a family-like structure. Later that year, the controversial feature *The Warriors* boasted a brief appearance by a gang who closely patterned themselves after the Dead End Kids. The Dead End Kids, Eastside Kids and Bowery Boys live on.